**ROCKS
IN THE
WATER**

**ROCKS
IN THE
SUN**

OUR LIVES: DIARY, MEMOIR, AND LETTERS

Social history contests the construction of the past as the story of elites — a grand narrative dedicated to the actions of those in power. Our Lives seeks instead to make available voices from the past that might otherwise remain unheard. By foregrounding the experience of ordinary individuals, the series aims to demonstrate that history is ultimately the story of our lives, lives constituted in part by our response to the issues and events of the era into which we are born. Many of the voices in the series thus speak in the context of political and social events of the sort about which historians have traditionally written. What they have to say fills in the details, creating a richly varied portrait that celebrates the concrete, allowing broader historical settings to emerge between the lines. The series invites materials that are engagingly written and that contribute in some way to our understanding of the relationship between the individual and the collective.

SERIES TITLES

A Very Capable Life: The Autobiography of Zarah Petri
John Leigh Walters

Letters from the Lost: A Memoir of Discovery
Helen Waldstein Wilkes

A Woman of Valour: The Biography of Marie-Louise Bouchard Labelle
Claire Trépanier

Man Proposes, God Disposes: Recollections of a French Pioneer
Pierre Maturié, translated by Vivien Bosley

Xwelíqwiya: The Life of a Stó:lō Matriarch
Rena Point Bolton and Richard Daly

The Teacher and the Superintendent: Native Schooling in the Alaskan Interior, 1904–1918
Compiled and annotated by George E. Boulter II and edited by Barbara Grigor-Taylor

Mission Life in Cree-Ojibwe Country: A Memoir of Mother and Son
Elizabeth Bingham Young and E. Ryerson Young, edited and with introductions by Jennifer S.H. Brown

Rocks in the Water, Rocks in the Sun
Vilmond Joegodson Déralciné and Paul Jackson

ROCKS IN THE WATER

A Memoir from the Heart of Haiti

Vilmond Joegodson Déralciné AND Paul Jackson

ROCKS IN THE SUN

AU PRESS

COPYRIGHT © 2015 Vilmond Joegodson Déralciné and Paul Jackson
Published by AU Press, Athabasca University
1200, 10011 – 109 Street, Edmonton, AB T5J 3S8
doi: 10.15215/aupress/9781771990110.01

Book design by Natalie Olsen
Cover photo © arindambanerjee / Shutterstock.com
Printed and bound in Canada by Marquis Book Printers

Library and Archives Canada Cataloguing in Publication

Déralciné, Vilmond Joegodson, 1983–, author
Rocks in the water, rocks in the sun : a memoir from the heart of Haiti /
Vilmond Joegodson Déralciné and Paul Jackson.

Issued in print and electronic formats.
Text in English with glossary of Haitian terms and Haitian sayings ;
translated from the spoken Creole.
ISBN 978-1-77199-011-0 (pbk.). — ISBN 978-1-77199-012-7 (pdf). —
ISBN 978-1-77199-013-4 (epub)

1. Déralciné, Vilmond Joegodson, 1983–. 2. Déralciné, Vilmond Joegodson, 1983–
— Childhood and youth. 3. Fathers — Haiti — Port-au-Prince — Biography.
4. Haiti — History — 1986-. 5. Haiti — Social conditions. 6. Haiti — Economic
conditions. 7. Haiti — Religion. 8. Haiti Earthquake, Haiti, 2010. 9. Haiti —
Biography. I. Jackson, Paul, 1955–, author, translator   II. Title.

F1928.23.D47A3 2015   972.9407'3092   C2015-900130-7
                                                 C2015-900131-5

We acknowledge the financial support of the Government of Canada through the
Canada Book Fund (CBF) for our publishing activities.

 Canada Council   Conseil des Arts
               for the Arts   du Canada

Assistance provided by the Government of Alberta, Alberta Multimedia Development Fund.

Alberta
Government

This publication is licensed under a Creative Commons licence, Attribution-Noncommercial-No Derivative Works 4.0 International: see creativecommons.org. The text may be reproduced for non-commercial purposes, provided that credit is given to the original author.

To obtain permission for uses beyond those outlined in the Creative Commons licence, please contact AU Press, Athabasca University, at aupress@athabascau.ca.

Woch nan dlo pa konn mizè woch nan solèy.
Rocks in the water don't know the misery of rocks in the sun.

CONTENTS

Preface
IX

Acknowledgements
XIII

Rocks in the Water, Rocks in the Sun
A Memoir from the Heart of Haiti
Vilmond Joegodson Déralciné
3

Commentary
An Essay on Haitian Politics and History
Paul Jackson
319

Glossary of Haitian Terms
369

Pawol Granmoun / Haitian Sayings
373

Chants
375

PREFACE

In the course of *Rocks*, Joegodson will describe from his perspective how this book came into being. Beforehand, allow me to briefly introduce ourselves from my point of view. My intent here is to answer questions that might nag at you and distract you from his story.

Joegodson and I met in Port-au-Prince in January of 2006. The city was, literally and figuratively, on fire. The popular classes were in a death struggle with the powerful for control of the country. The battlefield, this time, was an election. The poor won what turned out to be a Pyrrhic victory. Joegodson will describe the circumstances of our meeting in that context. He also describes how we exchanged our maternal languages in a fair-trade deal: English for Creole.

Four years later, the earthquake left Joegodson homeless and jobless. Everywhere there was work to be done. The Haitians had all the skills needed to rebuild their country to their taste. But there was very little money in circulation. Especially in the city, Haitians needed money to survive. The formal economy was organized around sweatshops subcontracted to supply multinational clothing corporations with merchandise for sale in the consuming countries, like the United States and Canada. (Joegodson will describe the wages and conditions there.) Meanwhile, Joegodson was a talented furniture maker. He had friends in desperate conditions who were skilled tailors and artisans. We considered the possibility of establishing a kind of fair-trade enterprise to connect Canadian consumers with Haitian workers. While he organized them into a potential workforce, I researched in Montréal the logistics of establishing an import business. This project had been thrust upon me, however, rather than chosen. The idea of handcuffing Haitian workers to a capricious foreign market seemed short-sighted to me. The Haitians would still be dependent on the wage for their survival, except that it might come more directly from Canada. But they were desperate.

In Canada, I worked with Foreign Affairs, Trade and Development Canada to learn how goods are imported from the "least developed countries." I discovered that products from peripheral countries are exempt from tariffs. The government claims that this regulation is intended to help the poorest countries develop their industrial base. It was easy to see, however, that the policy was a gift to the wealthiest multinational corporations that exploit the most vulnerable workers in the world. Not only do they have negligible production costs but the government allows those products to enter Canada as if there were no border. It is as if the production was located in Canada; however, they do not have to pay any of the social wages that Canadian workers had forced on the capitalist class over centuries of struggle. The environmental and social costs of production are displaced to the Global South, when possible. Nevertheless, and regardless of the real effect of the tariff exemption for products manufactured by Haitian workers, would it be possible for us to actually benefit from it?

We came up against obstacles in both Canada and Haiti. In Montréal, I researched the viability of retailing furniture, clothing, and art. For practical advice, I went to see an entrepreneur who imported similar merchandise from Africa. Several years earlier, I had purchased from him an attractive plant stand made by Moroccan artisans. He had installed in the boutique a video that showed the actual production process; I remember having watched how the Moroccans produced the stand. Now, years later, I found the shop had expanded. It was still full of attractive furniture from around the world, but no longer did the proprietor promote the fair-trade aspect of the enterprise. The store manager told me that few customers were interested in the production process. In fact, promoting merchandise in terms of fair trade could actually handicap items otherwise in demand. Price was the critical factor in moving merchandise. Ultimately, we would be in competition with the multinationals.

Meanwhile, there were bigger obstacles in Haiti, where it is extremely difficult to register a company. Moreover, the Haitian customs office is rife with corruption and controlled by powerful interests that operate in the shadows. Joegodson had already been forced to pay bribes to customs agents for things I had sent to him in Haiti. More ominously, the customs office was in the hands of the same people who controlled the assembly industry. In his first term as president, René Préval had unsuccessfully attempted to make Haitian customs accountable. Any successful effort to raise the Haitian workers to a decent standard of living would undermine the formal economy controlled by the people on whom we would be completely dependent to export products. Joegodson's friends were not concerned with these complications; they just wanted decent wages. Beyond that, Joegodson and I would be on our own.

At the same time, Joegodson and I were already working together on a blog that we set up so that he could describe post-earthquake conditions in Port-au-Prince. A few times, people who followed his writings sent him money. In his text, he talks about how he put those gifts to use. It was clear that these readers were not wealthy and were making financial sacrifices out of compassion for his ordeal. They encouraged Joegodson. He liked organizing his thoughts to produce posts for our website. And so, we devised the project that has culminated in this book. It was the one thing that we could produce that, as Joegodson put it, "allowed us to exploit each other equally." I was enthusiastic about the idea. The voice of the most vulnerable link in the global division of labour is silenced in the consuming world. Members of the growing global pauper class — slum dwellers with no prospective source of income — are systemically shut out of discussions about the future of the world. When they appear, it is through the voices of academics, journalists, authors, activists, and filmmakers. In Haiti, the literacy rate is approximately 50 percent. Even for the poor who are literate, like Joegodson, books and journals and Internet access are extremely rare. There are many reasons that the poor don't enter into our consciousness. Sometimes, it is because we would rather not hear them. But even where that is not the case, no infrastructure exists to support their intervention in the world of ideas, let alone policy. How would Joegodson have written his narrative alone in the circumstances that he describes? Even the pens and paper would have represented a big investment. Where would he have sent it for publication? The cost would have been prohibitive even if he had found a potential publisher. How would it have been received? In the culture of celebrity, who would care about the lives of some nameless slum dwellers? Beyond all of that, we are speaking of a world that, until we began to post items on our blog, was simply not within Joegodson's field of vision. Our world is constructed of many solitudes.

And so, Joegodson sneaks us into his social circles in Cité Soleil, Delmas, and Saut d'Eau, and we have a chance to see how life is experienced there. He is not speaking for Haitians any more than I am speaking for Canadians in this preface. We are both critical of our compatriots and reject the proposition that anyone could speak for everyone. Joegodson describes how Haitians act within the context of the choices before them. The value of appropriating the voice of the victims of global capitalism is that you can portray them in a way that serves your agenda. I find Joegodson's story happily devoid of the sentimentality and romanticism with which opponents of global capitalism discuss the world's most exploited classes. It is equally free of the demagoguery used by proponents of the empire to justify suppression of the subordinate classes that try to improve their position or free themselves of capitalism altogether. Those creations are instruments of a political agenda. Joegodson speaks about life in Haiti from within Haiti. Those familiar with the writings of Gary Victor, Danny Laferrière, and Edwidge Danticat may recognize his Haiti. He has not written fiction, however, but a memoir through which he has tried to describe his actual experiences, as well as those recounted by his friends and family, as faithfully as possible.

From a logistical standpoint: we wrote *Rocks in the Water, Rocks in the Sun* in Haiti in the fall of 2011 into January 2012. Joegodson formulated the story by choosing experiences from his life and the lives of his family and friends. They cooperated. We changed their names for obvious reasons. We spoke in Creole or French and I wrote in English; in that way, we could both express ourselves most freely. We both thought it best to publish in English. We went over every passage together. I tried to minimize my role as mediator as much as possible. However, the fact that we discussed our project constantly over the months of its creation means that I played some indeterminate part. If he had worked with someone else, the emphasis might have been on other aspects of Haitian life. In other words, this is one of a number of memoirs that Joegodson might have produced. There are many more books to be written by each of us.

Acknowledgements

A number of people and organizations have contributed to the realization of our book. Funding from the Social Sciences and Humanities Research Council of Canada made possible our initial encounter and intercultural exchange in Haiti in 2006. Although that postdoctoral scholarship had originally been granted in support of a very different plan of study, the committee accepted its conversion into a transnational project. After the earthquake of 2010, Cy Gonick and James Patterson posted our reflections on the situation in Haiti on the *Canadian Dimension* website. Soon after, we decided to create our own blog, www.heartofhaiti.wordpress.com, to introduce many of the issues that we would develop in this book. We were motivated to continue by readers who supported our analysis and approach as well as those who rejected us. Those articles that most pleased some readers invariably outraged others; all responses educated us. Once we decided to write this book, we needed material support. Joan Jackson helped from Canada in a number of ways and kept our project alive at crucial moments. In Haiti, Yves and Wilberta Gardel opened up their home to us. Antonia cooked, cleaned, and took care of Joenaara, which allowed us to write the manuscript. Back in Canada, Alvin Finkel saw the value in our work and encouraged us to submit it to Athabasca University Press where Pamela Holway made some important suggestions relating to its organization. After that, and most critically of all, Connor Houlihan oversaw its maturation to its final form; he kept it from going off track. Two anonymous reviewers made insightful observations that improved the manuscript. Ann Klefstad helped to make the text clearer. Megan Hall captured the spirit of our book in the graphics arena. Outside of AUP, Louise Velazquez was our most perceptive friend. She read the manuscript before anybody else and engaged us at every level, probing the boundless meaning concealed in daily life. On a different plane, Joegodson gives thanks to God, who granted him the ability to accomplish the book and who never lost confidence in him.

PAUL JACKSON AND VILMOND JOEGODSON DÉRALCINÉ

**ROCKS
IN THE
WATER

ROCKS
IN THE
SUN**

chapter one

MY DAD WAS BORN IN 1963 in a village called La Hatt Polikap in Ville Bonnet, a few kilometres from Saut d'Eau, which means "the waterfalls." Water abounded there. The local peasants knew how to exploit all the different types of soil in the area. Some parts were dry, others swampy, still others well drained. The mixture meant that the cultivators could grow all kinds of crops and raise livestock too. The local rivers were good for crops like rice, sugar cane, bananas, and some legumes.

The peasants stayed in the countryside. There was no need for them to go to the capital where they were ill at ease and mocked for their lack of refinement. Even if they wanted to visit Port-au-Prince, it was difficult because agricultural work took all their time. To migrate to the capital meant a complete change of life. Migrants depended on the support of their home communities. Family and friends would bring provisions to them while they tried to adapt to life in the city where they needed money. Peasants saw little money and lived well without it.

There were no fences in Saut d'Eau. There were little pickets placed at the corners so that peasants knew which plots they were responsible for cultivating. People respected each other's land. Everyone knew which plots belonged to which family. More important than expanding claims in relation to their neighbours was maintaining order in the system that supported the community.

The section chief was responsible for keeping order. He didn't carry a firearm. To demonstrate his authority, he had a baton and wore a special cap. He too would be a cultivator who walked around barefoot with his shirt unbuttoned, just like everybody else. Sometimes the section chiefs had whistles. It was the whistle and the baton that could instill fear in inhabitants, because behind those symbols was the Duvalier regime.

The peasants worked together all the time. To cultivate the soil, they organized what they called a *konbit*. As Haitians said, *Men anpil chaj pa lou* — many hands make the load lighter. A *konbit* was a group of cultivators who came together to work the land of one of the members. Working together, they would motivate each other. Also, there was more pleasure in working together than alone. The peasants loaned their time and effort to the cultivator whose land they worked. He or she would pay back the loan by working the land of each of the others in turn. A *konbit* was a full day's work. The peasants assembled at sunrise to work until the sun had almost completed its arc across the sky. The family that benefited from the *konbit* was responsible for feeding the workers. The women of the family would take care of that. The other women worked in the *konbit*, but the work was divided according to gender. Men worked with the heavy tools like picks and hoes. Women followed, gathering and twining the cuttings or planting the seeds, depending on the season. A *mera* was the same as a *konbit*, but it was only a half-day's work.

When a cultivator organized a *konbit*, he sought out the most reliable workers. He would prepare so as to make the best use of everybody. The peasants would trade their days to each other. So, if I worked for your *konbit*, then you would work for mine in turn. Each person needed to work well in order to expect the same of the others.

The inhabitants controlled their days and their work. No one had a clock or a watch. They wouldn't have had the time to check a watch. The shadows that the sun cast were the hands of their clock. By following the trajectory of the sun across the sky, they knew how much time remained in their workday.

Their horses were reliable means of transport if they had to travel outside of their community. The river was their source of life. It offered them clean water whenever they needed it. They bathed in it and used it for cleaning. The springs offered pure drinking water.

Peasant life was simple on the surface. But if we dig a little, we find an infinitely complex world. So, let's dig.

-•-

In his youth, my father, Deland, was impressed by the nice clothes that people wore. He wanted to be a tailor. He shared this goal with his young friends: "Someday, I'm going to learn how to sew and I'll make nice clothes for us all." Such a goal separated my father from most of the other peasants. He didn't renounce the cultivation of the land, but he wanted to master tailoring as well. Few of the peasants dreamed of mastering another skill along with agriculture.

Deland was motivated to succeed as a tailor for a number of reasons. His parents were separated and his mother was raising her five children alone. Not only did he want to make her proud but he hoped that if he was a successful tailor, her stature would be elevated. People would say, "There goes Suzanne. She is the mother of a fine tailor." She too encouraged Deland. Parents who raised a child who contributed something useful to the community were respected. Deland wanted to help his mother Suzanne; she wanted to help him. When he became a respected tailor, each would be helping the other.

In my father's youth, all the young people in the community worked hard in the fields every day. Sometimes they courted while working together. At night, the young men would gather together and if someone had a flashlight, they could travel around to visit the young women. The parents did not prohibit these nightly visits, except where a youth had a bad reputation. In that case, they refused to allow their daughter to see him. Reputations counted for a lot. Each family tried to maintain its good name by respecting their responsibilities to the community. It took only one member to behave badly for the entire family to lose its reputation. And so people watched their own behaviour and that of their relatives.

Even when two young people fell in love, the final decision about their marriage belonged to the parents. Timid boys could escape the fear of approaching the object of their attraction by asking their parents to arrange a meeting. In fact, it was a perfectly legitimate and respectable way to court a young woman. The parents would get together to discuss the practicality of the marriage. If one set of parents had an objection to the union, they would stop the courtship before it started. Otherwise, they would arrange for the youths to meet.

Families that had been marked as thieves as a result of the actions of only one member, or those who were known for domestic violence, had a difficult time finding partners for their children. This was not a local custom; it was similar in all the departments of Haiti.

Parents in local communities would watch the youths closely as they grew. They noticed boys who were lazy and unreliable and girls who were untidy and rebellious. Arrogance and disrespect were also unattractive attributes. Infidelity in girls was especially badly viewed; virginity was highly regarded. If a family knew that their daughter had already had sexual relations with a man and the parents of a courtier should arrive with a serious offer, it was best to acknowledge the truth. If they lied, the entire family could lose its status and possibly be required to compensate the family that had been misled. However, if a youth seduced a young woman with promises of marriage that he renounced the moment that his sexual desires had been satisfied, the family could hold him responsible. If they succeeded, not only would he be imprisoned, but the young woman would have her reputation restored. Sometimes, a family had no interest in the courts but would accept nothing short of marriage. If the young seducer refused, he might find himself the object of magic that could result in his death.

Sometimes, parents could take note of a young man whom they considered an especially good catch for their daughter. They could take the lead in the affair, courting the young man in the place of their daughter, doing what they could to bring them together. Young men would be very cautious in these circumstances, knowing that magic could be used not only to avenge a seducer, but to assure a seduction. When he entered the home of a family that he suspected of trying to entice him into courting their daughter, a young man was cautious about every move. If he sat on a hexed chair or drank from a charmed cup, he knew that he might fall under a spell designed to bend his will.

Parents could use sorcery directly on their daughter so that a certain man would be overtaken by desire when his eyes fell upon her. On the other side of the ledger, young men who were maladroit or timid could use enchanted perfumes to make them irresistible to the object of their desire.

Deland did not come from an intellectual family. But his mother taught him what was important: respect for others — especially his elders, working for peace in the community, and helping people in trouble. Deland lived up to her standards. He learned from her that the most important principle in life is to help others. He believed that good actions would always, somehow and eventually, be repaid.

I remember times when I personally saw how Dad put into practice the lessons that his mother had taught him. Once, my father was in a state hospital visiting my brother James who had had a serious accident. I was on the way to meet them, a few minutes away from the hospital. Inside was a young man who was in a terrible state. On top of whatever sickness he had, he had pooped his pants. He sat on a bed in utter humiliation as the patients and visitors in the ward distanced themselves from him, making theatrical gestures to register the smell and their disgust. My cellphone rang. My father said, "Come quickly, my Godson, we have a job to do here." I hurried to meet him. He was helping the hapless young man remove his soiled pants. I started to assist and was overtaken by a need to vomit that I successfully resisted. But my father kept working until the young man was cleaned. I saw that his hands were covered with the young man's feces. It didn't bother Dad. When everyone else had rejected the young man and added to his humiliation, my father acted in love without any hesitation. He was always like that.

This kindness marked Deland in everyone's eyes. In his youth, all of the parents of Saut d'Eau aspired to have their daughters marry someone like Deland.

In his travels in Saut d'Eau, young Deland found himself visiting the family of Cécile Robert, of whom he was very fond. But he was deflated when he thought of how her family was better off than his own. He decided to stop visiting, but without explaining why to either Cécile or her parents.

But Cécile's parents had been impressed by Deland. One day, they confronted Cécile severely, saying "What has happened to the young man who used to visit us? What have you done?"

"I have no idea. He didn't say anything. He just stopped coming."

When Cécile next saw Deland, she told him that her parents were holding her responsible for his sudden disappearance. Deland was too ashamed to discuss it. But Cécile insisted. She said that she refused to leave until she had an explanation. Finally, Deland was forced to explain. She was surprised. She had heard nothing from her parents but praise for Deland. Now, he was telling her that he had withdrawn on purpose because he judged himself unworthy.

"In any case, I'm going to explain the situation to them just as you have told me. I don't intend to be thought of as an accomplice in this," she said.

The Roberts were as surprised as Cécile had been. Finally, they told Cécile to bring Deland to them. Bashfully and against his will, Deland came. He felt that it would have been a sign of disrespect to refuse.

"Deland, we are not looking for wealth. From the first time you visited us, we could see in you the results of the education that your parents have tried to instill. Money does not make a man. We think that wisdom and goodwill are the most valuable traits and that they always take a man in the right direction."

As usual, the Roberts were respectful. They seemed to have already chosen Deland for their son-in-law. They invited him to dine with them. Then, in a small sack, they packed rice, beans, and avocados to take home for his mother. They had a couple of their young sons accompany Deland back to his home, another sign of respect and goodwill.

When he arrived home, his mother was overjoyed by the gift. Her land was planted, but it wasn't ready to be harvested. So, the bounty from the Roberts assured that the Déralciné family would eat well that evening. Later, when her harvest had come in, she sent to the Roberts a healthy package of her produce.

One day, Deland told Cécile, "We must hypnotize our parents. You must do everything possible so that my mother sees you as her own daughter, and I'll make sure your parents call me their son."

The two families started to collapse into one. Sometimes, Cécile would come by to do the laundry for her future mother-in-law. Deland responded by helping Mr. Roberts in his fields. They started to turn their marriage into an inevitability.

Meanwhile, Deland followed his dream to be a tailor. He encouraged Cécile to learn to be a dressmaker. In that way, together, they would be able to clothe both sexes. They both committed their time to develop their skills. They were taught by other cultivators skilled in the needle trade. Sometimes, Deland told his mentor, "If sometimes you have some work to do in your garden, you only have to ask me and I'll help out."

The cultivator judged that Deland was ambitious. He decided to hide none of his skills from Deland. He taught him all of the little techniques that he usually kept to himself.

As Deland was spending more time learning his new trade, he had less time to work his mother's fields. She was working harder. Deland's sisters were taking care of the domestic chores. But with less produce from the fields, there was no surplus to pay the cultivator who was mentoring Deland in tailoring.

Normally, Suzanne took the harvest from the family's land to the market to sell. She would load up her mule with the produce and lead him to the local market where, like the other peasant merchants, she laid it out on the ground for sale. This was the only activity that brought cash into her household. It was with that money that she paid Deland's tailoring teacher. The problem was that, without Deland's help, there was less to sell and less time to sell it.

Finally, because of these sacrifices on everyone's part, Deland came to master his skills. Cécile, for her part, made much progress as a dressmaker. Sometimes, they sat together to share the techniques that they were learning independently. Deland was eventually able to sew both men's and women's clothes.

―•―

July 16 is a great fête in Saut d'Eau. Haitians come from all over the country. Even members of the diaspora — Haitians who have emigrated to other countries — come back to Saut d'Eau. For Vodouists, July 16 is the most important date of the year, and Saut d'Eau is the spiritual centre of the celebration.

What Haitians celebrate on July 16 depends on their point of view. Both Vodouist and Catholic Haitians converge on Saut d'Eau at the same time for their shared but distinct celebrations. Vodouists celebrate at the waterfalls and Catholics in the local church. Why should there be two versions of one event?

While the Vodouists congregate at the waterfalls, the Catholic church in Saut d'Eau overflows with Haitians from all over. In the church are statues of the Virgin Mary. Several stories circulate about the origin of the miracle that occurred in the middle of the nineteenth century. Some say that the form of the Virgin appeared in a rock. Others say that she appeared in the leaves of a palm tree. Still others say that it was in the bark of a tree. In any case, while the Vodouists commune with the spirits at the waterfalls, the Catholics come to the church to ask the Virgin for help. Others lay bouquets of flowers at her feet in thanks for prayers that she has already fulfilled. There are different ways to ask the Virgin Mary for services. The church has built a special room so that, for fifty gourdes ($1.10 US), the faithful can light candles to Mary.

At the waterfalls, the Vodouists parley with the spirits. They bathe in the water under the falls. I was marked once by the sight of a young woman who disrobed and entered the water under the falls. Soon, a *lwa* — a Vodou spirit — entered her and took control of her body. She writhed violently under the power of the *lwa*. Another woman came to help her to the shore, worrying that she was in danger of drowning, or being drowned by the *lwa*.

Spirits surround us all. When we idolize material things, we open ourselves up to be possessed by the spirits that can inhabit them. Anything and everything. Our obsessions and idols can make us vulnerable to the *lwa*. Once possessed, a person ties his life to the spirit. It is very easy to become possessed by a *lwa*, extremely difficult to liberate yourself.

The *lwa* look for our weaknesses. We allow ourselves to be possessed. For instance, the Vodouists who come every year to Saut d'Eau light their candles at the trunks of the huge trees all around the falls. They pray to the trees. So many people participate in this practice that the trunks of the trees have become dangerously thin. They are diminished by the fires of the countless candles that burn all around them. Currently, the trunks are unequal to the weight that they have to support, for the trees are mature and stretch to the top of the waterfalls. Some people idolize the trees, obsessed by the need to light the candles. But, in doing so, they can put themselves and others in danger of being injured or killed by a falling tree. The *lwa* that inhabit the trees have entered those who idolize them. Once they allow themselves to be taken over by the *lwa*, people can fall victim to the very thing that they adore. Trees are one example. The *lwa* can use anything at all to gain entry and to control the life of a person: money, alcohol, drugs, fame, the search for youth, pride, material possessions, and so on. Whenever we begin to idolize something, we become vulnerable. We stay free by refusing the temptations that allow *lwa* to enter us.

The main difference between the Catholic and Vodouist worshippers is their social class. The Vodouists celebrate outside in the waterfalls, the Catholics inside a big building. The Catholics are better dressed, but the spiritual practices are indivisible. The Virgin Mary in the Catholic Church is the *lwa* Erzulie Dantor at the waterfalls.

The Church did all it could to keep itself untouched and superior to the unrefined Vodouists who made such spectacles of themselves. The Catholic authorities insisted that the Virgin Mary was legitimate and her appearance in the nineteenth century a real miracle. The civilized priests resented sharing their symbols with the savages. But the Catholic followers could not always see the difference. Many of the pilgrims went from the church to the waterfalls. Only the snobs refused to see the connection.

My family was, at the same time, both Vodouist and Catholic. Where my grandmother lived, there were four other houses, or *kay*. In those *kay* lived her mother, her son and his wife, her eldest daughters and my father. As was the custom, once he reached his twenties, Deland began constructing his future home in the courtyard. The courtyard where the extended family lives is called the *lakou* in Creole. Since my family were Vodouists, they served a *lwa*. In the *lakou* was (and is) a huge fig tree. The *lwa* that my family served lives in that tree and so my family used to perform ceremonies at its trunk. They would sacrifice animals there, for instance.

The *lwa* had helped them in different ways. It cured a child with a mystical sickness; it helped their crops grow; and it assured abundant harvests. Their success as cultivators provoked the jealousy of some of the other peasants. The resources were limited and so, for our crops to flourish, our *lwa* had to sap the strength from other fields. Even if my family members were ignorant of the actual methods that their *lwa* was using, the other peasants understood what was happening. Their crops were floundering while ours thrived. But my family was unable to counter the actions of its *lwa*. In fact, it was a disturbing sign that the *lwa* began to steal from others to enrich us. It is known that a *lwa* fattens its servitors before devouring them. My family was being threatened by its success.

The day came when our *lwa* was ready to take its restitution. Deland's elder sister awoke as usual on the morning of July 16, the day of the great celebration in Saut d'Eau. She went to the Catholic church and then proceeded to the waterfalls for the Vodouist part of the celebration. She spent several hours bathing in the waters and then started to return home. Normally, young peasant women buy things from street merchants for the family meal. She intended to buy pastries, mints, biscuits, and some *marinad,* a kind of seasoned dumpling fried in oil. But when she came out of the water, she was already mad. Instead of buying food, she filled her basket with inedible leaves that she collected randomly. When she arrived home, her mother looked in the basket and was stupefied.

"What have you brought us?"

Her daughter replied, "I brought all I could find."

My grandmother tried to soothe her, saying, "It's not important. It's just the heat of the sun and the excitement of the fête. Go and lie down to settle yourself."

After a few hours, the others saw that she was behaving strangely. They called my grandmother. Everyone knew that this kind of sickness was the result of a *lwa* acting on the victim. My grandmother tried to heal her, using a few methods that the *lwa* share with their servitors. But nothing worked. It was too late. The *lwa* had already begun its malevolent work, nullifying the powers that it had once delegated to the family. My grandmother was powerless.

Things deteriorated quickly. A few hours later, my grandmother received word that my father had also fallen victim.

Despite her folly, my aunt remained calm. However, Deland was stark raving mad. No one could subdue him and few were willing to try. He fought like a madman and showed no signs of connecting with reality.

My grandmother was bedevilled, struck by the fickleness of the *lwa.* After all their years of faithful service, the family was being destroyed by the very force it looked to for protection. When they understood what was happening, everyone panicked.

With my grandmother stymied, the other inhabitants came to the rescue. They looked for a way to save Deland from the spell. Several peasants were consigned to each of his arms and legs. Deland's normal strength was multiplied by the power of the *lwa* working inside of him. But they succeeded in subduing him. Other peasants arrived with ropes and wrapped him from head to foot. They wrapped the thick rope everywhere, including his neck, and then pulled the ends, placing Deland's life in real danger.

The *lwa* are extremely devious. This *lwa* had taken control of my father to provoke the peasants to harm him. The sneaky *lwa* was a spirit and, consequently, was suffering none of the effects of the human body of Deland. In fact, once it had provoked his friends to kill Deland, the *lwa* would be free to continue its malicious work.

Among the people who were pulling the ropes that were suffocating Deland were those who resented the recent agricultural success of our family. It was not that they were our enemies, but, nevertheless, the *lwa* was making use of their rancour. The *lwa* had very effectively set its trap. All the innocents were playing the roles that it had written for them in the drama. Meanwhile, Deland was at the centre of its complex machinations.

As soon as the *lwa* saw that my father was almost dead, it left his body to enjoy the drama from a different perspective. The peasants remained afraid of Deland and did not relinquish the tension on the ropes. Deland tried to speak. He managed to find enough air to say, in a tiny humble voice, "I'm choking."

The peasants replied, "You want us to release you? What do you take us for? We're not stupid. You will redouble your attacks as soon as you are free."

Deland had no more air in his lungs. He fell silent.

One of the peasants was following the drama with compassion for Deland. He intervened and implored the other peasants to release the pressure on the ropes. He said that Deland was dying.

They replied, "You want us to let him go? If something happens to one of us because of him, are you going to compensate us?"

He said, "Okay. I'll take the responsibility. Just, let him go because he's dying."

Against their better judgment, the peasants released their ropes and immediately lurched back to distance themselves from my father.

Deland was so weak that he could not remain standing. He fell to the ground, his arms and legs useless. The others who had been watching the event came to his aid. They took Deland and put him next to his sister, the two crazy people together.

Meanwhile, my grandmother went in search of an *houngan* or *mambo* who might have the power to counter the *lwa* that had turned against her family. When such things happen, the Catholic-Vodouists never go to the church. They know that the civilized world of the Catholic Church has no power to fight the *lwa*. Instead, they turn immediately to the *houngan* for help.

The cost of the cure would be high. Since the *lwa* was no longer a friend of my family, but the force that menaced its existence, my grandmother needed to sell everything that had come during the period of its beneficence. Everything now had to be sacrificed to free the family. So, the cows, goats, and chickens that were the family's wealth would now be, literally, sacrificed. The time had come for the *houngan* to profit.

Some neighbours accompanied my grandmother, Deland, and his sister to the *lakou* of a local *houngan*. They spent several days there; it was a sort of hospital for the spiritually sick. Cures are not profitable for *houngan*. The longer the treatment lasts, the more the patient has to pay. On the other hand, *houngan* do not like to admit that they have no cure. They have to carefully coordinate the "cure" with the resources of the patient. As a result, it is the sick person who has to diagnose the *houngan*. If the *houngan* has no cure, it is best to make a clean break sooner rather than later.

My grandmother was experienced in these things. She quickly left the first *houngan* to try out another. Each *houngan* has his own diagnosis. One might determine that a zombie has taken over the patient and attempt to exorcise it by beating the body, bound to a stake, with a cane. Needless to say, some cures can be costly in a number of ways. And the patient may question the motivations behind some treatments. It is wise to dispute the treatment plan of a rancorous *houngan* or *mambo* who insists on beating the spirit out of the patient's body.

My grandmother, Suzanne, went from *houngan* to *mambo*, *mambo* to *houngan*, looking for a cure for her children. She was reduced to financial ruin and her children were very close to death. She had sold everything that she had. There seemed to be no hope.

Finally, she sought the help of an *houngan* who was a member of our family. He gave her advice different from all of the others. He told her that no *houngan* or *mambo* could help her children. He too was powerless.

He explained that the *lwa* that the family served was very powerful. In fact, only that *lwa* had the power to help the family and, it was clear, it had decided to abandon us.

He counselled my grandmother to try one final desperate act. He said that she should go to the Protestants. Either the children would recover or they would die. If they died, the Protestants would help her bury them.

When she heard his words, she started crying. The most honest advice she had been able to find prepared her for the funerals of her children. However, since she had nothing left to pay for her children's burials, she decided to accept his advice. But, before she did, she knelt down to pray before the *peristyle* in her *lakou*. "I have heard of You," she said to God, "I don't really know if You have the power. If You heal my two children, my family and I will dedicate our lives to serve You."

Suzanne found a few Protestant brothers to pray along with her. She agreed to go to church with the children. With the aid of the other believers, and because they believed, my father and his sister were healed.

- ● -

During the entire time of the insanity of my father, Cécile never once abandoned him. Some of the other young men used Deland's descent into madness to court Cécile. She was deaf to them. Her parents also refused to allow other suitors to take his place. People told them that Deland would not recover. Moreover, Suzanne Déralciné was now ruined financially. But the hand of Cécile remained betrothed to a crazy man from a penniless family. They would have it no other way.

After his recovery, Deland discovered that Cécile had remained faithful to him throughout all of his sickness. And so he proposed marriage. In keeping with custom, Cécile left her family before the marriage to live with Deland in the house that he had been preparing in the *lakou* of his family. His elder sister, who had shared the madness with Deland, decided to marry at the same time.

In their new home, Deland and Cécile gave birth to my brother James in 1982. I came the following year. Both Cécile and Deland worked as cultivators and tailors at the same time.

As is the case with many lovers, Deland and Cécile found that living with their betrothed was very different than courting from a distance. Cécile started to have problems with Deland's family members. Sometimes, her mother-in-law, Suzanne, would leave quantities of rice and other produce from her fields in her home. She would often store them under her bed in a big metal tub, a *kivèt*. Her daughters would enter and take what they wanted. However, they left the impression that Cécile was taking it. "Have you noticed that since Cécile has entered the *lakou*, things go missing from Suzanne's house?" they would ask the other peasants. Before long, Suzanne came to believe that Cécile was stealing from her. No actual accusation had ever been made, so no denial was possible.

These kinds of machinations were unknown in Cécile's family. They were respectful of each other and did not stoop to petty gossip. Cécile did not have the experience that might have helped her cope with her new environment. My father understood the difference and was ashamed. But he was helpless to resolve the growing tension between Cécile and his sisters who lived in other houses in the *lakou*.

My father worried that if Cécile's family should learn of the way that their daughter was being disrespected in her new home that his own status would fall along with that of his family. His new marriage was on a train heading toward a disaster. He looked for a way to escape before it was too late. He decided that the only answer was to move with Cécile and his two sons far from the *lakou*. He planned to migrate to the capital. His main problem was that he had no economic means to leave. To begin, he would need to pay for a room in Port-au-Prince. He would have to find a way to support his family. His new path was filled with huge obstacles even before he took a first step.

However, if he was unwilling to accept sacrifices, he would have no right to expect to succeed. To prepare the way for the migration, Deland would need to go to the capital alone. That meant the worst of all possible worlds: he would be on a reconnaissance mission in an unknown place while Cécile was alone with her two babies in the heart of what had become enemy territory for her. Deland tried to build up her courage to make the sacrifice along with him.

My father walked three-quarters of the way to the capital until he found a *taptap* that took him to Carrefour-Feuilles. There, he stayed with another peasant from Saut d'Eau who had already migrated.

As soon as he arrived, Deland recruited his friend to help him find a job. Knowing that most peasants had some knowledge of sewing and that Deland was highly skilled, he led my father to a factory that made clothes for foreign companies. He would make nineteen gourdes ($3.98 US) a day. Even though the pay was unreasonable, Deland decided to accept it for lack of other options. He needed to get his family from Saut d'Eau to Port-au-Prince as soon as possible.

He began his new Spartan existence. He worked twelve hours a day in the terrible heat of the factory. He ate the absolute minimum; otherwise, he would easily have spent everything just on his survival. Nothing would be left to achieve his goal of bringing his family to the capital. He spent several months working in the factory until he had made enough money to buy a sewing machine. He still needed money to find a room. The rents in the neighbourhoods of Port-au-Prince varied enormously. The only place that Deland could afford to live was Site Solèy. There, close to the Route Nationale, he found a room made out of rusted corrugated iron and cardboard. The floor was simply cardboard laid on top of the dirt. There was no water, no electricity, no toilet. The local inhabitants used a narrow ditch at the side of the street as their toilet. As a result, all human waste flowed freely through the neighbourhood. For privacy, some of the elderly people would hold a piece of cardboard in front of themselves when they relieved themselves. Most didn't bother. People threw their dirty water in the same ditch to help keep the waste moving. Only the mosquitoes flourished in Deland's new neighbourhood. But he paid a price that corresponded with its value: 1,000 gourdes ($209 US) a year. That was my father's limit for the moment.

He had made a promise to Cécile that they would move to the capital. He would keep his word. But whether Cécile would find this preferable to her situation in Saut d'Eau was an open question.

He returned to Saut d'Eau to bring Cécile up to date. He didn't hide from her the reality of their new room in Site Solèy. She agreed to follow him anyway. She said that she would prefer to live in a desert in peace than in the poisoned atmosphere of his family's *lakou*. Deland sold the home he had built to one of his youngest sisters, underlining his intention to not return to Saut d'Eau.

He put my brother and me in two straw sacks that straddled the back of his mule. Cécile sat on its back. Deland led the mule over the mountains and down the valleys until he arrived at the big market called Titanyen just outside the capital. Peasants from all over come to sell their produce at Titanyen. From the summit of the mountains above Titanyen, we could see the capital for the first time. We could see cars moving back and forth.

My father left the mule in the hands of another peasant who had come from Saut d'Eau to sell produce. He would lead the mule back to

Suzanne. Then he piled us all onto a *taptap*, the first time we had ridden one, to take us to our *tikounouk*, our little hovel.

When we arrived in Site Solèy, our new neighbours took stock of the peasants who would be living among them. Dad had paid a man ten gourdes ($2.00 US) to carry our sacks on a *bourèt*. Finally, my mother bravely entered her *tikounouk* for the first time. She looked around at the rusting walls and cardboard floor.

Because my father had returned from Saut d'Eau with provisions for us, he decided to quit his job at the factory and to begin working as a tailor.

It was 1986 and Jean-Claude Duvalier was fleeing the country as we entered the city.

Everything was in chaos. We would hear the *tontons macoutes* running through our neighbourhood, firing their rifles in the air to terrorize us. Our doors and walls were made of corrugated iron. The bullets passed through it without any problem. My parents would throw James and me under their bed when they heard the *macoutes* coming. Hiding under the bed, we came up against huge cockroaches that showed no signs of conceding the space. We had a choice: we could face the *macoutes* or the roaches. We took our chances with the roaches.

I called that period *La Chasse aux Macoutes*. Haitians who had suffered under the Duvalier regime were taking their revenge against the *macoutes*, who had been his personal police force. The *macoutes* used to kill people in the prison of Fort Dimanche and then throw the dead bodies in our neighbourhood to make it look like we were the savages, not them. Now, the tables had turned. When the people managed to find a *macoute* who was hiding for his life, they would place a tire over his head and slide it down to pin his arms by his side. Then the people would douse him with gasoline and light him on fire. That was common enough to be given a name: people called it *Père Lebrun*. (The practice was called "necklacing" in South Africa during the same period. It was a form of rough justice imposed by local ANC communities against blacks who collaborated with the apartheid regime. In Haiti, the same custom was called *Père Lebrun* after a contemporary tire commercial on billboards in Port-au-Prince in which the salesman, Père Lebrun, appeared with his head through a tire.) In some neighbourhoods, such was the hatred for the *macoutes* that the local people hacked their bodies to bits and left the pieces on public display for weeks.

When we were playing in the roads, sometimes protests would pass.

They sang, *Grenadye alaso! Sa ki mouri zafè a yo!* — "Charge grenadiers! Those who fall, that's their own business!"

They meant to say that everyone was involved in the civil war. As such, each person was responsible for his or her own life and welfare. The protesters passed on foot but in great numbers. They carried machetes, pitchforks, and picks: their everyday agricultural tools transformed into arms of war. Others filed branches down to the sharpest points. Still others carried tires and gasoline.

When they passed, we kids were terrified. Even if we were not their enemies, they were telling us that if we were trampled underfoot, it would be our own business. They were pitiless and we were scared. If we were on our way to the ditch to pee-pee or poo-poo, we would turn in our tracks and throw ourselves under the bed until the protesters passed. We would wait until they passed and were out of earshot and then start out again for the ditch.

Once, we were out for a second attempt to relieve ourselves when we were surprised by the protesters who had turned around. They were on fire with excitement. I saw one protester brandishing the burning leg of a *macoute*, cheering. Others carried other parts. I stared for a second and darted back into our little house, launching myself directly under the bed with the poor cockroaches.

They chanted a new slogan this time:

Lafanmi Chilè siye dlo nan je'w,
Chilè pa mouri, se nan plàn li ye,
demen a katrè al telefòne'l,
al devan Sen Jan Bosko w'a jwenn Chilè.
Lafanmi Toto siye dlo nan je'w,
Toto pa mouri, se nan plàn li ye,
demen a katrè al telefòne'l,
al devan Sen Jan Bosko w'a jwenn Toto.

Wipe away your tears, Chilè family,
Chilè is not dead, he is at the pawnbrokers,
At four o'clock tomorrow you should telephone him,
In front of Saint Jean Bosco Church you will find Chilè.
Wipe away your tears, Toto family,
Toto is not dead, he's at the pawnbrokers,
At four o'clock tomorrow you should telephone him,
In front of Saint Jean Bosco Church you will find Toto.

Chilè and Toto were two notorious *tontons macoutes* who had caused much suffering among the people of the capital. They had been involved in all sorts of crimes to enrich themselves under the Duvalier regime. That regime had been built upon terror. The people had been terrorized into submission. The *tontons macoutes* were responsible for controlling their sections. Some *macoutes*, like Chilè and Toto, had earned reputations across the capital. They knew that the Duvalier regime was behind them and so they could terrorize the people without fear of repercussions. News that they were coming to a particular neighbourhood caused crowds to disperse and people to run for cover. They killed young men regularly to show that they could. Not surprisingly, with the regime in free fall and Duvalier en route for France with hundreds of millions of dollars to soften the blow of losing Haiti, the local people took their frustration out on the *tontons macoutes*. Chilè and Toto were two of the most despicable examples of the regime of terror and so they merited a special place in the chant of the protesters. Now, the victims took their revenge.

chapter two

IN SIMON, a district on the edge of Site Solèy, Deland found a little school called La Providence near our *tikounouk* for my brother James and me. It was a pitiful school but was connected to the Salesian Brothers, a Catholic congregation that helped us poor kids. They used to come to La Providence each day with two big sacks, one full of bread and the other of large hard biscuits. Their aid was very helpful because my father didn't have enough money to send us to school and to feed us. James and I were saved by the daily visit of the Salesian Brothers. For us, school was more about food than education. The biscuits were especially nutritious. One single biscuit filled me up.

James and I learned to read before all the other kids. As a result, they used to come to us for help. In gratitude for our help, they used to share with us the bread and biscuits that they got from the Salesians. We would eat our own portions at school and then take what our classmates gave us home for Deland and Cécile. That strategy helped us to relieve the pressure on our parents and also made us good students.

Sometimes the teachers kept sacks of bread and biscuits for themselves. They could sell it to street merchants and pocket the profits or they could take it home and feed their families. As a result, there wouldn't be enough for all the students. We students were affected differently, depending on our situation at home. For James and me, it was a minor catastrophe. The teachers would distribute a portion of the bread and biscuits. Then, we would see them start to tie up the sacks. Whatever remained inside was destined for the market or their homes. If we hadn't got our portion, it was too late. We wouldn't eat.

I used to cry when I realized that I was not going to get a biscuit. But I was too ashamed to tell the teachers why I was crying, that we were too poor to eat at home and my family depended on me. Mostly, I didn't like to be hungry. If a teacher asked me what was wrong, I would invent scenarios to explain my tears. I would lie that one of the other children had hit me, for instance. Once, the student I accused of hitting me yelled that I was lying, that the reason I was crying was that I hadn't received a biscuit. The teacher asked if that was true and I acknowledged that it was so. To keep me calm, if she saw me crying, she would undo the sack and find a biscuit for me. I wouldn't wait for the tears to stop streaming down my cheeks before I dug in.

One day, my grandmother Suzanne came to Simon to spend a few weeks with us. Since we couldn't eat the whole biscuit, we would keep a portion to take home for Suzanne. Sometimes, we managed to get an extra biscuit and we would give it to her. She started to get used to her daily biscuits, just like us kids. The first thing I used to do upon returning home was to greet my grandmother. After awhile, her response was, "Where's the bread and biscuit for your grandmother?"

One day, when we were especially looking forward to the arrival of the *taptap* that usually brought the Salesians with their bread and biscuits, it simply didn't arrive. All we school kids were crushed. School turned into hell that day. When we returned home, my grandmother was waiting for me at the door like a customs agent. She asked me hopefully, "Where are the bread and biscuits that you have brought your grandmother?"

I had already passed customs, but I had to take two steps back to deliver the bad news. I lied, "Mèmè, it's not just for bread and biscuits that I go to school, you know."

She was shocked by the response. I had always been a good grandson who shared his biscuits with his grandma. She never knew what I had to go through to make sure I returned with something for her.

"Okay, okay, my child," she responded. "I won't ask you anymore for a biscuit. I see that school also teaches you how to be mean to your grandmother."

Deland learned through the neighbours that the only strength of our school was the bread and biscuits. It was not strong in academics. So, he sent us to a primary school called Le Progrès, also run by the Salesian Brothers, in a neighbourhood called Site Limyè in the centre of Site Solèy. There, they gave us bread along with a little carton of milk. The school only operated during the dry season, better understood as the dusty season. During the rainy season, there was so much mud in the area that the school had a difficult time operating. So it closed its doors until the worst of the muddy season had passed.

In Le Progrès, we made lots of new friends. I was lucky to make a friend named Molière who was in my class and lived near the school. There were many days when the Brothers did not hand out milk and bread and I had not eaten at home. But, before going to school, Molière used to prepare a pot of kongo or black beans and leave them on the *rechau*, a little oven that the local men made out of sheet metal. When recess came, he invited me to his home for a plate of rice and beans. I asked him wherever he found the money to cook beans each day. In my own household there was seldom a meal in the morning. He told me that his mother was a street merchant who sold agricultural products. She left him the beans every morning.

—•—

Deland was now using his own sewing machine to support his family. He decided to buy his own house instead of renting. He found a place in even worse condition than the one we rented, but which he could afford. He paid in instalments. He did his best to make the new place habitable, but there was only so much he could do.

Deland was trying to build a life for us in Site Solèy, but we seemed to be going backwards. The new place did not have enough space for his sewing machine. The only logical place for him to locate his business was on top of the ditch where the human waste flowed. It was about thirty metres in front of our new home. At the time, the road that led to downtown Port-au-Prince passed next to that spot. Deland wanted to attract as many potential customers as possible. So he laid plywood across the ditch and built a little shop with corrugated iron. On a board, he wrote the name of his business and affixed it to the new structure: "Bethesda Shop Deland."

When my father began to build on top of the ditch, the neighbours and passersby thought he was crazy. But he continued. Finally, clients began to visit his new shop. Why? Because it turned out to be the best location. So what if human waste flowed underneath the shop? That was just a part of our neighbourhood. Inside the shop, clients did not think of its location. Not only did people reconsider their criticism of Deland, but many started to follow his example and build their homes and little businesses on top of the ditch.

Among them was a man from Cap Haitien and his family. He built a room of corrugated iron on top of the ditch not far from the Bethesda Shop. Olvè had no money, even to feed his family, but he wanted to start some small business. A friend lent him a little money to buy some oil, a sack of rice, one container of butter, another of tomato paste, and some beans. He divided his produce to sell to the poor who could afford only a small quantity at a time. He set up a table between the ditch and the road. Like Deland, he was visible and people took advantage of the convenience.

Everyone knew that Olvè was a Vodouist. One day, he decided to put the extreme poverty of his life behind him. "Better that I die than continue in this state," he said.

He went to an *houngan* who was known to be very powerful. Olvè wanted a "point." A point is a contract with the devil. One can enter such a contract, but with conditions attached. The devil can make someone enormously rich, but in return for years of life. The benefits that might come from such a contract — money, fame, youth, power, talent, protection — are unimportant in themselves. The devil uses human needs to trap his prey. The conditions are also diverse. You may have to sacrifice a member of your family, for instance. People always think that the devil is stupid, that he'll take the black sheep of the family, whereas he can take your fondest and closest member. He can take an eye, a leg, or an arm in payment. These payments depend on how much you want and how badly you want it. People think that they can escape the contract. The devil knows better. As long as you live, you are in his service.

Some people make contracts to travel abroad. Each year, the person must return for a big Vodouist ceremony. Or burn a portion of his money in an intersection. When the contract includes the loss of an arm or a leg, it is not simply a matter of the *houngan* taking out a machete and lopping it off. Instead, you may be climbing onto a bus when it is hit by a truck. The other passengers might escape without injury, but you will be gravely injured and lose your leg.

For Olvè, less than a month after his contract, all of the neighbours were amazed at his success. No longer was he selling little packages of provisions. Now, he was receiving truckloads of rice, oil, beans, tomato paste, and butter. Everyone knew that he had taken a point. Olvè bought up the little houses that people had built on top of the ditch after my father had broken ground. He used these little houses as storage units. He announced that he didn't need to hire security guards. He said that anyone who tried to steal from his storage units would be sorry. Everyone knew what that meant. His contract came complete with protection. Moreover, no one would accept any gift from Olvè, fearing that they might unwittingly be including themselves in the contract. People feared Olvè, but they did not respect him.

Olvè's family changed their appearance, like snakes shed their skin.

After three years, Olvè was dead. His business disappeared overnight. His wife confirmed to us that he had entered into a contract with a *lwa*. She was frightened. She and the children fled to Cap Haitien. We in the neighbourhood never knew their ultimate fate. Since they were accomplices in the contract, we knew that they were marked.

●●●

Meanwhile, the Bethesda Shop flourished. The local Catholic school required that children wear uniforms. At the beginning of the school year, Deland was inundated with orders from parents to prepare their children. So much work came in that he needed to hire some apprentice tailors to help him.

With his new success, he bought another sewing machine for my mother. She joined him in making the uniforms for the local girls. Together, they worked night and day. As the business grew, they were able to rebuild a proper shop with cinder blocks. Behind, he built a real toilet: a concrete floor with a hole that opened onto the ditch. People crouched just as they did outside, but the concrete walls offered privacy.

It was the only actual toilet in the neighbourhood. Not only his family and clients, but our neighbours started to visit his shop when they felt the call of nature. With this new luxury, they increasingly rejected the open public toilet.

In the heat of Port-au-Prince, clients appreciate any business that can offer cool drinks. So, my father sectioned off a small area at the front of his shop with cinder blocks. He bought some soft drinks and then covered them with blocks of ice that he purchased each morning from the ice factory in Simon. He protected the ice from the heat by covering it with old nylon sugar sacks. There were more and more reasons for visiting the shop. The Bethesda Shop became a focal point in the neighbourhood.

The school uniforms were the basis of my parents' business. However, those orders came just before the school year began and they swamped my parents with work. My father wanted to attract business during the rest of the year, when he and Cécile were not overworked. So, he stocked the shop with linens of bright colours. He hung in front of the shop examples of designs that he and Cécile had created. Dresses, skirts, and shirts gave his shop a lively and attractive allure. Everyone who passed stopped to admire the samples. Although they could seldom afford to buy a new article of clothing, they could dream. Before long, they would be saving their money in order to buy the item that they had seen everyday hanging in the front of the Bethesda Shop. At the time, Deland was the only tailor to promote his work in this way. Only street merchants of second-hand clothing displayed their work in the open, for lack of a shop. However, Deland had the distinction of both owning a shop and displaying his original work for passersby to see.

Over the Bethesda Shop, Deland built an awning to offer passersby a refuge from the pitiless sun. Underneath it, he built a bench. Many people stopped for a few minutes to rest before continuing on their way. The shade only added to the appreciation that the local people had for my father's business. It also helped to increase the activity around the shop, which could only help in the long run.

Deland and Cécile slept in the home across from the shop with the youngest kids. My brother James and I slept in the shop, on top of piles of soft fabric, along with the apprentices who now worked with my parents. One evening, some people came by to try to set the wooden door of the shop on fire. That might have spread to consume the fabrics and clothing inside, not to mention my brother and me. My father's success was provoking jealousy and resentment among some of our neighbours.

Sometimes, we awoke to find *vèvè* traced in the soil in front of the shop. A *vèvè* is a Vodou symbol that is used to communicate with the *lwa*. Each *lwa* has his own *vèvè*. They are used to call forth a *lwa*, but there can be a number of intentions. Sometimes, *vèvè* can be traced out of white flour. When people see a *vèvè* before their door, they might respond with fear. In that state, they are more vulnerable to falling victim to misfortune. They know that a spirit has been called forth to act upon them; that can't be good news. But Deland simply swept the *vèvè* away and carried on with his life and his business.

Finally, Deland was able to rebuild the old shack where the family lived. He bought cinder blocks and constructed two rooms across from the business. That was now our family's home in Simon, a section of Site Solèy.

Fortunately, Cécile was not materialistic. She was content with her two rooms and family. At the time, local produce was not expensive, and it was nutritious. Deland sometimes returned to Saut d'Eau to collect a part of the harvest that came from the land he still owned. He would return and stock our home with manioc, legumes, potatoes, corn, and other foods that had a reasonable shelf life. Moreover, it was what Cécile and the family were used to eating. During this period, when the Bethesda Shop was flourishing, my mother economized and we ate healthily.

Deland and Cécile were one in working for their family. Our home was separated from our next-door neighbours by a flimsy wall of corrugated iron. When our produce arrived from Saut d'Eau, Cécile used to share it with our neighbours. The two families often ate together. This worked as long as both families shared the same spirit as well as the actual things that passed between us.

―●―

Eventually, the administration of Site Solèy came by to mark all of the buildings built over the ditch for demolition. The Bethesda Shop was marked in red. We were told that city hall intended to enlarge the road. Those in the neighbourhood who were jealous of my father's business were content. Some prepared to begin the destruction with the Bethesda Shop.

Some people were sanctioned by city hall to carry out the demolition. However, a number of others wanted to participate so that they might recover the iron bars and other materials from the wreckage.

One of our neighbours whose home was also marked for demolition was a policeman. He placed himself in front of his door with a gun, threatening the crowd, "The first person who advances on my house will be shot."

The crowd backed up, deciding to leave the home of the policeman alone and to concentrate on the others. *Makak sou konn sou ki bwa li fwote* — a drunken monkey knows what tree he is rubbing against. Only the policeman's home remained standing. In fact, it is standing today. He lives there still with his family.

No one was compensated for their loss. Everyone had to start over again. Construction began on the road six years later.

My father was discouraged and sad. He thought of all that he had invested in the Bethesda Shop. It was destroyed. He had little to show for all his sacrifices. He got sick.

He thought of returning to Saut d'Eau. But given the problems that had precipitated our family's departure several years earlier, it seemed unfeasible. Moreover, my father had already sold his home there. But he decided to return to Saut d'Eau to work the land for a few months in order to return to Port-au-Prince with provisions.

Meanwhile, my mother took charge in Site Solèy. The house was still standing. She put her sewing machine in front of the house and continued to receive clients there. She managed to cope with the setback and to keep us all alive while Deland worked in Saut d'Eau.

Eventually, Deland returned with enough provisions to last several months. My parents decided that Cécile would continue to receive clients in our home while my father would go to work in a foreign assembly plant in the Industrial Park. He made fifty gourdes a day (about $3 US) if he succeeded in achieving the quota. Even if he made the quota, his pay was far from adequate to support his five children.

He intended to work for several months to earn enough money to rebuild his shop from scratch. Nothing had changed in the factories. He arose at five o'clock in the morning to walk a few kilometres to arrive at six o'clock. If he was fifteen minutes late, either his pay would be docked or he would simply be refused entry for the day.

In the factory, Deland was required to stand for the entire twelve-hour day cutting slacks out of the fabric. He was exhausted at the end of the day. When he returned home, he had to help my mother with her work.

After five months, he could no longer stand work in the factory. It was time to rent a room somewhere in the neighbourhood to rebuild his old business. He found a room for 5,000 gourdes (about $330 US) a year that was closer to the road than our house. Even with the money he had saved from the factory and that my mother had managed to put aside from her sewing work, he still needed to borrow from our neighbours to rent the room.

The new location was not as propitious for his business as had been the Bethesda Shop; it was not as visible. The same tactics that had worked so well to draw clients to Bethesda would not work in this new location. Even though the new room was not as lucrative as Bethesda, he made the same amount of money in one month that he had earned in five months in the factory.

After a year, my father decided not to renew his lease on the room. Next door to it was an old workshop that was in financial trouble. My father saw this as his opportunity and bought it. He transferred his sewing machine to get started even though the building was still arranged to make aluminium pots.

Over time, Deland was able to transform the old workshop into a tailoring business.

— • —

It was 1999 and Cécile was pregnant for the eighth time. As she was anemic and had developed varicose veins, the doctors had warned her not to give birth again. But it was too late.

One morning, my mother sat before her laundry tub washing our clothes.

She called me over to tell me that I had to finish it because the time had come for her to give birth. She packed her bags and left for the hospital. She never returned.

I was sad and cried a lot. I went to a friend of my mother with tears flowing down my cheeks. I had thought that she would be sympathetic. Instead, she was harsh. "What are you crying about?" she demanded in a severe tone. I didn't know what to answer because I thought it was obvious. "Your mother is gone now. You are still here. You have to learn to live without her, so get busy!"

On our *lakou* in Saut d'Eau, there is a big fig tree. My family used to worship it because the *lwa* lived in it. A fig begins its life by climbing up another tree. It is dependent on that tree. It leans upon it. As time passes, it outgrows its host tree. It leaves it behind as it stands on its own.

Cécile left my father with seven children. He and my mother had been leaning on each other. Now, Deland had to stand on his own, like me.

Deland spent everything he had, and went into debt, to pay for Cécile's funeral. When it was over, he decided that he could not manage the family without Cécile, so he had to find places for us. The fourth child, Roselèn, went to live with her uncle in Delmas 4. I would soon go to live with my father's sister in Delmas 33. Only James and Christla remained with my father in Simon. He sent the three youngest to an orphanage in Croix-des-Bouquets.

Gloria was the second-youngest child, smart and pretty. In the orphanage, there were malefactors — people who delight in doing evil and seeing others suffer — who came sometimes to prey on the children. They gave Gloria a dreadful illness. She would be overcome by seizures and fall unconscious to the ground wherever she happened to be standing, sometimes several times a day. When the directors of the orphanage saw that she had changed, they called my father to take her back. Back in Simon, my father went to the hospital to see if doctors could help her. They couldn't.

When she was thirteen, my father sent her to Saut d'Eau to spend her vacation with her aunt. They left Gloria alone in their *tikounouk*. She was overtaken by her sickness and fell on a fire. Although her hand was directly in the fire, she was unaware that it was burning. However, when she regained consciousness, she felt her flesh burning and called out. Some neighbours came in to see that her hand was already burning. They called my aunt who was still within earshot. She took Gloria to Saut d'Eau on the back of a donkey to look for medical help. The doctor couldn't do anything but bandage her hand. My aunt brought Gloria back to Simon to try to find help. But it was too late. My father couldn't afford the medical costs to save Gloria's hand.

Gloria spent all of her life with her sickness and her deformity. Her seizures led to nasty falls. Her face, arms, and legs were constantly bruised and cut. She was only aware of the pain when she recovered consciousness. But my father felt every pain when Gloria fell. She was constantly in danger and always in need. She took up much of my father's attention. He always hoped that she would recover and become healthy and normal. Deep down, I think he knew that she would never be well.

chapter three

IN OUR NEIGHBOURHOOD, kids were expected to learn a trade even while they were still at school. There were lots of little businesses around us where the young could be taken on as apprentices: mechanics, furniture makers, ironworks, electronics stores, and, of course, tailor shops.

My parents had been arranging for James and me to learn trades even before my mother died. Our home had no furniture. And so, I thought it would be good for us if I could become a furniture maker.

One day, sitting in our barren room, I asked my mother which she would prefer, a china cabinet or an *ofis*, which was similar but does not have three doors in the upper section. I was dreaming, because I didn't yet know the first thing about making furniture.

She replied, "My son, I will leave it up to you. You decide what would be better for us."

I felt proud. She spoke to me as though I was already a furniture maker. And so I wanted to fulfil her confidence in me and become what she wanted me to be. I could imagine her pride in me as she opened her beautiful china cabinet filled with real tableware.

My father had already planned with the bosses in the local furniture and mechanic shops to teach my brother and me. He took James to the garage and then me to the furniture shop.

"I am leaving my son with you," he said to the master cabinetmaker. "I hope that he will learn to be as skilled a cabinetmaker as you are."

That day, I watched everything that was going on in the shop, but the boss gave me nothing to do except sweep the floors and keep the shop clean. And so it continued, day after day. What's more, I soon found that, if I hadn't been able to eat at home, I would pass the entire day with nothing in my stomach.

One day, I was overcome by stomach cramps. I had left home without even tasting some coffee. The boss had given me the job of drilling holes in the legs of chairs in order to fasten them to the frame with dowelling. When I felt the cramps strike, I told my boss that I couldn't stay because I was in pain. He said that I could go home to see if the cramps would subside. I could return if I was feeling better.

So I went home. My mother was cooking. She asked what I was doing at home. I told her as I fell onto the bed in pain. My mother woke me up a short while later to give me a plate of *mal moulen* (cornmeal with oil and whatever vegetables and/or edible leaves are at hand). When I finished, the cramps disappeared and so I went back to the shop.

"Ah, you've come back then. You're feeling better?" the boss mocked me.

I said, "Yes."

"Did you eat at home?"

I told him that I had. The other workers in the shop all laughed, saying that it was a strange sickness that could be cured with a plate of *mal moulen*. I laughed along with them and went back to work. But my stomach and heart were not laughing. I decided that I would no longer work unless I had something in my stomach.

After a few weeks, the bosses taught me how to saw. My first effort was a mess. I was supposed to saw a straight line, but I couldn't guide the saw and the result was a zigzag.

My progress was slow. Meanwhile, James was already making money as a mechanic. He was able to buy things for my mother and for our younger siblings. But I was bringing nothing home but myself. I started to feel that I must be a great disappointment for my mother. But my father kept saying that, in a few years, I would be a great cabinetmaker. He was the only one who had faith in me.

Deland bought me a plane, a saw, and a hammer. My boss had told Dad that it was the same as buying books and pens for students in school. But I left the tools at home where I could practice alone and keep them shiny and new.

I was now arriving at the shop at about ten o'clock in the morning, because I always waited until my mother had prepared something for me to eat at home. Even though we always got up before dawn, if we ate, it was in the mid-morning. One day, the boss sent me home for arriving late. He said that he would call me when he needed me.

I left and went to hang out in the other furniture shops in the district, without making it known that I was already an apprentice. The following day, I returned to one in particular and offered to help the furniture makers with sanding or other small jobs. No one asked me to come back. I just showed up every morning and made myself available. I started to bring the tools that my father had given me. Since my tools were brand new, the main boss, whose name was David, preferred them to his own. Maybe my tools were more welcome than I was.

I made a big mistake. I didn't tell Dad that the master furniture maker that he had secured for me had expelled me from his shop. It was in passing one day that my parents saw me working in David's shop. They were angry with me, but they didn't force me to stop going.

The new master was an *houngan*. His mother and his sister were *lougarou*. *Lougarou* are humans that can transform themselves into other animals. Like vampires, they can fly and, at night, they suck the blood of babies. During the day, a *lougarou* looks for babies separated from their parents in order to pull a strand of hair from their heads. Along with the hair, the *lougarou* steals the soul of the baby who is thus doomed to die. Sometimes, they can innocently arrive at the home of a neighbour who has babies. They ask for matches or salt. Once these things are in their possession, they can use them to control the domestic life of the family from a distance. *Lougarou* do not act to enrich themselves, but simply to spread misery. Normal people can be inhabited by *lwa* that transform them into *lougarou*. A family can unknowingly have a *lougarou* in its midst.

David's family appreciated me because I was polite and did whatever they asked of me. But my father was concerned. He knew that the family were malefactors and saw that I was becoming attached to them. I knew he was unhappy with my presence in their household, but somehow I couldn't leave. Worse, the *houngan* didn't pay me for the little jobs that I did for him around the shop. Sometimes, as an act of rebellion, I took my tools and returned home. I knew that the *houngan's* tools were inferior. But, each time, I returned to offer him my tools again, never understanding why.

This *houngan* mixed magic with his work as a furniture maker. After he had taken money from clients for an order, he would use materials inferior to those he had promised and craft a piece smaller than that contracted. When clients came to pick up their orders, they were at first angry at the quality of the work. But, as they spoke, the *houngan* would put the client under his will until he accepted the work.

In the absence of David, clients came to argue with us, who were innocent. "I ordered a large china, and look at what you have made. This is a *kokorat* of a piece of furniture! I'm calling the police! I'm not leaving until I speak to David and we resolve this! I'm going to give him a piece of my mind."

We would say, "You'll change your tune when David returns. Wait and see."

They would argue even louder. But, sure enough, when David arrived, the clients would soften their tone. Although they might continue to complain, they argued with far less force. When he saw that, David would go on the offensive.

After my mother died, I worked all day every day in this shop. Even when David had no work, I visited to pass the day there sitting on a bench, as though I had been zombified.

My dad became increasingly anxious about the situation. He called his brother-in-law who was also a furniture maker, asking him to take me into apprenticeship. Dad's only concern was to make sure that I was freed from David's hold over me. My uncle had just opened a shop in Delmas 19 and had only one nephew to help him, but they couldn't get along. They fought constantly. I was to take his place. My uncle was happy to find a replacement, so much so that he immediately got into his old Volvo and drove to Simon to get me.

As he spoke to Dad in our home, I was at David's as usual. My Dad sent someone to get me and I told them that I would come home later. My father came himself to David's workshop and grabbed me by the collar and handed me over to his brother-in-law. I was crying.

My uncle took over, "Why are you crying? You are going to be with your family now where you belong. Everything is going to be fine now."

My Dad told my uncle that he would bring me to him the following week after we had made plans and prepared my clothes.

My uncle insisted that I leave then and there. I said that I had no shoes; he said that he would buy me some. He countered every one of my excuses.

"What do you know how to do so far?" he asked me.

I answered, "I know how to saw, to plane, to sand, and to connect joints."

My uncle gleamed. He was saved.

In the presence of my father, he made a show of opening the door of his Volvo for me to enter. He appeared to be a chauffeur, waiting upon the pleasure of royalty. Clearly, he wanted to convince Dad that I would be in good hands. I got in and he closed the door on my former life.

On the way to Delmas 19, he bought two-by-fours, plywood, and a few planks so that I could start working as soon as we arrived in his little shop. He could see the tears falling down my face in his rear view mirror. He looked for words to calm me.

"Listen, if you stay in my shop, I will teach you how to drive. You will be the chief of the workshop because there are no others. You will be the boss!"

He miscalculated, thinking that I was ambitious for power. But his offer to teach me how to drive hit home. It was my dream to be able to drive a car. But, for the rest, I knew in my heart that my uncle was lying. I had seen enough of the world to know that people don't take on little apprentices so that they can take control of their businesses.

When we arrived in Delmas 19, I saw his workshop made out of rusty sheets of metal. It was pathetic. He had me take the building materials inside the shop.

"Tomorrow, you will start working. Today you can rest."

We sat together. He bought us each a plate of rice and a soft drink from a merchant close to the workshop. He wanted to make me believe that I was in good hands.

At sunset, we got into the Volvo again and went to the home of his wife, Dad's sister, in Delmas 33. I felt uncomfortable. But my two little cousins were happy to have me with them. I ate and then went to sleep on a mat on the floor.

My uncle got me up at six o'clock. He told me to clean the Volvo before we left for Delmas 19. When we arrived at the workshop, he got me to start sawing the planks to make doors. The doors were not to fill an order, but just to sell to passersby. After we had made six doors, he put them outside on the side of the road. Each morning, my first job was to take the doors out to the road.

Every morning, my aunt would prepare a bowl of food for us. At work, my uncle would eat what was in the bowl and put a small amount on the lid for me. However, I was the one working. It was just as he had said: since I was the only worker, I was also my own boss.

As we climbed back to Delmas 33 that first day, he told me that I should carefully remember the route, because I would soon be going alone to the workshop . . . and on foot.

I soon discovered why. My uncle lived not only with my aunt and cousins. He also had an apartment where he lived with a mistress. When he was staying with his mistress, my aunt would give me the lunch for us both each morning and I would walk to the workshop in Delmas 19. My uncle would come from the other direction. He could arrive at any hour of the day because he used his Volvo as a taxi in the mornings. Sometimes, he was so late that the lunch had gone bad in the heat. But I had to wait until he arrived. If the lunch was still good, he gave me my part on the lid.

•●•

When I started to work at the shop, we were in the middle of the summer vacations. My Dad said that when school started again, I should attend during the afternoons. However, my uncle didn't accept that part of the agreement. The moment that I started school, the workshop would suffer. He was obliged to accept the agreement, however. *Se kondisyon ki bat kòk* — you can't change the rules in the middle of the game.

Nevertheless, my uncle arranged for my cousins to attend school, but not me. When all the other kids went to school, I continued to go to the workshop. So, I prepared my bags to leave my uncle's house, saying, "Dad told me that I should return to Simon to go to school."

My uncle got into his Volvo and drove to Simon where he asked Dad if this was so. My father replied no, but if there was a school in Delmas 33, I should attend it.

My uncle was obliged to agree to send me to school in Delmas 33. His intention, though, was that I work all day in his workshop as I had been doing throughout the summer. As he saw that I was determined to go to school, he decided to look for one close to the workshop.

So I began my new schedule. I worked at the shop in the morning and went to school each afternoon. Each day at noon, as I prepared to go to school, my uncle became angry. Needless to say, I was prohibited from doing my homework at the workshop, but there was no other time to do it. School ended at sunset and then I had to return home on foot to Delmas 33. Sometimes, I could barely stay awake on the way home.

My aunt was a street merchant. She would go to the big markets to purchase fig bananas that she resold in Delmas. It was my job to bring the sacks of bananas into the house when I arrived home. I had to clean my clothes at night by candlelight while everyone else slept. I slept on a carpet on the kitchen floor. There was no time to do all that was required of me. I was exhausted.

chapter four

MY UNCLE HAD TO LOOK for other workers to help make up for my absence at school in the afternoons. The first had been an apprentice in another shop. My uncle offered him a few little jobs. Josué believed that he would be able to make more money in my uncle's shop. Moreover, it was very close to his home. But my uncle didn't have too much confidence in Josué. His skills were not yet developed.

A number of different craftsmen can work on any one piece of furniture. Josué was expert at sanding and varnishing. My uncle employed certain sculptors to carve designs in the furniture once the form was complete. Sometimes, I would design furniture on paper just for fun. My uncle asked me if I would really be able to build the things that I was sketching.

When my uncle was out driving his Volvo as a taxi, I traced designs in the wood and then sculpted them. Like that, I designed and finished a buffet. When my uncle saw the designs that I had carved into my buffet, he asked who had done that. When he found out that it was me, he was upset rather than complimentary.

"Oh! You know how to sculpt like this and yet you let me waste my money hiring outside people to do it?! From now on, you do the sculpting."

It was understood, of course, that I would not see the money my uncle saved on outside sculptors. I was simply taken for granted. Worse, I got into trouble for not allowing him to exploit me more effectively.

From then on, he had me decorate every piece of furniture that he made from my designs. Although I was not compensated at all, I was happy that my skill was being recognized, albeit begrudgingly. Moreover, I was now able to practice my talent and passion for design. My uncle's exploitation would ultimately be to my advantage. My uncle was not talented in designing the pieces he built. That was my strength. I loved to imagine different pieces of furniture and always kept my sketchbook by my side.

In the workshop, there were several catalogues of furniture of different styles. Clients would browse the catalogues and point to a piece that they liked. Before he continued with the contract, my uncle used to come to me to quietly ask if we could do it. Then, he would go back and repeat what I had told him word for word. His methods were reasonable. Since I would do the work, he knew that if he accepted an order that I could not build, he would be stuck with a dissatisfied client.

Josué was not a regular employee, but was brought in to do the sanding and varnishing when my uncle needed him. So, most often, I worked alone. One day, I was building a china cabinet. As I was sawing planks of wood, the saw flew from its path and cut through my hand, almost detaching my thumb. The neighbours heard my scream and ran to help me. They poured alcohol on it. It was extremely painful. Like me, they were shocked to see the thumb of my left hand mostly detached. They told me to wait. When my uncle returned, they said, he would take me to the hospital for stitches, since the gash was deep. It was clearly beyond bandages.

My uncle did return. He looked at the little progress that I had been able to make on the china cabinet rather than looking at me. "What have you been doing all morning!?" he bellowed. "You've hardly done anything since I left!"

I held up my left hand so that he could see the extent of my injury. I had thought that even my uncle would soften his tone in the face of my pain. But no. He offered only a dismissive gesture, as if I was faking. Meanwhile, I was in real danger of losing my thumb.

"*Se sòt k'ap soti, lespri ap antre,*" he said: my "cut" would allow the idiot in me to exit my body, and wisdom to enter. It was a callous use of a good aphorism. The neighbours who had come to my aid earlier called themselves into my service once again, saying that it was abominable that an uncle should treat his nephew in such a manner.

I hadn't said one word since he returned. Now, I went into a corner to try to think and to cry. My uncle left the shop.

My uncle's reaction reminded me of the time when Haiti was a French colony. The slaves were brought from Africa and were treated as pieces of property. My uncle behaved as I imagined a slave-owner would have responded to the loss of a slave from an accident. But now, slaves were brought from Site Solèy to Delmas. I was of the poor race of Haitians. Now, the slave-owners like my uncle had only to wait for us to fall into their hands.

Two different ideas battled inside of me. One voice told me to leave the workshop; my uncle was a brute and I should simply escape. The other was aware of the crowd around me that was ready to take up my cause. How much could I rely on them? In the time of slavery, there were *mawon* who sought to flee and live in the mountains of Haiti, free from the French plantation owners; there were also revolutionaries, who sought to inspire their fellow slaves to defeat their masters. To fight or to flee: both strains existed in me as I sobbed in the corner.

Sometimes the *mawon* gave up their solitary existence in the mountains and came back to live on the plantations. Sometimes, they were caught and forcibly brought back. In either case, they were treated harshly for their rebelliousness. They could have a hand cut off, for example.

While still waiting in the corner, I decided to remain in the shop. But I would not forget this. My uncle would pay somehow.

Eventually, my uncle returned. He didn't ask me about my injury, but he told me to take some window panes back to Delmas 33 that he wanted me to install in his house. Then he left in the Volvo. He didn't offer to take me or the window panes in the car. He expected me to carry them back to his home on foot.

By now, my left hand was very swollen. There was no way that I would be able to carry the tools I would need to install the windows, even if I could carry the windows in my right hand.

All of this was taking place while I should have been in school. There was only one reason that I was not in school and that was my injury. In profiting from my absence from school to assign me work, my uncle implicitly acknowledged its seriousness. But he just as quickly denied it in order to get more work out of me.

In any case, I left the tools behind, thinking that I could return early the next morning to fetch them so that my uncle could install the windows. I had to walk to Delmas 33, because I had no money for a *taptap*.

As soon as I had put the window frames in the house, I went to the market to find my aunt. When I found her selling her bananas, I showed her my hand. She was shocked. She could see the exposed flesh. All of the merchant women gathered around us to look at the wound. They assumed it had been made by a machete.

"But what did my husband do?" my aunt asked me. "Didn't he take you to the hospital to have them stitch it?"

When she heard my answer, she passed her kerchief across her forehead. "You should go to the hospital. But I don't have any money," she fretted. "I have spent the whole day here and I have sold almost nothing."

We went home together. My uncle had already arrived and was in bed. We all turned in. Even though my thumb throbbed, I managed to sleep. *Domi pa konn mizè malere* — the wretched can sleep anywhere.

− ● −

The next morning, my uncle asked me where the tools were to install the windows. I told him that they were still in the shop, since I hadn't been able to carry them. He was livid.

"What!" he yelled. "All you had to do was bring a few tools. What kind of weakling are you?!" He treated me as though I was not suffering from a serious injury.

I put on my shoes and ran to Delmas 19 to get the tools as fast as I could and bring them back to Delmas 33.

I returned in no time with the tools. He grabbed them from my right hand and gruffly told me to return to the workshop and continue sanding the base of the china cabinet I was building and apply a coat of zincromat, a product that protects inferior wood from being infested by insects.

At the shop, I was so out of my mind that I did the opposite: I gave the china a coat of zincromat first, and then prepared to sand it.

While I was looking for sandpaper, my uncle showed up in the workshop. He saw that I had already given a coat of zincromat to the base of the china. He bellowed, "What am I going to do with this piece of shit! This pig!" He was referring to me rather than the china cabinet.

Some neighbours were in the workshop. I felt ashamed. I couldn't look anyone in the eyes. If I didn't respond to my uncle, then the crowd would have categorized me as a *restavèk* who had had his own will beaten out of him. I stared at my hand.

"Look. I have been injured working for my uncle. I am still working. But in return, he calls me a pig. It takes a lot of courage to respond to my uncle." Then, turning to my uncle, I said, "It would be best that pigs remain with pigs, and human beings with human beings."

Without waiting for any response, I left the workshop. He had mistreated me in order to show others the power that he had over me. Since I had talked back, he seemed to have lost the power that could only come from my submission. Now, my uncle was ashamed in front of the neighbours. I could hear him running behind me.

"Get back to the workshop! I'll give you the cane for that demonstration."

But I kept walking forward, refusing to acknowledge the barrage of venom that he was hurling at me. I was so determined that it may have looked as though I knew where I was going. In fact, I only knew that I was not going back to the workshop.

As I walked along, my mind was overwhelmed with worries about what I would do and even where I was going. I seemed to be burning a bridge from a place I did not want to return, but there were no others to take me somewhere better or worse. I decided to go to my aunt in Delmas 33 and to explain to her what had happened.

"My aunt, I have tried to behave correctly with my uncle and to respect him. But I can no longer accept the abuses that he has forced upon me. In public, he called me a pig. I can no longer stay if I want to retain my dignity." My aunt claimed that she was surprised to hear this. But, as we talked, it was clear that she was afraid of him and was really not surprised. With the humiliations that he forced upon her every day, how could she expect him to treat me well?

She advised me to stay home with her until I could make plans.

"You are kind," I replied. "But we know that men are the kings of their castles. He is really angry with me. When I am not working in his shop, he won't allow me to stay here."

But she surprised me, "No. You are my nephew. He cannot stop me from allowing you to stay here if I invite you. I paid for this land with the profits from my work as a vendor. I am the one who can say who can stay here and who cannot."

I said, "Okay. But I don't want to be the source of trouble in your home."

But she insisted, "No, no. It is thanks to your father that I am here in the capital. Deland helped me get started here. So it would not be decent for me to leave his son when he needs me. If my brother were to die before me, then I would feel responsible for his children."

"No, my aunt. A family is a family and a household a household. You already have two children. Your nephew should not be disturbing your lives here."

She started to cry. She called on some of her merchant friends to complain about her husband. She showed them my hand as proof of her husband's brutality. They all agreed that he was a brute. I was the centre of their pity. That was kind of nice.

After awhile, I said that I had to go. They wanted to know where I was going. "Are you going to Simon? To your father's?" I said no. I wasn't sure where I was going to go.

My aunt insisted that I give her my coordinates. All I could tell her was that I would be in Haiti. I would manage to survive. But my voice was shaking. I was really afraid, because I knew that I was going to join the *kokorats* for the first time. *Kokorats* are homeless kids who live on the streets of Port-au-Prince. They are like feral human beings.

I didn't want my aunt to be angry with me. She told me to come by whenever I needed something and she would help me.

— • —

The days were not a problem. I hung out in Delmas 33. I talked with people, watched soccer games played in the field, and just walked around. But as night approached, my stomach started to feel queasy. I did not want people to know that I had fallen out with my family. I didn't want them to know the state to which I had fallen. I would check out the abandoned cars for the possibility of sleeping in them. I found a *taptap* that had been abandoned in an intersection. An intersection, or *kafou*, is especially meaningful for Vodouists. Many of their ceremonies take place there during the night.

There is a group of Vodouists called *san pwèl*. They come out at night. Sometimes, they transform themselves into animals. Haitians who find themselves out in the middle of the night are very cautious to avoid all animals. A hen and her chicks crossing a *kafou* at night are most probably a group of *san pwèl*, with the queen presenting herself as the mother hen. A fool may make the fatal mistake of taking the hen for his pot. Foreigners can foolishly pick up a chick, thinking it a fluffy little innocent. But nothing is what it seems to be. The *san pwèl* also have the ability to transform any human being walking the streets into an animal by lassoing him or her with a mystical cord. The person is then fated to continue his or her existence in that form. The *san pwèl* emit an invisible breeze, called a *kout lè*. If a human comes into contact with a *kout lè*, he is in serious danger of dying. Or they can *flash* their victim from a distance. They have a kind of flashlight that sends out more than rays of light. If the *san pwèl* succeed in flashing a victim, he is doomed. However, an *houngan* or *mambo* can counter the spells cast by the *san pwèl*. The *san pwèl*, like *lougarou*, are nasty. There are many people and spirits who prefer to not be seen. In Haiti, with no streetlights, the nights belong to them. Policemen stop anyone who is out at night, assuming that all decent citizens are safe at home.

Every one of these dangers terrorized me as I entered the back of the *taptap* for the night. On top of that were the human malefactors: thieves and murderers. I had no other choice. Somehow, I managed to fall asleep in the back of the *taptap*. I awoke whenever I heard footsteps or packs of dogs running across the *kafou*. All over Port-au-Prince, the dogs that lie around in the heat during the day come together to form packs at night. Needless to say, my heart would beat double-time and I always longed for the sunrise. I laid face down on the wooden bench in the back of the *taptap* with my hands over my ears, not wanting to see or hear all the dangers that surrounded me. Every morning, at four-thirty, I was awakened by an early mass that was celebrated at a local church. They had loudspeakers that publicized the prayers inside. As soon as I heard them, I arose and stayed inside the church until sunrise.

Once inside the church, I used to kneel in order to give the appearance that I was particularly devout. I put my head in my hands as though I was deep in prayer. In fact, I was fast asleep, knowing that, although I was not comfortable, I was safe. In fact, I always overslept the mass. I would awake alone in my pew with my head in my hands resting on the bench in front of me.

I spent days eating nothing at all. In my pocket was a handful of salt. Each time I felt weak, I would put a few grains on my tongue. My main prayer was that I not allow my hunger to drive me to steal. Sometimes, it passed my mind to ask people for money, but I was too proud. Instead, I would just drink water dripping from the pipes that I could find. Sometimes, I visited my aunt to find bananas that were overripe and could not be sold. They were my staple.

One day, I went to visit her in the market where she sold her bananas. She alone knew my secret that I was living on the streets. She asked me how I managed, what I ate, and so on. She said that my uncle asked about me. Each time I went, she tried to get me to come back to live with her family. She said that my uncle would be different now that he had seen my reaction.

Finally, I gave in to her. In part, because she was my aunt and I owed her respect, but also because I had to do something. Her supplications were a relief to me. I spent several days back in her home. I didn't like the idea of living there without contributing to the household any more than I had liked being exploited. I was ready to start at the workshop again.

My uncle made the first move. He said that I could come back to work. I decided to forgive his past behaviour. At the same time, I didn't want to forget what he was capable of. If he treated me as before, I would have to leave for good.

The first week back in the shop was uneventful. My uncle made an effort to treat me better. However, I could not trust him. I liked to joke with the neighbours who hung around, but the moment that my uncle joined us, I stopped laughing. He avoided humiliating me in public and overtly treating me with disdain. But my uncle did not pay me. On Saturdays, he would give the workers a very small sum of money that we could not stretch to the end of the day.

He accepted that I should go back to school. But I couldn't pay the fees and my uncle wouldn't. The director would sometimes visit our class to announce the names of those students who hadn't paid their tuition. When he finished, we were sent out of the classroom. But we just hid until we saw him leave the class and then we would sneak back in. I was working hard at my studies and wanted to continue.

One of the neighbours of the shop saw my dedication to the work and was aware of my uncle's nature. He asked me often why I remained working there. I had to reply that, in order to flee, you needed a destination and the means to get there. I had nothing and nowhere to go.

This neighbour, Jelo, worked as the guard of a property owned by a doctor who lived in Thomassin. The doctor did not live in the house, but left the management of the entire property to the guard. In the courtyard was a large reservoir of water. Jelo used to let me bathe there in between working in the shop and going to school and, sometimes, after school before returning to Delmas 33.

When my uncle saw Jelo visiting me in the workshop, he would be angry. He feared that it might take me away from my work. Moreover, he wasn't sure what influence the guard might be having on me. What did he want? In the courtyard of the doctor's property were a number of fruit trees, including some mangoes. Jelo would bring some mangoes to me as a gift. I appreciated them of course. And although my uncle did not like to see the guard around the shop, he ate the mangoes. So he didn't protest the guard's presence too severely. Besides, as long as someone else was feeding me, he didn't have to.

chapter five

A NEPHEW OF MY UNCLE who lived in the countryside wanted to become a furniture maker. And so, in 2002, Willy came to join us. Now we were three apprentices: Josué, Willy, and I.

Willy and I both stayed in Delmas 33 and went down together every morning to the shop. From time to time, Willy returned to the countryside to see his family. He would come back with some provisions, thanks to the peasants. Once, he returned with a gallon of sugar cane syrup. When we added it to water, we found that it was enough to keep us going throughout the day. This became the staple of our diet and we budgeted together to make sure that Willy could buy a gallon from the peasants regularly to keep us supplied. With that, we didn't have to starve while we waited for my uncle to arrive to eat the lunch that my aunt prepared in the mornings. He still would put some in the lid for the employees. The problem was that it had never been enough for me alone and now I had to share it with two co-workers. Our work was physically demanding and the few grains of rice he threw our way — if and when he showed up — were far from sufficient.

After a few weeks, Josué was still learning the terms of our trade. One day, our uncle told him to bring him the *madriye*, thick planks of wood. Although it was right in front of him, Josué couldn't identify it. He said he couldn't see it. My uncle came to get it himself. He picked up the *madriye* on the floor behind Josué and threw it violently at his head. Josué reacted quickly, grabbing a piece of wood to protect himself. With an extraordinarily athletic move, he managed to deflect the *madriye* from its trajectory and save his head from serious harm.

Willy watched the violent act and understood the danger that our uncle represented.

Willy was not used to city life. He became sick with a fever. While he was still sick, my aunt decided to visit our family in Saut d'Eau for a week. She had not seen her mother, Suzanne, for several years. She left with her three children early one morning.

The day after her departure, my uncle left as well, but without telling Willy and me that he was going somewhere. So, Willy and I were responsible for the workshop, although our uncle had never made any mention of this. In the shop, we all assumed that our uncle was driving his Volvo as a taxi and that he would show up anytime. At sunset, we decided to call his other apartment in Delmas 30 to see if he was with his mistress and children. She said that she didn't know where he was. So we started to worry. We didn't know what to do.

Since it was already night, we decided to sleep in the workshop and return home to Delmas 33 at sunrise. There, we got a call from his children in Delmas 30 to say that they had heard that he went to Saut d'Eau to spend the week with my aunt and cousins. Since we had nothing to eat and Willy was too sick to move from his bed, I went out of the house to search for some food for him.

I explained the situation to some friends. One was able to give me enough money so that I could buy some sugar. I contacted the guard Jelo and he contributed some rice and money to buy some herbs. I returned to put our ingredients together for Willy.

Willy was suffering from malnutrition. We drank the sugar water together along with the rice. We didn't have enough money to eat properly, let alone enough to visit a hospital.

Willy's condition made our situation clear to us all. We worked hard and invested our imaginations and our skills to make our workshop stand out among the furniture shops. We worked physically hard for long hours. But our uncle showed only contempt for us. Even the French colonists fed their slaves.

I suggested to Willy and Josué that we should teach our uncle a lesson. We should go on strike. When our uncle understood that we were serious, we could then insist he address our grievances. Willy and Josué welcomed my strategy. They said that when he returned, he would see that we hadn't progressed in our work since his unannounced departure. He would be forced to treat us like human beings.

We spent three days playing dominoes in the courtyard next to the workshop. During that time, our friends in the neighbourhood supported us by offering us food and drink.

When the family returned, my uncle came to Delmas 19 to see how much money we had made for him in his absence. The first thing he saw was the door of the workshop closed. He opened it to discover that nothing whatsoever had been done since his departure. He then saw us outside playing dominoes. He didn't speak to us, but went back inside and sat down. We assumed that he wanted us to come to him. He waited about thirty minutes, but we didn't come. So he appeared at the door.

"Messieurs!" he called out brusquely.

Josué and Willy went to him. I remained seated.

He apologized to them for his absence. Josué and Willy explained the reasons for our rebellion. We had been left with nothing to eat. Willy had fallen sick. Our uncle acknowledged that he had been wrong and said that he would not do that again. Then he bought some coffee and bread and shared it with them, leaving a portion for me inside the workshop. So far, I had not been involved in the discussions.

As I watched Willy and Josué go to speak to my uncle without me, I felt abandoned and powerless. In the planning stages of our strike, they had led me to believe that they were highly motivated. They had pushed me along. I thought that I had an army behind me. Instead I was a general with an army of deserters. When the time came to act, I was left alone with my shadow. Alone, and with the traitors working with the enemy, I was doubly defeated.

I was still sitting where Josué and Willy had abandoned me. My uncle called to me harshly from inside the workshop, "Come Joegodson! I have something to explain to you."

I didn't enter the workshop. I stayed at the door. As I stood there, I saw Josué and Willy drinking coffee and eating bread inside. I felt betrayed.

"How is it that you didn't come when the other two did? What are you still doing outside?"

"Everyone has the right to do what he decides. Like them, I am free to make my choice."

"What do you have against me?" he demanded to know.

"I have nothing against you," I said. "But I have a problem with your attitude."

"What 'attitude' are you talking about?" he questioned. "I decided at the last minute to go with my family to Saut d'Eau. That's all. But that's a little thing. Besides that, I don't know what you're talking about. I understand that you were left a few days without enough to eat, but that's all settled now." He gestured to Willy and Josué, slurping their coffee and gorging on bread.

I answered, "If you have bought off Willy and Josué with a couple of cups of coffee, it's only because they have no respect for themselves. Put yourself in our place. How would you respond? Even your nephew, Willy, you don't respect. He was sick from malnutrition for three days. His sickness is really a symptom of the lack of respect that you have for us. That is the disease that we have to heal. You are sick and we suffer from the symptoms."

"But why don't the others think the same way? Maybe you have another problem with me. If you do, you only have to say so. What is it?"

"Maybe they don't value their own dignity. Imagine that we had decided to leave for the countryside for a few days without telling you and then return when we felt like it. Is that what you expect of us?"

He simply said that he couldn't understand what I was talking about. Ignorance is a good tactic. He simply couldn't understand me. In that case, how could I expect him to change?

I left the entrance to the workshop and returned to my game of dominoes. After a few minutes, I saw my uncle leave. Willy and Josué were working once again inside.

Soon, Josué and Willy came to me. They wondered what I had said to my uncle. They said they had been afraid to explain themselves. I congratulated them on their cowardice.

"What did you want us to do?" Josué asked.

"I wanted us to remain together. We had already discussed our grievances and our strategy. We did that together. But you left me alone."

They replied, *Ou jamn tande pòt an bwa goumen avèk pòt an fè?* — you ever hear of a wooden door fighting an iron door? How did I expect them to defend themselves against someone who had much more power than they did? Wooden doors cannot fight iron doors.

"Human beings only distinguish themselves as wooden or iron by their actions. I see that you have decided to be wooden doors. Wooden doors never transform into iron. You need to be careful."

They retorted, "Really? Just look! We managed to get some coffee and bread. And you got nothing."

"I see that he has also left you with lots of work to complete once you have finished your coffee. I hope that was a powerful cup of coffee, because it will have to last. . . . Good luck. I'm on vacation."

They went back to work. I returned to Delmas 33. My aunt started to complain to me. She said that her husband had explained to her that it wasn't his fault. He had told her how I had spoken very harshly to him. I had shown no respect. She accepted his word even though she knew — somewhere — that it was worth nothing. It allowed her to maintain a kind of lopsided peace with him.

After a week, when he saw that I would not submit, my uncle got in his Volvo and went to Simon to speak to my father. He complained bitterly about me. I was insolent and a rebel. I had poisoned the minds of the other workers and plotted against him. My father accepted it all. He called me to come to see him. He grilled me as to my motives. Was I jealous of my uncle's money? What was it?

When I saw that my father had condemned me before even hearing me, I was disheartened. Imagine that demanding to be fed should be seen as a claim on the "legitimate" wealth of my uncle. I was vitally responsible for whatever money his shop was taking in. My father had somehow allowed himself to be hoodwinked by my uncle's greed. How was it that, by demanding to be treated with dignity, I should be accused of avarice?

All around were doors that might have offered me an exit. But my friends and family closed each one of them in my face, leaving me in a dark prison. The doors were labelled inertia, fear, cowardice, and greed. How could I act morally in this prison? The devil had set this trap skillfully.

Feeling powerless and without support, I returned to the workshop. There was a small change. My uncle had learned that I could not be bought with coffee and bread. He didn't treat me like the others.

A few months later, my aunt became pregnant and she had to stop her commerce as a street merchant. Consequently, her household was deprived of the cash that she contributed. It was that money that she used to feed everyone and to make lunches for my uncle and us in the workshop. My uncle always found it easier to take than to give. Now, as the pregnancy advanced, my aunt needed support.

Believing that people could be bought, my uncle was also for sale. As long as my aunt brought sums of money into the foyer for his benefit, my uncle was pleased. Now that she was pregnant, she turned from an asset to a debt in my uncle's ledger. He changed toward her. He stopped coming to Delmas 33. Instead, he spent his time with his mistress in his apartment in Delmas 31. He withdrew all support that he used to give to my aunt and their children, and focused on the other household.

Now, my aunt was going days without eating. She would appear at the workshop to ask my uncle for something. He showed only contempt toward her. He hated to see her arrive there.

He would snap at her, "What are you doing here?!"

"The children have nothing to eat. We haven't seen you for weeks."

"What's the use in coming here? What do you want? You've got rice. Can't you cope on your own to cook it?" His answers were curt and heartless. People who did not enrich him directly were of no use to him until they started producing again.

Finally, he might take a crumpled hundred-gourde note out of his pocket and toss it toward his wife in contempt. Then he would turn his back on her. Sobbing, she would have to scramble on her knees to pick it up off the ground.

My aunt's ordeal touched me personally. This was her fourth pregnancy. She had earned his contempt each time she turned from creditor to debtor. Someday, I would leave his employ, but how could a pregnant woman with four children escape?

Scrounging on the floor of the workshop for a small gourde note while weeping reduced her to a beggar. That was how the clients and passersby might see her. I would go to her and ask her to return home and to cry there, so as to protect her dignity as much as possible.

Since my aunt was malnourished, it was clear that the baby too was suffering. I knew that emotional crises like the one my uncle was precipitating could lead to complications that could put the lives of both my aunt and the baby in danger. My uncle was doing all he could to provoke a tragedy.

—•—

Next to our workshop, there was a little *kokorat* who used to wash cars using the water that passed in the open sewer and then wipe them shiny with old rags. In early November 2003, he told us that he needed money for the Christmas season. He said that he had only 4,000 gourdes (about $103 US). Willy, Josué, and I listened, dumbfounded. Our three hearts sank as one. We had learned a trade and were constantly developing our skills. We were now producing superior pieces of furniture that were enriching my uncle. Here was a street kid, a *kokorat*, who complained that he had only 4,000 gourdes while we, altogether, did not have 115 ($3 US). We couldn't shake the humiliation. A *kokorat* is, in principle, at the bottom of the Haitian social order. Where were we?

The very next day, Josué, Willy, and I took some time to plan the rest of the year. December is a busy month for the furniture makers. There was lots of work for the shops, including my uncle's. That meant that we apprentices were in demand. If we stayed in my uncle's shop, we would be worked into the ground and have nothing to show for it. But what if we could find a shop that paid better?

Willy said that he wanted to return to the countryside for good at the beginning of December. He could no longer stand working or living with his uncle. He hated the city — everything about it. Josué wanted to work in another atelier. I suggested that I would stay in the shop to see how things went. If I worked hard to keep the shop going, would my uncle not finally appreciate me and compensate me?

At the beginning of December, Willy left the capital for home and Josué found work in other furniture shops. I stayed behind. I worked harder than ever to keep up with all the orders.

—•—

One night in December, my aunt woke me up to tell me that she was in labour. It was two o'clock in the morning. My uncle was, of course, staying with his mistress in his other household. My aunt asked me to get her husband. Although scared of all that could happen at that time of the night, I went on foot to get my uncle. When I arrived, I knocked on the door. At that hour, they were afraid to open the door. I heard a voice yell, "Who is it?"

I replied.

"What do you want? What are you doing in the street at this time?"

I told him that his wife was giving birth. He told me to wait. He went to get dressed. When he returned, he was in his usual ugly mood.

"Don't think I'm going to congratulate you. If you had any wits, you would never have come here, you would have looked for a *taptap*."

Since all the *taptap* drivers were at home asleep at that time, his reproach made no sense. Its sole purpose was to deflect the shame that he must have buried in some corner of his heart. And, as usual, to underline the fact that I was useless.

His Volvo was broken down so he had to find another car. He walked with great anger, stamping his feet harshly on the Haitian soil. I kept my distance. Anyone would have thought that he was begrudgingly offering me a great service; that it was my wife in labour and that I had been too incompetent to make arrangements.

He managed to find a friend who lent him a car. We picked up my aunt. He refused to even give her a hand as she entered the car. Then we drove to the hospital. He was less careful than the *taptap* drivers in avoiding the potholes, fissures, and rocks strewn everywhere. You might have thought that he was trying to provoke a miscarriage.

The first hospital was so full of women in labour that they wouldn't take us. He was obliged to drive to Sainte Catherine Hospital in Site Solèy. There, the nurses gently helped my aunt to pace in the corridor to help the birth along. My uncle got in his borrowed car and returned to his mistress in Delmas 31.

My aunt did not have the physical force to aid in the birth. She was malnourished and very weak. She spent hours walking up and down, holding my arm for support. Other women were also walking the halls with the same objective. It was like a competition among them to see who could arrive first at the birth of her baby.

The nurses were tired and went somewhere to sleep. But the pregnant women did not have that luxury. A couple of those women did not make it through the night. They had complications during the birth. I was afraid that my aunt would also succumb because I knew all that she had been through during her pregnancy. It was a miracle that she and the baby were still alive.

Before they left to sleep, the nurses had put my aunt in a special bed that is used for childbirth, called a *ti bourik*. While the nurses slept, the hospital was quiet and somber. The only action was here in the maternity ward where the women awaited the birth of their babies.

My aunt felt that her baby was finally coming for real. She sent me to get a nurse. I had to go all over to find where they were sleeping. I entered a number of rooms.

I opened the door to one room and saw a young man with a revolver who I took for a security guard. He looked at me harshly and asked me what I was doing. I told him that there was a woman about to give birth and I needed to find a nurse. He said okay and led me to another room where the nurses were resting.

As we went down the hall to get to my aunt, the nurse asked me why I had been talking with that young man. I asked if she meant the security guard. She said he wasn't a security guard but a thief. The hospital had no guards. In that neighbourhood, where I had been raised, gang members can have little patience for people who intrude on their work. For some reason, he took time out of robbing the hospital to help me find a nurse. That was lucky for us all, because the nurse helped my aunt to give birth to a baby girl.

I left my aunt in the hands of the nurses at Sainte Catherine's. Since the hospital was not far from Simon, I went to get my father who took a *taptap* to bring her some food. He was very fond of his little sister.

At noon, we were still at the hospital. After my aunt had eaten and been bathed and was resting with her new baby in her arms, my uncle arrived and saw Dad with us. He asked how we were. I said that my aunt had given birth. He said he knew that. I asked how. He replied that he had returned home to pray for her after he had dropped us off. He knew that his prayers were powerful and sincere. He asked us if we had eaten. I said that Dad had brought something. That too, my uncle claimed to have known in advance. It was a performance for Dad.

My dad, for his part, couldn't see through my uncle without opening a can of worms. I was in that can and it stank.

My uncle put his wife and new baby and me in the Volvo, working again, and drove back to Delmas 33. I went to look for some leaves. In Haitian culture, after giving birth, women bathe in water infused with certain leaves: papaya, maskriti, and several others. A few women from the neighbourhood came over to take care of my aunt as I prepared to return to the workshop. They remained with her until she was strong enough to take up her life again.

I returned to my work in the shop at an accelerated pace. Josué and Willy were gone. I carried on for the rest of the month alone. I built a bed and night tables, a dining room table and six chairs, and repaired another set. On 31 December, I was in the shop. I waited for my uncle, because it was the day when workers traditionally receive a bonus.

He came late in the afternoon, scratching his head. He said that, unfortunately, he was not in a position to offer me much in the way of a bonus. But he took my hand, placed some bills in it and then enclosed it inside his two hands, in a gesture of gratitude and bonhomie.

Had he come through after all? I opened my hand and counted 150 gourdes ($3.68 US). My thoughts went to the *kokorat* who had saved 4,000 gourdes from washing cars with sewer water. Maybe it had taken him time to save that amount, but he was living in a different income bracket than me. My uncle's bonus was so small that it was not even conceivable as an insult or a joke.

The next day was New Year's 2004, the two hundredth anniversary of Haitian independence. The glorious victory of the slaves over the French masters. My uncle came to offer me another surprise. He had bought some clothes for his two families. He included me. He offered me a shirt. But before giving it to me, he wanted to recount an inspirational story.

"There was a mason who worked for a businessman. The businessman bought plots of land and invited the mason to design houses for them. In each case, the mason would hand the businessman a list of the materials that he would need along with their cost. The businessman gave the mason the money and, together, they constructed many homes. While the businessman became rich, he paid the mason a miserable sum for his work. But the mason continued to work. He thought that the businessman would offer him a bonus. But no. The businessman bought a nice plot of land and asked the mason, as usual, to design a beautiful house for it. But by this point, the mason had become discouraged. He decided to make the businessman pay the price for his exploitation. This time, he used inferior materials but charged the businessman for the best. When the work was finished, the businessman arranged a public celebration of this special house. In his speech, he said, 'My mason partner and I have worked together for many years. Through thick and thin, we have persevered. I have become rich because of this man. He has always been faithful and honourable. Today, it is my turn to thank him.' He called the mason and said, 'For all that you have done for me, I want to thank you with this gesture.' He handed him the keys to the house and said, 'This house is for you.' Everyone applauded the gesture. The young mason began to cry. Not tears of joy, but of regret and shame. He was unworthy of the praise that his boss had offered him."

Maybe it had occurred to my uncle that I might be discouraged as a result of his exploitation. I tried on the shirt. It was *pèpè*, a second-hand article of clothing sold by the street merchants at reduced rates. It was so big that there was room for another Joegodson to join me inside. The sleeves hung over my hands. I looked like a clown. But it was fitting. Only a clown would accept to be treated as I was.

He said, "How do you like it?"

"It's the perfect gift. Look at how it fits me," I replied.

He registered satisfaction, proud of himself for his taste and his great generosity. "I never make mistakes, even when I buy things without taking measurements."

I folded together his gift, his story, and my entire history with him, and I put them in an envelope that I addressed Progress Toward Death. I wondered how my uncle expected people to respond to his lies. In his world of lies, what difference would the truth make?

After he left, I stuffed the shirt under the rug on the kitchen floor where I slept. It gave it a little padding. Since it was the holiday season, I didn't go to work. On 3 January, I went down to Delmas 19 to see some other furniture makers. They knew of my competence and asked me to help them come up with a design for the cupboards in an apartment. I agreed and, within a week, we had finished the job.

During that one week, not only did I eat, but I made 1,500 gourdes ($36.77 US). That was more than I had made in four years with my uncle, running his shop, designing and building furniture. After one week away from him, I was able to buy a bike with thick tires built to withstand Haitian "roads."

My uncle noticed that I had stretched the holidays into the second week of January. There was little he could do for the moment. He was now living in his other house in Delmas 31. He came periodically to see how the shop was going. But each time he came by, the door was locked. Normally, even big party-goers eventually recover from the holidays. But weeks went by and there was no evidence that I had yet unlocked the workshop doors.

Sometimes, he came by to meet a client, to make sure that he didn't lose any contracts. However, some came to demand the same style of table that I had designed and built. He was not able to accept the orders without me. He told the clients that the worker who normally did that work was unreliable. He offered them something in another style. They would reply that they were making enquiries for friends who had seen the work at their homes. He had to turn them away.

These experiences led my uncle to find out what was going on with me. He first made some enquiries in the neighbourhood to find out that I was working with other bosses. So, he came up to find me in Delmas 33 where I was living with my aunt and he was not. But I was never there when he came by. After a month, he became seriously concerned. I had rebelled before, but never for a month. He went so far as to decide to sleep at his wife's house in order to assure himself that he would run into me.

That night, when I returned home from church, my uncle was sitting in front of the entrance to the house. I greeted him in passing and entered the house. I went to bed. After a few minutes, he called for me. His daughter told him that I was already asleep. He told her to wake me up.

"Are you still working in my shop or not?"

"What do you mean?"

He said, "For several weeks now, the shop has been closed. If you have decided to finish with your trade, then you can return to Simon. I didn't take you out of Simon in order that you could just live here. It was to work. If you aren't going to work, then go back to Simon."

I said, "Okay. Thanks for all your patience with me . . . and your hospitality. Since you have decided to not allow me to stay here, I will leave."

I went to the kitchen to put my things in my backpack. My aunt came to see me to say that I should not leave that night. She wanted me to at least wait until the morning and to have a destination in mind.

I decided to accept her offer. I left my bag there and went out to talk to a friend from church about the situation. My friend was upset to hear the news. He knew my uncle and understood that I had been mistreated for years. He was worried about me, thinking that I could become a *vakabon*, as we say in Haiti: someone who lives outside of his community, someone with no morality.

He invited me to live with him. However, he lived with his brother who had just married. My friend didn't live inside the rented room, but slept on the roof. He had found an old mattress whose springs had broken through the lining that he tried to make less offensive by covering with cardboard. But the springs were stronger and would pierce the cardboard. He enclosed the mattress within walls of rusty old sheets of metal. That gave him a room that was exactly the dimensions of the mattress and that rose about one metre above it. Since there were other buildings all around that rose higher than our rooftop, we were always on view from above. From their perspective, we must have looked like rats scurrying into our sordid little bedroom.

I went to Delmas 19 to ask Jelo, who guarded the property of the old doctor, if I could leave my bag in the property while I slept on a rooftop up in Delmas 33.

I didn't want people in Delmas 33 to know that I had no work, so I came down to Delmas 19 to pass every day in the courtyard of Jelo's property. But at night, I was frightened to sleep on the rooftop. It was 2004 and the country was in an uproar. President Aristide had just been forced into exile and we poor were under attack. There was much violence. At night we could hear the exchanges of gunfire all over. At any time, a stray bullet could pass through our miserable little shelter and kill us. Worse, rumours were circulating that certain groups were ripping out the hearts of living victims for their sacrifices. We would have been sitting ducks for such malfeasance.

On top of those fears was the rain. When the tropical storms came, my friend and I looked for the least leaky spot in the shelter. We crouched with our heads up against the rusty iron ceiling, waiting for it to end. It was a life of trying to stay alive, without knowing why.

In the village of Solidarite, Josué would sometimes find some small jobs for us, repairing furniture or building night tables. In 2005, a member of the diaspora saw me working in Solidarite. He offered me a job building doors with wood imported from abroad and repairing furniture that had been rejected for sale in the United States because of imperfections. My job was to repair this *pèpè* furniture so that it could be sold in Haiti. The work was difficult, because the wood was of an inferior quality to that I was used to. However, the Haitian, who lived in Miami, was satisfied with my work. He left me in charge of the shop when he returned to the United States. I soon finished all that he had left for me. He told me he would return with more work, but he never did. Instead, his son arrived and proposed a number of jobs. He showed me photographs of furniture from foreign magazines and asked if I could reproduce the designs. I succeeded. I continued to work for him for a year, reproducing all sorts of furniture. Although he wasn't as abusive as my uncle had been, neither was he more generous. A couple of times a week, he would bring me a plate of rice and *sòs pwa nwa*. He paid me by giving me a cellphone that was not activated and that was, therefore, of no use to me. Finally, I gave up.

Sometimes we had to pass through exchanges of gunfire and protests that turned violent on our way to Solidarite. To avoid the risks that surrounded me, I decided to remain in one place. Jelo accepted my request to stay in the property in Delmas 19. I would be able to use a room in a building on the property that had been built for the groundskeeper. The house had been built during the early Duvalier years when the neighbourhood was middle class. Since then, it had deteriorated and was now largely inhabited by paupers. The doctor retained possession while he lived up the mountains in the security of Thomassin. Perhaps he hoped that Haiti would come out of its descent into insecurity. Meanwhile, the large two-story house remained in the centre of the property, uninhabited.

My room was only a short distance from my uncle's shop. Sometimes, he would see me as I walked down the street. From time to time, I even dropped in to say hello. He would get excited and ask me if I would like some work. He proposed a number of contracts. I always said sure, that's a good idea. Then I left and never followed up. He hadn't changed.

—•—

I decided to put all my energy into creating a *chef d'oeuvre*. I threw myself into the construction of a vanity. The design. The work. I thought about it all the time. I didn't have enough money to buy the materials. So, it was a long process. Whenever I had a few gourdes, I would buy another plank for my vanity. I was like a bird that builds its nest one twig at a time.

Eventually, it was finished and I was proud. It was beautiful. I left it outside of the gate by the side of the road where everyone could see it.

On our street was a school for children of the bourgeoisie. It was surrounded by concrete walls. Armed guards protected it. Every morning and afternoon, SUVs came down from the mountain. Big, burly men in black got out to collect the children of their employers. They carried a shotgun in one hand and, in the other, they held the hand of a little child that they led back to the SUV. Their job was to protect the children from being kidnapped. But sometimes, the parents of the children came by. They would see the cabinet.

One day, Jelo came running to me to say that a bourgeois was out in front of the property. He wanted to talk to the *ebenis*. I felt my heart pounding. This was my plan. The vanity was the bait. He would pay me for the true value of my skills. And, with that, I would construct another, and then another, and another. I would be recognized as a craftsman. And I would build my own business.

I walked calmly towards the gate. I refused to run. But I could not hide the pride that I felt in my creation. I couldn't suppress my smile.

He stood next to his expensive SUV. He was cold. He didn't smile like I was smiling. He asked if I was the *ebenis* who had made it. He said he would be interested in buying it. Then he proposed an amount that I am ashamed to repeat. It was well below the cost of the materials.

I thought maybe he was negotiating. I didn't want to play that game. I just told him how much it would cost. I priced it at its true value. Calmly. Honestly. My heart was beating again at its normal rhythm.

I saw him look me up and down. I could not hide my poverty. My clothes were made to fit someone bigger than me. My pants were held around my little waist with a rope. They frayed at the bottom. My shirt was ripped.

I could see his mind calculating. He would not pay me for what the vanity was worth, but for what he had decided I was worth.

If I had sold it to him, it would have been like agreeing that I was worth nothing. I refused.

From time to time, I saw one of our poor neighbours admiring the vanity. Eventually, he asked me how much it was worth. I asked how much it was worth to him. Instead, he told me how much money he could pay. Before I answered, he apologized. It was a little less than the amount that the bourgeois had offered. But it was a great sum for this man. I agreed. We took it to his *tikounouk*.

•●•

Jelo was both kind-hearted and shrewd, always looking for ways to make a few gourdes. From time to time, he let people sleep on the property that was enclosed behind big concrete walls. Once, he let a group of shoeshine boys stay on the property. The boys came from Bel-Anse in the countryside to look for any kind of work in the capital. They were peasants like Jelo.

Once they had arrived in the capital, they talked to other young peasants to find out how they made a living. The most common answer was shoeshine boy. In Haiti, they are called simply "shine." It was an easy job to enter. They just make a little box out of wood and fill it with a brush, a powder called aniline to mix with water, another container full of soapy water, a little fabric to shine the shoes, and two kinds of wax — one for dark shoes and the other for light. The most important tool was the bell they ring constantly to advertise their presence. They know where to set up their stands to get the most business — in front of schools, churches, and businesses, for instance. There is always a line of shines in front of the airport for travellers to wipe Haitian soil off their shoes before they leave the country. Where shines don't exist, people often carry their shoes in a bag and walk to their destination in sandals. Otherwise, they arrive with their shoes covered in dust or mud.

Sometimes the shines stop to pass a couple of hours in a lucrative spot and then continue on their route, following the rhythm of Port-au-Prince. They become dirty and sweaty as the day passes. In order to make their wages, they start before the sun rises and finish after it sets. Some feel humiliated to be working at the feet of their clients for a token sum. Some dislike being called "shine" and preferred to be called *bòs*. In Haiti, those who have mastered a vocation are called *"bòs."* There are *bòs mason, bòs ebenis, bòs mekanik,* and *bòs tayè*. The problem is that there is no way to complete the *bòs* title for a shoeshine person. *"Bòs shine"* only highlights the fact that the vocation does not require much training, even while shines can be proficient.

Often, shines have no place to stay. A number of shines can unite to rent a little *tikounouk* together. Sometimes, they allow more time to pass than is recommended between bathing sessions. Five or six shines, working for long hours in the heat and squalor of Port-au-Prince at people's feet and living in a tiny room together, can emit a powerful odour.

The shines didn't pay Jelo rent, but they were customers for his rice business. He used to prepare rice every night and the local poor people would pay just enough so that Jelo could squeeze out a small profit. But he had a difficult time with the odour the shines left in the courtyard. He didn't want to insult them. "Does anyone smell something funny?" he would ask them as they sat around. They would look at each other and shake their heads. Nothing smelled peculiar as far as they were concerned.

We liked having them living on the property. They joked. They were friendly, unpretentious spirits.

One Sunday morning, I was leaving my church in another part of Delmas when one of the shines who lived with us passed by. I was dressed in my church clothes that I had prepared carefully. He was covered in dust. Even his eyebrows were dusted white. When he saw me with my church brothers, dressed in their best clothes like me, he looked for a corner to hide himself away so that I would not have to greet him. I left the church brothers to go to talk with him. I took his hand in mine. "What are you doing here? It looks like you're trying to avoid me," I said.

"No, no, patron . . . I could see that you are with some people in clean clothes. I just . . . well . . ."

I told him, "Ah ha! I see that if I was in your place, and you were in mine, that you would humiliate me by not deigning to speak with me. Not so?"

"No, no, it's not that. Just . . . I didn't want to dirty you," he tried to assure me.

"You are more important to me than my clean church brothers over there. You live together with me. If I have trouble in the middle of the night, I'm going to count on you to take me to the hospital. You wouldn't let me down, would you?"

"No."

"If the church brothers ever have to respond to my problems, it will be when I'm already dead. But you, you'll be the one to assure my survival."

He accepted my argument in defence of solidarity. He promised me that, in the future, he would not take me for someone superior to him. He agreed that friends should respect each other regardless of what they looked like and how clean we were. How strange that he should see me, of all people, as socially superior!

chapter six

EVEN IN MY CHURCH IN DELMAS 33, when I would say that I was raised in Site Solèy, they thought that I was lying. Since I was a comic with a baby face, they knew that I couldn't be from Site Solèy. While those neighbourhoods were nearby Site Solèy, they might have been in another country for all that they understood about us.

In Delmas 19, we could always hear the violence in Simon. It was like we were getting the news directly. When the radio reported that there had been a shoot-out in Simon, we already knew because we had heard it in progress. One day, in Delmas 19, we heard long exchanges of gunfire coming from Simon. We were sitting around and one guy, a young mechanic, was standing. While we were listening to the gunfire, he thought that someone had thrown a stone at him. He touched his head to see that there was a trickle of blood. He followed a Haitian custom of massaging the small injury with a coin. Despite the massage, the little bump remained. The others that had been sitting around him advised him to go to the hospital to have an x-ray taken. When he went, the x-ray showed that a bullet had lodged under his skin, but had not pierced his skull. The doctors removed the bullet, telling him that he was not in danger. They said that the bullet must have come from a distance and had lost its momentum. When he returned with the x-ray as proof that he had been shot, people started to be careful about where they assembled. Simon was too close for comfort.

The young mechanic kept the bullet as a souvenir. We couldn't know if it had been fired by the MINUSTAH soldiers or a Haitian. The United Nations Stabilisation Mission in Haiti (MINUSTAH) soldiers were sent to Haiti by the United Nations to — so we were told — make it stable after President Aristide had been forced out of the country in

February 2004. In fact, they kept the country unstable, as if that was their job. But even the MINUSTAH troops, at least at first, were worried about how much the Haitian bourgeoisie hated us poor. The bullet may have come from somebody working for Andy Apaid or Reginald Boulos — who owned the sweatshops where people worked. Hating us and hating Aristide was the same thing for them.

People in Delmas decided that it was of little importance who fired the rifles. The fact that bullets from Simon could land in Delmas 19 increased their fear and contempt for their violent neighbours. They resented living in fear. For my part, I felt that every bullet fired in Simon was aimed at my reputation. While the people of Delmas would simplistically insult the inhabitants of Simon, I knew what was really happening. Each time I visited home, I saw the effects of the violence in the eyes of the old and young of Simon. The exchanges of fire became so intense that the air was putrid. It was impossible to avoid it. The eyes of everyone in Simon were a sickly yellow-orange colour.

I felt sorry for the elderly. And pity for the youth. The eyes of the elderly revealed not only the physical effects of the poisoned atmosphere, but the despair of being powerless to influence the community they had built. They had lost their place in Simon. They lived in fear. Where they had once had influence over the youth of the community, they now watched helplessly as the young were drawn into violence. When the boys arrived at adolescence, it was normal for them to enter into a gang. Their standing among their peers depended upon them proving themselves. Once planted, the violence reproduced itself. The parents watched as their role was eclipsed by violence. They were no longer the mentors of their children. Their counsel was no longer sought. In the face of the deadly violence, they seemed almost foolish. Their fear only discredited them further, because now young men judged everything in terms of recklessness — which they called courage — in the face of violence. The less respect you had for life and for other people, the more you were respected.

In Simon, there were schoolchildren, innocent pedestrians, and both older and younger citizens who refused to accept the new violent order. Many people would have left Simon and Site Solèy, but the cost of living prohibited them. It cost very little to rent a small room there, and very little was what everyone had. So they remained even as the world fell apart around them. Religion became more important than ever. Pastors preached Christ's message of peace as a counterpoint to the violence around them. And some of us hoped that religion could defeat the violence and hatred that was taking root.

The people were extremely poor. The violence was making their poor lives miserable. But they wanted above all to guard their dignity. People outside of Simon and Site Solèy had already discredited them, however, because of the violence. Everyone was thrown into the same boat. In their eyes, the people of the violent zones had no dignity. Outsiders never understood the courage that it could take to struggle against violence in that environment. Or to live with that poverty. The poor continued to work harder than ever to retain their dignity in their own eyes. Those outside would never understand. The rich, even the less poor, could not know the challenges that we faced.

Many people liked living in Site Solèy. Why? It was not expensive to live there. By identifying and filling a local need, you could earn a living. There were honest and dishonest businesses. For example, in the centre of Site Solèy, gangs were in control. Each block had its own gang. The blocks fought against each other. Each local gang fought to increase its power in relation to all the others. Sometimes, gangs sought to align themselves with political parties. Sometimes, political parties looked for the support of gangs. Local civil wars were initiated from outside when gangs were able to find material support from one party or another. Political parties, in other words, used the local gangs as proxies to fight their battles.

Many Haitians wanted to know what role MINUSTAH was playing in the local wars. Each time that MINUSTAH's mandate was approaching its end, there was suddenly an increase in the violence. Who was behind it? It appeared that some people wanted MINUSTAH to remain and were fuelling the violence to ensure that.

Some gangs were involved in kidnapping. But the origins of kidnappings were never clear. Who ordered them? The objective was usually financial. And the process was simple: target someone with money to demand a ransom. But anyone from any class could initiate a kidnapping. The children of the very wealthy could enter into partnership with gangs of Site Solèy to target someone from their own class. Policemen could be involved, knowing that they would not be discovered. Conservative politicians were known to initiate kidnappings in order to discredit the poor zones like Site Solèy by associating them with criminality. Site Solèy and Bel Air, for example, were used as a cloak to hide many crimes. The rich could distance themselves, literally, from the crimes that guaranteed their wealth.

In my childhood, the parents of Simon were a collective authority. My father, for instance, would delegate his authority over us to the neighbours if he were to leave us in their charge. They had the authority to discipline us, to hit us even, if we misbehaved. And so it was with all the parents and all the children. The arrival of MINUSTAH in Simon in 2004 changed the dynamics. Simon was caught in the crossfire. Kids grew up seeing that real power was connected with mortal weapons. The leaders began to recruit even young children into their gangs. Sometimes, they were assigned the most dangerous jobs. The communal authority of the parents that I had known throughout my childhood was undermined.

It was easier for the children to follow the gangs than to follow their parents. They wanted to fight MINUSTAH. MINUSTAH represented a foreign occupation. To submit to MINUSTAH was, for the younger generation, a sign of defeat, a loss of self-respect and dignity. To fight the foreign occupiers was a sign of strength and courage. MINUSTAH, simply by appearing and staying in Simon, assured that the violence would intensify. MINUSTAH became the main opposition of all the gangs in the poor districts of the capital region: Bel Air, Site Solèy, Boston, Pele, and so on. MINUSTAH was the key gang. It had access to the most modern war materiel: tanks, automatic rifles, and helicopters. MINUSTAH raised the level of the violence. Now, all of the gangs had to match the firepower of the foreign occupiers. But they couldn't. So they had to outsmart them.

The children and youths of Simon began to judge each other according to the size and destructive power of their personal arms. But arms were expensive. By entering the right gang, a youth could assure himself of a weapon that increased his standing and self-importance. He would be given orders by the commandant of his gang. Having replaced the parents as the local authorities, the gangs had to accept certain responsibilities in the communities in order to build a base of support.

One family in Site Solèy that I would get to know had fallen on hard times, even more than most. Economically, the family was destitute. They had a cute little boy named Zakari. When he was ten years old, Zakari had already taken a leading role in providing for the family. Nearby was a wharf. He used to go there to "fish" for birds. He would hook the small fish and throw the line into the water. Birds would come down to grab the fish and fly away. However, Zakari would have hooked them. He reeled them in as though he was fishing the sky. The birds brought a pretty good price in the local market.

Sometimes, he caught birds that had rings attached to their feet. He didn't know what purpose these identification rings served, but he said that he was "fishing" out of necessity and couldn't worry about disrupting somebody's scientific experiment. He normally kept a couple of the birds for his own family to eat and sold the rest to buy staple ingredients: rice, oil, water, and coal. Sometimes, he needed to catch more birds to buy other necessities. At ten, Zakari was a successful provider.

Zakari had lots of little friends in the neighbourhood. He was popular. The older boys also took note of him. All of the children are watched and judged for their utility. The commandant of one gang chose Zakari to act as his main antenna. An antenna is a young child who acts as a spy for the gang leaders whose movements and actions are limited as a result of their notoriety. Antennas are chosen for their intelligence, fearlessness, and apparent innocence. Zakari was the perfect antenna: intelligent, bold, cute, and small even for a ten-year-old.

Before each operation that the gang mounted, Zakari would check out the terrain. He would appear to be an innocent little boy playing in the street. Actually, however, he was on a reconnaissance mission, noting the strength of the MINUSTAH troops, what space they were occupying, how the mission could advance or retreat if necessary, for instance. For kidnappings and robberies, Zakari would have to see who was around and imagine what might interfere with the mission. To do his work, this little boy had to be well versed in all of the activities of the gang.

As time passed, the MINUSTAH soldiers came to see Zakari's appearances before the gang's operations as more than a coincidence. They knew that Zakari was the gang's antenna. One day, Zakari's gang was planning an attack on MINUSTAH. Zakari appeared first, as usual. He exited from one of the narrow corridors that separated the concrete houses. A MINUSTAH sniper was waiting for him and shot him in his lower spinal column. Zakari fell to the ground. The MINUSTAH soldier ran towards Zakari to take him into the military base. But the gang members had already recovered him and hid Zakari from MINUSTAH. After a period of time, they took him to the hospital, Lakou Trankilite in Simon. It was there that I would get to know Zakari several years later; he would have an important impact on my life.

chapter seven

FÉDRIK WAS BORN IN GROS MORNE, in the north of Haiti. During his childhood, he sometimes visited his cousin in Site Solèy. One day, his cousin asked his mother, Joseline, to allow Fédrik to live with her in the capital. Everywhere in the Haitian countryside, the peasants believe that things are better in the city. So, Joseline thought that she was doing her son a service by accepting the proposition.

When his cousin used to visit her home community in Gros Morne, she would bring *pèpè* and other stuff from the capital. The peasants were always impressed. In fact, the *pèpè* was inexpensive: second-hand clothing from North America that street merchants sell to their poor clients. Site Solèy was the most populous and squalid of all the slums in the capital. But the peasants only saw that their cousin seemed to have things they did not. They did not take into account that they had things — more valuable — that their urban cousin did not.

Very little money circulated among the peasants around Gros Morne. They had little need for money, since they grew what they ate. Their survival was assured as long as natural disasters like hurricanes and droughts did not destroy the balance of their lives. They raised livestock that they could sell for money. Peasants call cows, pigs, and goats their bank accounts. With the money that they might earn from their sale they could repair a roof or build a home. When peasants moved to the city, they needed to make a quick adjustment. There, they were dependent on money for their survival. They needed to sell their time and skills in exchange for the money that they needed to keep their families alive. When they looked at their relatives who returned from their homes in the capital and saw that they had money, the peasants assumed that life in the city must be wondrous.

But the money that is a luxury for peasants is an absolute necessity for urban Haitians.

In fact, the peasants could not understand the depth of the problems of their cousin in Site Solèy. What's more, the cousin contributed to their misapprehension of the real state of affairs in Site Solèy. She wanted to present herself in the best light, to not acknowledge how badly things were going for her in the capital. Instead of explaining to her relatives the real state of affairs, she pretended that her life was improving. So, she would bring *pèpè* for little Fédrik. The family was impressed. It was a small expense for her. She gave them a false impression. Simple, uncritical people judge by appearance. They can't put the puzzle together if they have only a couple of pieces.

After Fédrik had moved to Site Solèy, his cousin used to return with him to Gros Morne during the school vacations. There, Fédrik's mother asked the cousin if she could find some work for her. She said that things were going badly in Gros Morne. Her cousin agreed to look for a job for her in the capital.

The cousin worked as a street merchant in Site Solèy. Like many others, she sold whatever she could find: *pèpè*, produce, rice, coal, and anything else that she could resell to bring in a few gourdes. She would sometimes pile her merchandise in a basket and carry it on her head through the streets of other neighbourhoods in the capital. One day, while working in Petionville, she encountered a fellow merchant who told her that she knew of a family that was looking for domestic help. She thought of Fédrik's mother and went to Gros Morne to tell her of the opportunity.

Fédrik's mother came to the capital and began working as a domestic in Petionville. There, she became involved in a romantic relationship with the gardener on the property. He had a small property of his own in Bourdon, close to Petionville. She left her work for the family and moved in with him. There, he looked to set her up in business as a street merchant.

Fédrik left Site Solèy and joined his mother and her new partner in Bourdon.

Sometimes, his mother bought sacks of *pèpè* for resale. Fédrik would help her carry the bales of second-hand clothes to her room and sort them. Members of the diaspora buy the cast-offs by the kilogram in

North America. Then they ship them to Haiti where they are unloaded on the docks and distributed around the island. Merchants buy the box — sight unseen — and then separate what can be resold from the pieces stained or ripped. Usually, they can recover about 70 percent of their purchase. They take it to their public location and try to resell it to recover their investment and make a profit. That profit is never assured.

Once Joseline was established in her new commerce, her second son joined them in Bourdon from Gros Morne. He wanted to become a mechanic. Now that his brother had settled with them in the capital, Fédrik decided to join him in learning to be a mechanic. Until then, he had just been helping his mother set up her *pèpè* business. His new stepfather helped them find a garage that was willing to take them on as apprentices.

Once they began their new trade, the boys had to withstand the initiation rites of the established mechanics. Sometimes, they would have to put up with humiliations and abuses. His brother took it all in stride, but Fédrik found the atmosphere offensive. After awhile he decided to leave his brother and the garage. When there was electric current, he would watch Chinese kung fu movies badly dubbed into English. All he could understand was the martial art that impressed and impassioned him. He wanted to become an expert.

Fédrik found a karate class in the village of Solidarite and began his lessons. The school gave two different classes each day. Fédrik was so motivated that he took them both. He became obsessed with developing his karate skills. His mother and brother were as unhappy as he was excited. They wanted him to learn something that would bring money into the household. His skills would not translate into an income. But, obsessed, he could not stop. In order to reach each new level, Fédrik had to train and to compete. After he had achieved his goal of reaching a new level, he immediately set about to gain the next coloured belt. So hooked was he that it would have been easier to leave his family than karate. He carried on until he had his black belt.

Fédrik wanted to make himself invincible to his opponents. So he turned to magic. He bought a couple of books on magic from street merchants. Then, he visited an *houngan* to make him invincible in combat.

Still, his passion brought no money into the household economy. In fact, his martial arts cost the family. Moreover, his successes in karate left him with black eyes and bruises, despite his invincibility. He looked for ways to turn his passion into a way of life. Now that he had reached the level of a master, he thought of opening up a martial arts school of his own. However, with the Haitian economy going from very bad to far worse and people working full time to stay alive, it was impractical to conceive of such a future in his own country. It was equally impossible to enter a rich country: even if he had a passport, there is only one answer waiting for poor Haitians who ask for a working or visiting visa. So, he decided to try the only country that someone of his class could possibly enter: the Dominican Republic. He would take his skills across the border and see if he could parlay them into a career.

In order to find out how to enter the Dominican Republic, he visited some relatives in Delmas 33 originally from his home community of Gros Morne. There, he made the acquaintance of a young peasant woman from Verettes who was working as a maid in the household of his relatives. For a minute, she made him forget about karate — no small feat. Soon, he was rethinking karate, the Dominican Republic, Haiti, and his life as a single man.

chapter eight

I WAS FINISHED WITH THE JOB IN SOLIDARITE. It's a strange job that pays you a cellphone that you can't use. I needed money to activate it. But why did I need it? None of my friends had any kind of telephone. Besides, why would I spend money to call someone when the main thing I needed to tell them was that I had no job and no money? Why feed the cellphone when I was hungry?

There was another problem. Cellphones were just becoming popular and this was a big clumsy thing. But my friends wanted me to carry it around, even though it wasn't connected, so that they could hold it against their ears to impress total strangers, showing that they were cool. Which they weren't. Next, they all wanted to have their pictures taken using the cellphone. Then they could pass the picture around to prove to people that they were the kind of people who spoke on cellphones. They were all holding the same phone. And they were all, in fact, the kind of people who didn't speak on cellphones. It was sad.

How would I earn money to feed my baby cellphone? And to feed me?

One night, I was sitting in an abandoned car joking with some friends. We were in between my uncle's shop where I would never work again and Jelo's courtyard, where I lived. Near us was a big fire burning in an open sewer. We didn't think anything of it; it had been burning for years. Every week the neighbours would set it alight to get rid of the garbage that piled up in the sewer. Also, we liked it because it kept the mosquitoes away. But a couple of white people came by to look at it as if it was significant. They seemed zombified, lost in the flames that shot five or six metres above the street.

I judged that they needed help. I said, "Look, a couple of *blan*. Maybe this would be a good time to test my English." Haitians imagine that *blan* are American. So we address them in English. That's because Americans come to Haiti most often, whether invited or not. But I didn't really know what kind of *blan* was illuminated by the fire.

My friends said, "Go ahead. This is your big chance."

I walked cautiously up to them until I was between them, pretending that I too was looking at the fire. I then looked at them and threw a question into the air for whoever would respond, the man or the woman. "May I help you?"

The woman was especially impressed, "Oh, he speaks English. He can tell us."

The man replied, "Can you tell us what is burning like this in the sewer? Where we are from, we aren't used to seeing big fires like this in the streets. And no one seems concerned."

I didn't really understand them. For me it was strange that burning garbage could interest anyone. Maybe they had the spirit of children who are curious about everything.

I answered, "That is garbage they burning."

Their eyes opened wide. "Really! That's amazing." They seemed to be impressed by the mundane.

We Haitians were still standing there while the *blan* spoke between themselves. It seemed that the conversation was over for them; it hadn't begun for me. I asked them, "Who are you? Where are you from?"

The woman responded first: "My name is Patricia." The man after: "I'm Paul. We're from Canada." Then he asked me in French my name and I answered.

I searched through my head for some other words in English to impress them.

"Do you believe in Jesus?" I asked.

Paul answered, "No." Patricia said, "Yes."

I posed another question, "Do you know Martin Luther King?"

They both said that they knew of King. I admired Martin Luther King and was searching for a topic that could lead us in a promising direction.

A few minutes went by without conversation. They stared at the fire.

Paul took up the conversation again. He asked me if I could help him learn the Creole language. He offered to pay me 500 gourdes ($11.92 US) to spend an hour to teach him Creole. I was amazed. I had never worked for such a sum of money. I took a little time before responding. I didn't want to appear desperate. But I was desperate.

I tried to make it sound like I was judging the offer. Cautiously, and taking all the excitement out of my words, I said slowly, "Okay . . . that would be possible."

Paul and Patricia were ready to leave. Paul asked if I lived far from here. I pointed to the gate of the property where I lived.

"Okay, how about if I come by tomorrow morning?"

We separated. I went to my friends to explain to them what was happening. They were amazed. They thought I was joking. They hadn't known that I could speak any English. They were jealous. "Look at how lucky he is!"

I went to tell Jelo of the strange encounter. Listening to the story, I could see Jelo's mind operating double time, trying to figure out how to transform this into a jackpot. A *blan* meant money.

—•—

The next morning, Paul knocked on the gate. My room was in the back of the grounds, behind the big empty house and out of sight of the gate. I sneaked a peek to see a *blan* standing at the gate. Quickly, I took the keys to the gate and invited him to enter.

As soon as Jelo saw a *blan*, he realized that I hadn't been joking. But Jelo had no language to communicate all his projects with a *blan*. He spoke only Creole. I made introductions, but Jelo and Paul were like a couple of babies trying to communicate without a language in common. For each question that Paul asked, Jelo responded in the affirmative, "Uh hmm. Uh hmm." Always the same, without a clue what he was agreeing with . . . or to. I finally had to declare the conversation a draw so that Paul and I could go to the guest house where he was staying to begin our lesson.

Paul knocked on the metal gate to the guest house. The security guards came to answer. They looked at me with contempt, as if I was a beggar. I had never met them and they knew nothing of me. But they were clearly unhappy about my presence with a *blan*. I had to ignore them in order to continue with my agreement with Paul.

We went to a large room where there was a big blackboard. He brought chalk. I asked him to be at ease and to ask whatever he wanted. I taught him some vocabulary and grammatical rules. We also touched upon Haitian history and culture. We came to the end of our hour. He gave me 500 gourdes and I left him. He said that I could come anytime to the guest house to see him.

When Paul accompanied me to the gate, the security guards were angry. They clearly did not like to open the door for a poor Haitian. My class was written in every rip of my clothes and in my undernourished body. They told my story. My pants, frayed at the bottoms, were kept from falling by a rope tied around my waist that was wasting away. But the guards heard me speaking French, the language of the rich, with the *blan*. Who did I think I was?

The next day, in the morning, I went back to see if our class would become a course. I knocked on the gate. The security guards snarled, "Who is it?" I replied that it was the friend of Paul. They already knew that. There was a small slit in the metal door of the guest house. I peeked through it. I saw they were angry. I was bothering them. They took a few minutes before even getting out of their chairs. It was supposed to be their job to respond to the gate. They said, "Paul isn't here." However, when I turned my back to leave, Paul came to the gate. He had heard me from inside the grounds. He asked me why I hadn't entered. I had to explain. He got me through customs and we went again to the big room and we picked up where we had left off the day before.

With these attitudes, from black and white, I started to ask myself how I might survive this course.

But Paul and I continued. This time, we decided to spend half the class at the blackboard and the other half just walking the streets. On the streets, he asked me how to say things, how to buy from the street merchants, and so on. He wanted to know how the local people lived. I explained everything honestly. We returned to the guest house at lunch time. Paul told me to just line up with the *blan* and to take what I wanted. The whites took salads and meats with a minimum of rice. I piled my plate with rice and *sòs pwa nwa* with a tiny piece of chicken. Even my plate was the opposite of the *blan*.

The security guards could see us in the dining room through the forged ironwork surrounding the veranda. If there was extra food after the guests had eaten, then they would get it. Otherwise, they would have to pay for their own food. So, I decided to take my plate and offer it to the guards. I told them not to take it as a gesture of humiliation, but rather just what they would do for me if the situation was reversed. They accepted it and ate it ravenously. They thanked me and became friendly.

A few hours later, I decided to return to see if things had changed. This time, when I knocked at the gate, they jumped up and answered it without any resistance.

We communicated through our second language, French. Paul suggested that we exchange our maternal languages, English and Creole. I did want to learn how to speak English; it could help me in the future. So, we ended the Creole classes almost before they began. Instead, we decided on a fair exchange of languages. As an exchange, there was no more payment. It changed our relationship. Now we were both teachers and both students. However, from time to time, Paul would share some money with me, understanding my condition.

chapter nine

A WEEK AFTER WE BEGAN our language exchange, Paul and I were at ease with each other. I would visit him in the guest house and he would come to see me where I lived at Jelo's. Sometimes, we would go on little trips to explore the capital region or the markets. Each time I returned, Jelo would start complaining to me.

"Ti bòs, we don't have any rice or oil. We need provisions," Jelo would complain. His attitude toward me had changed. Since I now had a *blan* friend, he believed that I should take the responsibility of supplying the foyer.

I started to feel pressured. I held him off, "Okay, okay. I won't forget," I would say. But each time I returned to our property, he would be waiting for me at the gate to see what riches I was bringing home. He imagined me returning with a sack of rice on my head, carrying a gallon container of oil. I always disappointed him. He always had recriminations for me.

He would press me on the subject, "Ti bòs, you don't understand what you've got. This is a big occasion and you're letting it slip through your fingers. You have to ask him for what you want. If you don't tell him, he won't know that you need food."

Sometimes, I would respond along the lines, "Okay, what if he takes me for a liar? Obviously, I've been eating. He'll ask how it is I'm alive. I must have been eating something."

Other times, I tried to educate Jelo, "What are you thinking? Why do you assume that all *blan* are rich? Paul isn't rich."

Jelo was ready, "Are you saying that? Or did Paul tell you he isn't rich?"

"Not only did he tell me, I can see. We talk about things and I can see that he isn't rich. In our conversations, I can see that material things are not the most important for him. Just, he wants to live in dignity like everyone has the right."

"Okay. So he's not rich. But he can buy a little sack of rice. Even for a *blan* that's not rich, a sack of rice is nothing."

I asked him, "And you, what do you know about *blan*? A *blan* can be even worse off than you. You think that if a *blan* lands in Haiti, that every strand of hair represents a gourde that has to be plucked before he leaves?"

"Voilà! Now, I see. You are afraid to go to the *blan* to ask for something. I can see that going to school was a great waste of time for you. You didn't learn anything about getting ahead. . . . It's true you have an education, but it's got you all in a muddle. Things are simple: just get a sack of rice. If I had gone to school like you, I would already be rich. Even though I never went to school, I find ways to get ahead. When I came here to the capital, I had no support from my family. This little job I have pays only 750 gourdes ($17.88 US) a month. You can't feed a mouse on that! Each time the doctor comes by, he gives me fifty gourdes ($1.19 US) for food. But then weeks go by when he doesn't come. So, tell me: if I had to depend on those fifty gourdes, would I still be alive? Hardly! He knows that food is expensive. He and his family are just mean. They spend many thousands of gourdes on their food every week. Me — they give fifty! They tell me not to waste it. Buy some bread, they say. They have no idea how hard I work to get out of this situation. I have to fill the reservoir with water and then sell buckets of it to the people around here who don't have any. I have to be clever to stay alive. To eat each day, I need to buy a marmite of rice and to share it with the other poor people around here. They pay me just enough so that I will be able to do the same the following day and keep going."

The strategy that Jelo had devised was beneficial to the poor, and to himself. The local poor people paid him a small sum for the plate of rice that he made available every day. When he put all that money together, he was able to buy a full marmite of rice that he would cook the following day. If the poor had purchased their rice separately, it would have cost more. Jelo saved by buying in bulk for a number of people. The scheme assured him that he would eat every day. Also, it was a pretty good deal for the local poor people. Otherwise, they would each have had to buy coal and water for cooking if they did it separately. Only the street merchants, who depended on selling little sacks of rice and coal, lost a part of their market when Jelo bought in bulk.

Jelo's question made me think. For Jelo, the word "intelligence" referred to one's success at exploiting others. If I couldn't do that effectively, then he questioned the value of my education. However, "intelligence" could also refer to wisdom, to understanding how society and the economy and the environment function so that we make wise choices. And adapting to new information, to new facts. That would be a different kind of "intelligence." Jelo had no patience for that line of thought.

The doctor who paid Jelo 750 gourdes a month to protect and care for his property was also demonstrating Jelo's kind of intelligence. He had been educated many decades earlier in Saskatchewan, in Canada. However, when the poor targeted the bourgeois homes, including his property — three different times over the previous decade — he would finally pay a big price for his privileged position. This had been a middle-class neighbourhood under Duvalier. As time passed, however, his home was increasingly surrounded by penniless peasants who couldn't easily integrate into life in Port-au-Prince. There were no jobs, no services, no infrastructure. These paupers built shacks along the ravines, alleyways, and anywhere a couple of square metres stood vacant. His neighbourhood become uninhabitable... for him. He had to move way up the mountain for security. The doctor was bitter. "I was only trying to help the poor," he lamented, looking at the violence and insecurity in his old district. The doctor wanted to help the poor and profit very well from doing it. When he could no longer live there, he asked a friend from his church to find him a peasant who could act as a security guard. He was looking to pay peasant wages to an employee in the city. But Jelo did not stay innocent for long.

For the doctor, medicine was first and foremost a business, not a service. When the poor targeted the clinic, it was because they were the most in need of its services, but excluded by their very poverty. They couldn't afford the clinic. It would be difficult to find a poor family that had not lost someone because of the lack of medical care. The paupers in that neighbourhood suffered from all of the diseases of the poor. For them, the clinic was an insult.

Once you exploit, you have to accept being exploited. Once you accept being exploited, you learn to exploit. You have to refuse both at the same time. Neither the doctor nor Jelo would call that intelligent.

Jelo was frustrated with my reluctance to exploit my new *blan* friend. "Okay. Since you refuse, I'll show you how to do it. Watch and learn."

One day soon after that, Paul and I returned to the courtyard of the clinic. Paul greeted Jelo. In response, Jelo took Paul's hand and led him to a private corner of the yard. "Ti bòs doesn't need to know what we're talking about," he started.

I tried to hide myself. I knew that Jelo was about to address his favourite subject: rice, beans, and oil. Above all, I didn't want Paul to think that I had organized this. I was ashamed. But I couldn't stop it.

After a few minutes, they returned. Jelo was beaming with satisfaction: he had succeeded where I had failed.

Paul explained that he would buy a sack of rice for Jelo and me. Jelo had told him that there was no rice to eat and that I was suffering. He had played upon Paul's fondness for me. He talked about my recovery from a recent injury. I had fallen out of the mango tree and spent months in bed recovering. That was true. Jelo explained that I needed to eat to recover my strength. He said that we were poor and could not afford to buy rice. If Paul could just help out with a sack of rice and a container of oil, then I would be able to continue with the language exchanges. Otherwise, my participation was uncertain.

Jelo carried on with his old business as before. Each afternoon, he prepared plates of rice for the local poor. And he charged them as always. Nothing changed except the amount of rice that Jelo had to offer. There were more plates than usual. That meant that there was more money for Jelo. However, this time, Jelo didn't need to use those profits to buy a marmite of rice. Instead, a week later, he nonchalantly raised the issue of my health once again with Paul.

"Monsieur Paul," he began, with his brows furrowed in concern, "Ti bòs needs to eat well to keep up. We need more rice. The one we had is already gone."

Paul was shocked. It made no sense that our little household could have finished twenty-five kilograms of rice in a week. The only answer that he could see was that all of the people who had taken to hanging around the courtyard were also benefiting from the windfall.

He tried to find a solution. "You are sharing it with everyone, then," Paul said, touching only a part of the truth. Many people were eating the rice, but they were all paying, except for me, my brother, and Josué. "Oh boy... That's good. I understand. The problem is that I really don't have the means to feed all the poor in Haiti. And, when everyone understands that they can eat at Jelo's courtyard for free, then they will all come. In fact, those who aren't even poor or hungry will be the first in line. I will have spent everything I have and then I will just be another poor person in Haiti looking, like everybody else, for the next meal. Look — we'll get another sack of rice and container of oil, but this time, you'll have to economize better. Okay? Make it last."

"Okay, okay, okay," Jelo agreed. He pretended to understand the problem. He was especially happy to hear that another sack of rice was coming before his clients would arrive hungry in a couple of hours.

Paul was not ready to let the subject drop. "Only one thing, Jelo. Why don't you buy Haitian rice? Why is it you always buy American rice?"

Here was a problem. Jelo needed American rice for his plan to work. Haitian rice was better. It was more nutritious and much tastier. Haitians prefer their own rice by far. However, American rice is cheaper. Jelo could buy twice as much American rice with the same money. Also, American rice was more profitable. It puffed up when it was cooked. It took up twice as much space as Haitian rice that is more dense. In other words, Jelo was making more profit by feeding the local poor rice that was less nutritious. In reality, the spongy American rice provokes gas in the digestive system that, over time, can lead to hernias. Also, the high glucose content of American rice can lead to diabetes since it is a staple of the Haitian diet. None of these issues concerned Jelo. He was calculating how many plates of rice he could sell and the price of each.

"No, no, no, no!" Jelo insisted. Here, he had no answer. But it had to be American rice.

"I don't understand. How can a Haitian peasant prefer American rice?"

Paul tried to lecture Jelo on the politics of dumping American rice and its effects on Haitian agriculture. Jelo was simply waiting for Paul to finish so that he could get his rice. He was uninterested in the American assault on his country's rice industry.

Finally, in the face of an obstinate Jelo, Paul conceded. He would buy the American rice, but he asked that we economize.

This time, the rice lasted only a few days. The business was going well. Jelo was getting his stock for free and selling it at market rates. This was a perfect commercial enterprise. He cooked the rice himself, so there were no labour costs. He had a little basin where he could clean the plates between clients. The line kept moving. His pockets were as inflated as the American rice that he was serving.

The only problem was the source of rice. How to keep the rice flowing? In fact, the problem was resolved before Jelo had to face it. As Paul became more proficient in Creole, thanks to our language exchanges, he learned from the local people that they were paying for their rice at Jelo's. So Paul put an end to the donations.

I saw the problem take form around me. Having a *blan* friend was going to be a problem. It was as though I was becoming an honorary *blan*, even though my skin couldn't be much darker. I was guilty by association. When Paul and I had our language exchanges in the guest house, using the big blackboard, sometimes the workers lingered on the other side of the gallery to observe. They could see that we were deeply engaged in our work. It was clear that I was teaching him and he was teaching me. Even if I had been offering a service, they would have been jealous of my "luck." But since this went both ways, with us teaching each other, it was difficult for them to place either Paul or me.

Everyone had come to the same conclusion:

Blan are rich.

I had a *blan* friend.

Friends share.

Therefore, I was rich.

Josué, who used to work with me at my uncle's workshop, started visiting us in the courtyard to the point where he seemed to be living there. He would bring his furniture projects to work on them. Just hanging around meant that he would benefit in some ways from the presence of a *blan*. My brother James and others came by frequently. I didn't hesitate to share with them whatever material things came my way. I would keep some juices in the clinic fridge, for instance. Sometimes, Paul and I bought *pèpè* clothes. When I returned, I said that everyone had the right to wear them. Of course, they did.

One day, Josué saw a passport and a bank account book that Paul had helped me to get. Paul said that I should have a passport, because I never knew when it might be necessary. It took months to get the passport. We had to pay bribes. None of my friends had ever thought of opening a bank account. I hadn't told anyone yet that I had a passport or a bank account, because I had just got them. I just left them in a buffet. I left the key in the drawer of the buffet so that people could use it as usual. Josué opened it to find the strange documents. He showed them to Jelo secretly. "Look, Jelo. Joegodson is a traitor. He has a passport and a bank account."

Since neither of them could read, they might not have seen that there was almost nothing in the account. But they decided that I was leaving Haiti for Canada and taking a fortune with me. Josué told Jelo that he had seen me dress one day to go to the Canadian embassy to finalize my visa plans. He could, apparently, tell by the clothes that I was wearing where I was going and what I had in mind.

He also decided, upon my return, that the embassy had not accepted me. That was evident from the expression on my face. Jelo asked how he knew that I had gone to the embassy. Josué simply assured him that he was certain. Josué returned the documents to the buffet. But he kept it from me. They assumed that I had been keeping a secret from them. Now, it was their secret from me.

Jelo opened up to me about the gossip that was taking root. He recounted to me everything that Josué had told him about my secret plans to leave the country.

I started to worry. They were trying to understand these strange developments. What to do? How could I explain to Jelo that to have a passport was a human right? He was more likely to believe the gossip of Josué, that I had planned to emigrate without telling anyone. I explained to him that Paul had just suggested they could be helpful in the future. If this was a secret, why would I have left them so visible? Jelo accepted my explanation. But he told me to be careful in relation to Josué, who would not have confined his gossip to the courtyard of the clinic. It was likely that the news was making the rounds of the neighbourhood. If people came to believe that I was wealthy and connected to wealth, then I could be kidnapped and held for ransom. When kidnappers don't get the sum of money they ask for, they often kill the victim. It would be easier for them to kidnap me than the *blan*. And it would be easy to find the *blan* to demand the ransom that he couldn't pay.

As usual, Jelo had carefully surveyed the situation with sharp and cynical eyes.

It was logical to keep Josué at a distance, as Jelo advised. On the other hand, maybe he would become more suspicious and even bitter. Maybe it would reinforce his assumptions. In that case, Jelo's concern might become a reality. I thought that maybe it would be wiser to tell Josué the truth.

One morning, while speaking with Josué, I was secretly searching for a way of introducing the subject. But I just said, "Josué, I have a passport and bank account. Want to see?"

"Okay."

I went to the buffet and returned with the documents. "See," I said, handing them to him. "We poor don't give any importance to these things. Some confuse a passport and a visa. But everyone should have a passport. For identification. It's also important for everyone. We are living in this world, but we are excluded from even visiting it without a passport. Anyway, no one knows what the future will bring. Paul helped me get them. If you want, I could help you to get one too. I think it might be important."

Josué replied, "Ah! Maybe you have another idea that you're keeping from me. Maybe you are planning to leave Haiti."

"You think that getting out of Haiti is as easy as entering it is for the *blan*? For the poor, their appearance is their visa. It can take you from Simon to Site Solèy, but that visa makes it difficult to travel further, even from Site Solèy to Delmas. The border between those worlds is already difficult to cross. To get out of Haiti is almost inconceivable when you can't get out of the slums."

"Maybe for you alone. But with a *blan*, you could do it."

I asked him, "The documents that they ask for, do I have them already? How can Paul get them? Do you think he has a wand to give me a job, an apartment, a diploma, money?"

"If it's hard for you, what about us? You've got a *blan*."

"Maybe you don't see that we're in the same boat."

Josué conceded, "Okay, maybe your idea about the passport is good."

We left it there. "I will help you if you ask me. I'll show you how to go about it."

I was relieved. Maybe that would put an end to the gossip. Still, I knew that he remained bitter. Even though I offered to help him, he knew that he was excluded from this world of passports and bank accounts. And he was not happy that I was refusing to be excluded. In Creole, it's called *jalouzi*, jealousy. It helps keep the border between the rich and poor in place.

The first obstacle to travelling outside of Haiti would be my immediate social circle. Josué, who had refused to support me in demanding decent working conditions at my uncle's workshop, was now suspicious that I was going to leave the country to make a fortune just because I knew a *blan*. What luck! he assumed. He didn't want me to improve things in Haiti and he didn't want me to leave Haiti.

How difficult the struggle must have been for Jean-Jacques Dessalines! Not all the ex-slaves appreciated his plans for independence two hundred years ago. How much had changed since then? After the revolution, the great generals took the Haitian soil for themselves. Dessalines, however, could not accept the egoism of the generals, who looked down upon the ex-slaves. In their eyes, once victory had been assured, the slaves who had fought for their freedom had served their purpose. But, after independence, the former slaves were still crucially important in allowing the generals to amass fortunes and build their chateaus. As with most wars, the victims were the lowest ranks. The generals wait for the victory, gained by the blood of the soldiers. Then the generals claim the victory along with the riches that follow. When Dessalines proposed that all the ex-slaves share the new nation, that Haiti be divided among those who had fought for its independence, he was soon ambushed by the generals who had been waiting for their opportunity. Dessalines was killed by those who didn't want to change the system. The ex-slaves had not finished liberating Haiti. They haven't finished yet.

chapter ten

AFTER PAUL LEFT HAITI, things changed for me. I lost some friends who had become jealous of me. They were sure that I must be rich. The one thing that Paul was able to do was to pay for me to complete my secondary education. The following year, I went back to school. He paid for my uniforms, books, and tuition.

By February, a number of the students were questioning why we were getting an education in the liberal arts. We would be able to read and write French and have a foundation in the physical and social sciences. But since none of us had any connections, we could never use that knowledge to get a job. There were no jobs in Haiti for those without mentors in the upper class. We were from a class that the bourgeoisie detests. There were no jobs for us. What were we doing?

Anyway, I finished the year and then found myself just as I had been before it started, except now the local people were even more jealous. I continued to stay on the property with Jelo as before. I crafted some furniture to try to make some money. I was lucky to recuperate my costs.

•●•

One day in the autumn of 2008, I was being jostled along with other passengers in the back of a *taptap* on the bumpy road leading to downtown Port-au-Prince. One passenger stood out. He was a white-haired old man who carried himself with dignity. He seemed to be more affluent than the rest of us. He spoke. He said he was from Les Cayes. He had come to Port-au-Prince to deliver Bibles for a mission. In Petionville, thieves had stolen everything: the Bibles, his wallet with all his money, and even his glasses. Not only was he in an unfamiliar city, but he could see nothing and had no money to get back to Les Cayes. He told the passengers that he was at the end of his rope.

I decided that if I offered the man something it might inspire others to help also. I had seventy-five gourdes ($1.92 US). I gave fifty ($1.28 US) to the old man. It worked. The other passengers decided to contribute. Before long, everyone had given the near-blind old man something.

By the time the *taptap* arrived at Aviation, the driver stopped and came around to the back. He asked the old man why he was still there. The man had recounted to him his story way up in Petionville when he asked the driver to drop him off at Carrefour Aeroport. Since we were well past that stop, the *taptap* driver smelled a rat and said that he was going to take him to the commissariat of police.

Meanwhile, a woman embarked and was solicited to contribute by the old man's story. She offered him fifty ($1.28 US) of her 250 gourdes ($6.41 US). But she would have to get change. So, she descended at the next stop, which was the commissariat, to get change for the old man.

The driver told the police that this passenger who had first said he was going to Carrefour Aeroport was now continuing to downtown Port-au-Prince and had paid nothing. He left the man with the police and carried on his route.

I decided to stay with the old man.

Inside the commissariat, I watched the old man transform himself. He asked the police if they had been soldiers in the now-disbanded Haitian army. They had been. He told them that he, too, was a veteran soldier. He energetically reproduced some old military manoeuvres to convince the police and to bond with them. It worked. He repeated the story of his theft in Petionville. He told the police that he was trying to get back to Les Cayes, but he could see almost nothing. The police decided to give him 100 gourdes, veterans to veteran.

Then he and I left the commissariat. The woman returned with change and gave 100 gourdes ($2.56 US) to the man. Before embarking on the next *taptap* to continue on her way, she asked me for a favour. Would I take the poor old man downtown to where the buses left for the countryside to assure his safe departure for Les Cayes? I agreed to do that.

The old man and I took a *taptap* downtown. When we arrived, I wondered aloud about a group of buses, a distance away, that were in very rough shape. "I wonder if those buses are working?" I asked rhetorically. The man replied in the affirmative. I wondered, then, how he would know this without his glasses.

"I'll be alright now," he told me. "You carry on, young man. I'll call you when I return home to Les Cayes to assure you that everything worked out alright."

I told him my phone number. He didn't write it down.

A *taptap* passed in front of us. I bid farewell and crossed the street to board it to carry on about my business. Once on the other side, however, I decided to hide behind some buses and watch the old man's progress.

Well hidden, I saw the old man watch the *taptap* drive away. Then he changed his manner. His aimless stare that suggested blindness disappeared with the *taptap* that he thought was carrying me away. He looked all around until his eyes settled upon a young man crossing the street. Then, the blindness descended upon him just in time to stretch out a vulnerable arm and ask for help.

"Young man," he said, "could you help me please find a *taptap* to Aviation. I have no money and I have lost my glasses."

The young man, immediately concerned for the plight of the old fellow, slowed his pace and offered his arm.

Maybe it sounds like a simple — even amusing — little story. But it stayed with me. Soon after, another con artist, this time a beggar woman, fleeced me of all the money I had. I became depressed. Who can you trust? When liars and con artists preyed on the noblest of human instincts, on the generosity of kind people, what was the use of doing anything?

I was losing my will to go on in life at just the wrong moment.

—•—

I awoke with a cough. A second cough. Then a coughing fit. With each cough, my mouth filled a little more until it was full. I got up and went outside. Next to the banana tree, I spat out what was filling my mouth. It was blood.

The coughing continued. My cough was a pump pumping blood from my lungs to my mouth to water the soil. Jelo came to stand next to me with his hand over his mouth, silent. It was the first time he had encountered this. He asked me what he should do. I continued to cough and to spit up blood each time. Jelo looked for water to douse me, trying anything to stop the pump. After I did stop, he took me away from the pool of blood around the banana tree. He was afraid; I could see that he saw death in me. He didn't want me to die. Even more, he didn't want me to die on his watch. We say *Responsab se chaj* — the person responsible is also accountable. Finally, he decided to call my father in Simon.

After a few hours, Dad arrived. Jelo brought him to me and told him what he had witnessed. Seeing Dad leave his work for me, I understood that something really serious was happening. I felt the tears flowing down my cheeks. Dad looked at me tenderly and asked why I was crying. He insisted that I would recover. He said, with the help of God, I would not die. But I couldn't stop crying. My tears weren't just because of my fears, but because of the trouble I was causing. My father had no money to spend on a hospital. Or a funeral.

Jelo made some soup, calculating that I had to replace the blood I had lost. *Sak vid pa kanpe* — an empty sack (as I was) cannot stand upright. After the soup, Dad asked if I could walk back to Simon with him. I said I would try. And I made it back.

When I arrived in Simon, I saw the neighbours lined up in two rows. Dad and I passed through the gauntlet. They asked Dad all kinds of questions, but he was too overwhelmed to answer. His immediate goal was to get me to bed so I could rest. As soon as I lay down, the cough came back and offered a demonstration for everyone. I asked for a pan to collect the blood. Then the neighbours started muttering among themselves, saying that I wouldn't live. Everyone was an expert. No one wanted to be left out by not having a good tuberculosis story, so even if they didn't have any experience, they made something up. All that medical talk started to have a terrible effect on my father. Everyone had advice and no two people had the same idea. Everyone was willing to play the role of doctor with me as patient. I wasn't playing a role, though; I was really, actually sick. Also, they never asked Dad if he could afford what the free advice would cost.

Later, they advised Dad to go to a hospital that treated tuberculosis. Dad tried to raise money. Meanwhile, our neighbour Darlin took me to Gheskio medical clinic. I was so weak, I couldn't stand in the line-up to enter the hospital. Darlin saved me a place while I sat on a rock until she arrived at the front of the line.

The doctors gave me tests and said that the results would be available in three days. The tests were meaningless because I knew I wouldn't last three days. The next morning, I felt very weak. I coughed blood all night. I couldn't sleep. Very early in the morning, I wanted to go to the toilet. I got out of bed to go to the bucket. But I fell down, blind. I spent about twenty minutes with my eyes wide open, but I could see absolutely nothing. I had lost too much blood. I called my sister Roselèn to take my hand because I couldn't walk the ten metres to the toilet. I asked Roselèn to bring a pan for me to do my business, since I couldn't see and couldn't walk. From time to time, I could see little flashes of light. Roselèn stayed next to me after I did my business. But after twenty minutes, I could see again. Then she took me back to bed.

Even the rats sensed my weakness as I lay on my makeshift mattress. We have an expression, *rat mode soufle*, referring to the way that rats blow on the bite they make on sleeping people to keep them from waking. The blowing soothes the wound. I incorporated the experience of the pleasure of the gentle breeze on my arms into my dreams. But when I awoke, I would find that the cloth I was sleeping on had turned red with my own blood. I was becoming rat food.

chapter eleven

I CHRISTENED THE NEIGHBOURS who offered free and foolish advice Doctors Without Diplomas. They counselled Dad every which way. They advised a bath with various leaves, a kind of universal remedy. They counselled him to first rub salt into my hands and feet. I was ready to die, but I didn't want to enter into magic. I assumed that everything that was silly or complicated was magic. Dad told me that the bath salt remedy came from the neighbours. I said it sounded like magic, so he agreed to leave out the salt. I saw that Dad, under stress, was vulnerable to any advice, good or bad.

I felt really calm and free after the bath. But I was still sick. The Doctors Without Diplomas advised that I go to the Children's Care Hospital in Delmas 31. They told Dad that it was better than Gheskio. They would say that a brother or cousin had been there and been cured, and so on. I couldn't walk, so Dad paid for a motorbike to drive me. James went with me. When I arrived there, I filled out the admitting form and I paid seventy-five gourdes ($1.92 US) for a consultation. After that, they sent me to a technician who could test my phlegm. When I arrived, there were fifty people waiting for this specialist. I saw each person trying to produce phlegm to fill a little receptacle they each held in their hands. I coughed and coughed until I managed to produce a little, mixed with blood. The specialist gave me a rendezvous in three days.

When I returned with James to Simon, I couldn't stand the bumps of the motorbike. I thought I would die because I couldn't breathe. I breathed little air between Delmas and Simon. What I did breathe was the dust mixed with all the pollution that passes for air in Port-au-Prince. I arrived closer to death than ever.

I returned to bed. The Doctors Without Diplomas were waiting for juicy news. They never stopped diagnosing and prescribing. They next told Deland that there was another hospital nearby, Lakou Trankilite. They said that the treatment was free there and it was run by Catholic brothers. They had new stories now to show that this was the place I should go: anecdotes about people who left the hospital cured.

I was sick of the Doctors Without Diplomas and the way they were using Dad. I had just enough force to tell Dad, "If they are going to advise fifty hospitals a day, are you going to send me to all fifty? There are people who are happy to see someone fall. Some of them are more interested in their advice than in my health. You can listen to them all, but judge for yourself which advice is wise."

Sometimes, while lying on my bed of Dad's fabrics, I was content to see my brothers from church come to pray with my family for me. But I wasn't happy to hear them ask God to heal me. Because God is no child. It's His will that will be done. When I heard, "Heal Joegodson so that he can work again," I intervened in their prayers, saying, "God, I put myself in Your hands. If it is Your will that I die, so be it." How did my friends know what God wanted? How did they dare tell Him what to do? I was ready to die if that was the will of God.

But, really, I was almost relieved. My disillusionment with life on earth had only grown since my encounter with the old man on the *taptap*. I didn't tell anyone that I was thinking like this. Maybe they could sense it.

Dad decided that Lakou Trankilite was the best option. We had no more money to pay for tests. I said okay but that this was the last hospital that I was going to visit. This was the third in three days. Each wanted me to return for my tests after three days. I never went back for any of them.

James and Roselèn went with me, because they already knew Lakou Trankilite. I arrived on the same day that the doctor was there. There was only one doctor for Lakou Trankilite. He had a contract with several hospitals. Once a week, he spent a maximum of an hour to diagnose and prescribe for all of the patients in the hospital. He left instructions for the brothers. He consulted with me the day I entered and said I needed an x-ray to check my lungs. After the x-ray, during his next visit, he would decide on a treatment. He left. After the consultation, the cough wanted to make a demonstration. I coughed until my mouth was full like the first time in Jelo's yard. As I was close to the room where the most serious cases were, I motioned to a patient to hand me his bedpan. I coughed a mouthful of blood into it. The patient said, "Look, this one isn't going to last."

When the brother came to see the blood that I had coughed up, he said that I shouldn't go home to wait, but that I should have a bed in Lakou Trankilite. He gave me bed number twenty-four in the room for incurables. The beds were numbered in order from one to fifty around the room. The patient whose receptacle I had filled with blood was in bed twenty-five.

I began to worry. This room, it seemed as I looked around from bed twenty-four, was for people ready to die. In my semiconscious state, I could hear the other patients talking. My neighbour in bed twenty-five, named Rènel, told me they had just changed the sheets, since the guy whose bed I now occupied had died that morning. The brothers took my clothes and dressed me in the uniform that all the patients wore and shaved all my hair off. I was now an incurable.

During the days, I prayed that the night would come. But then, all night long, I lay awake, because my eyes couldn't stay closed. I heard every little sound: the mosquitoes, the anole lizards biting into insects, everything. Mostly, I couldn't stand the ceiling fan that chilled me and provoked my cough. I coughed all night long, disrupting the other patients. They didn't complain because they saw the state I was in. They had to accept it.

Each day, I saw the other patients eating. I saw it like a miracle, the ability to eat. I could only drink water. Everyone tried to force me to eat, my family and the other patients. I tried, but only vomited. The sick said that someday I would eat more than them, especially with the vitamins that the brothers were forcing me to take. But the medicine was so strong that sometimes I vomited it.

One day, at sunset, I was in conversation with Rènel, next door, and getting to know other patients. We told each other our stories, how we came to be there. It wasn't just tuberculosis cases. There were cases of AIDS, victims of accidents, and others. Rènel had been a mechanic who had been sitting under a car that was jacked up. The jack gave way and the entire weight of the car came down on his shoulders. His vertebrae acted as the shock absorber. His spine was crushed. His kidneys no longer functioned. Rodriguèz had been the victim of a bullet while he was trying to sell cosmetics in the city in 2004. He had been fourteen years old. There had been a firefight between MINUSTAH and their enemies. The bullet went through his neck and broke his spine. He was now completely paralyzed. There were some elderly blind people who had no family. They had been in the hospital for decades. And Zakari whom we have already met: he had been the antenna for a gang in Site Solèy who was shot and crippled by MINUSTAH in 2004.

Zakari delighted in tormenting the elderly. There were a couple of old blind patients named Bòsadriyen and Bòsjoe. One typical incident: Zakari quietly rolled his wheelchair next to Bòsadriyen, hit him on the head with a plastic container and then retreated as quickly as possible. Bòsadriyen demanded to know who had hit him. Zakari, from a distance now, said that he had seen Bòsjoe do it. Bòsadriyen then kicked at the bed of Bòsjoe who was sleeping soundly. Bòsjoe awoke: "Who kicked my bed?" The other patients started to laugh. Only Bòsadriyen remained angry. Zakari, who was directing the scene, quietly returned, hit Bòsadriyen again, and retreated. Bòsadriyen retaliated by striking Bòsjoe with more force. Bòsjoe, for his part, rose, grabbed the railing of Bòsadriyen's bed, shook it forcefully and demanded an explanation. And so it carried on.

The other patients, instead of calming the situation, laughed. That encouraged Zakari. Despite my weakness, I asked them to stop this kind of prank. I thought the devil was behind it. It could only lead to anger and finally injury when someone was actually hurt. The devil would be content to see such an outcome. If the show had come from God, He wouldn't have written it so that the humour should derive from the pain of the old blind men. We are all in the same boat, I said. Instead of spilling blood, it would be better to see how we could help each other. There was only one enemy here and it was death. We needed to unite to fight it together. That was the first time that I had spoken.

Zakari was unimpressed. "Ya, we know you, pastor. We're not in church now." From then on, everyone called me Pastor Pastor. I continued anyway.

The room was unhappy. It was as though death had everyone in its grasp. Every day, another person died. I wanted to change the way we viewed our situation. So I started a game where we tracked the passage of Death through the room. That way, we knew what bed Death was going to strike next and, by calculating the time, we could know when. It was a game we all played. After all our calculations, we would announce that Death was going to strike bed thirteen at seven o'clock. So, the patient in bed thirteen would tease Death and remain in place until six fifty-nine. Then, he would leap out of the doomed bed just in time. We all came to believe that we were beating Death by making a mockery of it. We could come together in solidarity to outsmart this devious and unseen enemy.

•••

I didn't have my balance yet. I could stand, but nothing more. I was as helpless as a baby. James would come to bathe me and take me to the toilet. I was so skinny that you could see all the bones protruding from my body.

We had a schedule. Every patient had to bathe at five o'clock in the morning, at noon, and in the evening. At five in the morning, the water was cold. Water was the friend of some patients and the enemy of others. Some patients who were really sick died during the morning bath. The water was so cold that the shock pushed them over the edge.

The patients were bathed by Haitian volunteers who were hoping to escape their poverty by joining the brothers. They took out their frustrations on the patients. The brothers sometimes gave gifts to the Lakou Trankilite patients. Cookies, for example. If they received these things, some patients shared them with the workers. If a patient dirtied himself, he could receive bad treatment from workers who didn't like him — with whom he hadn't shared his cookies. They could use the cold morning water as a weapon against a patient they didn't like.

I had lots of friends from outside who brought me little things to eat. People from my church came to visit each day. I was like a depot of milk, juices, cookies, and so on. I shared it all with everyone.

Some of the brothers were mean. One day a blind patient asked a brother for something to eat. The brother picked up off the floor a cookie that had been trampled on and put it in the hands of the blind patient. I looked at him to see his intention. He saw me watching him. He read in my eyes that I was not happy with his gesture. He turned to the blind person and took the cookie back that he was about to eat. Maybe the brother was demonstrating the power he had to control the lives of the patients. My displeasure was like a mirror that reflected the real meaning of his action back to himself. He was ashamed by the humiliation that he was imposing on another. He left the room quickly, trying to get away from me and, perhaps, himself as quickly as possible.

I asked the patients, "If he was in the place of the blind person, or a member of his family was, would he offer a cookie like that?" The blind person remained innocent of all the discussion that was centred around him. Zakari replied that the same brother had done something similar on another occasion. He had entered the room with a dead mouse. He asked Bòsjoe, "Do you want some meat?" Bòsjoe said yes. Then the brother held the mouse by the tail over the mouth of Bòsjoe. The other patients giggled. He asked the blind man to hold out his hand instead to take the meat. He put the mouse in his hand and told him to eat it. Bòsjoe threw it away, saying it was a mouse. I put myself in the place of the blind man. How could I live surrounded by such nasty people? Or good people behaving maliciously?

There was a Catholic chapel in the court of the hospital. Everyone had to go to church. If you didn't agree to go to church, they said that you would need to take your things and return home. So we all went each evening and Sunday morning. At first I was exempt because I was too sick to leave my bed. But afterwards, I had to go. We weren't allowed to go in our own clothes, but had to wear our hospital gowns. The services were attended by people from the neighbourhood and even farther away. They were all dressed in their best clothes. We patients stood out. We felt humiliated, because Haitians always wear their best clothes to church. Rodriguèz, Rènel, and Zakari were exempt because they were confined to wheelchairs and there were stairs at the entrance of the church that they couldn't climb. That was the only blessing that their handicap afforded them.

chapter twelve

FRANCHESCA LIVED IN THE NORTH of Haiti in a mountain community called Varettes. She sold the produce from the cultivators in the local market. Carrying heavy baskets on her head under the merciless sun, Franchesca would walk kilometres through mountainous terrain to reach the market. Her goal was to return home each day with the basket empty.

Franchesca had a cousin named Monique who went to school in Port-au-Prince. After she graduated from secondary school, she studied pharmacology in a professional school.

One summer, Monique came back from the capital to live with her relatives in Varettes. Franchesca was surprised to see how Monique had changed in the few years that they had been separated. Monique had finely coiffed hair. She wore makeup to accentuate her facial features and her clothes were stylish, clean, and pressed. When Franchesca looked at herself, she saw dirty clothes and the mud of the mountain paths caked into her skin. Her hair was unkempt: what was the use of fussing when she would only carry a heavy load on her head for hours every day? She had no time to apply makeup and no makeup to apply. In any case, she wouldn't know how.

Franchesca asked Monique, "Do you think that there would be room for me to live with you and your mother in the capital? I would only stay for a short while until I find a job and can rent a room."

Monique was obliged to accept Franchesca's request. "Of course you can stay with us."

"Oh ... okay ... when are you going back? I'll have to get ready ... I'll travel back with you, okay?"

A million thoughts darted back and forth in Franchesca's head. What career would she pursue in the city? She had always been impressed by the floral arrangements at marriage ceremonies. She was sure that she could make celebrations even more festive. She would need to find a floral shop that was willing to take her on as an apprentice. Throughout the summer, Franchesca's thoughts would transport her to the city where she imagined herself in a tidy little shop, designing magnificent arrangements for wealthy, cheerful clients. She would be well paid for her talent and her work and would send money back for her family. There would be money to hire peasants to help raise cattle or goats. Not yet conversant with banks in the city, she imagined those domestic animals as her only logical investment. Once this dream took root, it kept repeating itself with variations.

Monique led Franchesca to believe that she was delighted. But, in her heart, it was bad news. The room she shared with her mother and sisters in Delmas 33 was tiny. Already, there was not enough space. Whatever would they do with Franchesca? However, if she told Franchesca the reality, she feared that the news would spread through Varettes like a hurricane. Everyone would be talking about the bankruptcy of her family in the city. So she kept up the pretence that things were going well. Peasants believed that the move to the capital would be for the better. Any migrant who disabused them of that risked exposing himself or herself as a loser. It was easier to keep up the pretence. And so the makeup, clothes, and hairstyles — superficial signs of success and affluence — hid the reality of life in the city.

The day arrived. Franchesca packed her bag and waited in great anticipation for her new life in the nation's capital. She prepared provisions that would last them awhile in the city. Together, they climbed aboard a *taptap* and headed through the mountains.

In Delmas 33, Monique and Franchesca disembarked from the *taptap* together. Monique immediately walked ahead of Franchesca, not wanting to be available for Franchesca's questions. In fact, no questions were asked and no answers required. Monique knew that Franchesca was seeing the reality of Port-au-Prince. The narrow alleyways. The crowded slum. The garbage. And not a trace of green.

They arrived at her new home. It was nothing like she had imagined. It was a drab little room of porous cinder blocks under a roof of sheet metal. Although the blocks had been laid years earlier, they had never been plastered. As a result, the rain had driven holes in them. The walls were weak from lack of resources to finish this tiny box of a room.

As she entered the room, her cousins and aunt were trying to figure out what they would eat, since there was nothing in the house and they had no money. When Franchesca entered with bags of food from Varettes, she was greeted as a conquering heroine. Her cousins rifled through the produce as if it was all a great luxury. This was the stuff that she carried on her head every day and that she resented for giving too hard a tone to her muscles.

Monique immediately went to a corner of the floor and fell asleep. Franchesca began to prepare the produce for dinner along with her cousins and aunt.

"Where can I get some water?" she asked. It seemed a mundane question. In Verettes, she could fill her buckets at the spring whenever she wanted to bathe or cook.

"The water is just about finished. We should have bought some, but we ran out of money."

Buy water? But if you need water to live, what sense could it make that her cousins were telling her that they had no money for it? It was clear that there was no spring in this neighbourhood. But what did all this mean?

Her cousins were too ashamed to ask a peasant newly arrived from the countryside for a few gourdes to buy water. But, without that water, no one would be cooking the rice that came, like Franchesca, from Varettes. Finally, she asked directly, "How can I get some water?"

They lied a little about money that was owed to them that had not come. If Franchesca had five gourdes (13 cents US), they could get enough to fill their needs for the evening. They would, of course, repay that tomorrow. In reality, they would not repay that or any other gourde they took from Franchesca.

As her cousins went out to buy the water, Franchesca tried to get her head around her new life. Why was she so ignorant about all of this? If she needed money for water, what would she do when the few gourdes she had saved for her new life were gone? What would happen when the provisions were gone? There were no fields and trees here.

After the feast from Varettes was finished, Franchesca was tired and ready to sleep. But her cousins and aunt kept eating as though they had been waiting for food for some time. Franchesca asked her aunt where she could sleep.

"As you see, there isn't much space. You will have to move the pots and the *rechau,*" they said, pointing to the plates and utensils and dirty pots and cuttings and peelings strewn across the floor that doubled as a counter top. Once cleared, that would be her bed.

After a week, Franchesca's provisions were finished. She had imagined that they would last much longer, but since there were several mouths to feed and nothing else in the house, they went fast. With the provisions finished, her relatives started to resent her presence. The food she had brought was forgotten once their stomachs were empty. At that point, she began to shed tears and couldn't stop.

"What are you always crying about?!" they complained. "Stop it!" That didn't help.

Looking for an escape, she asked Monique if she knew of a family looking for a maid. She knew how to do laundry, cook, and take care of children.

Monique explained that finding a job was not easy. "I'll find you a *koutche*. That's someone who knows what is available and should be able to help. If he finds a household looking for domestic help, he'll let us know and you'll have to pay him a fee for his referral."

A week later, the *koutche* replied that he had found a family that was looking for a maid, not far away. Franchesca was happy. A little good news helped to resuscitate her dream. The *koutche* drove her to a family with five children originally from Gros Morne. Since the husband was a policeman and his wife worked at the Ministry of Culture, neither could stay home to care for their children. The matron offered Franchesca the job, but for a very small salary. Because of her situation, Franchesca was obliged to accept.

It was a live-in position. Compared with her aunt's tiny room filled with her cousins, Franchesca now had more space. She even had her own small bed. She would get up early in the morning to prepare breakfast for the kids before they left for school. Then she would start the laundry. Because of the mud and dust of the streets, the children's clothes needed to be cleaned each day.

Doing the laundry in Haiti means sitting on a cinder block or a little bench in front of a large plastic tub, soaking a special bar of soap in water. Women soak the dirty clothes and rub them between their wrists and forearms, tossing soapy water on them. They work around each article of clothing until they have cleaned it all, focusing special attention on any stains, of course. It is far more efficient than a washing machine that just stirs clothes in soapy water, and easier on the fabric. For hours, they continue the same movements, bent over the tub until they feel the strain in the small of their backs. Franchesca's back became sore because of this daily chore. She was not used to doing the daily laundry for seven people, but she continued because that was her job.

She used to return to her aunt's house on the weekends. As she was no longer living there, she was welcome to visit. They often asked to borrow money. That was difficult for her, since she earned almost nothing. Besides, none of the small loans were ever repaid.

One day, a young man named Fédrik visiting the household where she worked took notice of Franchesca. He began to court her. She was afraid to respond. She had been warned that the young men of the capital could not be trusted. But, as he shared his goal with her of going to the Dominican Republic to establish a martial arts school, she came to believe in his sincerity. She learned as well that he was a cousin of Mme Bolivar, her boss and the head of the household.

She took Fédrik to meet her aunt. Often, the young men of the capital reject the customs of the peasants. They don't like the tradition of meeting the parents. In the countryside, the criteria are clearer. But in Port-au-Prince, the young men are seldom sure of their futures and often have unstable pasts. It is unpleasant to present yourself before a court when you have no defense and you know the verdict will be negative.

Fédrik opened a little part of his heart to answer the questions of Franchesca's aunt, not wanting to give too much away. In most cases, he confined himself to "yes" or "no." His guarded answers led Franchesca to question him. What were his real intentions towards her?

Since Fédrik was also not certain about Franchesca, he proposed that they go to Bourdon to meet his mother. When he asked her, Franchesca understood for the first time that he was serious. In Bourdon, she was impressed by the way that his mother spoke of him. Franchesca declared openly that she wanted to build a family with him. Now, they both started to think along the same lines.

chapter thirteen

BECAUSE OF THE DAILY HUMILIATIONS in Lakou Trankilite, I didn't want to stay there. It was better to go back to Delmas 19. The food in Delmas was uncertain, however. I would need to eat. Also, I was increasingly on the bad side of the Catholic brothers. Why? Lots of reasons.

One day, a few Americans came to visit the hospital. They had already visited from time to time. They had promised Rodriguèz and Rènel to send some things to help them pass the time: a DVD player and films, Nintendo games, and so on. But the boys never received them. When the Americans came this time, Rodriguèz and Rènel asked me if I could interpret for them to find out whether or not they had sent the things they had promised. The *blan* said that they had sent them and also wondered why the patients hadn't received anything. They decided to talk to the brothers. They called the brother superior and asked whether the things that they had sent had been distributed. He replied that everything had been shared with the patients. The brother asked if the boys were saying they hadn't received them. The Americans lied, saying that they didn't know.

The Americans made some promises to Rodriguèz, Rènel, and Zakari. One said that he would deliver the stuff personally. I don't know if the brothers had seen me speaking with the Americans and probing the irregularities in the distribution of gifts. But, soon after, the brothers met to decide which patients were ready to leave. I was still really sick. Zakari had a friend among the brothers who told him that I was first on their list. I wasn't surprised to hear that, because I knew already they didn't like me, not only because of my interpreting for the Americans. There had also been the episode with Jeff.

Jeff was a patient of fourteen years old from Site Solèy. He was asthmatic. His mother was dead. He lived with his father who had no job and no money. He couldn't care for Jeff. He brought his son to the hospital with two goals: to get Jeff food and to treat his asthma. Normally Jeff lived with his father, but from time to time he stayed overnight in the hospital. I chose Jeff for a friend, even though he was sometimes disruptive. I identified with him. I too had lost my mother when I was about his age and Dad had trouble feeding us.

One day, the Sisters of Kindness, who manage a hospital in Delmas 31, wanted to celebrate the anniversary of their establishment. They were from the same congregation as the brothers who ran Lakou Trankilite. They told the brothers to prepare all the sick in Lakou Trankilite for the celebration. The sick, me included, thought that the brothers would take us to Delmas 31 to the sisters' hospital, which was much bigger. The brothers prepared everyone, shaving our heads. They bathed us and changed our uniforms and we waited in the court. We assumed we were going. But they had already left without us. Only the brothers went to the celebration. Around eight o'clock, the Sisters of Kindness brought the Brothers of Kindness back.

They brought a cake with them to share with the patients. We were back in our rooms when we heard the announcement to go to the dining room. We all went. Jeff told me he didn't feel well. Maybe he was having an asthma attack. A brother started to cut the cake for each patient. Jeff returned with his father. His father would stay overnight sometimes with Jeff. When Jeff got to the table, the brother had not yet finished cutting the cake. He got angry at Jeff for not being there earlier. He told Jeff that he wouldn't give him any cake and that he didn't want him in the hospital. He told him that his father could take him away. A quarter of the cake remained, but the brothers had already started to pack it up to take away. The brother then prohibited anyone from sharing his cake with Jeff. I decided to disobey the order and to share mine with Jeff.

When the brother saw that Jeff was eating, he thundered, "Who gave their cake to this guy?!"

All the sick remained in suspension. They knew it was me, but they didn't want to denounce me. I raised my hand and said that I had. He asked why. I just said that I couldn't eat it all. But then I added that Jeff had left because he wasn't well and that the brother was still cutting the cake when Jeff returned. In other words, I tried to defend myself and inculpate the Brothers all at once.

He told Jeff's father to take him away. He should have taken his anger out on me. But he sent Jeff away instead. I knew the problems that Jeff's father was having. It was another of many burdens. In any case, the next morning, Jeff and his father had to leave.

I spoke to them all night. I told them that Lakou Trankilite was not where life began, it was rather where it ended. I encouraged them both in their future. I had received 1,000 gourdes ($25.44 US) from friends from church. When the morning arrived and they were preparing to leave, Jeff had an asthmatic attack. He couldn't control his breathing. He was three-quarters dead. I tried to assure his dad. I gave them the 1,000-gourd note and asked them to return 500 to me when they could. After they left, I just sat there thinking about them for hours. Suddenly, Jeff's dad returned to the hospital. I was happy to see him, but the news that he brought was that when they returned home, Jeff was already dead.

I felt guilty. If I hadn't offered to share my cake with Jeff, he and his dad wouldn't have been evicted from the hospital. All I had offered them was a few empty words about how everything would be fine. And now, just hours later, Jeff was dead. How would his dad afford a funeral? He couldn't feed Jeff and care for him in life. Neither could he in death. I had nothing else to offer. He returned the 500 gourdes to me. I told him to keep it. I knew how expensive the funeral of a child could be. I tried a few more words of encouragement. But what can you say?

•◗•

After that, I passed a number of days with my heart elsewhere. I wondered what I could do to leave a trace of me behind in the hospital. From time to time, new Brothers of Kindness would come to the hospital for training. Their job was to give needles, injections, medicine, change bandages, and so on. They came from all over the world. They found employment or meaning by working at Lakou Trankilite. What motivated them?

Some would try over and over to find a vein to give an injection. One brother just couldn't manage to give an injection. A patient tried to explain how to do it, what vein to use and how to insert the needle. But the foreign brother wouldn't take instructions from a Haitian patient.

There was a class structure that those above wanted to keep in place. Everyone entered the hospital according to his place in that structure. The poor sick Haitians had to remain on the bottom rung. The foreign brothers wanted to guard their place. If they too were poor, the same as the patients, then there would be nothing to distinguish them. I think that many of them, in their home countries, might have escaped the fate of the paupers in Simon by joining their "charitable" order. Maybe they were honoured for their choice of vocation. But there was no spirit of charity. They needed us more than we needed them. We would happily have given up our poverty. Would they have given up their place on the ladder to see that happen?

There was another brother who came to replace the brother superior. He spoke English and Spanish. He wanted to get to know the sick in our room, but unfortunately he couldn't speak to them. I tried to speak to him. We could speak together in English. He would look for me to ask me how to say this or that in Creole. That made me feel almost at ease with this brother. He needed me and so I felt useful. Mostly, he wasn't too proud to admit that I could be useful.

I still dreamed of leaving. But I wanted to have a profession before I left.

I asked him whether, if I left the hospital, he would be able to pay for a course for me so that I could get a diploma in English. He said that when it was time to leave, he would see about whether they could arrange something. He said I should choose the school and return with the information. With that promise, I was ready to leave that day. I asked my friends in the hospital. They said to wait to be sure that I was cured, because if I left before I was cured, not only would they never take me back, but even the members of my family would be blacklisted from the hospital. I decided to take their advice and not leave until I was discharged. After a few weeks, I felt almost well enough to leave. But the new director had not decided if I was ready to go.

During the two days that they changed bandages, local people came to the hospital for treatment. That was good publicity for the hospital. Serving outpatients from the neighbourhood reminded everyone that the hospital was active. It was also helpful for the local sick.

Also, local Haitians sometimes were engaged by the hospital to help the brothers. They weren't paid, but they professed an interest in entering the Brothers of Kindness. They sought to escape their poverty in the same way that the brothers had. They slept in Lakou Trankilite and helped with a number of jobs, including taking care of the patients. There were also two patients in the hospital who found a way to help the other patients, transforming themselves into health providers. They were very efficient. I too wanted to help the brothers bandage the local people. Unfortunately for me, the same day that I was put to service helping them, the brother who was in charge of all staff saw me. In front of all the local people, he said that he had not authorized me to treat people. I was humiliated and returned to my room.

That week, I received a call from the director of the hospital to say that my health had improved and that I could return home. I was a graduate of Lakou Trankilite. He gave me a card that allowed me to get the medicine I needed in a hospital in Site Solèy, and 250 gourdes ($6.30 US) to buy it.

I folded my clothes and said good-bye to my friends, promising that I would always return to see them. I returned home to Dad's house in Simon.

chapter fourteen

ZAKARI'S FAMILY WAS HIT HARD by losing him after he had been struck by a MINUSTAH sniper's bullet. They came to visit him in the hospital often.

Zakari had a talent for understanding what made people tick, including the Catholic brothers who administered the hospital. One of the Brothers came from an Arab country. He was weak in the Creole language. Although Zakari couldn't understand this brother, they found a way to communicate through hand gestures and such. He understood that this brother was a womanizer who especially liked young Haitian women. Zakari obliged him by inviting some young women from Sitey Solèy into the hospital to introduce.

The brother also understood both poverty and human nature. It was therefore easy for him to seduce the poor Haitian women that Zakari invited. The brother had access to the gifts that foreigners sent to the hospital for the benefit of the patients. He could choose the most attractive items to offer to the most attractive Haitians. Some pretty young women, both single and married, allowed themselves to be bought by the latest phone technology or other material things. Sometimes, they managed to get enough money out of the brother to start a business as a street merchant.

It was a precarious game for the young women. The brother had no interest in forming a relationship. He could be seduced as much as he was a seducer. But if the young woman made herself too available, appeared too loose, the brother rejected her immediately. She would need to play the brother along until she had succeeded in negotiating a fair exchange. She needed to assure herself that he traded fairly before sexual relations put an end to the affair. The brother was insatiable, but he never drank from the same cup twice.

Zakari profited more than the young women from his new business. The brother took a special liking to him. Zakari too understood that the brother was fond of him and would make sure that his needs were met. In this way Zakari could provide for his family from his hospital bed. The brother quietly passed Zakari not only some of the gifts that the hospital received, but enough money to make up for his absence from the family home.

The business was visible to all the other patients. Neither Zakari nor the brother worried about hiding it. Some became jealous of Zakari. They had never believed that they could be anything but victims in the hospital. But they saw that Zakari was controlling not only his own life from his wheelchair, but that he was providing for his family and initiating a number of commercial enterprises for young Haitian women. Some patients began to look for how they might repeat Zakari's success. Did the brother have another Achilles' heel besides women?

One patient discovered that the brother had a weakness for gossip. This handicapped man hoped that this weakness might be strong enough to replace Zakari's business. Unfortunately, gossip was a secondary pleasure for the brother and could in no way take the place of his main interest, which was sex. In that area, Zakari had the market cornered. Moreover, this other patient's entrepreneurial initiative turned against him. As the other patients learned that he was speaking maliciously about them, he became detested by everyone. He had indeed found a weakness in the brother, but it was one that profited no one and harmed many. Zakari's pre-eminence was never in danger. The poor patient wound up loathing Zakari out of jealousy as much as he himself was loathed by the other patients for his petty scheme.

Twòp magi gate sòs — too much seasoning ruins the sauce. Too much success can lead to failure. Zakari became contemptuous of the other patients. He was a little guy confined to a wheelchair, but the others were afraid of him. No other patient had managed to wield such power. He could make life difficult for the other patients by complaining to his friend among the Catholic brothers.

Zakari did not behave like a patient, but like a director of the establishment. He thought himself above the rules and regulations of the hospital. He refused to follow his own treatment program. For instance, the hospital had a certain schedule for changing bandages, twice weekly.

If Zakari brought himself to accept one application, he would refuse the second. He had attained an elevated status among the patients. To allow himself to be treated like them would bring him to their level. He became the victim of his own pride.

Sometimes, the other patients who liked him tried to convince Zakari that it was for his own good. Rodruguèz and Rènel would say, "Come on, Zakari. In this case, you need the doctor more than he needs you. You are acting as though you are not handicapped like us. But we all need to accept this about ourselves."

Zakari would have none of it. "Leave me alone. I'm almost cured. I don't need any help."

In fact, Zakari had open sores from spending all day in a wheelchair. Only in his mind was he healing.

No human power is eternal. And Zakari's was fleeting.

All of the Catholic brothers who worked in the hospital were foreigners. Eventually, their time would come to an end and the congregation would send them to another posting in a different country. And so, the time came for the Arab brother who had entered into business with Zakari.

When Zakari got the news that his special friend was leaving, he became visibly sad. He stopped eating for days on end. He stopped his daily travels around the hospital. He confined himself to his bed until the day the brother left. The sadness intensified his illness. He refused treatment and allowed himself to sink into deep despair.

Zakari's health deteriorated. The loss of his brother made him see that he was not in charge, but sad, sick, and powerless. He thought of the good times he had known, and saw no possibility in succeeding again. He could never help his family again. Against all odds, they had come to rely on their handicapped son for their survival just as he had provided for them when he was a healthy ten-year-old. Without the brother, his business shut down. The girls stopped coming. He came to see himself as a patient, the victim of a bullet to his spinal column.

A couple of months after his friend left, Zakari died.

chapter fifteen

FRANCHESCA WAS NOT WELL RECEIVED by Fédrik's family. Fédrik's cousin, Mme Bolivar, was Franchesca's boss. When Franchesca entered the family, it had been as a poorly paid maid newly arrived from Verettes. Mme Bolivar was trying to separate her family from the peasantry and the urban pauper class. When she learned that her cousin Fédrik was seriously courting her domestic servant, she was upset that her family, with one foot on the first rung of the ladder, would fall back onto Haitian soil.

Franchesca and Fédrik, too, both understood the problem. Franchesca knew that she could be either maid or fiancée. Fédrik encouraged Franchesca to find any other work in order to protect her reputation within the family. If she was seen as a maid, their union would never be accepted.

So Franchesca resigned from her new job and returned to her aunt. Her cousin, Monique, who had studied pharmacology, was working in a sweatshop. She advised Franchesca to take a course in operating the industrial sewing machines. The course, called *degoche*, took a week and cost 500 gourdes ($12.57 US).

When Franchesca had finished the course, Monique went with her to the Industrial Park, SONAPI, close to the airport. When she entered the Park, Franchesca saw a large sprawling complex of many factory buildings. In front of each was a crowd of about forty Haitians milling around.

Franchesca stayed apart from the crowds while Monique went into one of the factories to speak to a supervisor. After a few minutes, she returned with a middle-aged Haitian man. The crowd came to a standstill immediately. All eyes turned toward the man who passed through the crowd as if it was made up of ghosts. He went directly to

Franchesca. Monique introduced them and the supervisor brought Franchesca into the factory, once again passing obliviously through the crowd. Slowly, the unemployed returned to their aimless rambling and small talk.

Inside the factory, the supervisor took Franchesca to a kind of sewing machine that she had not seen before. It was larger, more powerful, and more complicated than the ones she had seen in her course. She focused all her attention on the machine with its threads moving in complicated and incomprehensible geometries. She had seen the aimless crowds outside and knew what it meant. If she failed, she would find herself among them. For some reason that she would never know, the supervisor was beholden to Monique and was doing her the favour of accepting Franchesca. The dynamics that ordered the sweatshops' human resources were complex. Supervisors had something that people wanted: a job as poorly paid as it was demanding, but a job nevertheless. They used that to their personal advantage. Depending upon their characters and priorities, the criteria could change from helping people in real difficulty, to favouring members of a religious sect, to seeking bribes, to gratifying sexual desires, and so on.

She glanced from side to side at the other workers to see how they had threaded their machines and how they operated them. Never had she focused her attention with such concentration and intensity. But she managed to keep her place.

At break time, Monique led Franchesca out of the factory to a street merchant selling rice and juice. Monique addressed her, "Client, I'm here."

The merchant replied, "That's ten," while handing Monique a plate of rice and a cup of juice.

Franchesca did not understand what was happening. Was this woman employed by the factory to feed the employees? She followed Monique and said, "Client, I'm here."

The merchant frowned and said, "Who are you? This is the first time I've ever seen you and you address me like you know me! . . . What if you take my food and then never come back. Who do you suggest I go to for my money?"

Monique took up Franchesca's cause. "This is my cousin who has just begun to work in The Well Best building. She will be able to pay you on payday. I'll take responsibility for her. If anything goes wrong, I'll pay you." Payday was every two weeks.

The merchant did not exactly welcome Franchesca. "I know your type! You take my food and then when payday comes, you take flight. You'd better not disappoint me," she warned, thrusting a plate of rice at Franchesca.

Franchesca stood for a moment without accepting the plate. Obviously, she was paying the price for employees who had deceived this merchant in the past. *Chat brule nan dlo cho, le li wè dlo frèt, li pè* — a cat that burns itself in hot water fears the sight of cool water too. Cautiously, she accepted the plate and begrudgingly entered into a contract with the nasty merchant. She ate it standing next to Monique. It was insufficient and, served with humiliation, it had a bitter taste. Each morning, she went to the same grouchy merchant for either spaghetti or bread before beginning work. At break time, eleven-thirty in the morning, she would have a plate of rice and a cup of juice.

— • —

Payday came. When the workers exited the administrative building where they received their pay, Franchesca saw the street merchants who served them their lunches all waiting with their little account books in their hands. They formed a formidable flank and workers could evade their trap only with a predetermined escape plan. Franchesca's merchant wasted no time. She charged up, showed her the page where her purchases had been documented and took most of Franchesca's pay for two weeks of ten-hour days. Other workers got away from their merchants, refusing to arrive home with nothing.

Franchesca had to decide how to carry on. What did the other workers do? What was the point in eating if you made no money? What was the point of working so hard to simply remain alive? If she tried to stiff the merchants, then she would earn their contempt and harm her reputation. So, she decided that she would not eat so that she could retain her salary. Some of the other employees entered into different agreements with the supervisors who covered the cost of the food. But these arrangements usually cost dignity and self-respect. She would try to go hungry.

Franchesca kept up her resolution for several weeks. She resisted the desire to eat each morning and at each midday break. She tried to avoid hanging around where the merchants cooked and the employees ate so as to not provoke an appetite. But she weakened. Her body reacted badly to her paltry diet. She started to fear that she would fall seriously ill, in which case she would have to see a doctor. That would cost even more than the price of food. She would have to go into debt in order to pay for medical treatment. She was surrounded by vultures that would, one way or another, separate her from her paycheck.

The company deducted from each employee a certain sum for ONA, national insurance. It was supposed to cover medical costs and life insurance. When Franchesca started suffering from headaches and muscle cramps, she went to the administrative building and asked for medical help. She assumed that since she was paying for health insurance, they would send her to a hospital for proper care. Instead, the clerk reached absentmindedly into a little cardboard box, handed her a pill, and sent her back to work.

She suspected that she was suffering from malnutrition. Also, she worked under intense lights that added to the stifling heat of Port-au-Prince. Franchesca's physical troubles did not subside. Each time that she went to the office, she received the same pill. It was prescribed for all maladies that affected the workers at SONAPI. Sometimes, she felt too weak to work. Once, she stayed at her aunt's home and slept for a couple of days. When she returned to SONAPI, she found that her place had been taken by one of the people who had waited outside of the factory door. She, in turn, took the place of her replacement in the crowds. She chose another factory and joined one of the other crowds, knowing that it was unlikely that she would be rehired by the same supervisor who had replaced her. That, of course, was common practice among the workers who, for reasons similar to Franchesca's, found themselves unable to continue.

The other factories assembled other items for the foreign market: luggage, bags, and all sorts of clothing. But the working conditions and salaries were consistent. They were controlled by the Haitian bourgeoisie that subcontracts all of the assembly work from the international corporate class. Their role is to assure that their foreign partners pay Haitian workers as little as conceivably possible. Also, they assure that the workers do not eat into their windfall profits. Once you know one factory, you know them all. There is no competition between factories, or companies, for employees. The workers have very little choice.

Sometimes, on Sundays, when Fédrik visited Franchesca at her aunt's, she would complain about her life at SONAPI. But Fédrik felt powerless in the face of Franchesca's complaints. Even though they were not yet married, Fédrik was supposed to support her, according to tradition. But Fédrik could not think of how to help himself, let alone anyone else. His problem was of a different order than Franchesca's. While she was overworked and underpaid, Fédrik couldn't even get to that point. There were no factories for martial artists, and that was his only skill.

But Franchesca's complaints pushed him to speed up his plans to go to the Dominican Republic. He found some friends who were used to crossing the Dominican border without passports. They would show him how to get to Santo Domingo. Crossing the border was always risky, but they advised him on how to minimize those risks. In 2009, he made his final plans. He tried to encourage Franchesca to do her best in his absence. Since she saw that he was sacrificing for their future together, she was encouraged. She knew that foreign countries had the one thing that barely existed in Haiti but that Haitians needed to exist in Port-au-Prince: money. Fédrik was going to the Dominican Republic to come back with a sack of money. That was a noble and brave adventure. She would wait.

chapter sixteen

WHEN I LEFT LAKOU TRANKILITE, I returned to church for the first time on 25 December 2008. The choir had organized a concert. I was kind of the star of the concert just because I was still alive.

I started to resume my activities in the church, in the choir, and in the *coeur d'adoration*, whose job was to inspire the congregation to participate in singing the hymns, like cheerleaders. The choir rehearsals began. I joked with my friends as before. We used to talk about all kinds of subjects, including our romantic lives. One of the other members was named Annie. Sometimes, she would discuss with me the problems that she was having with her boyfriend. I encouraged her to remain faithful to him. We became intimate friends. Since she had confided in me about her relationship, one day she came to tell me that she had broken with her boyfriend. He was a policeman who had a roving eye. She knew that he had girlfriends all over and wanted to keep them all. Annie decided that she could not continue with him.

Now our close friendship changed. Up to this moment, one of the intimate subjects that we discussed was Annie's romantic problems with her unfaithful policeman. Now, she had taken him out of the equation. That meant that things shifted between us. For the first time, I went to the house in Delmas 33 where she lived with her elder sister, Mme Bolivar, the wife of another policeman. The house was large. I thought about my poor miserable father and my family in Simon and I felt intimidated. I came and went without saying anything. Each time I visited, it was the same. Never could I bring myself to talk with Annie's family.

I was so numb that I even started to spook Annie's three-year-old niece, Lucy. Every time she saw me she started to cry, saying, "Go back home." I tried to smile to comfort her, but she would reply by hitting me. If my presence was eliciting such a reaction from a three-year-old, I despaired to think what the adults were thinking about me. Moreover, I couldn't blame them.

One night after church, I walked Annie back to her sister's house. She told me that this time I couldn't leave without saying why I was there. That was going to be tough because I hadn't yet said anything to anyone. Once in the house, she called her brother-in-law, the policeman. When he came, Annie told him, "Joegodson has something to tell you."

He said, simply, "I'm listening."

I collected all my courage to announce, "Perhaps Annie is better placed to tell you what we have to say."

He boomed, "No! If it was up to her to tell me something, she would just call me to say this or that. She says that it is you that is going to tell me something. What is it?"

I started to speak, "Normally, you are used to seeing me here visiting Annie. But so as not to hurt my reputation, it's best that I explain our relationship. That is to say, Annie is my girlfriend."

He said, "Well, I am delighted. She has spent much time here with us. We have never had any problem with her. But I am only one member of the family. You must discuss this with the others. For instance, my wife Mme Bolivar and also their mother Mme Dieumerci, since Annie has no father."

To help me out, he called his wife to the room. I repeated the same speech to Mme Bolivar, only this time, as things were not going as badly as I had supposed, I filled in some empty spaces with details.

Mme Bolivar told me that I was welcome in her house. She said that the family was not rich. The only strength they had was in unity. They were nine sisters who were raised by a single mother who worked as a street merchant, selling the *manba* (a kind of spicy peanut butter) she made herself. When one has a problem, it touches all the others. She said that she appreciated my comportment. She left to continue with her chores, assuring me that I was welcome.

With that, I left to return to my little room in Delmas 19.

Now that I was officially accepted, the fears that had kept me silent disappeared. Only Lucy remained to conquer. I tried a number of tactics. I started with the easiest. Each time I visited the house, I brought candies for her. She would accept them, all the while insulting me in terms impressive for a three-year-old. She was going to be tough. Each time I returned, she was waiting at the door with her steely eyes, defying me to proceed. But now I had a weapon to use against her. I knew her weakness. As long as she was accepting the candies from me, I was certain that she would sweeten up.

One day, Annie's mother came from the countryside to stay with her daughter Mme Bolivar. They gave her all the details and she asked Annie to bring me to meet her. When I got the message, I hopped on a *taptap* and headed for Delmas 33. By the time I arrived, her mother was preparing to leave. We met in the entrance. She had the appearance of the elderly street merchants I was used to seeing. She had white hair and an assured character that came from careful business dealings to protect a tiny profit margin. No nonsense.

Mme Bolivar's husband, the policeman, was also on the gallery. As soon as I arrived, he asked me if I recognized this woman.

I replied, "Perhaps I should know her."

He said to Annie's mother, "And you, do you know this young man?"

Mme Dieumerci replied, with a somewhat suspicious look in my direction, "No! I don't know him. Why are you asking?"

I sensed that I had already failed to impress Mme Dieumerci by my physical presence. Whatever she was looking for in a son-in-law, it was clear that it was not the slight man from Simon that stood before her. Perhaps the bar had been set by those who preceded me. Annie had already dated a policeman and, before him, a bank clerk, and, earlier, a Haitian who was important enough to live outside of Haiti. Me, I was in Haiti to stay. I dreaded the questions to come.

Now Annie had entered the gallery. She greeted me. Then, she turned to her mother, "Mother, this is Joegodson. He is my brother from church and also, he is my boyfriend." She continued the formal introduction, "Joegodson, this is my mother."

I offered my hand and said, "Hello, Mme Dieumerci. Now you have a new son."

I stood like a statue with my hand outstretched. She kept her two arms by her side.

"Where is your father? In the capital or in the country?"

I answered, "My father lives here in the capital in Simon."

"You live with them?"

"No. I live in Delmas 19."

"And your mother?"

"My mother died in 1999."

"How did she die?"

"She was giving birth, even though the doctors had ordered her not to. She was anemic. By imprudence, she became pregnant. Both my mother and the baby died in childbirth."

"Oh! Your father is heartless. He should have listened to the doctors. He killed your mother!"

She continued, "But if your mother is dead and your father lives in Simon, why do you live in Delmas 19? Who do you live with?"

"I have lived with some friends since 2003. The person with whom I live has become like my family for me."

She then asked, "Do you have a job?"

"I am simply a little cabinetmaker. Sometimes I work alone, making furniture in the courtyard where I live to sell to passersby. It's not easy."

I could understand why my answers were filling her with doubts. Separated from my family, she assumed that I must be a *vakabon*. With a voice full of apprehension, she said, "When you have a child, you have to leave her to make her own choice. There is nothing that I can say, but Annie has chosen you."

No words could have deflated me more. She was trying to reconcile herself philosophically with a great disappointment. Clearly, if she believed that parents had the right to choose their daughters' husbands, I would not still be in the race.

"I have nine daughters. I don't direct their lives. I follow their collective will. They will have to consider this situation first. After I listen to them, we will have more to say. We don't do things haphazard. You will have to introduce us to your father also so that we can judge. I have more confidence in the older generation than in the young."

When she had finished, she left in a calculated sadness.

Annie came over to me. Perhaps she saw that her mother's questions and my answers were weighing heavily upon me. She wanted to reassure me. But that was not in the order of things. "Why did my mother ask you all those questions?" she said innocently.

I answered, "She was right to ask all that she did. She is doing what any mother should. But my answers were disappointing in their honesty. She has the right to think anything she wants because she is protecting the interests of her daughter.... Only, I noticed that her questions were really focused on improving her family's condition. They were not about sharing, but rather advancing.... After all, her questions don't discourage me. *Au contraire*, they make me even more determined to protect my reputation."

Annie said, "Okay, but still, I simply introduced you. Over time, she will get to know you. It's not by asking questions like that that she can know you."

I answered, "Maybe some day my family will hurt you. People sometimes say things that they should not. It's best to try to understand the mentality of each person. If you don't, you cannot live on earth. The same person that encourages you one day can deflate you the next. Best to take both in turn."

chapter seventeen

FÉDRIK LEFT DURING THE NIGHT with his friends. They jumped up on the top of a rickety bus piled sky high with sacks of something. They looked like cats balancing themselves on the sacks as the bus swayed from side to side along the Haitian roads, seeming close to tipping over when the potholes were too abrupt and the rocks too large. When they arrived at the border, they pretended that they were merchants selling the stuff they sat on. As money is the key that opens many doors, Fédrik and his friends paid the driver to bribe the border guard to cross into the Dominican Republic.

Then, they followed mountain paths and rivers to finally arrive in a territory where there were many other Haitians who had taken the same route, sometimes many years earlier. They welcomed Fédrik and his friends. They told Fédrik that if he attempted to live openly, he would not last two days here. They told him that Haitians survived in the Dominican Republic by living like rats, hiding from the light of day and scurrying away from all authorities and enemies. It was the only way of life possible.

Fédrik was intimidated by the advice of the experienced Haitians, called *viejo* (old ones). They told him that he would need to be strong to protect himself from the Dominicans. They hated Haitians. They will come at you with machetes, they told Fédrik. If you are meek and show fear, they can kill you. Fédrik did not come to the Dominican Republic to fight Dominicans — except in sport. His goal was to help Franchesca escape her peonage in the sweatshops. It was to build a future life, not face a violent death. This was bad news.

They also told Fédrik that he needed to be willing to work very hard. The only work available for Haitians was cutting sugar cane.

If you are afraid of snakes, like most Haitians, then you should return now, they said. In the fields where we work, the snakes are huge, they warned Fédrik, who was starting to wish he had never left Port-au-Prince.

During the first week of his unofficial apprenticeship in the Dominican Republic, Fédrik cooked for the *viejo*. They gave him a little money for this service. After that week, he decided to accompany them to work in the fields. Since Fédrik could not speak Spanish, the *viejo* negotiated with the Dominican bosses on his behalf. Fédrik had to accept whatever pay the *viejo* said he was earning.

In time, Fédrik became a part of the *viejo* community. It was an uncertain existence. After several weeks in one place, they would hear a police vehicle coming for them. They would pack up and flee in minutes. They would find another location in the fields or forests where they could camp until they were smoked out again. Scurrying through the Dominican forests, Fédrik understood what they had meant when they said that he would see life from the perspective of a rat.

He learned from the *viejo* by following them. He learned how to work, how to communicate in Spanish, and how to avoid the authorities. From Fédrik, the *viejo* learned something about the martial arts. They were motivated students. The Dominicans were exceedingly racist toward Haitians. They made good on their threats to attack and beat Haitians. Fédrik taught the *viejo* how to protect themselves physically from such attacks. The *viejo* felt more secure, knowing that they could defend themselves.

Among the Dominicans were young men whose job was to control the Haitians . . . to terrorize them. One of these thugs worked with the Dominican patrons who hired the Haitians to work their fields. He had heard of the new martial artist. One night, he came to their campsite and told them all to flee, as was his custom: a show of his authority and his brawn. When Fédrik remained seated, he sat next to him, "You didn't hear me? I said to get out of here."

Fédrik gazed calmly at the flames before them.

"Haven't you heard of me?" said the Dominican henchman.

"Maybe you haven't heard of me," answered Fédrik without bothering to look at his tormentor. He showed no signs of leaving.

The Dominican was impressed. Instead of pushing the issue, he offered his hand to Fédrik, saying "Yes, I have heard of you." He asked

Fédrik if he would be interested in taking on a different job in the enterprise. Instead of the backbreaking work of cutting the sugar cane, would he like to learn how to drive a vehicle? It was farm work, but of a higher status. And he would earn the salary of a Dominican.

Henceforth, Fédrik lived and worked apart from the *viejo*. He was paid a real salary and was able to rent a room in the fields. When he wasn't working, he shared his skills in the martial arts with the Dominicans. They didn't pay him for the lessons; it went without saying that the lessons were part of his exchange for his new job, which surpassed the normal status of Haitians. He had offered the same skills to the *viejo* for self-protection from the people he now taught.

He wanted to go back home, but now his higher salary was holding him back. When he returned to Port-au-Prince, he wanted to bring enough with him so that he and Franchesca could unconditionally break the chains that held them in servitude. Franchesca would be free from the sweatshops once and for all. And so he kept working. He would make her happy. She would thank him.

Also, the thought of returning reminded him that he had no papers. Leaving the Dominican Republic posed more problems than entering. If they found him trying to leave the country without papers, the police and customs agents would rob him before kicking him out. Alternatively, he could take his chances with the bus drivers who specialized in smuggling people across the borders. Either method would be expensive.

chapter eighteen

AMONG DELAND'S NEW NEIGHBOURS in Simon back in the 1980s was a woman named Marie. She had worked in La Société Nationale des Parcs Industriels (SONAPI), the large consortium of factories in Port-au-Prince, since she was a young woman. She and her mother had come from Jeremie, the southwest tip of Haiti.

In the factory, she met another peasant named Pierre, a young man also from Jeremie. He courted her and they became a couple. Because of the very low salaries they received, they couldn't help each other. But they hoped that, together, they might be able to save enough money to start a family. The young man wanted to continue his academic studies. After a few months, instead of sharing his factory money with Marie, Pierre took courses to advance his academic career. This was fine by Marie. She encouraged him in everything that would lead to a better future for them both. The young man, however, never asked Marie's mother for her approval, as he should have. He appeared, rather, as a friend from work.

After a few years, Marie was pregnant with Pierre's child. That is how her mother discovered the nature of their relationship. As her pregnancy advanced, Marie continued to live with her mother. Pierre came by from time to time to offer some material help. Like Marie, he continued to work in the factories in Sonapi. However, the expense and care of Marie during this time fell upon her mother, a widow who took in laundry to make ends meet.

When Marie was reaching term, she left her job in the factory and stayed home at her mother's house. She gave birth to a girl. Pierre could not take care of Marie and the baby. He could barely take care of himself on his salary from the factory. He came by from time to time with a little money. He was ashamed of his impotence to help them. After a few months, he disappeared.

Marie's mother had a difficult time coping with the new situation. Her house of corrugated iron was tiny and insufficient. She could not make enough money taking in laundry to support Marie and her baby. She chastised Marie, telling her that girls in the countryside respected customs. They would not have found themselves in Marie's position.

Marie cried all the while that she took care of her baby. Having a baby without a father was her first shame. But she had also made things difficult for her mother, who was now forced to pay, literally, for her romantic mistake. Her only option was to return to the factories to take the pressure off her mother. However, she had to leave her baby in the care of her mother during the days. Her mother watched over the baby while doing laundry for the neighbours.

On her days off, Marie searched for Pierre who had left SONAPI and broken his old ties. Marie understood that she was looking for someone who did not want to be found. But she succeeded in finding him. He was living with his sister in Petionville. He was ashamed to see Marie and his daughter. While Marie wanted him to take responsibility for his daughter, her visits to Petionville showed her that it was a lost cause. He was living, like others, on the provisions sent from his peasant family in Jeremie. Marie saw that she was trying to get blood out of a rock. He could not care for the baby any more than she could. He was trying to set himself up in such a way that he could become a respectable head of a household. But he had very little to offer meanwhile.

After a couple of years, Pierre found an orphanage willing to take the baby girl from Marie. That was as close as he could get to taking responsibility. Marie agreed. Pierre advised Marie to leave the factories and to return to Jeremie to work as a merchant. The land in that department was fertile and she could build a better future. When she was established, Pierre would send for her and they could start over with a chance of living decently.

Marie rejected Pierre's suggestion. She asked him, "Are you crazy?! How could I return there when the other women know my history, how could I look them in the eyes? You think they'll just accept me?"

Pierre resumed, "Are you going to live for them or for yourself?"

Marie insisted, "How do you think that they would see us, when they all assume that things are going well for us in the capital? When they see us return to Jeremie — starving — to eat their harvest, can't you see what they'll say? We will be great failures.... If you were in my place, would you feel comfortable, returning with nothing? Especially when everyone is waiting with anticipation for me to return with lots of money to spread around."

"Marie, they have to know, we are just straw and life is the wind. It sends us where it chooses. We have little power when we are caught in that wind. We may as well accept it."

Marie conceded, "I know, I know. But tell me, what is this about really? What is going on? Sending our child to an orphanage ... advising me to go back to Jeremie ... Are you trying just to free yourself from your ties? Are you trying to get rid of me?"

"No, no, no. Marie. All I'm trying to do is to free you from that factory. It doesn't allow you to even live independently of your poor mother. It's a trap."

Marie replied, "You think so? Well, you have no plan. I do. After two years, I will have saved enough to begin my own commerce. You'll see."

"Okay. If that's your decision, you'll have to carry out that plan alone. I don't see it as a solution."

Pierre left disappointed that he and Marie could not agree on a plan together.

Marie continued to work at Sonapi. Pierre worked on his studies, paid for by his sister.

Marie worked hard, motivated to prove to Pierre that he was wrong and that her work in the factories would allow her to launch a business of her own. But no. Pierre had calculated correctly: when your salary cannot pay for your food and lodging, then you will never be free of it. She made sacrifices, secretly putting aside a few gourdes each week into a box that she kept hidden. Unfortunately, from time to time, she was forced to take out everything when her mother's health declined. She was always starting from zero. She went to Pierre to tell him how badly things were going.

For a second time, Marie and Pierre expected a child. Pierre was upset. He said that if Marie had just gone to Jeremie as he had suggested, then everything would have been different. Not only was Marie always starting over trying to save a few gourdes, but now they found themselves where they had been with the first pregnancy. There was no sign that this one would be different.

"I'm still at school. I have no money to help with a child. You're going to figure out how to get out of this," Pierre said. "Do what you can to take care of yourself during the pregnancy. When the child is born, I'll have to leave my studies to find a job."

Marie went home. It was hard to tell her mother this news for a second time. But a pregnancy can't be kept secret. In fact, it was her mother who told Marie that she was pregnant. She was angry to the point of throwing Marie's things into the street. But when she reflected on the help that Marie had offered her during her illnesses, she softened.

Marie continued in SONAPI. She was ashamed before of her co-workers, who already knew of her situation. Some were sympathetic, others gossiped. Under that added stress, Marie wanted to die. She couldn't see another way out.

Although Pierre had very little money, he would come to the Industrial Park from time to time to pass along a few gourdes. These little gestures helped Marie out of her depression. She made it through and delivered a healthy little boy. She left her job to take care of her baby for a few months.

Pierre was true to his word. When the baby was born, he left his studies and found a job in a store that sold soft drinks. He put aside a part of his paycheck for Marie. He didn't make enough money to support a family. Far from it.

The little shack that Marie and her baby shared with her mother had a roof of old sheet metal with many holes. When the rain came, she had a difficult time finding a dry place for her baby. The rainy season arrived two months after the birth. Marie spent most of her time squished into a corner with her baby on a drenched bed. Sometimes water would pour into the *tikounouk* by the front door. There was a gap between the bottom of the door and the ground. When the water flowed, Marie's home put up no resistance. Since Marie's mother slept on the ground, the rainy season meant that she hardly slept at all. Rather, she tried to keep as much water and mud as possible out of her little house.

Marie's mother tried to figure out how to escape from the worst of their troubles. *Bourik fè pitit pou do li pose* — a donkey has foals to lighten its load. In this case, there was no rest for either the *bourik* or the *pitit*. Marie, in her corner protecting her baby from the rain dripping through the roof, listened as her mother complained while sweeping water and mud back into the street. Marie wanted to leave, to be anywhere rather than listening to her mother's complaints.

When the baby was three months old, Marie returned to the factory. Pierre came by to offer just enough help to take care of the baby. Marie's salary continued to pay for herself and her mother.

Marie changed from factory to factory, looking for one that might pay a little better or help her somehow. But they were all the same. Only the personnel and the work varied. The conditions and the pay were the same.

When the baby was two years old, Pierre paid for daycare in Simon. When he lost his job, he decided to return to Jeremie. That meant that things were even more difficult for Marie. She worked all the time. Sometimes, she asked for help from the church or from friends to pay the school fees for her son. She applied for scholarships to help defray the expense of educating him.

Marie tried to get fired from SONAPI. She had worked there long enough that she might qualify for a small severance payment. So she tried to provoke the bosses to fire her. But nothing worked. They were used to that strategy and overlooked her provocations.

A few times, she organized her co-workers into unions. Although some of the workers that she organized were fired, the bosses left her alone. They fired those who would not cost any severance.

She never heard any more from Pierre. After a number of years, she learned that he had a child in Jeremie.

Each year, Marie promised her son that if he succeeded in his exams, they would celebrate. My brother James and I grew up with Marie's son, Lòlò. Since our parents had seven children, they couldn't reward our successes in the same way that Marie could honour her only son. But we conspired with Lòlò to get what would serve us all. For instance, we told Lòlò that he should ask for a television if he passed his year. James and I were genuinely happy for Lòlò. His success was, literally, our success.

In Simon, electricity flowed erratically, but still more than in most neighbourhoods. That was because Simon was next to the factories that the electricity had been installed to serve. Like all neighbourhoods in Port-au-Prince, you know when there is current by the spontaneous cheer of the children playing in the streets. "Yahoo!" Then they rush to the home of whoever has a television set. In our area, Lòlò was on the cutting edge of technology as a result of his good grades. Sometimes there were so many of us in the room where Lòlò lived that Marie and his grandmother could not enter. We watched each film carefully, especially the Chinese kung fu movies. When they were over, we all poured into the streets and practised the moves that we had watched, trying to take each other's heads off with karate chops. Once, James struck Lòlò in the mouth during their kung fu battle and knocked out his front tooth. When Lòlò appeared with a handful of blood and a missing tooth, our father beat both James and me without the benefit of any kung fu training.

 We grew up together. We watched Marie go to the factory before dawn and return at dusk. We watched her hair go from black to white. Marie put all her life into Lòlò. His education became Marie's reason for living. He grew tall and strong like his father. Lòlò finished his secondary education.

 The *tikounouk* and his grandmother aged together. The walls and roof were barely enough to protect the television and other testaments to Lòlò's academic success. When we entered our adolescent years, we used to sit together and talk about our plans and our hopes. Lòlò always had the same priority. When he was finally able to earn money, his first priority would be to liberate his mother from the factories at SONAPI. His grandmother would not die in the same squalor that they had known.

 When I had left Simon, after my mother's death, I returned every Sunday to visit my family and friends. Lòlò remained a wise young man. He kept himself apart. He was in the service of his grandmother who had become weak in her old age.

 MINUSTAH arrived in 2004 and intensified the violence in Simon. From time to time, they would mount their assaults against us. They would arrest gangsters and others who had nothing to do with the gangs. They were as erratic as the electricity. But they could never find any cause to harass Lòlò, much as they might have liked to. Lòlò was a tall, strong young man, the type they saw as a threat. But he was focused on caring for his grandmother and mother and succeeding in his studies to help them permanently.

It was a rare event for a boy from Simon to finish his secondary education. But Marie and Lòlò had succeeded.

However, Marie could not find the money to pay for university for Lòlò. The factories didn't pay nearly enough. Because she had worked there for so long, Marie asked the directors to help her find a scholarship for her son. Despite her decades of service, the director dismissed the idea out of hand.

In 2008, a friend of Marie offered to pay half of the fees for Lòlò to attend a vocational school called Saint Gerard, a building five stories tall. Marie continued in the factory to pay the other half. Lòlò chose a two-year course in automotive mechanics. Marie was happy to have found a vocation for her son. Her mother was now aged and she was ageing. Both put their hopes in Lòlò for a future better than their pasts.

Lòlò always reassured them. "The day that I get a job, we'll leave this place. We'll be comfortable." Each time that he picked up his backpack to go to Saint Gerard, his grandmother was proud and hopeful. The hope was not for her, it was for her grandson. For her, four years was no different than four weeks. Things were heading in the right direction for her grandson. They had suffered their entire lives to live decently. Lòlò was as solid and reliable as the ground under their feet.

Marie sacrificed her own comfort for Lòlò. She lived as minimally as possible. She spent her money so that Lòlò could wear the best *pèpè*. She neglected meals at the factory so that Lòlò could eat well at home. His grandmother bought bread for Lòlò. Lòlò was like a tree that was still not providing fruit. But the tree was being fertilized, and pruned, and watered. The harvest would justify the cultivation.

Lòlò finished his first year with great success. He was the top student in his class. Marie started to look for contacts so that he could find a good job immediately upon his graduation. A couple of contacts agreed to accept Lòlò when he arrived in the second year. He could work part-time in their businesses while he finished his program.

Marie bought Lòlò a toolbox and began to buy the tools to fill it.

On 6 January 2010, Lòlò returned to school after the holidays. His exams to complete his second year were scheduled for 10 February. The course at Saint Gerard took place on Tuesday, Thursday, and Saturday afternoons, from two o'clock to five o'clock.

Early on Tuesday morning, 12 January, Lòlò asked his mother for the money to take a *taptap* in the afternoon to Saint Gerard. Marie gave him the money. Lòlò was approaching his second-year exams. He would start working the following month.

"Ah Manman, you already know that I am going to be at the top of my class. I work as hard as I can. We will get out of this hole. I only have three people in my family: you, me, and grandma. Before grandma dies, I'll pay her back for her patience with us."

"Okay, I'm leaving it up to you." And she left for SONAPI, smiling about their good fortune after all these years. She walked into the factory on top of the world, realizing that her years there had not been for nothing.

Marie spent the entire day in the factory. She didn't go outside for lunch. She spoke to all her friends about her son's success. They were used to her story, but Marie was now telling it with more conviction than ever. And her co-workers believed that her days in the factory were coming to an end.

At four o'clock, Marie started to feel unwell. Others replied that they too felt ill at ease, that there was something strange about the day. People guessed about what might be coming. Was it here in the factory? Would it be at home?

At a quarter to five, they heard a sound, like a breeze, outside. They sensed the earth begin to tremble. They weren't too worried. SONAPI is next to the road. Everyone thought that bulldozers were passing. Moments later, the real shocks arrived. People working on the industrial sewing machines were jostled; some got their hands caught. Those who were working upright fell to the ground. Boxes full of fabric fell upon them. Things fell off the walls.

"Jezi! Jezi!" people yelled.

Marie called, "Jezi! Lòlò is dead!"

Despite the shocks that rocked her from side to side, she tried to keep her balance so she could get out of the building.

She ran down the street. She saw nothing around her. All she could see was in her mind's eye: the vocational school, Saint Gerard, collapsing to the ground. Lòlò was on the second floor.

She panicked. She ran like a crazy woman. There were no *taptaps* running. There was no way to get to the school.

She went to Simon to check on her mother. Since their shack was made of sheet metal, she was not too worried. Her mother was lying on the ground, crying. She was crying for Marie whom she assumed was dead.

"Manman, I'm here. Lòlò! What about Lòlò? Have you heard from Lòlò?"

They each took a shirt belonging to Lòlò and tied it around their waists. They left the house and wandered the neighbourhood, mourning his death. But their neighbours encouraged them. "No, no. Don't say that. He'll be okay."

While they were crying, a friend of Lòlò came up to them. He and Lòlò often took the *taptap* together, since their schools were close by. He was white, painted by the dust from the rubble of a collapsed building.

When she saw him, Marie ran to him. She grabbed him by his shirt, "Where is Lòlò?! Give me Lòlò!?"

The young man was crying, "My school is destroyed. In my class, there were fifty students. Only ten of us lived and most of them have broken arms and legs. We were buried. We managed to dig our way out. We called out. Some people from the outside came to help dig a passage from the other side to get us out. In the other stories, no one escaped alive."

"Tell me! Lòlò!?"

"I passed by Saint Gerard," he acknowledged. "It was reduced to rubble. We tried to dig, but there was no sound from inside. We found only dead bodies. For someone to be saved, he had to be outside of Saint Gerard."

Marie fainted and fell to the ground. She lay there as though dead. Her mother couldn't speak. She was dumb with shock.

Some of the neighbours found alcohol to place under the nose of Marie to revive her. They used a spoon to try to unlock her jaw that was locked shut.

Finally Marie awoke. She arose and started running... nowhere. People thought she was crazy. Some people ran after her and brought her back, making a clearing in the crowd to create a little calm for her.

•●•

Two weeks later, all of the factories were up and running. Marie returned to work. She told the director that her only son was dead. He advised her to take some time off. She kept coming anyway.

Even the workers whose homes were still standing were afraid to sleep in them. A large number of tents were delivered to the Industrial Park after the earthquake. The tents didn't go to people like Marie. Instead, the workers saw them piled into big trucks inside the Park and taken away.

Marie continues to get up at dawn to work until dusk. Her mother no longer takes in laundry. On her eighteenth birthday, Marie's first daughter returned to live with Marie and her mother. After her years in the orphanage, she helped her mother and grandmother heal from the loss of their son with the return of their daughter.

chapter nineteen

TUESDAY, 12 JANUARY 2010, I passed half the day in Delmas 19 in the courtyard where I lived with Jelo. I was thinking about my future and it had drained all the energy out of me. The future was nothing but a word with nothing inside of it.

My church had a Bible study group that met at five o'clock each Tuesday evening. As I had nothing to do at home but mope, I left to arrive an hour ahead of schedule at the house where my girlfriend Annie lived with her elder sister, Mme Bolivar. Together, we would walk to the church that was just a few minutes from her place.

I was playing with the kids of the house. That always lifted my spirits. Then, since there was power that afternoon, I went to watch television until it was time to walk over to the church. Annie was taking care of Lucy, her three-year-old niece. I was lost in a war movie. During a gunfight on the television, I heard a little noise outside like a bulldozer passing. The house was far from the road; it was built into the hill with only little alleyways running through the neighbourhood. I didn't think further about it because my concentration was taken up by the film. The gunfight on the television intensified at the same time that the house began to shake. I was so into the film that the shaking seemed normal — but in the context of the film, not in real life in Delmas 33. My chair started to shake. Finally, I separated the film from my life. The entire house was rocking from side to side. Even the characters in the film finally joined real life, when the television fell to the ground.

I heard Annie cry outside. "Oh Jezi! My head, my head!" As the ceiling came down, a piece of concrete had struck her on the head.

Lucy heard her aunt scream and she imitated her, yelling, "Jezi, Jezi," and swayed her arms in the air.

Outside, everyone was yelling the same thing, "Jezi! Oh Jezi!" It was as if all the voices in the neighbourhood came together in one thought, one sound.

I did everything I could to get out of the room where the television was now crashed on the floor. I was trying to get to where Annie and Lucy were calling. But I was in the back of the house and the only way out was the hall. I called to them to stay calm. I tried to negotiate the hallway as the house swayed, balancing myself with outstretched arms on the walls on each side.

For a second, the earthquake calmed and I was able to get to Annie and Lucy in the hallway. Annie was crying. Lucy too was crying tears, in every way imitating her aunt Annie.

I told them, "Listen, it's not over yet. We have to find the other kids and leave the house."

When we got to the gallery, Annie's three nephews appeared on the stairway from the roof and joined us to leave the house. We didn't have time to listen to their stories. The important thing was that everyone in the household was accounted for. We all left together.

Standing on the pathway that led to the road, we were not yet safe. The houses rose on each side. We were still perilously close to them. So we descended the pathway to reach the road. There, we saw all the neighbours who had escaped assembled together. Everyone had come instinctively to this open place. Everyone was white with powder. All that was visible was the black of their eyes. Those who were weak were lost in their tears. Others thought of how they might help those who were trapped.

After a few seconds, the earthquake struck again. We saw houses around us collapse.

Annie, the kids, and I grouped together in the middle of the road, watching the walls sway back and forth with the shakes of the earth. We saw big fissures split the walls. Sometimes they collapsed and sometimes they didn't. In this neighbourhood, there were relatively few victims.

Once it was clear that we were out of danger in the middle of the road, my thoughts transported me to Simon. How might the earthquake have left my family? Other people seemed to be taken by similar thoughts about their loved ones. First, we tried to phone, but the connections were dead. I started to descend to Simon to find what I would find.

It was weird to see how it took just a few seconds to return to a world without technologies that we had come to depend upon. We adapted quickly. In the countryside, they would not have lost their means of transportation. Moreover, the peasants put less importance on telephones and similar technologies. They had less to lose compared to us in the city. In many ways, they were more resilient than us, because they were more self-reliant.

On my way down to Simon, I passed neighbourhood after neighbourhood. It was tough to pass some of the areas. More and more, it was clear that Annie's neighbourhood was almost untouched compared to others. Especially where my aunt lived in Delmas 31, there were so many dead that I needed to be careful to not step on the bodies that were spread across the streets. The people had never considered the effects that such an event would have on their poorly built homes.

The people laid out around me had had less luck than me. There was a young woman who, I could see, had tried to run out of her house. She had almost made it. Half of her body had been out of the house when the roof collapsed on her legs and hips. I could see that she had lunged to escape through the door just as the concrete was falling. That desperate action was now frozen in time as she lay dead, half in and half out of her home. The neighbours assembled around the poor young woman's body.

In another neighbourhood, I passed a hospital. I went into the courtyard to see how the patients were coping. For once, the sick were better off than the healthy. Their hospital was fissured, but it remained standing. They were okay. In the courtyard, so many injured had assembled that there was not enough space for a needle. Most of them were more dead than alive. It was clear that they would not survive to see the next day.

Some had simple broken arms and legs. Many had fractured skulls from falling concrete blocks. But the seriously injured were a different story. Some nurses from the hospital walked among the injured to see who was already dead so they could cover the body. Among the injured, I had the privilege of speaking with a young woman before she died. Her pelvic bones had been crushed. Her head was swollen grotesquely. She told me that she had escaped the earthquake and the aftershocks. She saw, in the house of a neighbour, a toddler all alone. Its mother and father were already outside. Maybe the stress made them forget the child, maybe fear. This young woman heard the child screaming inside. She managed to get to the child but, as she was leaving, a hydro pole fell over during an aftershock. It fell on her hips and crushed her. She protected the child in front of her so that it would not be struck. But she was trapped under the pole. Other people came and took the child from her. They freed her and brought her to the courtyard in the hospital. The medical staff said she had lost too much blood. She could not survive. Now, her only compensation was that the child had survived. She had succeeded.

I continued. I headed toward Delmas 19. I stopped at the home of my friend Jameson from my choir. I didn't see him. His house was reduced to rubble. No one could have survived. I tried to find his neighbours. They told me that he was alive. During the first shock, he had been inside the house. The moment he felt it, he ran as fast as possible for the exit. As he was running, the ceiling came down upon him and crushed his arm. He struggled with his good arm to try to free the other that was pinned under concrete. Finally, he yanked his arm from its trap and fled the house as it collapsed. Better to lose his arm to save his life, he calculated.

His arm dangled by his side, clearly beyond repair. Some other members of the choir that lived in the area would take him to a hospital. They went to Saint Marc, north of the capital, where a medical team was amputating the arms and legs of the victims. Waiting for his operation, Jameson sat with a woman whose head was swollen to the point of exploding, so much blood had collected. Jameson judged himself lucky at that point and raised what remained of his arm to thank God. His friends could not understand what he was thankful for. When the doctors took him into the operating room and told him he would lose his arm, he said that he already knew that, it was okay. He would return to the capital to continue life with one arm instead of two. Jameson never complained.

I had to pass by Delmas 19, where I lived, on my way to my family in Simon. But to get to Delmas 19, I had to close my eyes to everything around me. Finally, I arrived. It was surreal. In Delmas 19, there had been apartment buildings three stories high. They were rented out to a number of families. Now, in the place of the apartment buildings were piles of concrete behind clouds of dust. People were just returning home to their families from work. As they approached, everyone's eyes were full of dread, not knowing if they had lives to return to.

The tragedies of those who discovered the worst mixed together to make a nightmare. I continued on to see if my own friends were alive or dead. If Jelo had been in the main house, then he would not have been spared. It was a large, old structure. I had little confidence that it could have resisted the shocks.

When I arrived, I saw Jelo standing in the courtyard. The main house behind him was mostly destroyed, the second floor having fallen over to touch the ground. But parts of the house remained precariously intact. I could almost hear Jelo's heart beating. He had assumed that, if Delmas 33 was in the same state as Delmas 19, I would not have survived.

When he recovered his calm upon seeing me alive, he told me that he had been on the roof of the house when the earthquake struck. A young man from Tigwav was staying with him. The young man had been standing in the courtyard. From his place on the rooftop, Jelo could see a whirlwind develop in the courtyard below. It spiralled up to the sky taking dust and dry leaves. Then, he said, there was an eerie, deadly silence. He didn't know what was happening. Suddenly he felt the house move below him. It was as though it was trying to pull itself from its foundations and fly away.

Behind the main house, there was a one-story building that had been built for servants. It was in those little rooms that Jelo and I lived. Next to those rooms, there was a big orange tree. Jelo launched himself from the roof of the main house to land on the roof of the secondary structure. From there, he jumped onto the orange tree that led him to the ground, safe and sound.

Once on the ground, he looked for the young man from Tigwav whom he had last seen in the courtyard. He was okay. Jelo called to him brusquely, "Hurry up, let's get out of the courtyard!"

He left with Jelo to wait in the street, as far as possible from the falling walls and buildings. When the young man from Tigwav had sensed the land begin to tremble, he had grabbed onto a cherry tree and held on while the walls of the large building before him turned into concrete blocks and then rubble. He told us that he had taken comfort only in nature. He said that as he watched everything that was man-made crumble all around him, he believed reflexively that nature would prove resilient. And so he hugged the cherry tree for comfort and security.

He asked us to look around. He said, "Look, everything is destroyed all around us. But not a leaf has fallen from the trees. The mangoes are still waiting to be harvested tomorrow. We, human beings, we deserve what we are getting tonight. These big buildings were built badly with money that was taken from the work of the poor. This is the harvest. If we don't change, we are heading towards an even greater disaster. This is a warning."

After listening to this young man, I went into the courtyard cautiously, keeping a prudent distance from the main house, half standing and half collapsed. That day, water was rare. I was parched with thirst. Everyone must have been in the same state. In the courtyard, there was a reservoir that we could exploit. I thought I could offer a small gesture for the victims I had passed by bringing them water.

First, I entered one of the rooms in the service quarters behind the main house. It showed no fissures. It seemed stable. Five plates of rice and *sos pwa kongo* were lined up on a big metal box. Jelo had been preparing dinner for everyone. Not only had everyone's appetite disappeared with the catastrophe, but no one dared enter the courtyard now. I took two or three spoonfuls of *sos pwa kongo*. Then I saw that the flies and ants were going to devour the rest. For them, this was a great day. A feast! *Tout sa'k pa bon pou youn, li bon pou yon lòt* — things that are not good for one person are good for another.

I left with two gallons of water. I started to retrace my steps to visit the people who had been in the worst state. Thinking of those who had given so much, like the young woman who would die that night after saving a child, I could at least relieve some discomfort.

As I carried the water along, I found myself preaching to everyone. The earthquake had broken all that was material. It was time for us too to break with our egoism and greed. It was time to share. Time for compassion. I spoke loudly. People thought I had lost my mind. Looking back, I see that I had indeed gone crazy to think that a catastrophe would make people change.

I heard people muttering that I had gone nuts. But I wasn't sure what sanity would look like in this nightmare. Anyway, I knew that I was sane enough to see how to help people in distress. I went to ask them if they needed water, just to make clear what was important this evening. Some were grateful.

I carried on. People called to me for help. Parents who had saved the lives of their children and were lying in the middle of the street implored me to give them a drink. I explained that it was reservoir water and untreated. No one made the slightest distinction that night. Everyone was parched. The excitement, the efforts to save oneself and others, the dust, the heat — all of that descended on Port-au-Prince in the form of a great thirst.

I was only halfway back to Delmas 33 where I had started the evening when my reserves of water were empty. I carried on to Annie's. I went into the house. It was empty. Everyone was in the street, still keeping a good distance from buildings. They had taken only what was necessary from their homes: sheets and pillows. No one wanted to enter any building. But they weren't sure yet where they would spend the night.

Mme Bolivar and her family were there. A sister and her family had come from Bon Repos, a part of the capital where the water flowed just below the surface. In the time of the French colony, some of the richest sugar plantations had been located in Bon Repos. When the earthquake struck, the land literally opened up and the groundwater flooded the area. Immediately, the local people took refuge with their relatives outside of the zone.

Night was falling. Everywhere, people were gathering in the streets, frightened of every noise. Reflexively, they yelled "Jezi! Jezi!" But the noises were not the earthquakes that they feared and expected. The local people, traumatized by the earthquake, began to interpret every sound and every movement as an aftershock. Everyone was hypersensitive to anything that reminded them of the quake. People jumped out of their skin when a door slammed behind them. They lunged for cover when a helicopter passed — helicopters are notoriously insensitive to traumatized people.

The people started to claim the places in the street where they would sleep. The choices were limited. The roads in Haiti are all rocks and bumps and holes and, in the dry season, dust. Even cars find them barely negotiable. The life of a shock absorber in Port-au-Prince is nasty, brutish, and short. This night, not one person found a flat place to rest. But few slept indoors.

You could distinguish the different classes of Haitians in the streets according to the quality of sheets they brought from their homes.

Professionals and unemployed, police and thieves, nurses and patients, young and old, handicapped and athletes, religious and atheists: everyone was in the same boat. No one could sleep well because every thirty minutes a new aftershock woke us all. Each time, people would begin to pray. The aftershocks were like a button that turned on the prayers. They prayed so much that some continued to mumble to God even after they had fallen asleep. Everyone wanted to sleep, but the first order of business was survival.

The aftershocks also assured that no one overslept in the morning. Once we were all awake, no one in our group that had passed the night together left until we had prayed together. Nurses and police went to take up their jobs. Those without paid work had lots to do in helping the trapped out of the rubble and offering help to all the victims.

I started on my way to Simon to find what had become of my family. When I arrived at Delmas 19 again, Jelo told me that my father Deland had already been by to see if I had survived. I was so happy to hear that someone whom I was looking for was also looking for me. And I was relieved to find that my worst fears would not be realized when I arrived in Simon. My father had told Jelo that all of my family survived, even Gloria, my handicapped little sister.

chapter twenty

SIMON HAD NOT BEEN HIT BADLY. Most of the houses had roofs of corrugated iron. Even when the houses collapsed, there were fewer concrete blocks to crush the people below. The cinder blocks of the falling walls, however, took a major toll.

Deland had been at church when the earthquake struck. Two days earlier, his pastor had announced that on 12 January, everyone should arrive at four-thirty instead of five o'clock, as usual. Even among those who could not easily leave their jobs, like the workers at SONAPI, *taptap* drivers, and street merchants, he insisted that they arrive at four-thirty. He asked that everyone bring their friends and colleagues with them.

Deland, who was always punctual, took his pastor's request to heart. He was at the church even before four-thirty. Others arrived on time. Some members had given extra money to the pastor to pass along to those who said that they would not have the money for a *taptap*. At four-thirty, the pastor began a service.

They were deep in prayer when the church building began to rock. Because of the prior insistence of the pastor that everyone, without exception, attend the service and that they should even make sacrifices to be there, the church members immediately assumed that the pastor had been aware that something transcendentally important would happen before five o'clock. People believed that they were witnessing the Second Coming.

During all the powerful shocks, the worshippers kept their eyes firmly closed, afraid to look their Lord directly in the eyes. Some people started to fall to the ground, the pillars toppled over, and the walls began to fissure. Some members could not resist opening their eyes a little to sneak a peek at the end of the world.

The pastor fell to the ground. He opened both his eyes. He told everyone to lie on the ground in the centre aisle of the church. The perimeter of the church collapsed. However, those who had taken refuge in the middle, according to the pastor's advice, were saved. The collapse buried them in dust. They started to arise from the rubble, white and dumbfounded. The pastor asked everyone to thank God that He had saved them. Then everyone went home to see if He had saved their loved ones as well.

Deland hurried home with his head full of horrors. He did not have the heart to look at the people he passed carrying victims with broken arms and legs, crushed skulls, and those who had expired. Each terrifying scene filled him with dread for what he would find when he returned home.

As he approached, he saw that the front of his home had fallen to rubble. He had passed more expensive houses reduced to dust, but much of his was still upright. He entered and saw his family crying for him, having already given him up for dead. As soon as they saw him alive, the tears stopped.

Since the front of his house had collapsed and he had no money to rebuild it, he hung some drapes to serve as a wall. They continued to sleep inside as they had before the quake.

The house also served as his business. Since the space was small, he used to transform the table that held his sewing machine and material into his bed at the end of his workday. Next to his sewing table was a buffet that had a large surface where Deland would lay the fabric out in order to mark and cut it. Each evening, Deland cleared his work from the buffet so that his children could use it as their bed. The smallest kids crawled into the large drawers and snuggled themselves into their dad's fabric.

Deland never had a fixed schedule. He would work each day until he was overtaken by exhaustion. In the evening, he would often fall asleep over his sewing machine. Mosquitoes would bite his arms after he had fallen asleep. He could tell by the number of bites how long he had dozed off.

The mosquitoes also provoked the very exhaustion from which they profited. Deland suffered chronically from malaria carried by mosquitoes. He struggled against the fever in his blood and tried not to let it show in public, but he was always tired. After the earthquake, it got worse. The malaria had never been able to defeat Deland alone, but the earthquake created an environment favourable to diseases.

Deland could no longer cope. He needed medical care. The only option was state hospitals and clinics that offered free treatment. There, the consultation consisted of a brief "How do you feel?" Based on his response, someone would prescribe him some drugs. He tried to buy the prescribed drugs from the street merchants. If he couldn't find what the clinics had prescribed among the street merchants, he would have to buy them from a real pharmacy.

The drugs were useless. Increasingly, Deland was too weak to even begin his day.

The fever intensified and sapped the strength from his arms and legs. He did not want to give in. Rather than sleep on the sewing table where he wanted to be working, he tried to sit in a chair. He would try to stand up, holding onto the walls for support. The effort to show how well he was, however, had the opposite effect. It only highlighted to everyone that Deland was a very sick man.

Deland had always been strict with us children. He insisted that, regardless of how desperate the situation in the country had become, his children do their best to find honest work. In Simon, he watched others choose to follow dangerous and criminal paths, since the respectable path led surely to misery. He insisted that we work honestly no matter how discouraged and how frustrated we became. Now, however, he could not be a model for his own advice. He was unable to work. For Deland, the inability to work as a tailor to keep his family alive was the most degrading blow of all. Deland believed that working hard toward a better future would bring it into being. His lack of health and inability to get treatment undermined his own beliefs. What happens when you can't work?

Deland lived flush up against the road — rather, the alley — that led through Simon. Before the earthquake, there was a wall that assured his family some privacy. Now, only a sheet separated him from the neighbours passing by. When the sheet came down, Deland watched all that was taking place. Unable to work, he sat and watched the people pass. He listened as they explained to him what was happening in Simon. He despaired. What would become of Simon? What would become of Haiti? What would become of his children?

It hurt to see him fall into despair. If Haiti had no future, then Deland had no meaningful past.

chapter twenty-one

THE EARTHQUAKE CHANGED all of Fédrik's calculations in the Dominican Republic. Suddenly, saving money was of secondary importance. He thought of his mother and brother and of Franchesca in the factory. He knew little about what was happening in Port-au-Prince. He decided to take what he had made and return home. He and Franchesca, in any case, would have to discuss how to respond to the new crisis together. The earth had shaken up everyone's plans.

First, he bought some things to surprise Franchesca and his mother and some mechanic's tools for his brother. He found a bus driver whom he paid to smuggle him into Haiti. The bus driver had agreements with the border agents. He paid them to overlook passengers like Fédrik.

Still in the Dominican Republic, the bus driver stopped to pick up another passenger. When he did, a group of Dominicans ran out of the forest with machetes and guns and boarded the bus. Three of them trained their guns on the passengers while two others started to shake everyone down. They took everything that the passengers had. They even took the new pair of boots that Fédrik was wearing, leaving him barefoot. The driver then crossed the border and drove the passengers to Port-au-Prince. Fédrik had not been surprised to be robbed. He had always heard that the Dominicans were crafty thieves. But he was shocked to see the state of Port-au-Prince, reduced to dust and rubble. It was now two weeks after the earthquake.

Fédrik walked barefoot to Delmas 33, the home of his cousin Mme Bolivar. In the circumstances, there was nothing unusual about a young man walking kilometres barefoot. Once in Delmas 33, he tried to find a pair of shoes. Then, he went in search of Franchesca. It was difficult to distinguish one pile of rubble from another in the neighbourhood of her aunt's home. His heart beat faster as he approached her place, fearing that he would discover the worst.

Finally, he arrived at her aunt's home. All around, the little houses of cinder blocks had collapsed. Most of the walls and ceilings had tumbled, but the outline of Franchesca's was still evident. What was left was not secure, but they continued to live there for lack of an alternative. Her cousins told him that Franchesca was back at work in SONAPI.

He was relieved to find her alive, but disappointed to hear that she was working as usual in a city destroyed. How could business go on as before in this state of disaster?

He waited all evening to see Franchesca. When she arrived, they were ecstatic to see each other alive and well. Seeing Fédrik allowed Franchesca to forget about the earthquake for a minute. The sight of his face filled her with hope.

They could not tell each other all the news at once. Franchesca related how, when the earthquake struck, she had been finishing work in the factory. Everyone took the first rumblings to be the result of the big trucks that used to lumber into the Industrial Park. But when the earth shook, the tables overturned, the walls fissured, and things started to fall. Everyone ran for the doors. Ran for their lives. Some injuries occurred when people stumbled under the stampede of everyone racing away from the high walls. In relating her experience to Fédrik, Franchesca appeared to be reliving it, so excited was she to see him. There was so much to share about so many things. Each story was fuelled by curiosity about questions not yet asked and answered.

Fédrik listened to Franchesca. Each of her words was filled with hope. He thought she would explode with excitement. But he knew that underneath her happiness was the presumption that he had returned with a fortune. When she spoke of SONAPI, he knew that she was imagining that she would never see it again. His news felt like a hammer that would smash a joyous moment.

Fédrik feverishly searched through all his experiences for something that would make Franchesca happy. But every path led to the robbery. He was about to dishearten Franchesca who was so in need of hope.

"Oh Fran, we have gone through so many hard times together. We have crossed rivers and borders, and escaped the wrath of God.

When I arrived in the Dominican Republic, I found Haitians who have lived in hiding for generations. They were like another species. Their skin was blacker than black. They had no razors and so their beards grow naturally. They play hide-and-seek with the Dominican authorities."

Fédrik prepared Franchesca for the bad news while Franchesca waited for Fédrik's good news. He continued, "When I was in Haiti, I never liked cooking. But there, I had to spend a week cooking for those Haitians. Sometimes we were forced to pick up everything, including the hot pot, and run from the soldiers." Franchesca did not yet register enough pity. He continued, "It was amazing, Fran — after a few weeks, I started teaching them karate so that they could protect themselves from the Dominican thugs. Our Haitian brothers were really proud of me. For once in my life, I felt really important. . . . I had to put one of the bullies in his place. But he reacted by offering me a real job driving a kind of tractor."

Franchesca beamed. But Fédrik started to see that he was digging his own grave deeper with each new adventure. "So, you see why I had to spend so long there. I went through all of this because I only wanted to free you from that job. Unfortunately, because of the earthquake, I had to take what I had earned and buy some things and hurry back to you. . . . I bought you a beautiful bracelet, an expensive necklace, and a watch. I bought tools for my brother and a beautiful dress for my mother. Just the kind that she always wanted. And I treated myself to a sturdy pair of boots. After all of that, I managed to leave the Dominican Republic with enough money for you and I to get passports and visas to return legally. I made friends there so we could be legitimate temporary workers. Then, I was able to buy a ticket on the best bus that comes to Port-au-Prince. In the bus, even though all the Haitians were sad about the earthquake, they were all happy to be alive and able to bring things home to help. We had almost arrived at the border, when the bus driver stopped to take on a passenger. Behind him, four others charged into the bus with rifles. No one had a chance. They threatened to kill us all. The first one to resist would be killed . . . I thought of you and how hurt you would be if you had to receive the news that I had been killed by thieves. I thought to myself, 'Be careful Féd, because you know that Franchesca would far rather have you back safe and sound than have a bunch of material things and a pile of money. Better to let them take everything — even the boots that I liked so much — just to get back alive.'"

Franchesca stared with wide-opened eyes. Her mouth too was open but no words came out. After she had digested the story and its meaning, she dropped her head in her hands.

Fédrik understood that the hope that had rested upon Santo Domingo was lost. He had known for some time, but Franchesca had to catch up with him all at once.

After a long silent moment, Franchesca said, "I would rather have died than have to continue in this country. Things were already intolerable. Now, they're worse. And now I have no hope for anything to change... except for the worse.... Why did you bother coming back? You just bring more misery with you."

Fédrik said, "No, Fran! Don't say that! Try to remember why I went to the Dominican Republic in the first place. That hasn't changed. The Dominican thieves are just obstacles in the way. They haven't changed my heart. I will still work to make us a better future. Please don't give up."

"You speak of hope, Féd, but I don't see it. Our only hope is death — to escape from all of this."

"Is this what you call courage? We need courage to face these problems. What kind of hope hopes for death? Maybe it's not our fate to go to the Dominican Republic. Maybe it's somewhere else. Maybe it's right here in Port-au-Prince," he said. "Maybe, we'll find some magical spring that allows us to forget this past."

Franchesca replied, "What are you talking about? A magic spring?! If there is anything magical in Haiti, it's going to destroy us. Each day for me is like the one before. And they all stink. How can I forget the past? It's just like the present!"

"Are you telling me that there are no happy moments in your life? Nothing but misery?"

Franchesca protested, "Nothing but! Think about you. I was proud to have a fiancé abroad. I thought that you were going to change things. But here you are — even worse off than when you left. Is this a happy moment? My happy moments were the ones when I hoped for something better. You have brought a magic spring all right. Your news makes me forget about that hope. Stop this talk about magic springs. Let's get real."

Fédrik arose, disappointed. He was deflated to hear that Franchesca was discounting all that he had done, as if he were a ne'er-do-well. He had been proud of his achievements in the Dominican Republic, however modest they may appear to some people. But to have Franchesca call him a romantic and unreal was a harsh blow.

Fédrik left, dejected. How could he help Franchesca out of her funk? How could he avoid falling in himself?

chapter twenty-two

MME BOLIVAR WAS WORKING in the Ministry of Culture when the earthquake struck. She heard a loud noise. The ministry is in the city centre. The area can be violent sometimes, with gangs and police exchanging fire. But she heard something that she couldn't identify. She heard something big fall. When she left to see what was happening outside, the ministry started to collapse. She was barely out of the doorway when the room behind her caved in. It was then that she understood what was happening. She was still on the second floor. Below her, on the ground floor, she heard people screaming. Blocks of concrete were falling all around her. Somehow, she tumbled onto the courtyard without being injured. Others were around her, trembling.

In front of them, the office of the minister had not yet fallen in completely. The ceiling had collapsed in part, but was still standing. The minister called to a young employee. She said to him, "I forgot my briefcase on my desk. Could you go in and get it for me?" He obliged the minister and entered the building that others had just escaped with their lives. The ceiling that hadn't yet fallen had been waiting for the aftershock that came at that very moment. It fell upon the obedient employee. He didn't know that his wife was dying at that moment in another part of the city. Their four children lived, orphaned that night.

The other employers in the courtyard looked at the minister when the tons of concrete collapsed upon the young man. She said, "Oh my God, he's dead!"

Unable to bear the contemptuous gazes of the people around her, the minister instead removed herself from their company. The other employees spoke among themselves. "If that was my family, I would look for justice in the courts. She has destroyed his life for a sack of garbage."

chapter twenty-three

AFTER THE EARTHQUAKE, there were thousands of individual crises of the dead and wounded. But for a moment, a window opened for me to see a different world. It was a world of humility and of sharing. People were sleeping under the same stars together. They were sharing what they had. It seemed that everyone had seen how vulnerable they were and they knew that they needed others to survive.

Rich and poor took up the same amount of space under the stars. For that moment, they didn't need acres of land and, most important and atypical, they didn't need a big home to show off. All homes were equally dangerous. Only crazy people entered houses.

We all heard the story of a rich man who was the proprietor of a big store. He was inside when the earthquake struck. He survived the shocks and the collapse of his store all around him, but was pinned under concrete. A part of the floor above him was held tenuously in place by a column that had not yet fallen, but that resembled the Leaning Tower of Pisa. He watched people pass, people who were voluntarily rescuing those trapped in the rubble. He called out, "I'm here! Help!"

People stopped to survey the situation. They all came to the same conclusion: "We can't come any closer."

The man thought that money could solve his predicament, as it always had. "Just come to help. I'll pay any price to whoever frees me."

People looked and considered their options. Some realized that this could be an opportunity. Not one among the rescuers didn't have dreams of improving their impoverished lives. This could be their great chance. But they were stopped, literally in their tracks, by the danger. They were all making the same calculation as the wealthy store owner: what is my life worth next to riches?

One common answer came from all the rescuers, "We're sorry, sir. We're going to look for a tractor. Only that could be of help."

The man pinned under the concrete with all his stock around him saw that his wealth could not help him and could not buy others. The inevitable came to pass. A little tremor brought the remaining structure down upon him, putting an abrupt end to the rescue effort.

But there were other signs that it would take more than an earthquake to alter the social landscape of Haiti. For the *kokorats*, it was great fun to hear bourgeois families try to find a comfortable spot on top of rocks and potholes and dust. The earthquake had turned the social ladder upside down. The *kokorats* were on top. Why? Because what was unusual and difficult for everyone else — sleeping in the streets and living by one's wits — was their normal life. They were already schooled in the life that was strange to everybody else. While the bourgeois families were sleeping in the open, the *kokorats* would collect the plastic juice containers that litter the streets of Port-au-Prince and pee-pee into them. They would put the lid back on and puncture it with holes. Then, they would squirt it all over the bourgeois families, "watering" their campsites.

The wealthy families would complain, but there was no one to listen. The *kokorats* were applying the same justice that had always been used against them: they had been there first, no? If the homes belong to the wealthy, the streets belong to the *kokorats*.

After a few weeks had passed, the spell was already broken. The window on a world of sharing and equality slammed shut. NGOs arrived with ration cards. Each neighbourhood organized a committee to deal with the crisis. The committees prepared lists of the people living in their neighbourhood. These lists could include the dead as well as the living, because each name represented the right to aid. The NGOs would give to the committees ration cards equal to the number of names on the list. Then the committees would distribute the cards to the people in their neighbourhood. The surplus cards could be sold or distributed under conditions agreed upon in advance. For instance, someone could get a card upon the condition that he or she share with the committee member whatever benefits it brought.

At first, the cards were given to everybody. One card for each person, male or female. But the NGOs saw the disorder in the distribution of relief. The stronger young men were always at the front of the line. The NGOs decided to give cards only to women. The moment the new system was announced, poor families all over Port-au-Prince conspired how best to exploit it. If the NGOs believed that men were brutes and women were angels, then they would play the part.

I knew a pregnant woman who had a family member on a committee who passed her a number of ration cards. Since she was very obviously pregnant, they gave her priority in the lineup. The MINUSTAH soldiers who guarded the distribution had no idea that this same woman appeared a number of times in the same line. Each time she received her ration of a twenty-five kilogram sack of rice, she passed it to a male relative to take to their shelter made of sheet metal in one of the camps that had sprung up after the earthquake. Then, she joined the end of the line to begin the process again, spending the day lined up while her relatives stocked their *tikounouk*. She spent all day long in line under a hot sun, without having eaten in the morning. Eventually, she fainted.

The MINUSTAH soldiers went to the fallen, unconscious woman and addressed the crowd, "Does anyone know this woman?"

Someone in line knew her. The MINUSTAH soldiers put the unconscious woman in their jeep along with the sack of rice that she had been waiting for. They asked her neighbour to join them to show them to her home. They followed her instructions to the *tikounouk* of the unconscious pregnant woman. The MINUSTAH soldiers entered the shelter with the woman, who was still disoriented. When they entered, they saw that the woman had arranged her big sacks of rice to make a mattress. The soldiers returned to their post with all of the sacks, except one. For all of the cases where such schemes worked more smoothly, the rice wound up on the black market, purchased by the poor and those who did not want to take advantage of the suffering of others. The system of aid continued to divide the population into poor and less poor.

◆◆◆

The authorities decided to change the system again. They decided to go directly into the camps, to each person who had a tent. They kept to the idea to deal only with women. In the camp at Saint Louis de Gonzague in Delmas 31, two NGO authorities came to distribute ration cards. When they asked where the family was who lived in a vacant tent, a neighbour said that they were absent and that she would pass the card along. They gave her the ration card for the absent woman. She now had two cards and no intention of giving one up.

She went to get her own sack of rice that she brought back to her tent. Then she returned with the second ration card that should have belonged to her neighbour. While she was waiting in line for the second sack of rice, her neighbour happened to appear and discovered the distribution of rice. She was told by others in the line that her neighbour had her ration card. So she asked her for her card.

"No, no," said her neighbour, "they are mistaken. I didn't take a card for you. This is my own card."

The MINUSTAH soldiers could not understand what was happening. They wrongly assumed that the woman who had the ration card in her hand was its rightful owner and that the other was trying to steal it from her. They literally pushed away the woman who had no rice and no ration card. That woman said threateningly that she would wait for her neighbour in the camp. All of that was lost on the MINUSTAH troops.

When she got her second sack, the woman returned to the camp. Her neighbour attacked her to get the rice. The first tried to balance her big sack of rice on her head while fighting off her neighbour whom she had cheated to get it. The cheated neighbour was seriously scratching the face of the woman with the rice when I happened to be passing by.

I approached. Others in the camp were surrounding them and encouraging them to fight. I saw one woman balancing a twenty-five kilogram sack of rice on her head with one arm and fighting with the other. Her adversary bit the hand that had entered her mouth while they were striking out at each other. Startled and in pain, she let the sack of rice fall from her head and it burst open on the ground.

I squeezed myself between them, pointing to the rice on the ground. "Look," I said, "you are fighting each other and look at the result. Haitians should be sharing with each other. We're all hungry. Look at you. You're both hurt and both still hungry.... The NGOs would love this image. If they had known you would be so co-operative, they would have been here with cameras to show the world that Haitians are so hungry they are killing each other for a sack of rice. Maybe they could use that to raise even more money."

The people who had been goading them on now applauded my intervention, "He's right, he's right," they said, "as long as we fight among ourselves, the NGOs will be enriching themselves. They aren't here because they care about us, but because they saw that the earthquake could raise their importance."

The two women started to calm down. They both wanted to explain their positions to me. I cut them off. "The main thing isn't to judge who is right or wrong, but that we try to manage the situation for ourselves. If we fight among ourselves for the little that we have, instead of taking care of each other, then we only leave the NGOs and *blan* and rich the opportunity to take control."

While all of our discussions were going on, a *kokorat* had scurried out of the shadows to the place where the rice had spilled over the ground when the sack broke open. He turned his t-shirt into a sack and started to scoop into it all the rice he could manage. A *kokorat* like him had no access to the distribution of rice in the "civilized" lines. He hadn't reached the social level of a tent in a victims' camp. So he had waited for his chance to get his ration.

I directed the women's attention to the little *kokorat* loading his t-shirt, "Look. *Tout sa ki pa bon pou youn se bon pou lòt.*" (Meaning that someone can always benefit from the misery of another.)

They both looked at the boy and shook their heads. They returned to their tents.

I heard the *kokorat* say, "Today, I'm going to fill myself up thanks to those two women!"

Everyone laughed. He scurried into the shadows.

chapter twenty-four

SOON AFTER THE EARTHQUAKE STRUCK, we heard American helicopters and aeroplanes and saw them landing at the airport. Planes from other nations came as well, but the American military wouldn't let them land. It had taken control of the airport.

An old church sister of Deland, who lived abroad, was touched by the news of the catastrophe. She had become very wealthy. She tried to charter an aeroplane to bring relief to her native island. Her flight and all that it was bringing, like the others, was turned away from Port-au-Prince by the Americans and ordered to land in the Dominican Republic. Many Americans believe that Haiti, because it is situated in the Western Hemisphere, is under the authority of the United States. Other countries cannot have independent relations with Haiti. Haitian affairs, it was made clear during the crisis, pass through Washington. Even Haitians, such as my father's friend from church, had to go through Washington. The Haitian rich nurture the right contacts among the American rulers, so they can be sure of Washington's support. That can be unfortunate for the rest of us Haitians.

Some Haitians already understood, as a result of their daily lives and those of their families for more than a century, that the Americans saw Haiti as their own possession. Some assumed that Washington had somehow provoked the earthquake to take overt control of the country. The immediate response of the American military seemed to validate their suspicions. Some claimed that the Pentagon had exploded a weapon under the sea that set off the quake. They said that the loud bang that preceded the earthquake was not natural, but evidence of American treachery. All of these rumours were simply interpolations from what Haitians knew about American intentions over a century.

The earthquake traumatized the victims. The actual experience — the loss of loved ones to a violent death, the destruction of homes and buildings, the memories of the terror, and so on — was compounded by the knowledge that the bodies of the dead would soon start to decompose and emit foul odours. To that was added the combative sound of American helicopters constantly circling overhead, terrorizing the traumatized victims below. On the ground were American soldiers everywhere, running around with their rifles drawn and ready for combat. Against whom? We were in no mood for fighting. All of these traumas led people to seek peace outside of the capital. Many returned to their home communities in the countryside to escape the terror of the capital.

Many of those who remained in the capital thought they might be useful in the circumstances. Medical workers, drivers, engineers, masons, and so on imagined that there would be lots of work to put Port-au-Prince back on its feet. Those who could speak other languages also saw that they could be useful, and find paying work, among the *blan* invading the capital.

Josué had an uncle who told him that the airport was now full of English-speakers from the north. He said that Haitians who could speak English needed only to appear with their identity cards and they were assigned jobs. Josué remembered my language exchanges with Paul in 2006 and encouraged me to go to the airport to find work. He wanted to come along with me. If I were to find a job, he said that I would then be on the inside and could find something for him as well. I went to get my passport and Josué got his identity card. His uncle wanted to drive us to the airport, with the same idea as Josué — if I should find a job, then he wanted to be close by to profit.

We weren't alone. The streets were full of people going to the airport with the same objective. They were all on foot. The *taptaps* were not moving. Only the SUVs of foreign journalists and bourgeois Haitians were still circulating. When we got to the airport, we saw foreign journalists preparing to leave Haiti. I found a security guard whom I knew from Simon and asked why they were leaving. He told me that they were being turned away by the American military authorities. They had landed only to return to their native countries.

Outside of the gates was a big crowd of us Haitians. A few decided to organize themselves. They created a list of their names and competencies that they intended to hand to the foreigners who were taking control of our country. I asked a man to write my name on the list he was creating. He said it was full, so I found a piece of paper and asked to borrow someone's pen and wrote out my coordinates and my English skills. Josué then asked that I put his name down too, which I did. Then, everyone circled us like mosquitoes, shoving their identity cards in my face and insisting that I include them on my list. I couldn't keep up. Everyone who, like me, had been refused on the other list was determined to not miss this chance. Josué's uncle took out his identity card so that I could add him to my impromptu list. Unfortunately, he is short and when he tried to hand it to me, others batted his hand away, saying, "No, no, I was here before him. . . . No fair. . . . Me first." Even though it was his idea to come, and he had driven us, he had to wait until the more insistent people were on my meaningless list.

I was writing my list in conformity with the others that had gone before me. People told me that they had passed lists through the gate with ten names each. But there were forty people who were hollering at me that they had to be on my list. I politely told them that I understood that these lists should have ten names each and so they could begin one of their own. However, they insisted that they be on my list. Some told me that if they weren't included on my list they were going to beat me up. So, to save myself, I took forty names before no more would fit. I had not the foggiest notion where my list would go and what would become of it. I felt sorry for the poor souls who were putting all their hopes in a list with no destination, despite the fact that they were threatening me.

When I finished taking their names, I waited in front of the gate with the list in my hand. No one came to get it. I was frightened of the crowd behind me that had elected me their spokesman because I had a pen. Once they had put me in charge, they expected results. I waited for two hours. As time passed, some of the crowd got hungry or bored and started to disperse. Eventually, the security guard whom I knew came by again. I asked if anyone would take my list. He said no, that they had already taken lists of people looking for work. So, I just ripped up the list and left it in front of the gate. Those of us still there left, just as we had arrived.

chapter twenty-five

A FEW WEEKS AFTER THE EARTHQUAKE, we were all sleeping under the stars. To have a tent was a luxury. We were in the middle of the dry season. Everyone wanted a shelter from the dust. We were also thinking of the rains that were in store for us.

Some international NGOs came with tents. The bourgeois families, with the contacts that soften the blows of life, put up the best tents and distinguished themselves from the other victims and the *kokorats*. The wretched had to fight in lineups to get a tent. Many managed to get a tarp from an NGO or, if they had money, bought them from street merchants. Where did they get them? From committees that misrepresented the number of people under their charge. Or from other contacts that may never be known. Those who couldn't buy a tent or a tarp and couldn't get one through an NGO were left to fend for themselves.

A number of camps arose where people built their own shelters. All that was needed was eight long sturdy branches and some sheets to hang from them to represent walls: the kind of shacks that the very poor build for themselves in slums all over the world. These camps quickly became densely populated. The NGOs decided to visit them and to distribute whatever tents or tarps they still had. To qualify for those donations, or other aid, Haitians needed to have a place etched out in one of the camps and to have demonstrated some proof of residence. They would need to have put up some kind of structure. Inside these camps, every inch of land was taken up by people trying to establish a presence.

Everyone kept their ears open to find out where the NGOs were distributing the tents most generously. The objective was to go to that camp and demonstrate a presence. Then wait. Sometimes people squatted in a number of camps at the same time in order to cover all their bases. There were distinct classes of victims. For some, the objective was to accumulate as many tents — and whatever other forms of humanitarian aid might arrive — as possible. When they saw that material goods with a street value were coming into the country, their goal was to profit. To do that, they had to shut their eyes to the people who were actually in desperate need of the basic necessities of life: water, food, and shelter. They became even more callous than before toward those who were suffering the most.

Imagine that you are a single mother of seven children living in Delmas 19, like a friend of mine. Four of them were immediately crushed and killed when the building where she rented a room collapsed upon them. The other three were at school and were saved. But now, she had no home, no money, no food, and water was hard to come by. How could she battle others for the absolute necessities of life for herself and her surviving son and daughters while grieving the deaths of four children? She heard that the Red Cross was giving tarps out to people in a camp in Silo. So she managed to find the branches to build a frame for the tarp. There, she still lives with hundreds of others. From time to time the Red Cross comes by to distribute some soap. The residents have planted bananas and beans around their crowded camp that they keep spotlessly clean. Now, she suffers from depression and she is always in pain. But while she tried to cope after the earthquake, others were pushing her out and plotting how best to profit and advance their family's interests in the new circumstances.

In other cases, the owners of the land threatened the real victims with eviction and even hired *vakabon* to physically kick them from their land and return it to its vacant state.

Since I had no shelter after the earthquake, I was nervous about sleeping outside when the rainy season started. I didn't trust the structure where my room was located, behind the house that had collapsed. I wanted a tent. Moreover, I was dreaming of getting a tent that was large enough to protect my friends who were also homeless. I listened, like everyone, for where I might be able to find one. People told me that the camp at Saint Louis de Gonzague was my best chance.

I called my friend and fellow furniture maker, Josué. He too was homeless. Together, we arrived at Saint Louis de Gonzague where we found all kinds of activity. People were building shelters of all sorts, with whatever was at hand. All of the space was taken. Some people who had received real tents refused to erect them. They preferred to keep their pathetic impromptu structures in place, since that might qualify them for more tents and other aid. Sometimes, they took their tents and then sold their space to someone else who could use it to get his or her own tent and continue the cycle. I decided not to buy a space from someone who had already received a tent. Instead, I chose to find a couple of vacant metres where I could build my own shelter.

In a corner of the field there was a little open space. Josué and I didn't want to occupy it before asking around. Usually, a little vacant space like that in a camp had already been claimed by someone whom you would have to pay to take it over. There were often fights over such spaces. I wanted to avoid trouble. We found a young man who told us that he had already started to clear and level that space and so it belonged to him. He wanted 500 gourdes ($12.42 US) for two small spaces, each two metres square. I had 150 gourdes ($3.73 US). Josué had 250 ($6.21 US). We put it together and offered it to the young man, with the promise of paying the outstanding hundred gourdes later. We were happy. We'd have our tents, we thought.

We returned to Delmas 19 to take the branches off of some mature trees to build a frame. Then we found some *ranyon*, which are clothes and sheets worn and soiled beyond use, to use as the skin of our new shelters. We hurried back with our materials as well as a machete and a pick, because the little plot was on a hill that we would have to flatten. We passed a day working the land and building our structures. When we were nearing the end of our work, an anxious woman came up to us. "What are you doing on my property?!"

I was surprised, "Your land? What are you talking about?"

"This is my land. I was the first one here. I weeded this property. I even came across a snake that I had to kill. I'm not going to give it up now."

Josué said, "Joegodson, don't listen to her! She'll say anything at all to steal our land from us that we have already bought and prepared."

I was already listening to her. It was entirely possible that the land we had bought did not "belong" to the man who had sold it. Maybe she was as right as we were. I told her the story of how we came to be there.

"That young man is a thief!" she said. "He's from Site Solèy. That's the same guy who sold us the land. I'm going to call my husband and he'll tell you it's mine."

Her husband came and calmly explained how they came to claim the land. Josué and I told them our story, almost the same. She was sleeping under the stars with a three-month-old baby. She couldn't fight the crowds for a tent, so she had decided to come here to try the same method that Josué and I had in mind.

"Okay," I said, "since we have the same idea — that is, neither of us is in the camp to stay, but just to get a tent, maybe we can find a way to get three tents out of these plots. It would be a better use of our time than arguing over who has the right to be here, because we all do."

After a short while, we were all agreed. We went to find the young businessman who sold us all the same property. But he had already left with his profits. We left the two shelters that we had assembled in place. I gave one to the woman and I shared the second one with Josué. From time to time, we passed by Saint Louis de Gonzague to see if there was any talk of a tent distribution. The NGOs never came back to Saint Louis de Gonzague. Presumably, they had struck it off their list after the first tents had been distributed. After two weeks, we came by to find that our shelters had been removed, tossed into the woods by the camp committee. Our hopes were dashed of ever getting a tent. Josué and I let the idea go, but we wondered how the woman with a three-month old would manage. We were young men and we hated fighting for food in those lineups.

chapter twenty-six

EVERYWHERE, PEOPLE USED the pretext of 12 January to squat on a plot of land. In many cases, it was a necessity; in others, a strategy. There was often not much difference between the two. Even people whose homes mostly or partly survived were in a desperate situation. It would be necessary to get whatever food and water NGOs might distribute. One day, Franchesca's aunt approached Fédrik. She told him that she had claimed a small plot of land; would he be able to build a tent for them? Fédrik responded, "Of course."

"Great. Since you are here, I have already prepared a few things that you can use. I have these two tarps that a friend got from an NGO. I wasn't able to fight for one. The way they hand them out, you have to be strong enough to fight everyone. I let my friend fight for them and then I paid her. I also have some wood. It's not a lot, but try to prepare an *ajoupa* anyway. Then we will be able to sleep there at night. As you know, what's left of our house is fissured and could fall. We don't want to lose Franchesca."

Fédrik hoped to be able to impress Franchesca, knowing that he had fallen from her favour. The material that her aunt handed to him was not sufficient. He had to be clever in order to find all that he needed to build a decent *ajoupa*.

Franchesca's aunt was happy with his creation. Franchesca and Fédrik started to sleep there at night, while her aunt and cousins remained in the house. One day, Franchesca returned from work to find that the thick plastic tarp had been locked shut. Her aunt had bought a lock and poked holes through the two sides of the tarp to fasten them together, in the way that most people were locking their tents. When Franchesca went to her home, her aunt told her that she had decided that she and

Fédrik would be better off in their own tent. The aunt planned to listen for when the NGOs were going to distribute something, then go and unlock the lock and wait to benefit from the distribution. However, if Franchesca and Fédrik were living there, then they would profit and the aunt, whose idea this had been, would be left in the cold. So, she locked Franchesca and Fédrik out. They would have to build another place for themselves.

Franchesca asked that she let them continue to live there, since it would take a week to be able to construct another. Besides, they would now have to start from scratch. They would have to wait until Franchesca was paid before they could buy the necessary materials and to claim some land.

On payday, Franchesca handed her pay over to Fédrik to buy the tarps and other materials. Fédrik decided not to build it in the same tent camp where he had built the one for Franchesca's aunt. He found another tent camp a little distance away. Before the earthquake, the local people had used it for their pigs. They would throw their garbage in that space and, inevitably, the pigs and goats would root through it. The animals came to claim it as their pigsty. This sort of commons existed throughout the capital. Not at all a green commons; rather, its main attraction for the pigs and goats is the garbage. The odour of the local commons in Port-au-Prince is overwhelming. The garbage that offends human senses attracts pigs. Plus, they are comfortable on mattresses of mud. Now, humans were taking over from the pigs.

There were already sixty families living there. Each newcomer swept the garbage a little to the side, to the displeasure of the previous residents. Eventually, the pigs understood they were being evicted. They had not been disturbed by the earthquake, but now they were feeling the aftershocks. The pigs were ultimately working for their human masters without knowing it. Now, they had to manage for themselves.

Fédrik built a nicer *ajoupa* than the one he had made for Franchesca's aunt. They lived together there. Franchesca got up at dawn each morning to take a *taptap* to the Industrial Park. Fédrik found himself in the same situation he had faced before his adventure in the Dominican Republic. What to do? He dreamt again of karate, but that dream led in no profitable direction.

He couldn't stay in the tent all day. Physics made sure of that. As the sun rose, the tents became unbearably hot inside. From ten in the morning until six o'clock in the evening, no one could stay inside the tents because of the heat and the toxic gases they emitted. Inside, you were at risk of suffocating. Even mosquitoes expired from the toxic heat of the tents.

Both before she left for work and upon her return, Franchesca complained that Fédrik was still unemployed. As the days passed, she became like a bee in his ear, humming the same monotonous tune. She argued that, since she was working in SONAPI all day long, that he too should find something to do. Together, maybe they could begin to live decently instead of displacing pigs in order to sleep.

But the advice only frustrated Fédrik, "Well, tell me what to do! I spend all day thinking what to do. Do you want me to get into criminal stuff? It doesn't sound like you care what I do!"

"No, Féd! I didn't say to do something illegal. Just find something!"

"Okay. Here! I'll sell our lives to a *lwa* in exchange for a little food and a nicer place to live. Will that make you happy?"

Franchesca replied, "No. But since it's you that is suggesting it, you don't have to include me in the contract. If you want to deal with a *lwa*, that's your business!"

Fédrik disagreed, "Wait a minute! It's what you are asking me. You can see very well that the rich are doing better than ever while we live with pigs. Even the *lwa* are turning people away these days. Port-au-Prince is full of unemployed. More and more, we are unemployable."

Fédrik continued to look for work, but without success. Franchesca continued to complain, without relenting. Their time together became predictable, with Franchesca telling him to get a job and Fédrik not knowing how. Fédrik's frustration built to the point that he wanted to hit Franchesca. When he felt his anger rising to that point, he left the tent and came to visit me. As she complained to him, he complained to me.

I advised him to talk more with Franchesca . . . and with compassion.

I said, "Féd, I can see her point of view. I know the sweatshops. I've worked at SONAPI. She's working really hard in crappy conditions for almost no money. Above all, you've got to avoid fights where you're living in the tent camp. Your neighbours will enjoy a free show. It's the only entertainment for many of them. And it degrades you. Talk with her with compassion and find the best solution for everyone."

He was listening quietly, so I continued, "I think that if you just approach the problem right, you'll find a solution. It's not that she doesn't want you anymore — she's not talking like that. It's SONAPI that's eating at her. If you could spend just one day there, you'd see why she doesn't come home in peace and with patience."

"But you don't understand, Joegodson," Fédrik interjected. "She leaves no space for compassion and understanding and patience. She starts harping at me the moment she sees me and follows me around buzzing in my ear. She won't stop. I'd like to know how to have a civil conversation with her."

"Okay, Féd, okay, okay. It's a good thing that you've come here. You were wise. When things heat up in a relationship, the best answer is to cool down. For sure, when you go home, you're going to find that she has already calmed down. Then, she'll be ready to listen to you."

"No, Joegodson. I know what she wants and so does she. She wants me to work in the sweatshops with her. I don't want to. There's no answer because we don't want the same thing. She treats me like a child. If she could, she would take a strap and beat me all the way to the factory."

I said, "Then try to get her to understand that your old dreams still exist. Ask her if she would look for a way to realize them with you."

"Dreams?! You think she has any patience for dreams after my experiences in the Dominican Republic? She is not in the mood for dreams and hopes and inspiration. She is hard."

"Just try again. Maybe she has forgotten the Dominican Republic. Maybe she can listen to another plan. Just try."

Finally, Fédrik agreed to try again. He walked back to their tent.

— • —

"Franchesca, just listen. I understand you. Don't think that I don't understand what you're going through. I know that working in the factories is worse than slavery. We cannot accept it. That is the thing that's killing you."

Franchesca answered, "Féd, the only reason I go to work is to keep us from being ashamed in front of my family. If I go home and start complaining about you, they will start gossiping about us. We'll be finished before we start. . . . How can we free ourselves from this monster that is zombifying us? "

"We have to think about creating something together — a business. Like that, we'll be independent of the sweatshops."

"What if I were to enter a *sabotay*? I could put aside some money. I'll take the first place in the *sabotay*. I'll pass the money on to you while I carry on working just to pay it off. When it's over, I'll quit my job at the sweatshop and join you in the business."

A *sabotay* is a voluntary union of workers who are underpaid in the sweatshops of Port-au-Prince. *Sabotays* have been in existence for decades and there are, at any given time, a number available to join. When I once worked at SONAPI, I was the "Papa" of a *sabotay*. If a woman organizes it, she is called the "Manman." The Manman or Papa must be well-respected for their honesty and good judgment. The workers are motivated to join a *sabotay* because they can trust the organizer and the other workers to honour their responsibilities to the others.

The idea is simple in principle. A *sabotay* is organized to allow workers to save enough money to attempt to realize some dream. Each payday, the members hand the Manman or Papa a portion of their pay. Also, each payday, one member of the *sabotay* receives the collected amount of all the others. The amount depends on how long you have been paying and how much you contribute each payday. There are all sorts of *sabotay* available depending on what you can contribute and how big your dreams are. The *sabotay* pays you back only what you have contributed, less a small administrative fee for the Manman or Papa. So why bother? Why not just save the money yourself or hand it to a trusted friend or put it in a bank? Because no one trusts him- or herself to save anything. When you are hungry, you eat if there is any money available for you to buy food. If your money is in a *sabotay*, however, you cannot access it until the date that you had agreed upon when entering it. There are risks, of course. But workers trust the Manman or Papa to have stronger willpower than they have. The Manman or Papa will allow the participant to go hungry, knowing that in several months, he or she will be compensated for their sacrifices by their payout.

Fédrik was overwhelmed by Franchesca's idea. She would sacrifice everything and sentence herself to working at a job she hated to free them from a life of penury. Mostly, he was humbled by the enormous confidence she was showing in him. She would give him all her money from months of work, in the hope that he could use it to establish some business.

Franchesca entered into the *sabotay* as planned. She worked sixty hours a week and made 3,200 gourdes ($80.87 US) every two weeks. She paid 2,400 gourdes ($60.65 US) each payday into the *sabotay*, which would be paid back to her in July. She couldn't leave it until it was finished and all the members had been compensated as she would be. But there was no margin for error in this scheme. In order to be able to pay it back, she had to sacrifice food. It was a plan that ignored basic human needs. She soon fell sick ... but she continued to work. She had no other choice now that she was beholden to a *sabotay*.

One morning, as she prepared to go to work, her head was spinning and she felt exceedingly tired. Fédrik tried to comfort her by rinsing her face with cool water, but it didn't help. She tried to walk, but couldn't find the strength to go more than a few steps.

Fédrik had just enough money to pay for a *taptap*, and no more. He called me. I had only 100 gourdes ($2.50 US), which I gave to him. I encouraged him to take her to a hospital and let the doctors take care of her. We would find whatever money was necessary by borrowing from neighbours and friends.

Fédrik helped Franchesca into a *taptap* and then half carried her into a clinic in Delmas 19. Since it was a private hospital, they examined her and then admitted her. The nurses gave her an intravenous, not before reproaching Fédrik for having kept her at home for so long. They said that she was in an advanced stage of malaria. She was days away from death.

Franchesca asked the nurses if she would be well enough to go to work. If they were not informed, they would surely fire her. And she needed to keep her job.

The nurses were amazed, "Are you crazy or what? Aren't you aware that you are on the edge of death. What kind of work is so important that you have to be there? What's at stake in this job?"

"You don't understand. If I show any weakness, my place will be taken by someone outside. I can't afford that."

"Better that you go to work and collapse over the machines, dead? Not only do you have malaria, but you're suffering from malnutrition. You think that you are lucky to be working at such a job?"

"No, but we need it. The company helps us," Franchesca said.

"Help you! Help you how? Help you do what? I have never had a case of a bourgeois suffering from malnutrition. You don't even have enough in your system to survive, let alone work!... There are two vitamins that you need in your body. I can inject them into the intravenous. But you'll have to pay for them. If you give me the money, I'll be able to buy them for you."

Franchesca waved her hand, "I have nothing. Fédrik is trying to raise some money among the neighbours. When he gets back, maybe he'll have enough."

The nurse was amazed to hear that Franchesca was worried about getting back to a job that couldn't pay her enough to buy vitamins to treat malnutrition. Her life was literally in the balance and she was worried about losing a job!

Frustrated, the nurse left Franchesca. She wasn't sure if Franchesca was sane.

— • —

Meanwhile, Fédrik was able to find nothing among his neighbours in the pigsty camp. The people did not choose to live there because of their wealth. If they had a few gourdes, many chose to spend them on *klarin* in order to forget the smells and squalor of their hopeless lives. They didn't budget for medical costs.

Totally broke, Fédrik walked a few kilometres from pigsty camp to visit his mother in Bourdon. She was seated in front of her *pèpè* on the street corner. She could tell by the way that her son approached that he was not bringing good news.

"What ill wind is blowing you here?"

"Problems," he said quietly.

"Look at the son I have! I was hoping he would come to tell me that he finally had a job to help his mother escape her problems. Instead, he brings more of his own.... Well, all right. What is it?"

"Ah, Manman. This country is not for me. I've tried to find something. But I have failed. The more I try to make troubles disappear, the bigger they get."

"What troubles? Please don't tell me that Franchesca is pregnant while you aren't working."

He replied, "No. Worse. It's not about life, but death. She's very sick. She has been sick for awhile, but . . . again, it's my fault . . . I just thought it was stress from her work and living in the tent. If I don't act fast, she's going to die."

His mother dropped her head to the ground and sighed in despair. She said, "I can't lend you money, because you have no income. Tell Franchesca that I'll lend this to her," she said, as she handed Fédrik 3,000 gourdes ($74.57 US). "This is from my business, but it's more important to save a life than to keep a thousand businesses going."

Fédrik's despair gave way to relief. He left his mother free of the weight that made every step an effort. He went to visit his brother in the garage who contributed another 1,000 gourdes ($24.86 US).

Leaving the garage, he bought a few drinks and a container of prepared rice to bring to the hospital. When he arrived, he found Franchesca sitting alone on the side of her bed talking to herself, her head in her hands. "Fran, why aren't you lying down? What's wrong? Is it worse?"

"How am I going to get down to the factory to explain?"

"Forget about that for the minute. When you're sick, the only thing that matters is to get better. Listen, we are saved."

Franchesca thought that he had found a job. She sat up alert to hear the good news.

Fédrik said, "Everywhere I tried, people were in worse condition than us. So I went to Bourdon. I arrived just as my mother was preparing some money to buy her next package of *pèpè*. But she lent it to us. Then my brother lent us some more."

Franchesca was unhappy to hear about these loans. She simply slouched back into her gloom. Fédrik implored her, "Fran, say something."

So she did: "Don't you see anything? These loans have to be paid back. How?"

"It's not the time to be thinking of that. The first thing to do is to get you better."

"Féd! We were supposed to be starting a business together. I'm in a *sabotay*. Now, all of that is just to pay back these loans. We're finished before we have even started."

The truth kept Fédrik quiet. He walked out into the courtyard, dejected. He didn't want to continue that discussion. He waited until dusk and returned to her room.

"Fédrik. Listen. Tomorrow, what if you went to the factory for me? You can tell my bosses why I'm not there. Also, I'll give you my badge and you can pick up my pay. There are two weeks waiting for me. That'll be 3,200 gourdes ($79.55 US)."

Franchesca told Fédrik to ask me to help him at SONAPI. He had never entered the grounds. The next morning, he arrived early to pick me up in Delmas 19 and we carried on to SONAPI.

When we arrived, all kinds of merchants were lined up in front of the gates, as usual. It is so busy that you need to take care to not step in a pot of boiling rice or a pile of oranges or avocados. It is impossible to not step in the garbage, especially as the day proceeds and the piles grow.

In front of the main gates, armed security guards asked to see our identification. Fédrik showed Franchesca's badge. They took our national identity cards as ransom and gave us visitors' badges for the time we were in the Park. Then we passed by the MINUSTAH soldiers who also maintained a presence in SONAPI.

We passed by a number of factories before we found Franchesca's. Again, in front of the factory was a security guard toting a shotgun. His eyes were hidden behind dark glasses. We asked him if he could help us find the administrative office. He took off his dark glasses and told us to turn left as soon as we entered the factory.

We passed more armed security as we crossed the courtyard to the main door. As we entered, we saw all the employees in long rows inside a huge room working feverishly as supervisors walked slowly up and down, surveying their work. We turned left and saw the administrative office. There was simply a smoked glass window with a narrow slot in the middle. We stood there, not knowing what to do. We could see nothing behind the glass.

After a few minutes, a very stern female voice, already tired of our presence, growled at us from the other side of the window, "Well! What do you want?"

Fédrik couldn't speak. I took up the explanation and slid Franchesca's identity card into the narrow slot. "We are here on behalf of this employee."

"What's wrong with her? Where is she?"

We explained and said that we had come to collect her money that she needed for the treatment for malaria.

"This worker has been absent for three days. She is about to be terminated."

"That's what we're here about. Here's the document from the clinic that is treating her." We passed a document with the letterhead of a respected clinic stating that Franchesca was suffering from malnutrition and malaria. "She has no money for her treatment, so she has sent us to pick up her pay for her."

The female voice replied, "She'll have to come here to pick it up herself."

"Madam, maybe you don't understand. Look at the document. She is deathly ill. She cannot walk. She cannot leave her bed. That's why she has sent her husband and me to pick up her pay. Without it, she can't afford the treatment."

"Okay. Move away from my window. All your talk about malaria, husbands, documents, and pay means nothing to me," she snapped. "How do I know that you didn't find this identity card in the street? You could have got anyone to forge that document. There's nothing I can do."

"Put yourself in her place," I pleaded. "Imagine that you are in a critical state and that the only way to save your life was to have a relative come here to pick up your pay. Would you rather that they not give it to you?"

"A thousand times!" she said. "I'm responsible for the payroll money, not somebody's health."

This was a waste of time. This voice that snapped at us from the other side of the glass was treating Fédrik and me like thieves. Far worse, she was condemning Franchesca to death. It was unbearable. But there seemed to be nothing we could do.

Fédrik could barely control his anger. He stamped harshly around the grounds of SONAPI, kicking up Haitian soil in every direction. As he passed me, I caught the gist of his argument.

"That's why I keep saying to Fran . . . working in this factory. . . . She says that it's going to provide for her future . . . it will kill her. . . . She'll see how much they respect her. How much they need her."

He carried on in fury all the way to the hospital. I said nothing to avoid adding to a fire already burning out of control.

"How did it go?" Franchesca asked as we walked into her room. "Did you get my pay?"

Fédrik fumed, "Give us your money?! They're hoping you die so that they can keep your two weeks' pay! They have no interest in you whatsoever."

Franchesca was groggy from the serum that she was taking for the malaria. But she called a nurse and asked to be sent home to take the rest of her prescription there. She could not afford to stay in the clinic. The nurse wrote a discharge note for Franchesca. Féd and I helped her back to pigsty camp.

Early next morning, Franchesca was waiting before the door of the factory to resume her work.

chapter twenty-seven

ONE OF THE BENEFICIARIES of Haitian labour is Gildan Activewear, the largest manufacturer of sportswear in North America. It subcontracts its t-shirt production to Allain Villard, a member of a rich Haitian family. The bourgeois families work together to make sure that the working standards and salaries are equally terrible for all Haitian workers.

Paul told me what was happening in Canada after the earthquake. The news that all but two of the buildings in the Palm Apparel plant in Carrefour collapsed during the quake, killing approximately one thousand workers, was bad for the company. Gildan shareholders had to be reassured quickly . . . not about the thousands of lives, but about their investments. Would the company be able to continue production? How weak would it be as a result of this devastating blow? The company directors immediately made public the good news that its other contractors in Haiti had survived the earthquake with no serious injuries to personnel or damage to equipment. And they had resumed production.

Meanwhile, Canadian news was full of the devastation of the capital. Paul related how images on television were showing just how poor we are here. So Gildan's message had to be properly nuanced. It had to assuage investors' fears at the same time that it seemed to care about Haitian workers. Paul told me that at a shareholders' meeting in Montréal, the management said that it would financially compensate the families of its deceased workers and that it would provide food, medical, and psychological help to the survivors. We decided that I should go to the Gildan factories to see if any such promises were being honoured. It seemed odd, since the conditions don't vary among the foreign assembly plants. If one foreign company began to change working conditions and salaries, then people would not work for the others and all hell would break loose. In fact, we seldom know the name of the company we're working for or what country it's from. They're all just *blan* companies.

In any case, Paul and I would write up the results of our research and describe the situation — whatever I should find out — on a website that he was setting up for me to describe what things were like in Haiti. I decided that it would be best to have some support. I didn't want to do this alone. While I was mulling it over, a brother from church, named Mardi, appeared next to me. He was a teacher, but unemployed. He seemed a good candidate. I had already told Paul that I would need to have some money. Not only did I have nothing to buy food or to live, but sending photos on the Internet could be expensive from Haiti where I would need to have a connection — often slow and unreliable — at an Internet cafe. Plus, I would have to research and organize my part of the project. I asked my friends at SONAPI and they said that Gildan had a number of sweatshops around Port-au-Prince. It could take time to research. Paul was also struggling financially at the time. But he had fifty dollars, and his friend donated another fifty so that I could carry on. All I could promise Mardi was that I would pay for our *taptap* rides and our food while we were researching. He agreed. He said knowing that he would eat was already a service. We decided to start out early the next morning.

He was afraid of carrying out our project. So was I. How would we continue? We could be targeted. In Haiti, anyone who tries to speak a truth that interferes with the rich can be easily eliminated. And both Mardi and I sensed that we were targeting one of those truths.

When I saw Mardi's concerns, I suggested that we should just present ourselves as we were, unemployed Haitians looking for work. No one would take us for a threat. We would arouse their contempt or, at best, their pity.

Then I went to visit Annie at Mme Bolivar's house. She was very worried. She couldn't ask me not to do it. But she said, "Be careful!"

Afterwards, I returned home to Delmas 19. I prepared for our research. I decided that I would take a camera that I had bought with a gift of money from Louise, a kind woman who always read the website that Paul and I had started and whom we knew when she had visited Haiti in 2006.

The next morning, I went looking for Mardi. We took a *taptap* to Carrefour 3 Mains, to begin our research in SONAPI. We entered the grounds to see if we could locate a Gildan factory there. We asked the security guards in front of any factory that had no name affixed to it if they knew whether Gildan employed workers here. We were sent all over the place. Finally, we found a guard who knew that Gildan used to have a factory at SONAPI, but that they had moved a few months earlier. He advised me that Gildan operated in Carrefour Thor, the same address that Paul had given me. We decided to leave SONAPI in peace. We now would have to travel to Carrefour Thor.

Leaving SONAPI, I suggested to Mardi that we had better eat before we got on a *taptap*. One of the street merchants who sells to the workers sold us each a plate. Because there were no chairs, we had to crouch down to eat in the bustle of the entrance, among the garbage and the fumes of charcoal burning and cars passing. There was such little room that we had to get up each time someone passed. Then we bought ourselves soft drinks and started out again. It was now ten o'clock and the sun was rising fast. It was going to be very hot. We found a merchant who sold us a couple of caps.

We took a *taptap* to the main intersection to get a bus for Carrefour. In the bus, I asked people if they knew of a factory called Gildan. No one knew. So I asked them if they knew of a factory owned by the family Villard. That, they recognized. They told me that it was in the centre of Carrefour Thor. They told me that I would have to ask people where to find *Kay Villard*, rather than Gildan. Factories are known in Haiti by the name of the Haitian subcontracting family, not their corporate partners.

When we descended from the bus, I began asking people. One explained that it would be too complicated to give or remember directions. There were too many twists and turns and ups and downs through narrow alleyways. He said that he could send us in the right direction, but that we would have to ask others until we arrived at Kay Villard. I went as far as his directions took me. From there, I asked a child to show me where Kay Villard was. "Is that the factory?" he asked. He gave me another set of directions that I followed to arrive at the factory complex. Smart kid!

There, I saw a big gate. It was opened to let a car enter. I saw a big tractor working inside the complex. It had evidently already cleared piles of rubble away, as it was now preparing the land for reconstruction.

There were many containers that I assumed were loaded either with fabrics for the workers to transform or clothes ready to be shipped to Canada. The door closed on me.

I didn't want to look suspicious, so Mardi and I kept moving and spoke to the security guard who manned the little kiosk in front of the gate. We addressed him as if we were a couple of unemployed workers looking for jobs. Since it was the first time that Mardi was involved in espionage, he just listened carefully. I figured that if you want to arrive at the truth, you may have to take a long and complicated path. I could certainly not simply pose my questions and expect answers. I would have to move a little distance at a time, asking at each new twist and turn in the conversation for the way forward.

I greeted the security guard and said, "Hello sir. Could you please tell me if this company is hiring?"

He replied, "Today, they won't be taking anyone. But next week, they might be." He pointed in front of him, on this side of the gates, and said that the company was going to expand there.

I asked him, "But there is so much space inside where the tractors are working. Why don't they use that to expand?"

"That still belongs to the company. The factories inside were destroyed in the quake. Lots of people were killed. Now they're rebuilding."

I said, "We've come from Delmas. We went to SONAPI. I asked people whether there was a company that paid better than the others. Some people told me that Gildan paid more. So, that's why we've come here. Is that true?"

"You should have stayed in Delmas and worked at any of the factories. There's no difference. If you want to make more money, the only way is to try to make the quota. That's almost impossible to keep up. It's all the same."

He was much older than me, the father of a family. His dark glasses were just for show — to give him a tough look. Once he took them off, his eyes were kind and he was decent. He wore a uniform: green pants and a white shirt. The twelve-calibre shotgun in his left hand seemed at odds with his manner.

I put myself in his place: "You should be the best paid here. You should be paid more than the boss. If there is trouble, they'll kill you first, before they start looking for the boss."

"That's true," he said. "Normally, if I had another profession or something else to do, I would never choose to be standing here with a gun in my hand, trying to threaten people. Here, I hardly earn anything. The boss doesn't have any respect for me. But I have my family to feed."

I asked a more searching question: "But at least if you have an accident or are sick, you will have some kind of medical insurance?"

He smiled. "If you are sick, you are supposed to use the money you make to pay for whatever you need. The minute you can't work anymore, you are of no importance to them. The rich understand the situation this country is in. They will never value workers. The minute you show signs of costing them money, they replace you with one of the unemployed poor that wander the streets. They have no need of you."

I, counting myself among the unemployed poor wandering the streets, continued, "Maybe in the big meetings, the bosses talk about how well they treat their employees. But maybe if someone really wants to know, they should ask people like you."

"Of course. We are already condemned to never know a better life. Look at you. You are young. You have your life ahead of you. Maybe if your parents had some means, you wouldn't be looking to sell yourself to work for a place like this. That's why so many choose easier ways to survive, like kidnapping and theft. At least they don't have to feel like slaves.... Anyway, I'm not going to continue with this. It's too dangerous. There's no respect. There's no future."

While we were talking, the street merchants were setting up for the lunch break in the factory. It was almost noon. They arrived balancing big pots on their heads. They set them down and prepared the plates. The juice merchants too prepared for the moment when the factory doors would open. Mardi and I excused ourselves from the guard and went to stand with the merchants. We bought plates for ourselves. We heard the merchants complaining among themselves about all of their clients who had died during the earthquake with debts on their heads that the vendors would never be able to recuperate.

I asked one merchant, "Has the factory been open for a long time? When did it reopen after the earthquake?"

"After the earthquake, I had to go to the country. I returned after a month to start up my business again. But it had been open for awhile at that point."

Mardi spoke up. "Did you have any family who worked in these factories?"

"Yes, yes," she said. "Everyone around here had people in the factories. Some had broken arms and legs."

"Ah, well," Mardi continued, "at least you can be sure that they would compensate you and help the injured. A big company like this must have lots of money to take care of the victims."

"Oh really?!" she stared at him, as if trying to figure out what planet he was from. "Everyone who died, died for the patrons. Those who were injured simply added to the poverty of their parents. Because it was the families that had to do everything to help their injured. Not the company." She dismissed Mardi as if he was an innocent.

"But I thought there was a system of medical help for the employees. Maybe you didn't seek the right help," Mardi pushed.

She replied, "The bosses never listened to the sick any more than the dead! They don't have the time. Normally, if the workers were human beings, bosses should have brought the victims together to see what they could do. Even if it wasn't a lot, it could have been helpful. There were meetings after the earthquake. The company did suggest that there would be help in the future. But that future never came. And the talk has all dried up."

While we were talking, the workers poured out of the building. Mardi and I split up to talk to different groups. We searched for the people, wherever they could be found, who wanted to talk.

I went up to a man buying a plate from a merchant. "Excuse me, sir. Could you help us? My friend and I are here from Delmas. We were told that this factory pays better. Is that true?"

"That depends on whether you make the quota or not. Sometimes I make it but, when it is high, I can't. I normally make 150 gourdes a day ($3.73 US). Sometimes less. There are people who work overtime to make 200 gourdes a day ($4.97 US)."

I pushed, "If you are sick, is there any medical help?"

"No," he said, "they send you home rather than to a doctor or a hospital."

I asked the obvious, "That money can't take care of all the expenses of living. How do you cope with that salary?"

He said, "Even if the company would feed us, rather than forcing us to dig into our little salary, it would be better for us. But no. The bosses see only the quantity of our output. They don't care what we're going through."

While we were talking, I saw another group of employees arguing next to a juice merchant. I walked up to buy some juice from her, to listen in on the discussion. I was able to pose as one of them without them knowing, since no one could know all the other employees. This time, a number of people were talking. But all were frustrated.

One woman was particularly angry. "That's what I hate about the Haitian *sousou* . . . the sell-outs! . . . Look at the earthquake. God saved our lives, they say, but we were already mostly dead. Working here is a kind of death . . . the *sousou* do whatever they're told . . . even to go back to work while we were trying to cope with everything. If we had all got together to say no, we aren't ready to start work again . . . but no, we're a bunch of losers. . . . If we would get together to show that we're serious, then we'd be accepted as human beings . . . but no! We say *annavan* and everyone says yes, but there are always some sell-outs who run to the bosses to tell them who is plotting against them." I had the impression that she had a few sell-outs in the crowd in mind. On the other hand, would she really be reliable in an important struggle? I wondered.

Another woman spoke. But she was sad. She had tears in her eyes. "Every time I ask the bosses to let us out early so that I can get home before dark, they tell me to decide whether I want to work or not. I'm afraid to go home in the dark. And I have to take care of my kids. They don't care. I thought after the earthquake, things would change. Especially 'cause of all the aftershocks. But no. I can't even afford to make a miserable lunch for my kid to take to school."

Another said, "Look at our friends who died. If the company was serious, they should have helped their families. Some of us need tents. When tents arrive at the factory, they're taken away by people driving cars. Who is benefiting from these tents? It's not us, who need them most. They say they're sorry for us. But not sorry enough to change anything."

I said, "Maybe it would be helpful if there was some kind of psychological help."

"That's too expensive. Besides, it'd only apply to human beings. We aren't that important. They tell us they're gonna to help us. They never tell us how they're gonna screw us to make more profit. But that'd be the truth. Now they say there's gonna be some regulation to force everybody to make the quota no matter how long it takes. We'll have to keep working all night till it's finished."

Then she thought about her earlier argument and decided to take a stand. "This time, I don't care what the rest of you do. If you accept that, then go ahead. But I'm keeping my life. I'm not giving up my energy and my life to them. There'll be no limit to what they ask of us."

"Of course. If we agreed to stay here day and night, working, they'd be happy. But the minute that we fell ill, they'd fire us and replace us. There is no limit, like you say. Even the miserable minimum salary, we can't make it without working overtime."

A loud bell drowned out all the complaints. Everyone moved reflexively to the factory doors. I pretended to follow them, but that was the last place I wanted to be.

When they were all back inside, just Mardi and I were left standing in the dust. He had spoken to a number of workers and gotten negative answers in every case. No medical help. No psychological help. No food aid. The pay sucked. People told him that work covered their survival, and no more.

Mardi was surprised to see how the world looked from this perspective. He said that Haitians had long accepted the words of *blan*. Now, he saw that rich foreigners lied. Rich Haitians lied. Poor Haitians lied. He was discouraged to think that there was nothing but lies.

He asked me, "Who should I believe? Is this world reparable?"

I had no answer.

We found a bus back to Delmas. I shared with him the money that remained.

chapter twenty-eight

WHEN ANNIE TOLD ME THAT she had missed her period, she asked me what we would do if it turned out she was pregnant. It is not uncommon, despite the prohibition, for young Haitian men to dis-engage as soon as such news is announced. Many woman tell their partners that they are pregnant with much trepidation. Would I leave Annie to face her family alone, in shame?

I answered, "If it turns out that you are pregnant, I will marry you. If not, we should wait until we have a way to support a baby."

She remained skeptical, I know. She knew that I didn't have the means to support myself. It was not clear to either of us how I would support three people. She went to have a pregnancy test. We decided to leave the issue aside until we knew if there was something to resolve or not. That was the official decision. But I couldn't stop thinking about what I would do if indeed we had to deal with a pregnancy.

The following morning, Annie and I went to the clinic. The nurse asked me to wait outside. Oh-oh!

After thirty minutes, Annie came to tell me that the test was positive. She was scared. "How am I going to tell my sisters this?" she trembled.

"Stay calm," I said. "We have to figure it out for ourselves first and then things will fall into place."

We went to see a ring maker — the husband of a member of our choir — to find out how much a decent ring would cost. Wedding rings are important for Haitians. We explained the situation. He told us that the ring would cost 15,000 gourdes ($372.00 US). The price of gold had gone up. Neither Annie nor I said a thing. Our jaws dropped in unison. That helped him better than words to explain our situation.

"Try to find 10,000 gourdes ($249.00 US). I'll do what I can to get some gold and we'll leave it like that."

I called Paul to explain what was happening. I asked him if we could write an article for our website to see if some readers might be willing to offer me some help. We had never used it to ask for something, but just to discuss conditions in Haiti. After a week, no one had responded. I asked Annie if she would tell her sister, Mme Bolivar, the news. But Annie said no, that it was up to me to do it.

One afternoon, as I left the church, I dropped in to Mme Bolivar's home. After a short while, I asked to speak to her in private.

After some awkward preliminaries, I blurted out, "Your sister is pregnant. I have been thinking of how I can deal with the situation. We have spoken together and I would like to marry Annie."

Mme Bolivar cried out, "What!" She shook her head. "The country is in such an awful state and I know that you aren't in a position to marry."

"I want to do it, not just for Annie and to keep the respect of her family, but also that of my church."

"Well, okay... congratulations. You have courage. Just... Annie is my little sister. She should have told me before you. You are an outsider."

I replied, "Annie and I have decided. We just have to tell the pastor of the church and then my father."

Mme Bolivar said, "I will have to explain the situation to my mother and sisters. I'm not the head of the family."

A few weeks passed. I had stopped going to my activities at the church. No one asked me why. I was ashamed to present myself to people. The idea of telling the pastor was daunting. He was a middle-aged man with a severe disposition. He didn't joke. He was heavy, both physically and in temperament.

Each time the pastor passed me, I felt uncomfortable. But, one Sunday, I resigned myself to telling him.

"Pastor, I have something to tell you."

"What exactly?"

I explained, "It concerns my girlfriend Annie. She is pregnant."

"I'm busy at the moment. Come to see me on Tuesday at four o'clock... with Annie."

Monday morning, I started to search through the rubble of the main house in the courtyard where I lived for decent wood, with the idea of transforming it into furniture. Furniture is a necessity to begin a marriage. Without furniture, people don't view the union as serious.

Jelo was watching me. I had been nervous about addressing the issue with him.

He followed me quizzically, "Ti bòs, what are you doing?" Parts of the big structure were standing tenuously, and I was crawling around under massive sections of the second floor that hadn't yet collapsed like the rest of the house. These parts were held up by crooked and fissured supports. Without a very good reason, what I was doing was bordering on insanity. I had what I thought was a very good reason.

"I'm thinking of making some furniture with whatever I can salvage from this wreck," I said.

Jelo lit up, assuming that I would be building some furniture for sale. He was happy to think that some money would be coming into our little household.

He came closer, "Ah Jelo . . . listen . . . uh . . . Annie is pregnant."

"What?" he exhaled.

I explained the situation. I watched the life drain out of him. I have seen, and felt, that response when people have received news of the unexpected death of a loved one. He remained in that state for a period of time.

I watched this deathly sadness descend upon him. It only grew more agonizing as the day passed. It was as if the moment of our separation had arrived with this news. He said nothing to me for the rest of the day. I knew what he was feeling. It was impossible not to see and feel his sadness. And so I was drawn into it. It was painful. However would he manage to get through the actual wedding?

He walked around the courtyard to avoid being close to me. When I looked at him, I could see his hands trembling. His sadness had taken over his body. He couldn't have controlled himself if he wanted to. Even while he was avoiding me, I tried to get his attention to talk to him, to engage him in conversation and, hopefully, to make him smile. Not only would it be good for him, but it would free me so that I could continue to find my wood and plan the furniture.

I tried to pose questions that would provoke a conversation. Jelo answered with one or two words. He could not pump enough air out of his lungs to make a sentence. Finally, I decided to leave him to adapt to the new situation in his own time. I had to plan for the wedding so that I could erase the shame that our unplanned pregnancy could cause.

•●•

The next morning, Tuesday, I was talking with my friend Josué in Delmas 19 when another cabinetmaker came by to ask him if he would be interested in working as a carpenter for a group that was building temporary shelters in the neighbourhood. Josué agreed, although he had another small job to complete first. So I represented us both at a meeting that morning at the home of Mme Nicole, who was acting as the local agent for Cooperative Housing Foundation (CHF; now called Global Communities), a subsidiary of USAID.

I went with Josué's friend to the property of Mme Nicole, not far away. Out in front, a number of young Haitian men had assembled with their own tools, ready for the day's work. After thirty minutes, a foreman appeared telling us to enter for a little talk before heading out. I joined the meeting, even though I was not yet officially accepted onto the project.

The foreman began by welcoming everyone. He tried to sound formal and managerial, but he was miscast in the role:

> Dear friends, I have to talk to you about your complaints. I know that things aren't going very well for you, especially since many of you are fathers of families. Others have responsibilities even if you aren't fathers. I know that many of you don't live nearby; you have to take the public transport to get here and you leave nothing at home for your wives, children, and others. I also know that many of you work all day with nothing to eat as a result of having no money. But listen, brothers: try to build a bridge by borrowing some money from your relatives or your friends to get through the present period. It might take a few months, but CHF will not disappoint you because it's a reputable international NGO. Even if it takes a few months, you will receive your money and you will realize your dreams. The problem is that CHF has a lot of responsibilities beyond just

this project of building shelters, like stabilizing the area and so forth. You understand the situation and I think that with patience you will be fine.

When he was finished, an engineer took over and carried on in the same direction. It was clear that they had got their story straight. He said that each shelter cost $2,000 US, including materials and labour. Labour included three people: two bosses and one worker. Each boss was to receive thirty American dollars and each worker ten dollars a day. The workers had to build one shelter a day or risk losing their jobs. But after months of work for CHF, funded by USAID, no Haitian worker had yet been paid. Not one cent. I don't know how much the Haitian managers were getting.

When they had finished, one of the workers who was a foreman took the floor. He raised his hand and asked the committee to examine it:

There are five fingers, but they are not all the same length. Similarly, we do not all have the same financial means. It's true that we all have neighbours, but all neighbours are not the same. A neighbour may be able to help you for a couple of weeks, but not for several months.

He summarized the situation with a saying familiar to all Haitians: *woch nan dlo pa konn mizè woch nan solèy:* rocks in the water don't know the misery of rocks in the sun. He asked whether CHF would behave as it does if it were in the place of the homeless Haitian workers. He said that even half of the pay that was due to them would be enough to relieve the suffering.

Mme Nicole took the floor to explain to the workers how foreign NGOs function, from her perspective on the inside of CHF. She told of a worker who had worked for months for a foreign NGO with no pay whatsoever. Finally, however, the worker received, all at once, $3,000 US that he then used to buy a plot of land that he had had his eyes on for a long time. She continued, "My dear friends, I'm not saying that you have the same goals as that man, but rather that you must suffer in hope. When your wife and children ask what you're doing with the money, explain the situation to them and they will understand."

Another worker, not convinced, asked why CHF didn't have committees organized to deal with the various things that they were involved with in Haiti. Why the mismanagement? The spokesmen and Mme Nicole had no answer.

It was eleven o'clock. I went to find someone in the neighbourhood who was living in one of these CHF shelters. I found a local woman who had one. She told me that people had to say they liked the shelters because it was the only thing offered. But in reality, she said, people slept uneasily in them. They were plastic and robbers could enter them with a knife. If only they had been given the money that it cost to build them, she said, they would have been able to make themselves decent homes.

•••

It was getting late. I went to pick up Annie to go to the church to face the pastor. We went into a private room to talk.

He opened our little meeting with a prayer. He asked Annie what she thought about my idea to marry. Annie said that she was wholly in favour of it.

"Joegodson, you have done me much wrong. You are a young man in whom I had placed a lot of confidence. I am very disappointed."

I said, "But Pastor, I have chosen to marry Annie to do the right thing. I accept the error that I have made and we have found a response so that no one will suffer from it."

I had seen a number of youths leave the church when confronted with these circumstances. They knew the response they would receive in the church and they chose to simply absent themselves.

"Okay. Given the situation in this country, how are you going to support a family? Do you have a profession?"

Did this pastor have any faith? Any empathy? I had thought that he would be happy that I was acting in the interests of those concerned and the church. I thought I was tracing a path that he should have appreciated. Instead, his thoughts were purely materialist. How much money did I have? What kind of job did I have? He was not addressing any spiritual aspects of the marriage. I thought that was his job.

He continued, "What do you do for money?"

I was stumped because he knew that I was a furniture maker. But, to not be rude, I told him that. Then I told him that I had a project with a Canadian to write a book.

"A book?! A book about what?"

I responded, "About society and the economy and spirituality. About life in Haiti and our place in the world . . ."

"Okay," he cut me off with the hand gesture that people use to brush flies away from a plate of rice. "I know that you are a furniture maker. It's hard to find jobs now. Get in touch with some bosses and see if you can get some work. As you should know, there is an expert furniture maker in the church. He went to school to study. He has worked for me and is very competent. Sometimes, he has a lot of work and needs some help. Go to him and explain your problem. He's young like you. He should be able to understand. He might be able to help you prepare for the marriage. You'll need furniture."

It didn't seem that the pastor understood how furniture workers operated in Haiti. I did. The pastor was suggesting that I work for the furniture maker to make some money. I knew I would be paid enough to eat and no more. But as long as I was working for him, I would not have the time to make my own furniture. The pastor's advice would lead me to the worst of all worlds. Also, he spoke as if I was incompetent. I was burning inside but couldn't say anything. I was really much more talented than the guy he wanted me to work for.

There was no use in responding. This was not a conversation. He was issuing orders.

"Okay, I'll call the furniture maker and tell him that I'm sending you over." He took out his cellphone. "Hello, Gilles? I have Joegodson here. He needs some work. . . . Okay, then, I'll send him over to you. Okay, thanks."

Apparently I had nothing of any importance to say about my own life, about my own marriage. It seemed more like a funeral. But I, not the pastor, was going to have to live with these choices.

He closed his cell phone. "Okay. It's all set up then. That's it."

He meant "that's it" in the spirit of "you can leave now and follow my instructions." In fact, he told me that I should go over to see the furniture maker right away and get started. He said Annie should remain at the church while I went to get a job. I shouldn't waste a second. "That's it."

I left his office like a zombie. I walked down the stairs acting under the will of the pastor. What was the difference between my pastor and an *houngan*? What was the difference between the pastor and a *lwa* who controlled the soul of his victim? I was actually walking toward a *taptap* to go to see the furniture maker when, somehow, my own soul asked for re-entry into my body. "What am I doing?" I said to myself. "Who is in charge of my life?"

I went back to see Annie and pick up our plans together.

I thought about how long it would take me to build my furniture, plan the wedding, and find a place for us to live. We needed to set a date for the wedding. I decided I could get everything done by the first of October.

Now I could tell my father.

I went down to Simon. As usual, my dad was thinking about how our family might be able to get out of the mess we were all in. He was very anxious.

Each time that I opened my mouth to begin to tell Deland, I thought of all the problems that had come tumbling down on him since the earthquake. Christla, my little sister, was pregnant. None of us, perhaps not even Christla, knew who the father was. Roselèn, an even younger sister, had fallen into the same condition a couple of months later. Again, the father was unknown. Next, Suzy, Deland's niece, made it three. The moment that her boyfriend found out that she was pregnant, he kicked her out of his apartment. Deland took her in. So, under the roof of his half-collapsed two-room home were three pregnant girls with no prospect of marriage. Plus his other children. Then, thieves took advantage of the fact that the walls of his home had collapsed to steal some beautiful suits that he had been contracted to make. He was falling into depression. James, the eldest of his seven kids, had entered a *plasaj* with the woman who rented the second room in Deland's house. A *plasaj* is a common-law union. They had a young daughter together to go along with the tenant's other three children. Deland was disappointed in James as much as he was in the girls.

I feared that I could destroy Deland if I wasn't careful about how I told him the news. On the other hand, this news could uplift him. I knew that he looked to me to protect the reputation of our family. I wanted him to continue to believe in me. I wanted him to be happy.

"Father, there is a little problem, but not too big. I'm making the necessary preparations. The rings are already made. I am preparing the furniture. In other words, I'm getting married soon . . . well, the first of October . . . to be precise . . . because Annie is pregnant."

Dad was surprised. He took a while before saying a word. After a couple of minutes, he said, "Let God's will be done."

chapter twenty-nine

ONE DAY IN DELMAS 19, I had a surprise visit from Fédrik, who was sweaty and weary from his karate session. He spoke about the difficulties that he and Franchesca were having in the pigsty tent camp. He said the camp was rotten. People smoked marijuana. He couldn't stand that smell mixed with the lingering pig odour, coal burning, dust blowing, garbage piling, human excrement ...

Worse, there was an air of resignation about the camp, the soil, and the people that depressed him. But he had no means to move. Therefore, he had to find the means. He needed money!

Franchesca complained. Normally, people who smoke marijuana do so in private. But in the pigsty camp, they smoked openly. It was, she said, a sign that they had withdrawn from society. They were announcing that they didn't care anymore. Both Fédrik and Franchesca, wretched as they were, continued to see themselves as part of Haitian society. Their status in that society could hardly have been lower.

The pigsty camp was showing signs of developing into a *baz*. A *baz* is a group of people that withdraws from civil society to create a world unto itself. Maybe they just resist being oppressed by the bourgeoisie. But they can also enter into gangsterism. They can be kidnappers or thieves, for instance. The people are exceedingly poor and reject all social rules. They do not apologize to anyone for their criminal actions and they target everyone. But really, they steal from the poorest of the street merchants and kidnap local people who might have more affluent connections.

They depend on violence. The fear that they instill in others through terror protects them in the neighbourhoods where they live. People are obliged to pretend to accept their authority or else pay the consequences. But they do not endear themselves to their poorest neighbours who can fall victim to their schemes and their violence.

They used to visit my father from time to time in his tailoring shop. The youths would strike up a conversation, "How are you?" "How are things going?" All very innocuous. Then, they would tell my father that they were hungry. My father used to give them some money to buy food. They wouldn't overtly menace my father, but the consequences of not "paying" them were clear. It was sad, because my father really did share with people in the neighbourhood who were in need. He never needed to be threatened. In any case, his benevolence never saved him from being robbed from time to time by armed young men charging into his shop wearing masks to protect their identities.

Walking through Simon to visit my father one day several months after the earthquake, I saw a couple of boys grab what appeared to be a gold necklace from the neck of a young woman. They caused her considerable pain. She screamed for help. No one could do anything to stop the armed youths, who continued on their way normally, with the necklace in hand. That they didn't run was more disturbing than the theft. They, and others like them, were now so contemptuous of society that they felt no shame. Others noticed the same devolution. The gangs and *baz* were operating with more open contempt.

The members of a *baz* see themselves as revolutionaries; they are anything but. They accept the fundamentals of capitalist society. They are materialist and egoist. They seek all the trappings of status in our material world and want to outdo the bourgeoisie who use legal or untraceable forms of theft to accumulate wealth. The *baz* does not bother with the distinction. In private, neither do the rich. But they own so much of the culture that they can create fairy tales about their noble intentions and actions. Haitian films, like *La Pluie d'Espoir*, try to bury the reality of Haitian life under self-serving bourgeois myths. Otherwise, the *baz* and the bourgeoisie have much in common. Both use violence and both prey on the poor. Prey on the rich too, when possible. They are not looking to change society or the economy. They just want more. The gangsters live close to the violence that they create; the rich live up the mountain where the air is cool.

Fédrik told me that he was afraid for Franchesca. He knew these people. They were capable of rape. They also had no concerns about cutting through the tarps to pillage the few belongings of the poorest victims of the earthquake. Without walls to protect themselves and their possessions, Fédrik saw no escape from their lives in the pigsty.

While Fédrik was talking, my cousin Lorès from Bon Repos called. He told me about a friend who had a parcel of land in a place called Canaan. His friend was planning his marriage and could not afford a ring for his fiancée, so he had decided to sell his land. He invited me to come to see it, knowing that I too was planning my marriage and had no place to live.

I told Fédrik that I was going to see it. I would report back. If it was good for me, maybe it would be good for him too. I took a *taptap* to Bon Repos and my cousin Lorès and I carried on from there to Canaan. Interest in Canaan was exploding. The *taptap* drivers had begun to address the demand and had created a new route to Canaan. From all over the capital, people wanted to go to Canaan to explore the possibility of relocating there. In Bon Repos, there was a mad dash for each *taptap* headed toward Canaan. My cousin Lorès and I fought to get into one.

The area of Canaan, Corail, and Onaville had long been abandoned by Haitians. During the Lavalas period, Aristide had attempted to build a community there for civil servants. It was now called Onaville. The area was isolated, but there were sand and quarries that could be exploited. The development had a promising beginning. You can see from the superior construction that was completed — minimal though it was — the vision that he had had for the area. It appeared to be a good plan to relieve the overpopulation of the capital with its lack of infrastructure. The government paid for the construction. State employees paid for their homes through deductions from their salaries. The homes were designed to resist seismic activity. They were attractive and well-constructed. They did indeed survive the earthquake intact. The program ended, however, when Aristide was abducted in 2004.

Canaan was a deforested desert. Only scrub that could survive the intense heat grew there. Sometimes, religious people climbed to the tops of the mountains for celebrations and sacrifices. The remote mountaintops assured them of the isolation they sought. Others went there for religious fasts. No one ever considered living there. The religious who went to Canaan to fast, however, were obliged to build a rudimentary church in order to protect themselves from the heat.

Almost all the poor who were left homeless after the earthquake had been renters. Now, we wanted to own our own homes. The people who used to go to Canaan to pray now put up some tents. When others saw that a few people were going to live there, they started to come in numbers. Before long, there was a flood of people into this desert. They started to plant plants resistant to the heat, like papaya *mawon*, a kind of papaya that doesn't give fruit but that grows fast and protects the soil. Olive trees and *pwa kongo* also were growing and soon producing fruit. The problem was water. There were no wells or springs. In time, they would be built. Meanwhile, water would have to be purchased and carried some distance.

When it was clear that a large population was coming to Canaan, several people formed a committee to seek aid. NGOs do not give aid to individuals, but to organizations, so they decided to name themselves as representatives of the new inhabitants. Eventually, the committee would be recognized by the state. Each area of Canaan would create its own committee. They got badges to wear on their breasts. You could see how important they were by the way they acted. Others, like the friend of my cousin Lorès, started to mark out plots of land that they would then sell to people like me. They had no claim to the land except that they claimed the land. As the demand increased, they started to raise the prices. But they needed to demonstrate a presence to be able to claim possession of any property. Some people made themselves considerable sums of money by charging the earthquake victims for properties that they literally drew on the soil of Canaan.

Canaan is a mountainous deforested area. Below it is a large plain, the Plaine de Cul-de-Sac. It all appeared like a very hilly desert of rocks and brush. In the plain was a large area with rows of tents. That was Corail. A rich Haitian businessman, Aby Brun, wanted to establish some assembly factories in cooperation with a South Korean apparel multinational. In Creole, the words "Corail" (coral) and "Korea" sound very similar. As we approached Canaan, the *taptap* passengers said that Corail was poorly located. The plain was a natural pathway for the flow of water. When the heavy rains came, the plain would flood. I asked them why an NGO would go ahead with the project. They were supposed to be experts. Someone in the *taptap* snapped at me, "Experts in what?! Don't imagine that NGOs came here to help us."

I said, "They told us that they were responsible for the reconstruction."

Another passenger interjected, "Look. If they were experts, they wouldn't have needed anyone to tell them that this area is a ravine and a flood plain. You are going to see those tents replaced with permanent homes in the future. But those permanent homes will not last the first hurricane. Neither will their occupants. Some experts!"

A woman told me, "When money gets involved, people aren't logical. Those NGOs want to keep themselves in business. They depend on crises. If this project floods out, they'll just have another nice crisis to clean up."

While people were considering her argument, she continued, "It's up to Haitians to decide what they want. Where they want to live and how. Why are people who aren't going to live here and don't know us deciding where we should live and how?"

She had some clear ideas. "What's happening? Our misery is enriching a lot of people in other countries — that's what's happening. Why would they want that to change? Would they work to put themselves out of business? No! What careers would they take up afterwards?"

Another woman took up the argument, "You — you Haitian men — are like the NGOs. Even when you aren't available, you never let a pretty woman escape your notice. Instead, you make all kinds of promises, telling her that you will do this and that for her, provide her with all kinds of riches. You even make sure that your conscience doesn't intervene to spoil a good thing. Instead, you put your conscience aside to offer things that are not in the girl's interests and can even harm her."

As she finished, the *taptap* arrived at its final destination. The men looked at each other. Each one said, "I'm not like that. . . . That's not me. . . . She was exaggerating."

When she descended, she said, "No one ever claims responsibility for malice. But the moment that honours are being distributed, everyone is first in line."

As we started to go our separate ways, we saw that a number of people had already started to settle here. But they had used whatever materials were at hand: corrugated iron and cardboard, for instance. My cousin and I started to climb the hills. It was now noon and the sun took up all the sky and burned us little Haitians below. There were no kind trees to offer us a little shade. But we needed to keep going, having come this far.

When my cousin's friend saw that we were discouraged, he pointed ahead and said, "There, that's it. That's the property." Having a precise destination, he thought, would keep us from turning around. The mountains were high enough that we could have climbed them all afternoon.

So we kept going, parched and dusty. When we arrived at the piece of the mountain that he had claimed, we magically forgot the trouble that we had getting there. There was a steady breeze that countered the stifling heat of the sun. We stood on the crest of a hill overlooking the plain. In the distance we could see the sea that was thoughtfully sending us the gentle wind.

I looked down at Corail in the valley below with the warnings of the *taptap* passengers buzzing through my mind. Here, I would be far above the plain and protected from downpours and floods. This was rocky land while the plain was sitting on top of water. That was good news. Rocky soil is a natural protection against earthquakes. The rocks absorb the shock. At the same time, there were many crops and fruit trees that would thrive in this soil. Already I could see the pretty yellow blossoms of healthy tall kongo bean bushes that some pioneers had planted.

My heart had already chosen the plot of land. I now had to negotiate the price. I saw that he had made an effort to mark the four corners of his property with iron pickets. We agreed upon a price of 5,000 gourdes ($124 US).

The settlers were already reselling the properties that they had marked out for themselves to profit from the heightened demand. I was able to pay 3,000 gourdes ($74.50 US). He agreed to wait a month for the rest. I could see that he needed to sell it in order to buy his fiancée a ring, an important custom in Haitian marriages. Ironically, buying his property meant that I was going to have a difficult time affording a ring for Annie.

We had changed places. He now had a ring and no property. I had a property and no ring.

My cousin Lorès was happy to have helped me. He himself had not had the chance to buy a plot of land. When he had married, his brother-in-law let him build a couple of rooms on a sliver of land on his courtyard. He was not independent. Worse, he was persecuted by a *lwa rasyal*.

A *lwa rasyal* is a spirit that your ancestors served, sometimes generations in the past. Even if the family breaks off relations with the *lwa*, it can still find a host among other members of the family, including descendants. The person possessed may have no knowledge that his ancestors served the *lwa*. But the *lwa* knows. The *lwa* came to our country from Africa with the slaves. So, some *lwa rasyal* may trace their connection to our ancestors in Africa.

The mother of Lorès was my father's sister who had been possessed along with him in Saut d'Eau. Both had escaped the *lwa* when their mother Suzanne agreed to become Christian. But afterwards, the *lwa* sought out my cousin Lorès.

While preparing his marriage, Lorès had only enough money to finance the foundation of his two rooms. Things were not going well for him. He was rejected from all the jobs that he applied for. He started to think of himself as marked somehow. Sometimes, the *lwa* can plan their possessions carefully. They can make sure that their victim is in a precarious state. They can arrange his life so that he becomes insecure and unhappy and, therefore, more vulnerable to their machinations.

One night, Lorès dreamed that a man dressed all in black told him, "I know of all your troubles in finishing your house. Tomorrow morning, when you go to the foundation for your house, you will see a piece of paper. It will contain three numbers. Play those numbers in the lottery as much as possible with as much money as you have. You will win enough to finish your house." With that, the apparition disappeared.

The next day, Lorès did indeed find a paper with three numbers. He didn't play the numbers. Instead, he simply recounted the dream to some neighbours. They played the numbers and won the jackpot, just as the apparition had predicted.

The next night, he was visited by a serpent who spoke to him, saying, "I'm here to help you again. I want you to finish these two rooms. Tomorrow morning, next to the foundation, you will find a single sandal. Look for the size. Play that number and its reverse. If it is 06, then play that along with 60, and so on."

Lorès did see a sandal. Again, he told other people about the dream. They played it and won. Lorès did not play.

The *lwa* follow their prey to understand them. This *lwa* saw that Lorès was going to be a tough nut to crack. So, the following night, he visited Lorès in the form of a member of the family who had died long before. Nervously, the apparition told Lorès, "I am aware that you don't really know what you want. I have tried to find a way to help you escape your troubles. I am going to offer you a final chance. This time, it will be in Saut d'Eau, where you were born. Go there. Take a backpack. Go to a place called Govri on your mother's property. Hang the backpack from the orange tree there. Don't say anything to anyone. At midnight, go out to see what I have left you."

Lorès followed his instructions. He went to Saut d'Eau. There were not yet roads, so he had to take the mountain paths. When he arrived, he went directly to hang the sack and then went to his mother's house. At midnight, he was sleeping in his mother's house and he almost missed the rendezvous. The *lwa* appeared in the dream of a cousin of Lorès who was sleeping in the next room. He heard her talking in her sleep and awoke. Immediately, he remembered his rendezvous and went to Govri. Before he left, he told his mother where he was going. He went to see what the *lwa* had in mind, not to accept whatever it was. He knew what the *lwa* had done to his mother and his uncle, Deland. He knew the danger.

In the backpack hanging from the orange tree, he found bottles, handkerchiefs of various colours, a wand, two chachas, and money. Immediately, he set it on fire. Something began to move inside the burning backpack. Lorès felt a transformation. A kind of paranoia overcame him. His mother and other members of his family had followed him up to Govri to watch over him. When they saw that he was struggling with a *lwa*, they began to chant Christian hymns to undermine the *lwa*'s power. Then they took Lorès to his mother's house.

Back at his mother's house, the *lwa* seemed to be winning. The *lwa* feed upon the weaknesses of humans. Only a powerful faith can hope to defeat a determined *lwa*. The first evidence that Lorès was being taken over came when his grandmother, Suzanne, approached him. She wrongly judged that he was winning the battle until he kicked her harshly. Then he hit his sister in the stomach. Things were deteriorating quickly.

The others started to cry and scream. They had seen this before with Deland. It was the same *lwa*. The family had a choice: it could accept the situation and return to the *lwa* or renounce the *lwa* for good. The first option was inertia, the second required enormous strength of will. No weakness can exist in a spirit that chooses to fight the *lwa*. Neither choice was attractive. If you accept to serve the *lwa*, it will eventually destroy you. If you fight it, it will never leave you alone. It will persecute you, your family, and your descendants forever.

The family decided to fight. They took Lorès to live in a church in Bourdon in the capital. He never left the church for a moment for three months. Finally, the *lwa* left him for the time being. The *lwa* was not finished. Lorès lives with the knowledge that he is targeted.

―•―

When I arrived back in Delmas 19 from Canaan, I told Fédrik my good news. We made plans to go together to Canaan one month later to see if we could find a plot of land for him.

When the day arrived, Fédrik and Annie and I took a *taptap* to Canaan. Annie would see for the first time the plot I had purchased and Fédrik could explore the area.

Annie complained as we climbed the hill under the eternal sun, much as I had. But also like me, she had a change of heart when we reached the crest of the hill where we would build our home. The breeze was still blowing, diminishing the heat. She said, "Okay, I see. This is truly Canaan," pointing under our feet to the property that I had staked out. "This is the land of milk and honey, surrounded by desert."

Fédrik and I started to trace the perimeter with a pickaxe that I had borrowed from Jelo. We put up a little tent made out of plastic just to signal a human presence and intention. Meanwhile, Annie pulled out weeds. The perpetual breeze erased the terrible heat that we had felt while climbing the mountain. We had lucked into a natural air conditioning that would be a blessing in the future.

While we were working, the friend of Lorès arrived. I paid him the remaining 2,000 gourdes ($50 US) outstanding on the property. He said that he had one more plot of land close by that he needed to sell to have enough money for his marriage. We looked at it. I tried to negotiate for Fédrik. He said that he wanted 2,000 gourdes for it, but I talked him down to 1,000. I had only 500 left, which I gave to Fédrik. The balance was due in two weeks. He would have to get the second half from Franchesca to buy the property.

chapter thirty

MY MARRIAGE WAS OFFICIAL. Now I had to prepare for it. Normally, in my country, when parents enter into an agreement regarding the marriage of their children, things become very serious. Every minor problem becomes a droplet in a river that rages forward. Nothing can stop it. Calm comes only when it reaches the sea. I would reach the sea on 1 October. Until then, the river would rage.

Si ou pa pwason, ou pa dwe antre nan nas — if you aren't a fish, you shouldn't enter the net.

Once the date was set, everyone left the details up to me. They had to prepare their clothes and remember the date, but my head was exploding with all the things that I was responsible for. The problem was that I didn't have any money whatsoever.

Deland knew my state: no home, no money, no job, and no possessions. The news I brought him, however, reminded him of his own impotence. There was nothing he could do to help. My marriage made him feel worse about his own life. He looked for some way that he could be of help.

Deland said, "I will take care of making your marriage suit."

Although I knew that he couldn't work, his determination to do this touched me. He was weaker each day, but he assured himself that he would find the strength to succeed.

He had two potential fabrics: one grey and the other light chocolate. I chose the cafe-au-lait fabric.

He said that he and the mother of Annie would need to meet to discuss the marriage. Since Annie was still living in the home of her elder sister, I gave her 2,000 gourdes ($50 US) so that she could pay for the little celebration to mark the nuptials. Only her sister knew that the money had come from me. For me, it was a way to save the honour of my family. I wanted to encourage Annie's family to receive Dad and also to hide the fact that my sick father couldn't receive anyone in his little collapsed home in Simon.

Deland arrived at Annie's family with my brother James and a longtime friend who, like him, had lost her spouse in 1999. He bought two apples on the way to offer to Annie. The meeting began very well. All of Annie's family was impressed by the obvious fact that Deland was a poor but humble and decent man. It was through judging the quality of my father that they began to categorize me. Especially Annie's mother changed her attitude.

We prepared one table so that the two families could eat together. I took some pictures with my camera. I took this encounter to be a preview of the marriage.

I had taken three steps now toward the marriage. I had two months to prepare. Two main problems remained. We had no place to live and we had no furniture. Both problems needed to be resolved.

Mme Bolivar already understood the situation. She suggested that we take a room in her home after the marriage until we could find a place to settle. She knew that I had a plot of land in Canaan and that I intended to build our home there. That would be expensive and, as everyone knew, I had no way to begin building a home. I told her that I would reflect upon it. Now, I knew that at least I would have a room. But I had to make our furniture.

When I had been hospitalized in Lakou Trankilite, a brother from my church used to come to visit me every day. I asked him for his advice. He advised me that it would be best to keep a healthy distance from the family. Living with my in-laws, he cautioned me, was a minefield. We would be like children in their home. Moreover, our lives would be an open book. As I listened to him, I became more and more anxious. Better to suffer in silence in the present to ensure a decent future. I started to fear that, poor as I was, I might condemn my future family to the life of paupers. How could I avoid sinking my family into the same misery that my father and my neighbours in Simon knew? Which choice would lead me where? How was I to know?

Tout otan tèt ou poko koupe, espere met chapo — as long as your head isn't chopped off, you can hope to wear a hat.

He made a proposition. He said, "My uncle rents several rooms in Delmas 33. Each room goes for 24,000 gourdes ($603 US) a year. I could rent one to you for half the normal rate for a year. Even though you have the look of a youth, as soon as you marry, you will be categorized as a 'citizen.' You will have to fulfil your responsibilities. After a year, you may be in a position to take care of your family. Don't begin your marriage by demonstrating weakness. If you start by demonstrating independence, it will be easier for you to continue on that route. The first step should lead in the right direction."

Although I didn't have the money to rent the room even at the discounted rate he offered me, I agreed to his proposition. Somehow I would find the money in time. Now, I focused on the furniture.

I mulled over this new problem while staring blindly into the rubble of the main house that had collapsed on the grounds where I lived in Delmas 19. My initial idea to recuperate the big doors and cupboards and transform them seemed the best option. I had already begun the process the day that we were sure that Annie was pregnant — the day I told Jelo.

The old doors were going to open onto my new life. When I had recovered a decent quantity of wood from the wreckage, I sat down to take stock. I calculated that I would be able to build a china cabinet, a coiffure, a bed, and two night tables. I should have also considered crafting a dining room table and chairs. However, after I had been to see the little room in Delmas 33 where we would be living, I concluded that there was not enough space even for the three pieces.

First I disassembled the doors to recuperate the planks. Then I joined the planks together to trace the new furniture. Soon, I had traced the bed and two night tables, the coiffure, and the base of the china cabinet. For the upper part of the china cabinet, I would probably need to buy new planks. But the collapsed house had been very generous. Through its death, it was offering me new life.

Although the planks recovered were sometimes banged up, I had in my mind a way to build the new furniture so that it would appear even more expensive than the imported pieces that the Haitian bourgeoisie buys in the best stores in Petionville. Not only would my furniture be more attractive, but I would be able to build it to a much higher standard. The bourgeois look only for appearance. My furniture would be both beautiful and well crafted.

I didn't have good tools to continue the work. I had no electric tools, for example. But, then again, Delmas 19 had no reliable electricity. So, I used what I had: a handsaw, a plane, a few screwdrivers, a chisel, a hammer, a clamp, a drill press, and a coping saw. These were the essential tools to craft by hand all I wanted.

I wanted my furniture to speak. My philosophy teacher had recounted a story of Leonardo da Vinci. After he had completed his portrait of Moses, he struck the canvas, ordering the portrait, "Speak! Speak to people!" Me too, I always tried to infuse life into my creations so that they could speak for themselves. After my work as a craftsman was complete, they would then live on their own.

The pieces soon began to take on their life. Maybe because the banged-up wood was now considered worthless, I treated it with the greatest respect. I was able to recover some door frames that had remained more or less intact. I carefully took the nails out of them. I then took the plane and removed all of the parts that were scratched, crushed, or dented.

As the local people saw me taking the planks out of the rubble, they assumed first that I was going to use the wood for fuel. When they saw me caressing the planks, stroking them carefully with my plane and organizing them in a tidy pile, they started to say — not for the first time — that I had lost my mind. The same people who were now mocking me would someday congratulate me on this furniture.

I took some of the thicker planks. They had been a closet on the main floor that the doctor had used to store medicine. To protect the medicine, they had been made out of *madriye*, thicker than the other planks I recovered. I decided that they should be used for the bed, to make it stronger and more durable. I joined pieces together so that I could trace the design that I had in mind. I used a hand drill to connect the planks together with dowels. Then I glued and clamped them together and put them in the sun to dry. While they were drying, I started on the other pieces.

I took some pieces of plywood that I had recovered from a clothes closet to trace the coiffure. It was more complex. The two sides would close so that Annie could lock them. When unlocked, they opened up on each side. Each would have shelves where she could store perfumes and things. The doors had to be attractive whether opened or closed.

The next morning, I traced the form of the bed on the *madriye*. On the top of the headboard, I traced a heart in the wood. Then, I took another small piece of wood to trace an identical heart. I glued them together so that the heart would appear to have depth. I traced the form of the headboard into the wood, all to accentuate the heart at the centre. Then I took a piece of oak that I had recovered to trace the border of the bed. Oak is easier to sculpt. I would sculpt the artistic designs upon it, including the heart in the top centre and then, at the end, attach it to the headboard. Within that border of oak, I sculpted the words *Ouvres ton cœur à Jésus*, open your heart to Jesus. In the place of the word "heart" was the symbol I had drawn.

Next, I traced two night tables out of wood that I recovered from a buffet that had been crushed in the earthquake. It had once belonged to the mother of the old doctor and it had been of good quality. Now, I salvaged the parts that were not too badly deformed and prepared them for their next life as night tables. The main doors in the doctor's home had window panes of glass built into the centre. When parts of the house came down, some of the glass panes had remained intact. They were perfect for the sliding doors that I wanted to build into the night tables.

Now I traced the night tables with the coping saw. I made the tables with two levels. The top level was open so that we could place a lamp and other things that we would want close at hand. The bottom shelf would have the glass door. That way when our child started to crawl around, he or she would not be able to get into too much mischief. I used thick *madriye* to fashion four feet for each of the tables in the style of Louis XV.

For the china cabinet, I could recover only enough material from what was left of the rubble to make the base. A china is divided into two parts: a base with drawers and a display cabinet above. I divided the base into three parts. The middle section had three drawers and protruded about five centimetres from the two side sections that each had cupboard doors. Most chinas were built on one plane. Since mine had another dimension, it took on a special character that gave it, literally, depth.

I had to buy several planks of mahogany from some peasants to follow the same design in the display cabinet that I had built into the base. Someone who read the website that Paul had set up to keep people informed about my progress after the earthquake sent some money so that I could buy them. The display cabinet took a lot of work. I used the mahogany not only for the structure, but to sculpt attractive designs into the windows. I had to buy the glass for all three sides of the display cabinet. I was lucky that some of the small windows inside the doors had survived the earthquake. But all the other glass had been smashed. I needed to buy the glass shelves for inside the cabinet as well as three mirrors that I placed in the back. I bought some plywood to place behind them to protect them. I put a socket into the back of the china so that, if ever there was electricity all of the glass and mirrors would sparkle. Finally, my friend, who was an expert wood sculptor, wrote in mahogany, "Jesus love you." I placed that on the top of the china that was already more than two metres high. That way, my china cabinet could always speak to people. Well, maybe it was grammatically incorrect, but it meant well, much like my sculptor friend.

The sculptor was my old friend Molière who used to cook beans and rice for me when we were in primary school together in Site Limyè in Site Solèy. After the sixth grade, we went our different ways. But I had the good fortune to reconnect with him in Simon. He was working in the same shop that Deland had first sent me to as an apprentice furniture maker, where I was always hungry. Molière had become an expert wood sculptor.

We caught up with what had happened to us since our childhoods in Le Progrès school. He told me that he had become enchanted by the woodcarvings of a local artisan in Site Limyè. As is the case throughout Port-au-Prince, the artisans worked in the open because of the lack of infrastructure. A workshop is usually half indoors and half out, cobbled together out of sheet metal and spare boards. Molière often stopped to watch the sculptor carve life out of simple blocks of wood.

Molière was always timid. But one day he asked the craftsman if he would show him how to sculpt in wood. The man said no. Time and again, Molière asked the same artisan the same question and received the same answer. One day, for some reason, the artisan agreed. Molière began his apprenticeship as a woodcarver.

In 1998, Site Limyè prepared to celebrate the birthday of the parish priest, Père Volèm. The children were encouraged to present him with presents. Molière decided to sculpt the priest's name in mahogany so that it could stand upright on a desk. So impressed was the priest by the creation that he asked to meet with the artist. Molière was aflutter at the prospect of so much attention from an important person. The priest told him that he showed great talent. He offered to pay the fees so that Molière could learn a vocation.

"What would you like to learn?" the priest asked.

Molière was overwhelmed and thought of all the vocations considered acceptable for the boys of Site Solèy.

"Plumber," he said.

And so Molière entered the vocational school Saint Trinité where he learned the plumbing trade. After three years of hard work, he earned his license. He was a plumber. However, Port-au-Prince had few opportunities for plumbers. Those who worked were well connected within a small network that controlled the jobs. Moreover, Molière was the antithesis of a Haitian plumber. He is gentle, imaginative, and slight of build. Haitian plumbers cut quite a different figure.

In recounting his story, Molière thought about his response to Père Volèm. He asked me, "Why did I say plumber? I never wanted to be a plumber."

In fact, throughout his vocational training, he obsessed over his artistic creations. He continued to carve wood into imaginative shapes.

The priest had offered Molière a vocational scholarship on the basis of his obvious passion for sculpture. Molière had been too timid to admit that sculpture was his passion and was all he wanted to do. It didn't seem to be an acceptable answer and so he didn't dare offer it. Like most people, Molière answered according to what he thought people wanted to hear. But it was a lucky thing for me and my china cabinet that he reconnected with his love of woodcarving.

I was used to finishing my work with varnish. However, this time, I wanted to do something special, because I was secretly proud of the pieces that I had crafted. I wanted them to look special. When I received some money from another reader of our website, I went to see a friend who was an expert in decorating vehicles. For example, in Haiti, the *taptaps* are often beautifully painted in the most brilliant colours. I asked my friend to paint all of the pieces in a soft cream colour. He chose a durable paint.

The furniture had been built with every type of wood I could find: oak, mahogany, plywood, and pine. There would have been no way to varnish this mishmash of second-hand woods into coherence. However, the paint that my friend applied in layers married everything behind it in harmony. Finally, after a month of work, it was all finished. I had spent that month at peace when I was working on my furniture. When the stresses of my life were multiplying and my friends and family were confronting even more serious problems, I escaped into my work and allowed my imagination to calm me. The more confusing things became around me, the more at peace was my heart, as long as I could create.

chapter thirty-one

AS MY MARRIAGE APPROACHED, Deland was confined to bed. I didn't think that he would be able to participate. I continued my preparations for the marriage anyway. Deland, in bed, fought to see if he could control himself enough to attend. He went to a free clinic for help. The medicines they distribute are a gift to Haiti. They have expired or have been rejected for other reasons from the rich countries. They are fine for Haitians.

Deland was turning into a walking pharmacy of expired medicines — except that he could barely walk. How would he survive? *Sak vid pa kanpe* — an empty sack cannot stand. But whether horizontal or vertical, he was getting sicker and sicker.

When he arrived at the clinic, it was up to him to diagnose himself. "I feel hot, my head spins, my arms and legs are weak, it feels like my bones are breaking inside, and I have no appetite." The doctors never asked if he was allergic. They just gave him medicine for each separate symptom. "No appetite — take these; a fever — take these; weak — take these." They loaded him up with drugs. Innocently, he took them all. He didn't know what to do, and he believed the doctors did.

After a couple of weeks, as my marriage approached, he forced himself to sew my wedding suit. On the morning of my wedding day, 1 October, he sent my little brother Jean-Claude to deliver it to me. Jean-Claude told me that Deland wasn't well. He said that a nurse who lived down the street had been to see him. He was too weak to stand up. She went to buy three different serums for him and injected them to see if they would help him stand long enough to attend the wedding. I called him to see how he was doing.

"Father," I said, "Jean-Claude says you aren't well. Are you going to be able to come? This day is important for us."

He said, "My son, your old father is not well. Your soldier is in bed." That meant he was very ill.

"I'm taking some serums to see if I will be okay this afternoon. We'll see."

I answered, "Dad, this day is really important in my life. And your presence too. If you aren't there, it's like it doesn't even count for anything for me. You're the only person who can represent my family. You are my two parents at once."

"Okay, my son, we'll see. I think that maybe God will give me the strength. He will not leave me today."

Then I had to go to help Jelo who was also very sick. He was so unhappy that I was leaving his property — that I would no longer be living with him — that he became sick. I had to help him onto a bus so that he could go to Tiguav to recover in the mountains. Normally, he should have been helping me on my wedding day, but I understood his sadness. When he was getting on the bus, he handed me 1,500 gourdes ($37.74 US) so that I could buy some shoes. It was a miracle. Until that moment, I feared that I would be married in sandals. Now, I had the money to buy some decent *pèpè* shoes. Did I have the time?

Time is innocent. It keeps going, innocent of all the deadlines that are not going to be honoured. But no one would know that I had bought shoes on the way to the ceremony. Once they were on my feet, everyone would take them for granted.

While I was downtown, after putting Jelo on his bus, the hour was almost upon me. My cell phone wouldn't stop. Annie told me that she was now ready. Her sisters had helped prepare her. Where was I? I told her I was downtown. Already it was late. Both she and I knew that there could be traffic jams or that I could get on a *taptap* that broke down. I didn't tell her I hadn't yet bought any shoes. She was already anxious. "Oh! Hurry up!" she chided me.

I heard the frustration in her voice. I understood. Was I coming or not? Was this going to be a case of last-minute jitters? She wouldn't know until the last minute.

"Annie, I'm not going AWOL. Don't worry." I tried to calm her. I heard people laughing in the background. I understood that there was a team of Dieumercis waiting for me.

In the big market downtown, the merchants sell clothing in the section called La Guérite. There was a long row of booths for new clothing; other merchants sold *pèpè* on the ground next to them. As I walked down the line of booths, I was aware that every merchant — man and woman — was scrutinizing me to guess what I was seeking. Some started to call out to me, "Hey! You! Jeans — you want jeans? Sandals, mister? Look at these shirts!"

They targeted me as a potential client. I waved them off. When they became too aggressive, I had to avoid their eyes completely. If I had paid attention to everyone calling me, I would have been dizzy. I also had to be careful not to get too close to a merchant for fear of being physically pulled into a booth. These were professionals, and they were ruthless.

But when I knew that I was passing a shoe merchant, I had to take in the entire stock with one lightning glance. If I dwelt for even an instant on their merchandise, it would be over. I would be harangued by the merchants while Annie waited at the altar. If only I had dark sunglasses, like the smoked windshields of UN vehicles!

Finally, from afar, I saw some shoes. When I got to the merchant, I stopped, without betraying any interest. I was trying to keep out of the merchant's grip as long as possible. He literally grabbed me and pulled me into his booth. He put me on a little bench. He started to pour words of honey all over me until I was drenched. His flattery was taking up the few precious minutes I had left.

"Okay, okay, brother. That's enough. I don't have time. I want some shoes. And fast. Let me choose."

He said, "Okay, okay. Go ahead." But, as if he was terminally programmed to flatter and persuade, he started up immediately, "Here, look at these. These are made in Italy. Very good quality. And here, this is a good brand that would suit you perfectly."

I examined a few pairs. Each time I moved from one to another, he told me that the one I was examining at that particular moment was the best choice, better than all the others, the best of all his stock. At one point, I stopped the process, "Okay, this one is of superior quality to the one I was holding earlier," I said, summarizing his sales pitch. "So, I think I'd better go back to the inferior quality," I said, returning to the pair that we had passed by.

"Well, they're the same price," he said.

I chose a pair of brown shoes. In Creole, the word for "brown" is the same as for an uncivilized person. During the time of the French colony, slaves who escaped and fled to the mountains to live were said to be *mawon*. I waited for him to tell me that *mawon* was not a good colour for a wedding, given its connotations. Instead, he said, "Oh, *mawon*. That's a good colour for you. Perfect!"

They fit well. Now, for the price.

He started to negotiate. He started high. The merchant next to him overheard us. Normally, the merchants work together, even though they are in competition with each other. Once one is making a sale, the others can present themselves to bully the client in a number of ways. Maybe they share the part of the profit that was theatre.

"I have only 750 gourdes," I said. "If you take it, I'll buy them. If not, I'll go to another merchant."

"You have no conscience," said my merchant.

"I don't want to upset you. Maybe you'll find someone who can pay what you ask. I'll have to go elsewhere."

"Okay, okay," he softened. "Even though I'm losing money on the deal, I'll let you have them, but only because you'll come back here when you need something and you can pay a proper price."

I handed him the 750 gourdes. Immediately, I jumped onto a *taptap* to take me up to the courtyard where the wedding would take place in Delmas 33. The pastor had refused to wed us in the church because of the fact that Annie was pregnant.

I arrived with thirty minutes to spare. But I hadn't picked up the generator for the ceremony. So, I went to visit a church brother who owned a generator with which he made blended juices that he sold in the evenings. He loaned it to me as a favour. I carried it back and installed it for the ceremony. We needed it to play the music. The problem was that the noise of the generator mostly drowned out the music from the DVD player. Haitians are used to ignoring the noise of generators that pollute the atmosphere.

I still had twenty minutes. I bathed the parts of my body that would show: my face, hands, and hair — and also my feet that had picked up a lot of Haitian soil during the morning. For the first time, I put on the suit that my father had made me, with a coloured shirt and a cream tie.

I had a brown belt and, of course, brown shoes. For socks, I had a pair without heels or toes, but only my shoes and I would know that.

I wanted to stop the ceremony at one point to ask everyone to take off their shoes and show the state of their socks. I bet that, in the private space underneath their shoes, most would have been no better off than me.

When I was finished dressing, I started to sweat. It was extremely hot. In a few minutes, I looked like I had been dunked under water.

It was five minutes to four when the pastor arrived. The crowd assembled; brothers and sisters from our choir at the church, Fédrik and Franchesca, and Annie's family. Annie arrived in a white car. My father hadn't been able to get out of his bed and my family stayed with him. Some of the children went to borrow some chairs to fill up the courtyard. We put the four nicest ones in front of the pastor and covered them with a white sheet. They were for Annie and me and the witnesses, Mme Bolivar and the church brother who had rented me the room in Delmas 33.

After I had taken my place with the best man and Annie had walked down the aisle, I heard a *taptap* outside of the courtyard. My father had arrived. He was wearing a pèpè suit that couldn't hide the fact that there was little flesh left on his body. Some friends from Simon helped him onto a chair.

After the ceremony, everyone wanted to embrace and congratulate us. Deland hugged me and I felt his bones through the suit. I was both sad and proud to see him. Sad to see how the world had transformed him. He had worked so hard and with compassion to make a better world. That world had reduced him, a first-class tailor, to brittle bones inside of a second-hand suit. I could feel the heat of his body through the suit. I understood the strength it had taken for him to get here. It was heroic. He patted me on the back. He said, "We have won."

chapter thirty-two

IN THE NEIGHBOURHOOD OF PCS (Plaine de cul de sac) in Simon, where my family lived, there were many victims of the earthquake. Together with the neighbouring districts, the people of PCS formed committees to represent the interests of the victims. People chose those who were literate and most capable of dealing with the world outside of the poor districts. The committee members started to scour the streets to find help.

The victims in PCS chose my brother James as the person responsible for representing them and finding help. Choosing James, however, did not mean that they intended to submit to him. Instead, they remained aware and critical of everything that he attempted to do for them. Even inside a family, there are arguments and disagreements. Within the community of PCS, there were sometimes as many different opinions as people.

The local people wanted to see material changes in their miserable lives. If James could convince donors to supply tents, for instance, then they would be happy and praise him. If he asked for contributions to pay for his *taptap* rides to visit aid organizations, however, they complained. People wanted to delegate everything except the right to complain. When the committee was forming, it was hard to find people willing to participate. The moment that someone's name was put forward and he or she accepted the job, however, the people would start to complain. There were two positions available: critics and criticized. Almost everyone preferred the first category. Very few accepted the second.

I think it was preferable to remain in the crowd rather than to accept the responsibility of leading. The cost of accepting a role on the committee was high and the benefits small. There was never enough aid to fulfil the needs of the earthquake victims. Even when aid organizations helped, they gave only a percentage of what was needed. For instance, the committee members might find a humanitarian agency willing to supply the needs of a tent city in Simon. If there were two hundred people in the camp, then the organization would give enough for one hundred. Consequently, every bit of aid that the committee was able to find served to divide the victims. Those who were helped praised the committee; the others railed against its incompetence, fraudulence, or injustice. But the main problem was outside of the control of the committee.

Moreover, the changes that would have made a real difference were far beyond the competence of the committee. They would require revolutionary changes not only in Simon, but among everyone in Haiti and the rest of the world. The obstacles are overwhelming. And so people just want a free tent. That, they can understand.

In some districts, there were committees that worked wholly against the interests of the population that they represented. If the committee members were well-chosen to impress the international aid organizations (if they could speak some English and appear middle class), then they might be able to negotiate a donation for their camps. Once the donation was secured, however, they would sell it on the black market that was flourishing. The poorest victims would then have to buy the donations at an elevated price while their leaders pocketed the profits.

Chat boule nan dlo cho, li pè dlo fret — a cat that has been burned by hot water is then afraid of cold water.

People came to suspect that every committee was corrupt. It was assumed that the committee members were profiting from the misery of the victims who were suffering more. And that was often the case.

I remember one visit to Simon several months after the earthquake. There was a group of three boys whom I knew well. I had grown up with them. They called me and asked me to come and talk with them. They told me that they had devised a plot to profit from the situation. They said that many others had already tested it with success. They had invented an orphanage in Site Solèy, given it a name, an address, and a population. They had counterfeited the documents that verified its existence. They needed me to go with them to advocate for the imaginary orphans. They wanted me to present the project to an American pastor who had arrived in Delmas with a large amount of humanitarian aid: sacks of rice, beans, cooking oil, pasta, and so on. The pastor had already fallen for this scheme. Now, my old friends thought that they could succeed as long as they had the right front man. I could speak English and make a credible presentation, they figured. They told me that when we had the merchandise, we would separate it fairly among ourselves and sell it to the street merchants for resale.

The boys were not especially creative. If anything, they were well behind the curve. Everywhere in Port-au-Prince, the street merchants were selling the products that had come into the country as donations. The people who suffered were those who remained poor and were unable to buy it. If only the money had been put directly into their hands to buy the essentials, then the "aid" could have been sold on the market to help the street merchants in their businesses. Money would have circulated at the lowest levels of the Haitian economy. It would have remained there. When aid was given in the form of food staples and tents, the people were certain to remain poor.

I listened to the boys' proposition. I was surprised at their boldness. They weren't worried about being discovered. They were taking no special precautions. They approached me without fear, but with enthusiasm for the scheme that they had hatched.

I listened carefully. "You aren't afraid?"

"No way. This has already worked. Once we've finished with this one, we'll help you make up another charity so you can try it out yourself."

"But what will you do," I asked them, "if the donors tell you that they will visit the orphanage to see how things are going?"

The boys replied quickly, "No, no, no. Don't worry about that. They never follow up. The people who have already tried this have never had a visit. That's why we put the orphanage in the centre of Site Solèy. They won't go there. They will be afraid, not us.... We're doing them a favour. We're helping them get rid of their stuff quickly. Then they'll have more contracts since they are working so effectively. They'll be back all the sooner."

I said nothing. I was trying to find an exit from this conversation that was making me uncomfortable. If I made the wrong choice, then I could turn myself into a target. I was all the more disquieted by the presence of one of the brothers from my church. He knew me. I knew him. I knew that when I said no, he would be ashamed that he had said yes. This proposal that he and the others were making went against everything that we professed to stand for. But these guys weren't thugs or criminals or delinquents. They were good boys. Smart.

I had two choices. Say no and be a coward. Say yes and sell my soul.

They asked me, "You are afraid, aren't you?"

"No. I'm not afraid. . . . I just don't like to act without reflecting."

They bought that. "Okay. If you need to think about it, okay. You can think about it until tomorrow. We'll call you early. We're going to see him tomorrow morning at ten o'clock."

I had intended to spend the rest of the day in Simon, but I didn't want to see the guys from that group. I knew that I would say no, but I really didn't like either of the choices offered.

I told my father what the boys had proposed and that I wouldn't be cooperating with them. He was thankful to hear my choice. I excused myself, saying I didn't want to spend the day in Simon under these circumstances and that I would return soon for a proper visit.

When I returned to Delmas, I passed the rest of the day dreading their call the following morning. In order to allow my mind some peace, I decided to call them to officially withdraw from their scheme.

"Tomorrow, I have another rendezvous that is much more important. I'm sorry. I would have liked to participate, but it won't be possible." All lies!

I waited another week before returning to Simon. I really didn't want to know any more about their plan. My desire to avoid them was greater than my curiosity about the outcome of their scheme.

When I returned a week later, some of the boys saw me from a distance and waved. But they made no motion to approach me. I could see in their eyes a certain apprehension. I was neither friend nor foe. People like to know precisely where you stand. I was now an unknown entity in their eyes. It was better for everyone that we remain polite and distant now. But it was disappointing to have old friendships disappear into a kind of uneasy courtesy.

chapter thirty-three

ONE DAY IN OCTOBER, ten months after the earthquake, I was in Simon talking with my father and my brother, James. A few people came to speak to James. They told him that a meeting was taking place in the MINUSTAH base, the old ice factory, for all of the leaders of the local camps. James went to find out what was happening.

He soon returned to tell us that MINUSTAH was organizing a program for children between the ages of five and eighteen. Each camp should provide fifteen kids and three supervisors. The fifteen kids would be divided into three groups. Each supervisor would be responsible for five children. MINUSTAH would be giving the children courses in Portuguese, music, soccer, and theatre. Each supervisor would also participate in the course along with the children under his or her charge. The leader of each camp was also invited to participate in whichever of the four disciplines he or she chose.

He said that MINUSTAH would offer each child who participated a notebook, pencils, and a T-sheet to serve as a uniform. For the next meeting, the camp leaders were to return with the supervisors and the list of children who would participate. That meeting took place at four-thirty that afternoon. Even though James wasn't yet sure of the details of the program, he went around the camp to talk to the parents in their tents or *tikounouks* and to compile the list of participants from PCS. James recruited me first and then found two other supervisors.

I had plenty of reasons to be suspicious of MINUSTAH. Their headquarters, close to my father's home in Simon, was an old factory. When I was a child, it used to produce ice for the local people. Not only did we appreciate the ice, but some of us worked inside. Street merchants lined up before sunrise to buy big blocks of ice, two metres long. They then set up their blocks, covered by strips of wood to protect them from the sun, and chipped away pieces for their clients who would come by with thermos coolers to buy their day's supply. Other merchants came from farther away to return to their own neighbourhoods to sell ice in the same way. Many would have an agreement with a *taptap* driver to collect the ice first thing in the morning, before the *taptap* driver began his daily route.

The ice that the factory produced was invaluable. Especially for the poor, a block of ice could melt away the discomfort of living under the scorching heat of the Caribbean sun, compounded by dust and detritus, and without reliable electric current to run refrigerators or fans.

In February of 2004, President Aristide was forced out of the country. There were all sorts of rumours about whether he left, was forced out, or escaped. It was confusing. But when he was gone, there was no more ambiguity about who had control of the Presidential Palace. And it wasn't us in Site Solèy. Exactly who owned that palace was less clear.

After President Aristide was gone, the ice factory was shut down and the building taken over by MINUSTAH troops from the United Nations. It was a great disappointment. It seems that the owner of the factory arrived at an agreement with the United Nations to lease the factory. In my innocence, I said, "But surely, MINUSTAH will continue to make ice for us."

"On the contrary," my wiser neighbours replied. "They have not come to cool us down, but rather to heat up our neighbourhood. They will make trouble."

The factory was the most secure and sturdy building in our part of Simon, called PCS. Our neighbourhood was at the centre of a civil war between two gangs: Boston in Site Solèy on one side and Pele on the other. When the young people in Simon, like me, refused to take any side in the constant fighting, we were attacked by both sides. By putting the MINUSTAH troops in PCS, the authorities intended to control the population on all sides.

Marengwen ap vole ou pa konn mal ak femèl-while mosquitoes are flying, you can't tell male from female.

By that time, I was living nearby in Delmas 19. But when I visited Simon, I was used to seeing bullet cartridges lodged in the homes of old people who were neither criminals nor revolutionaries. It scared me. I thought that if old, harmless people were being targeted, then how would I escape the violence? From Delmas 19, we could hear the exchange of gunfire night and day. The people of Delmas were terrified of Site Solèy. Although they lived close by, they never visited Site Solèy and had developed strong prejudices against those of us from those miserable zones. When they found out that I was from Simon, they were often dumbfounded. They had judged me to be a man of peace. I couldn't be from Simon.

•●•

We went to the MINUSTAH base at four-thirty. Well-armed soldiers guarded the entrance as usual. All of the committee members of the PCS camp were waiting as scheduled, but the soldiers wouldn't let us enter. We were mixed up with the *kokorats* who always hung out at the gate, harassing the soldiers and begging for food. The soldiers couldn't distinguish all the types of Haitians that they saw before them. We were all frying under the same hot sun.

After a few minutes, the soldier in charge of this program appeared with a list in his hands. He spoke through a Haitian interpreter who announced the name of each camp from a list. The leader of each camp would be allowed entry into the base along with the supervisors. There were ten camps represented, which added up to forty people: the camp leader and three supervisors for each camp.

Entering the base, I saw on the ground floor half a dozen tanks and several military vehicles. Everything was marked "UN" and coloured pure white to remind us that it was the opposite of Haiti.

A soldier led us up to the second floor. We all thought along the same lines. We were the enemies of these soldiers and we had penetrated their fortress. We spoke freely together in Creole, knowing that the foreign soldiers were deaf to our language. We wondered if we were being led into a trap or whether we could spring one of our own. We joked, but there was a serious undertone to all of our imaginings. We could also see the unease in the soldiers. We were their enemy. The tanks were used against us. And now, we had penetrated. This building had once been ours. It had served us. We had relied upon it to supply us with ice. MINUSTAH had taken it from us and given only bullets and misery in return. They were ignorant of all that, of course.

We saw where they changed out of their uniforms when they returned from their missions of firing into our homes and killing our friends. Like Zakari. We saw a number of soldiers speaking to their families in Brazil through the computers. Some were downloading images of the poverty of our district from their digital cameras to send home. Others were eating at a table with plates piled with food. Some of us were really hungry. When those people saw the food before them, they started to fantasize that, after the meeting, they would be invited to take a seat at the table. They prayed that, after a short meeting, the MINUSTAH officials would suggest that we all retire to the dining table and eat for the rest of the evening. That would have been the best meeting of all time.

The sincere wish of every Haitian present was for the shortest meeting followed by the longest meal. The emptier the stomachs of the Haitians, the more full their minds with thoughts of rice, *sòs pwa nwa*, *pitimi*, goat meat, chicken, followed by gallons of cool fresh fruit juices sweetened with Haitian sugar: *chadek*, orange, lemon, sour cherry, pomegranate, poured over piles of ice.

The goal of MINUSTAH was also to keep the table full. However, it was MINUSTAH soldiers who profited from the bounty. There were no Haitians around the table, either in reality or in their mind's eye. There was no difference between desire and reality for MINUSTAH. For the Haitians, dreams were the opposite of reality.

The soldier had no idea that he awoke all the Haitians from their sweet and savoury dreams with his abrupt command, "Okay, let's get the meeting started."

Two MINUSTAH soldiers, a man and a woman, presented themselves before us. The woman translated from his Portuguese to French, leaving our Creole aside.

"Okay, maybe you don't know why you were brought here. We will explain why this meeting is very important for you. We want to gather together a number of children from different camps. We will give classes in music, soccer, theatre, and the Portuguese language. As we have already explained to the camp leaders, we need twenty kids from each camp, divided into four groups. Each group will have a Haitian supervisor to be responsible for them. The supervisor will be able to participate in the class also. The supervisor will be responsible for controlling and disciplining the children. If we have to travel to another area, then the supervisors will be responsible for the safety of the children. We want the supervisors to be strict. If not, they will need to be replaced. If a child misbehaves, we will expel both the child and the supervisor from the program. That's why the supervisors need to be responsible people."

Each group was scheduled for a different day. The supervisors were responsible for distributing the kits to their kids. The MINUSTAH soldiers then said that the meeting would end there. If there were any questions, we Haitians could now pose them.

I asked, "How much time have you set aside for these courses?"

They answered that the courses would last three months, to finish at the end of November.

I continued, "I am not an expert in music. But I understand that the subject is vast. Do you think that three months is a reasonable amount of time to impart even a basic knowledge of music? What kind of music will the students be learning? For instance, Haitians have their unique style of music called *konpa*. Will you teach that? Or will it be Brazilian music? Will there be instruments for the children? What kind of instruments?"

They said, "You say that you are not an expert, but clearly you have some musical knowledge. Our goal will be just to offer the students some basic principles. So, our lessons will not be based on any particular cultural style, but will impart what is common to all music."

Then they asked me if I had been assigned to a musical section. I replied that I had been asked to supervise a group that would learn Portuguese. So, they asked me why I was asking questions about the music instruction and not language.

"I am just starting with music. I have some questions for the language classes too."

Instruments were expensive. I wanted to find out if this was a serious school. I had a little cousin who studied music; she chose the violin. Also, my brother Jean-Claude had been learning to play the drums. I knew how difficult it was.

I wanted to ask my questions concerning the language classes, but they refused. They said that they wanted to let others pose their questions. That was dubious because no one else was signalling the intent to ask a question.

Another Haitian raised his hand tentatively. He said, "To follow up the questions that my colleague was asking . . . for language, in particular. You say that all of the courses will last the same length of time: three months. Because it is not possible to learn a language in three months, what method will you be using to teach the children to speak Portuguese? Languages cannot be taught without textbooks, especially a dictionary. We don't have the ability to buy these things. Even if we could afford them, it is hard to find them in our bookstores. In fact, it is hard to find a bookstore. Are you going to help us to find these materials to help propagate your language, Portuguese, in Haiti?"

He had learned from their treatment of me to ask a number of questions at once. His questions seemed to place the four feet of the two soldiers in one box. They looked at each other, the ceiling, the walls, the floor — everywhere except the eyes of the starving Haitians before them.

Finally, they were obliged to respond, "Your question is very important. You can't learn a language without textbooks any more than a soldier can go to war without a rifle. . . . After we start the classes, we will be able to see what resources might be available."

In other words, they had no idea what they were doing. Or maybe whatever they were planning wasn't what they were telling us.

All of this question-and-answer session was taking place in French, rather than our language: Creole. Most Haitians are uncomfortable in French, the language of our colonial masters. The female soldier was translating between French and Portuguese, the language of the soldiers.

While the female soldier was speaking, the other went to the table filled with plates of food. We Haitians watched with anticipation, no longer interested in what they were going to teach or how. Now, a much greater question pushed every other into irrelevance: what were we going to eat? What was the soldier going to collect from the table for us? Each large Haitian eye followed his every movement. They had memorized everything that was on that table. Each Haitian was preparing his or her own feast, choosing a chicken leg from one plate, savoury rice from another, vegetables of every colour and juicy texture. Then, they poured themselves a huge tumbler of fresh fruit juice trickling over a chunk of ice.

While they salivated, the soldier returned with a platter of little round cookies, inferior to those we buy from the street merchants. They were tiny, flavourless, and without any nutritive value. We poor Haitians would never serve such biscuits to our guests. We would be ashamed.

The soldier handed the platter to a Haitian in the front row who was supposed to serve himself and then pass it along. Then, the same soldier went back to the table and returned with another platter full of tiny plastic cups of orange juice. It wasn't natural juice. It tasted like chemicals were killing the orange. Anyway, after one gulp, the cup was empty. It couldn't have done too much damage.

When the soldier offered the platter to the hungriest of the Haitians among us, they looked at the cups, then at him, and declined his offer. The educational program and the food were the same: artificial, parsimonious, and unsatisfying.

Our feast was over. We were hungrier than when we arrived.

Next, the soldiers returned with the packets for the children. They gave each supervisor the kits to distribute to the kids in his or her group. The white plastic bags were marked "UNICEF." Inside were a ruler, a pen, a pencil and pencil sharpener, an eraser, and a small notebook. Everything was labelled UNICEF.

When everyone had the kits to distribute to the kids, the soldiers gave us the schedule for each discipline. With lots and lots of *blan* smiles, they showed us to the door. We left without understanding the motives behind MINUSTAH's sudden interest in the lives of us poor Haitians.

chapter thirty-four

IT WAS A TUESDAY IN OCTOBER, the day before before my kids would be going to MINUSTAH for the first time. I went down to Dad's place in Simon, to motivate my five students and also to find out how things had gone for the music group. My cousin Junette and my little brother Jean-Claude were both in the music group. Jean-Claude had chosen the drums and Junette, the violin.

I was talking with Deland as James arrived. James, in his role as leader, had spent the afternoon at MINUSTAH to see how the music session had gone. He handed me a t-shirt that MINUSTAH had provided as a uniform for all participants in the program, students and supervisors. It identified us all as accomplices of the enemy: "MINISTÉRIO DO ESPORTE" was written in bold black letters above a colourful "BRASIL." Below that was written, "UM PAIS DE TODOS" and finally, "GOUVERNO FEDERAL." On the back of the shirt, against a white background, was written "BRASIL" in bold letters.

As soon as he gave me the t-shirt, I wondered if I would be a marked man in Simon. But the MINUSTAH troops had not given us t-shirts that identified us as complicit with them. Instead, the shirts aligned us with Brazil. Brazil was not MINUSTAH, even if it had accepted the role of lead nation in the United Nations' force. Haitians were much more interested in Brazil as a soccer nation. Haitians are divided in their support for Argentina and Brazil, the two Latin American soccer powers. However, the Brazilians were not here in Haiti to play soccer. Maybe it was the subtext that was most important: "Brasil: um pais de todos" — Brazil: a country of everything. But it was not really honest to trade on Brazil's soccer image to promote the military occupation of Haiti. Soccer players had nothing to do with MINUSTAH. They don't carry guns. They don't fire on kids. Perhaps the Brazilian soldiers were ashamed of the reality of their actions, so they wanted instead to highlight their love of sport.

A few hours later, Junette and Jean-Claude returned from their first class.

I asked Junette, "How did the music class go?"

She grimaced. "Ah! It wasn't serious. They didn't have any instruments. I don't understand what they were writing on the blackboard. Maybe they know something about music and maybe they don't. The translator seemed to understand them. We couldn't make sense of the translator."

She said that the students didn't want to continue if the classes were going to be like that. They were a waste of time.

I interjected, "Maybe if you had instruments, it would be more challenging and interesting for you."

She said, "What instruments? They didn't tell us that we would have instruments. All we have is benches to sit on and some explanations that no one can understand. I don't know if the teachers understand what they are saying."

I asked by brother, Jean-Claude, if they had at least given him some drumsticks to tap on the benches.

He said, "No. I didn't even see a *tambou*. It was a waste."

I said, "Well, maybe your course is tougher than the others. They don't have instruments for you. Maybe they don't have much expertise either in music or teaching. . . . We'll see tomorrow how the language classes go."

I left them alone and went to motivate the kids under my charge. I spoke to their parents. They thanked me and said that they trusted their kids with me. The kids ranged in age from ten to fourteen years old. I asked them if they were enthusiastic about the upcoming class. They said they were excited about learning Portuguese. Maybe it could be useful for them in the future. I told them that they should be well behaved. They agreed.

At home that night, I prepared for the next day. I thought of how I would treat the children during the lessons. I took my role seriously. My reputation and that of my country were important to me. I would make sure that the children held themselves with dignity. Moreover, I would learn to speak Portuguese. My Dad thought that was great: "If you learn to speak Portuguese, you can teach us afterwards."

Walking home, I saw that people were noticing my new t-shirt. I decided that, the next morning, I would pack it in my backpack and change into it in Simon before taking the children to the school next to the military base where the classes were taking place.

•●•

The next morning, I took the kids to the school next to the MINUSTAH base. We met and joked around with the kids from the other camps who were waiting for the lessons to begin. We heard a big — and very loud — MINUSTAH vehicle arrive in the courtyard of the school. A bunch of soldiers descended with guns. They took up positions around the courtyard as if they were following a predetermined plan. The kids who had been joking together were stunned to see themselves suddenly surrounded by armed soldiers. The soldiers appeared to be there to protect the soldier-teachers from us.

Then the two soldiers whom I had met during the meeting in the military base appeared. As the female soldier-teacher prepared for the lesson, she was accompanied by a young Haitian man from Simon who had been engaged as translator. However, it was soon clear that he spoke very little Portuguese.

The female soldier-teacher began in French, "Do you know how to say hello in Portuguese?" she asked the class. "Portuguese is very similar to Spanish. In Spanish, you say Buenos Dios and in Portuguese, you say Boa Dia. And for Good Evening, you say Boa Noite."

She had everyone repeat Boa Dia and Boa Noite a number of times. Then she asked us how we would greet someone whom we were meeting for the first time. There were, among the students, a number of *kokorats*. They were used to hanging out at the gates of the MINUSTAH base in Simon to beg for food and to annoy the foreign soldiers. As a result, they had learned to speak Portuguese. A couple of them jumped up to answer, "Como você se chama? if it is a woman. If it's a man, Como você se chamo?"

The soldier-teacher forced a smile and told them they were correct. She was noticeably unenthusiastic to discover that the poorest and the dirtiest of the Haitians before her were already able to answer a question with more precision than it had been asked. I think she wanted Haitians to act like Haitians. She wanted to teach ignorant slum-dwellers. But the charm of the *kokorats* is that they aren't afraid of revealing what they don't know and what they do. They are innocent. She didn't like them; it was clear. They couldn't have cared less.

She had the students repeat the Portuguese greeting several times. Then she asked the students to pose any question they liked and she would translate it into Portuguese. We played that game until the session was over. It was clear that the teacher had prepared no class. If there were any grammatical rules in Portuguese, we would have to discover them on our own. This had been a parlour game, not a language class.

The class over, the soldier-teacher walked to the military vehicle and climbed aboard. Behind her, the armed soldiers mounted with their rifles drawn, surveying the courtyard as if they were a SWAT team on a deadly mission. Sixty Haitian students stood either terrified or dumbfounded until the troops drove away, invisible behind their dark-tinted windows.

After the MINUSTAH soldiers had left, some of the students went up to the *kokorats*. They were much more at ease with the *kokorats* than with the teacher-soldier. The class had whetted the appetites of the Haitians for the Portuguese language. They peppered the *kokorats* with questions: how would you say this, how would you say that? While the teacher-soldier had not appreciated the *kokorats* who illicitly understood Portuguese before the classes had begun, the Haitians wanted to exploit their knowledge.

The students who had come from the other districts wanted to know how the *kokorats* had learned Portuguese. The children from Simon already knew. "They are just *comida*. They hang out in front of the gates of the MINUSTAH base and beg. They learn Portuguese to talk to the soldiers."

Some students wondered why they were taking a formal class when the *kokorats*, or *comida*, had obviously found a more effective strategy to learn Portuguese. Meanwhile, they surrounded the *kokorats*, each with a question to ask and with a hundred in reserve. However, the *comida* had to get back to work in front of the gates of the MINUSTAH base.

Each of the supervisors had to return the children under his or her charge to their parents. The *comida* came from different groups, but all of the supervisors accepted that they were a separate case. We left them to resume their posts in front of the base, or anywhere else their spirits led them, and took the more domesticated children back to their families.

chapter thirty-five

ON THE MORNING AFTER MY WEDDING, I went to Simon to thank my father for coming to my marriage.

When I arrived, I saw him sitting on a bench with an intravenous in his arm. Next to him was a neighbour who was using his sewing machine.

I thanked him for coming to my wedding and for elevating me in the eyes of Annie's family. He said he was proud of me. And of himself for having made it.

I brought with me a piece of my wedding cake and a soft drink for him. He took the cake with two outstretched hands, as if it was sacred. When I handed it to him, he turned to his neighbour and said in a stern voice, "That is my son that God has raised in dignity. He has just married into a good family. No one would have believed it."

He gave a piece of the cake to his neighbour, sewing next to him. "Here, take this cake. This is a special blessed cake. You should eat it with respect. This is not just some cake that a *vakabon* bought on the street. This is an important cake."

When my sisters and brothers approached, he said, "I want to give it to Gloria. You others, I'm not giving you anything until you behave respectably, like your brother. You should try to follow in his footsteps."

My two little sisters had already shamed my father by going out with *vakabons*. They were both pregnant and neither could (nor would) say who the father was. They would both give birth within the month. They both decided it was best to leave us. James, too, who was living in a common-law union, was out of favour.

My father spoke to me, "My son, again, congratulations. Continue to live wisely and well. Now you should know that when I sent you from

Simon after your mother died, I had a plan for you. I knew that this area was going downhill. I saw that people were allowing themselves to be corrupted. Especially, I wanted to get you away from David and his family of sorcerers. I knew you would have troubles with your uncle. I knew. But I also knew that if you managed to surmount the difficulties, you would be stronger. Gold has to pass through the fire a number of times before it glistens. After I die, remember that you had a father who wanted you to be a great man."

When he said that, I was sad. He was speaking as if he would die. When he said "great" we both knew he meant "moral."

"Be good. Be respectful of everyone, of Jelo and your uncle in Delmas 33. And your friends that advise you. Keep yourself apart from this world that can lead you to despair. Pray to God to help you nurture a forgiving heart. Make God your father, because He will never abandon you."

He asked me to pray for his recovery. He said that, once he was well, we would look for ways to struggle for a better world together.

When he finished speaking, it was starting to get late. I said that I would encourage Annie and Mme Dieumerci to come to visit him.

― ● ―

A week later, Annie, her mother, and I returned to visit Deland. We brought some food with us. He started to rise. He was happy to see Mme Dieumerci. She reminded him of his own mother. They were both elderly merchant women with white hair. He had not been expecting company. He was ashamed of his broken-down house in a broken-down slum. But Mme Dieumerci was not judging him. In fact, she saw herself in the same boat. She was a poor peasant woman trying to assure the future for her children. Deland bought bread and an avocado to go along with the food that we brought. And we shared our humble feast together as one.

chapter thirty-six

ANNIE AND I WERE INSTALLED in our little room in Delmas 33. It measured three metres squared. We hadn't been able to pay any rent yet. There was not enough room for two bodies and the three pieces of furniture that I had built to celebrate our marriage and legitimate it in the eyes of the community. I had only enough money to finish the bed and the china. The coiffure remained behind in Delmas 19. I hope to someday reclaim it, finish it, and move it to a more permanent home.

One Monday morning, Annie was awakened by a disturbing dream. The fear did not subside with the sunrise and the activity all around us. So we decided to talk about it.

As she recounted the dream, she seemed to enter into it. She shook as she told me about the images that were too vivid and frightening to confront alone.

In the dream, Annie was the main character. She was suspicious of everybody except me. In front of her were the United Nations' troops. They were frightening. They drove enormous, impervious tanks. Which they do in reality. They were armed with huge machine guns. As they are. They dwarfed her, a defenceless, pregnant woman.

The troops were inhuman, anonymous behind dark glasses in the same manner that Duvalier's *tontons macoutes* had always presented themselves. These inhuman automatons separated the men from the women at gunpoint. Annie was corralled into the group of women, unable to communicate with the Haitian men. The MINUSTAH troops marched most of the men into confinement, behind an impenetrable wall. Others they led into forced labour. Annie said that it was like the colonial days and the Haitian men appeared to be slaves. When they were working, overseen by the armed troops, it was like the *corvée*, or forced labour, under the American occupation of 1915-34.

Annie saw me working under the surveillance of the lethally armed MINUSTAH troops. The work was exceedingly demanding physically. In the groups of Haitians, she identified someone who was our church brother in real life. He is exceptionally tall and strong. However, this powerful man was weakened to impotence by thirst. He asked for something to drink. If he did not drink, he would die.

From the other side of the barrier with the women, Annie was trying to get my attention. She wanted to tell me that our friend was in danger for his life. But I was too busy talking to everybody. I was asking how they felt. Were they going to accept these conditions or would they revolt? I was interviewing people about their situation while someone we cared for was expiring before her eyes! Annie was unable to make contact with me as I continued to "interview" people.

Then the lustful eyes of the MINUSTAH troops turned toward the Haitian women. They advanced on Annie and the others. The women were alone, separated from the men. Annie was terrified. Alone. Vulnerable. That's when she awoke in a sweat and fear that would not subside.

Once awake, she took stock of her actual situation. She was seven months pregnant. Her country was occupied by people with no knowledge or interest in its history. I couldn't find a way to make a decent life. Our lives seemed to depend on the capricious self-interest of people who only saw what they could get out of us.

In the real world, our classes with MINUSTAH had been going along for three weeks. That day, we had our first hint of the motivations of MINUSTAH in organizing the courses. A different soldier arrived that day to tell us that the following week, all of the groups would unite to learn a song that most of us already knew: "We Are the World" by Michael Jackson. He told us that this would be a very serious undertaking. We would be singing this song in the main MINUSTAH base in Tabarre during a big ceremony that would take place on a Wednesday during the first week of December.

"You have to understand how big this celebration is going to be," the officer assured us. "This ceremony has a huge importance for us. This is not just any ceremony. Do not underestimate this event where you will be singing. It is about our very presence and reputation here in Haiti."

He continued on like that, trying to impress us with how important the event would be to him. He was so insistent that we saw that he was trying to instill fear in us. We should be in as much awe as he was in the face of this event that meant nothing to any of us.

He was an officer. He had been trained to project authority. His job was to erase doubt and to discourage questions. It was a performance that needed an audience properly conditioned. He spoke in Portuguese and a young Haitian translated his words into Creole. At least, as far as we knew.

"This is not an event for any one country. It is for the United Nations. Many great countries will be represented during this big ceremony. Certain soldiers will be honoured with medals. We will give you medals also. That is why you will learn how to sing this song well, so as not to bring shame upon Haiti. You will be representing Haiti. If you want Haiti to have a good reputation, you should remain polite and respectful."

Of course, what he was asking us was that we show to the world the image of Haiti that his MINUSTAH troops had been sent to assure. The children would be the proof that the Haitian poor had been pacified. The rebels beaten. The resistance quashed. All that remained were quiet, docile, desperate people ready to pay homage to the great countries that he spoke of, the ones that wanted poor little Haitians to submit to their will. And, personally, he would surely take much credit for the pacification. His career would be assured along with our submission . . . and our misery.

"If the supervisors cannot perform their jobs, they will immediately be replaced. Any child who does not behave himself properly during the rehearsals will be expelled from the classes. We have a list of all the participants. If your name is stricken, then you will not be able to return."

Hearing this, the students were motivated to participate. Especially when they heard that they would be awarded medals in recognition for their efforts, they lit up.

"Next week, all the groups from all of the disciplines should meet here on Tuesday at five o'clock for the rehearsal. If anyone misses even one rehearsal session, then he or she will be excluded. Absenteeism will not be tolerated.... Okay. We will end there. You should begin to think about this ceremony and decide if you will participate or not."

I kept going over the officer's promise of medals for everyone. What kind of medals would they be giving us? As it turned out, everyone was wondering the same thing. For that was the only material benefit that we could see in this ceremony. Everything else that he said was meaningless. Moreover, after three weeks, we had all judged that the courses were a total waste of time. They were a pretext. Until now, we hadn't know what they were a pretext for. Now, MINUSTAH was laying another card on the table. We were slowly understanding. But we also understood that this officer had put his reputation in our hands. And he was scared.

MINUSTAH and UNICEF were united in this plot to demonstrate to the world how much progress they were making among the Haitian savages. The simulacrum of education would be followed by the presentation of medals. But medals for what? Who wanted to give us medals?

— • —

The following Tuesday, I picked up the kids in Simon for the first rehearsal. We wondered if MINUSTAH would now start spending its money on the rehearsals. If this ceremony was to be as big as the commandant said, then surely there would be a significant budget. Maybe now there would be instruments and even an orchestra. Maybe, this time, we would eat. If we were to be bought off to present a calm and non-menacing image of Haiti, it would be better to feed us first.

All of the kids arrived on time at the school. They were ready and waiting for MINUSTAH. A few minutes later, we heard the sound of a tank approaching. Haitians don't like that sound. We thought that maybe they were using the tank to bring the instruments, since in our minds they would have been considerable. Instead, only two soldiers descended from the tank with automatic rifles drawn and ready for action. The third man to descend was the officer who had explained the upcoming ceremony to us. Instead of a rifle, he carried a guitar. A fourth soldier, the female soldier-teacher we knew, followed him with a laptop.

We continued to stare at the tank door, expecting to see the rest of the orchestra descend. A final robust soldier appeared with a rifle, closed the door, and took up his position as humourless guard, rifle drawn and menacing.

The officer with the guitar called us to attention. He said, "We will not be singing the Michael Jackson version of the song, but the one that a number of stars recorded after the earthquake. I will need several people to sing the main part. The youngest children will then sing the chorus. How many of you already know this song?"

A few people already knew the song, including one of the *kokorats*. Others knew it, but were uncertain of many of the words. Even those who could sing it did not understand the meaning of the English lyrics. But the officer had only one copy of the lyrics on a sheet of paper that he held in his hand.

He asked for the attention of the children as he began to strum his guitar and sing "We Are the World."

He told the children, through the translator, to repeat each line after him. However, he sang with a thick Portuguese accent. His version sounded like nothing that any of us had ever heard. It was not clear that he was singing English. To repeat after him meant to reproduce meaningless garble.

Happily, as the officer strummed the guitar, the kids who knew some of the words sang them while the others made sounds approximating English, but in keeping with the melody. Since the officer's linguistic skills were undeveloped, he couldn't distinguish the real English from the fake. After the kids had got to the end of a stanza, he congratulated them on their mastery of English. However, it was only English to those who couldn't speak the language.

A few of us could see the farce that was playing out before us. The officer had already threatened us with extinction if we were uncooperative. At the same time, the officer apparently believed that he could speak and understand English. All of the evidence before us belied those claims. If the officer said that the children were singing in English, then the children were singing in English. Some of us began to exchange glances of recognition. The officer was digging his own grave with arrogance. Visions of the international ceremony in Tabarre flashed through my mind. I saw an audience of dignitaries from the United Nations and "the great countries" listening to a Haitian choir sing "We Are the World" in no language. The officer would then turn with pride to the officials, expecting to be congratulated.

I stood quietly while the choir sang incomprehensible sounds. The only part of the song that I knew was a part of the chorus. The officer soon took note of my silence and shot a threatening look in my direction. I was already marked as a rebel. So, when the chorus arrived, I was able to sing a few words. Then, I continued, filling the melody with the Portuguese sounds that were passing for English. The officer brightened up and shot me a thumbs-up.

I fought against the urge to laugh. The fact that this was no laughing matter only made it funnier. I was a supervisor and was supposed to set an example for the children. So if I fell to the ground in hysterical laughter, I wondered if they would shoot me on the spot. The soldiers already had their guns drawn. That, too, made we want to laugh.

For the children, the whole episode was just a game. They didn't know what was going on. They just closed their eyes and repeated the sounds that the officer was making. Since that seemed to satisfy him, they carried on.

Finally, the officer stopped playing and spoke. Unfortunately, he did not tell everyone that we would now break for lunch. Instead, he said, "Okay, you have got a good sense of the melody. Now, you are going to work with the computer. The music for this song is recorded on the computer. Not only the guitar, but all kinds of instruments are recorded."

He opened up a laptop. He started to play the music.

The officer wanted the children to listen to the computer; however the sound was very weak. Only those who could put their ears directly against the speakers could hear.

The song on the computer was not the same version as the officer had been singing. As the students listened to the computer, the officer told them that he was changing some of the words. At the end of the song, he had decided that the kids would sing, "*Ayiti, Ayiti.*" However, he pronounced *Ayiti*, the name of our country, Ayichi. The children followed his instructions and repeated after him, "Ayichi, Ayichi." That is how they would pronounce the name of their own country before the dignitaries of the United Nations at the famous ceremony: Ayichi. That was what they were told to sing. That's what they sang.

He told everybody that, the following week, the rehearsal would take place at the big MINUSTAH base in Tabarre. Later, when I took the kids home, I told them about the change in location the next week. MINUSTAH would provide two buses that would take the kids to Tabarre. For the rest of week, we thought about the trip to Tabarre. We were getting closer to our medals. But, the *kokorats* told us that the base in Tabarre was much better supplied with food. They used to wait outside that base to get the best handouts. Maybe our dream would come true and we would eat like the soldiers.

chapter thirty-seven

A COUPLE OF WEEKS AFTER MY WEDDING, my father called me to tell me that he was feeling worse. He was going to try to go to Gheskio, a large medical clinic downtown. The hospital treats tuberculosis, malaria, typhus, and AIDS.

At Gheskio, the staff gave him a number of exams. They told him to return in three days for the results.

The diagnosis was not good. They said that his body was fighting typhus and malaria and they were winning. He was lucky to be alive. They gave him some pills — very powerful medicine — and sent him home in the afternoon.

James called to tell me what was happening. He said that the doctor told him to eat well before taking the medicine. It's easier to tell a Haitian to take medicine on a full stomach than to actually fill the stomach. Anyway, after eating what he could, Dad took two pills. He began to sweat immediately. His face started to alter, as if he was a different person. You could hardly recognize him. He called James a devil! He spoke loudly and incessantly. He spoke to everyone with contempt, even his closest friends who came to use his sewing machine.

Early the next morning, I went down to Simon. He spoke calmly with me, as usual. He was reading his Bible. I prayed with him. We spoke about my website. "Excellent, my son. Keep at it," he encouraged me. I spoke to him about a project that Paul and I were developing for transforming *pèpè* into new garments for sale. I wanted his advice as a tailor. He said that it was possible. "Good, good thinking," he said, fully lucid.

Since I saw that he was okay, I left him. I was starting to doubt my brother James.

That afternoon, when he took his medicine, Deland reverted to the maniac who frightened the neighbours. James called me again. Same story.

I decided to go back the following day. But since Annie was in our room in Delmas 33, I didn't want to leave her alone all day long. I was obliged to leave Simon and Dad — who seemed fine — at noon to return to Annie. No sooner had I walked in the room than James was on the phone. My father was acting crazy again.

We started to wonder if my presence had something to do with my father's state of mind. There were two factors that were in constant conjunction: the medicine and my presence or absence. Which was the cause of my father's outbursts?

"Okay, tomorrow, I will come in the morning and stay until he has taken his medicine. Then we'll know better what's happening," I said.

The next day, I stopped to buy some fruit and sugar from the street merchants to make Deland some juices. I bought oranges, chadeks, sour cherries, and his favourite, lemons.

I arrived and, as usual, my father was sitting calmly on a bench. He was happy as ever to see me. He asked me where I had found the money to buy fruit. I answered that that wasn't important. If I could buy his health, I would. What was important was that he get better. Some nice juices couldn't hurt. As I prepared the juices, he spoke about whatever came into his mind.

"We have arrived in a world where money is more important than the work that people do. I have seen this sickness overtake our neighbours. They value money so much that they steal it from those who work. Work is no longer of any interest to them. It is like the owners of the factories who hated work and the workers, but took all the money that we made for them. *Bourik travay pou chwal galonnen.*" This means, "the donkey works so that the horse can prance."

He was quiet, lost in his past again. "The greatest mistake of my life was thinking that the *lwa* could bring happiness. In my youth, I accepted their authority and their promises. As an adult, I thought that having money would make me a man. But if I had stayed in Saut d'Eau, the land would have nourished me and the thieves and bosses would never have targeted me."

After this lament, he said, "It's time to take my medicine." He explained to me that he was uneasy about taking it. The doctors had explained it was strong medicine. He had to follow their instructions. But he didn't want to.

"Try anyway, Dad," I said. "If things don't go well, then we'll go back to the doctors and see if there is a better treatment."

He went through the process of taking the pills. He put each one separately on his tongue and then washed it down with a gulp of water.

After thirty minutes, he said that he wasn't feeling well. I asked him to lie down for awhile. Maybe he would feel better. While he was lying down, he started to look from side to side suspiciously. Then he addressed no one in particular, "Why have you come here?! Didn't I tell you that I'm not your friend? In the name of Jesus, leave! Leave!"

I didn't know what Deland was seeing or whom he was talking to. He had told me that when he takes the pills, even little children appear huge and menacing. Everyone becomes his enemy. So I kept the children away. He could react in a way that was outside of his normal nature.

He jumped up from the carpet that he was lying on as if he suddenly had strength. I went to him to see if he would accept my presence. I offered him a glass of the juice that I had prepared.

"No," he said sternly. "I haven't yet received the order."

Then he started to repeat a phrase over and over again: "If Jesus is alive, the soul of Deland is alive."

I tried to force him to take the juice. He resisted, saying, "Yes, I see you. This conspiracy is not going to work."

For three hours he spoke without stopping. Given the weakness of his body, it was amazing. From time to time, his voice diminished in strength. He rasped as his vocal cords gave way. But then he would start up again. Throughout this harangue, he connected with no one around him. He continued to speak to people and things only he could see.

It was hard to accept that my father was treating me like an enemy. Sometimes, some spectators came by to watch. They did nothing to help. They stood as if they were enjoying a free show, almost enjoying the fall of their neighbour.

I thought about the time that he lost his sanity in Saut d'Eau. I thought he was reliving it. As I couldn't approach him, and to make the spectators go away, I simply prayed that he might fall asleep and recover his wits and some strength.

Finally, he was overtaken by sleep. He slept for about an hour. I imagined he would be hungry. He was so visibly weak; his outburst must have sapped all his remaining strength.

He opened his eyes, "Oh, are you still here, Joegodson?" He spoke calmly, taking our conversation up from before he had taken the pills.

He ate and drank the fruit juices. I was so relieved to see him in control of himself again.

While we were speaking, my cousin Lorès called me from Bon Repos. Deland was his godfather. Lorès suggested that we move Deland to live with him while he recovered. We would need to bring him back to Gheskio medical clinic from time to time. But otherwise, we thought that Bon Repos might be a good idea. Simon was a loud and aggressive district. My father was responding to every noise. It was logical that Bon Repos might offer a good rest.

Since he was not far away at that moment, Lorès came to Simon to speak with Deland.

"What ill wind has blown you here?" he said to Lorès. My father would never speak to people in disrespect, even as a joke, so we knew that the medicine was still affecting him.

"What would you think about coming up to Bon Repos, godfather? It might be quieter and calmer for you."

"No, I have not yet received the order. When the order comes through, I'll let you know."

"Okay," said Lorès. "I'll be waiting for you."

When Lorès had left, my father started to talk again at the top of his lungs. Everyone who passed saw. Those who were surprised asked how long he had been this sick. We couldn't say. Deland kept his problems to himself so that we didn't know when he had first started to be this ill.

One of Deland's church sisters who had been particularly friendly with him approached to say that we couldn't leave him in this condition. She suggested that we take him to Ste Catherine Hospital. We agreed and she went to negotiate with a *taptap* driver to take him there.

When she returned with the rented *taptap*, my father said that he had not received the order to move from where he was. She asked some of the local boys to help get Deland into the *taptap*. Deland resisted.

The local young men had to wrestle with him to finally get him into the *taptap*. Although he put up a good fight, they succeeded in the end. They entered the back of the *taptap* with him and held him firmly. Throughout the entire trip, he continued to yell with all his diminished strength. Everyone along the route was drawn to the sight.

When we arrived at Ste Catherine's, someone jumped down from the *taptap* to get the security guard to open the gate. A doctor came to the gate and, upon hearing Deland's voice on the other side, said, "No, we don't take this kind of case. He'll have to go elsewhere."

By "this kind of case," the doctor meant to tell us that we should take him to an *houngan*. Deland's church sister said that it was just a fever that Deland had come down with that day. The doctor relented. We went inside, with my father talking incessantly.

It was already late. In that part of Site Solèy, it is a bad idea to be out at night. Moreover, I had left Annie alone. Deland's friend and her fiancé volunteered to sleep in the hospital with him. I felt I should get home quickly to avoid the insecurity everywhere. I was relieved, because the friend was a nurse and would be more effective than me in caring for him.

chapter thirty-eight

WE WERE LOOKING FORWARD TO Tuesday and our expedition. When the day came, we united as usual at the school in Simon. A Haitian was there to make a list of the names of all the students and supervisors. Then, he told us to go over to the MINUSTAH base close by. There, we saw waiting for us two white buses with UN markings, their windshields tinted black. The officer was also waiting. He told us that we were now entering a new stage in our preparations. We would now be rehearsing in the very place where the ceremony would take place in December. The children should not make any noise. Everyone would be under surveillance to earn the right to participate.

We got into the buses. Another MINUSTAH vehicle filled with the armed soldiers we were used to seeing around us took the lead. Inside our buses, armed soldiers took the front seats. Prisoners of war are probably transported like that.

For the first time, I entered the main military base in Tabarre, next to the new American embassy. It was as though we were crossing the Haitian border with Brazil. There were rows and rows of buildings. The buildings of each member nation of MINUSTAH were separated by fencing: Brazil, Nepal, Ecuador, Chile, and so on. Maybe they were all telling themselves that they were here in Haiti protecting their national interests. What kind of arguments were they each using to convince their citizens that they should come to Haiti? To do what exactly?

The bus had to drive for several minutes inside the base before we arrived at our place inside the Brazilian section, far larger than the other member nations of MINUSTAH. On the buses, we started to understand that we were in enemy territory. Some of the Haitians wondered if we were part of a plot to inject us with cholera and then send us out into Port-au-Prince again. Some suggested that we would, after all, be offered something to eat, but that the food would be tainted with cholera.

We dismounted the buses two by two. They took us to the enormous square where the ceremony would take place. Hundreds of houses could have occupied that space: not the houses that NGOs were offering, but concrete houses according to Haitian tastes.

Several acres were asphalted for the soldiers' exercises. There was a podium and a long area with metal chairs for spectators. Thousands of soldiers would be able to stand at attention in front of the podium. In the centre of the asphalted area was a huge metal pole with a big screen for projecting images.

The officer, accompanied by some soldiers, explained to us how the ceremony would take place. The boys and girls each separated into two groups to make four lines: two lines of boys and two of girls. Each line was organized from the shortest to the tallest. Then we learned how to organize ourselves into a half circle, again with the shortest people in the front and the tallest in the back. Then they taught us how we would undo the semicircle and leave the place in an orderly manner once our part in the ceremony was over. When we had rehearsed these actions, they took us to the actual spot in the square where we would sing our song.

We had just arrived on the square when I saw that one of the little boys appeared anxious. I went to him to see what was wrong. Normally, Haitians relieve their bladders in the open. The fact that there are no public toilets makes this a necessity and everyone accepts it. Here, inside the MINUSTAH base, the boy sensed that the same Haitian rules didn't apply. But neither did he know what to do. And so he became frightened. I went to a soldier and asked where the little boy might pee-pee. The soldier asked how many kids needed to pee-pee. The sixty kids said they all needed to go. Either they all actually did or else they didn't want to miss the chance to see a MINUSTAH toilet.

The soldier showed them the way. All the kids ran, each wanting to get to the toilets first so that they would not have to wait in line. The officer in charge watched in shock. Suddenly, he worried that his well-behaved little Haitians could be undone by a simple call of nature. The officer spoke to the interpreter who called to the children for order. "Don't you remember what the officer told you back in Simon? Behave yourselves! Calm down! Slowly!"

When the boys arrived at their toilets, another soldier pointed them to the urinals. They made two lines, but only one boy was allowed to use the urinal at a time. The others waited their turn to shoot themselves towards the urinal. After everyone had relieved himself, we joined the girls, who had returned from their toilet, to continue the rehearsal. We met three Haitians who worked inside the military base as interpreters and spies. Their job was to help MINUSTAH find their targets and to explain the local terrain for them. These three would join the officer and the *kokorat* as the core of the chorus. They were paid by MINUSTAH and had already demonstrated their loyalty to their paycheques. The officer, clearly, wanted to be surrounded by people that posed no threat.

It was getting late. When we returned to rehearse the song in the place where we would be presenting it, we shared the square with thousands of MINUSTAH soldiers going through their drills. They too were rehearsing for the ceremony that would take place the following week.

We were occupying the part of the square where we would be singing. It was in front of where the dignitaries would be sitting. The soldiers carried out their drills imagining that they were presenting themselves to those officials from the United Nations and "the great nations." As a result, they seemed today to be performing for us, the little group of little Haitians singing "We Are the World."

Groups of soldiers followed geometric patterns, coming together and separating according to a logic that only they understood. We started to feel dizzy watching them. As their drill proceeded, they marched along in a never-ending row about a dozen soldiers wide. Their feet raised and fell in unison, like a nasty millipede. From time to time, they turned abruptly and in unison to stare at us in defiance, all traces of friendliness absent. Their faces were dangerously blank. But it was hard, for all the seriousness they intended to project, to not see them as little plastic soldiers being manipulated by some ill-willed child. They slammed their feet on the asphalt with such force that we felt the earth move under us.

I thought of Dessalines sleeping below them. Two hundred years earlier, he had declared that Haitian soil was for Haitians. Could he hear this assault on his beloved country? It was as if each marching step was a new challenge to Dessalines, reminding him that Haiti did not belong to Haitians. And the violence of the marching, the intense pounding of the ground, told Dessalines that not only was his country occupied, but the occupiers would treat it in any way they chose.

The strange thing was that this great march past, in perfect unison and organized violence, seemed to be directed at us little Haitians, dwarfed by the size of the space. Our little song, a sentimental ode to world peace and unity, was completely drowned out by the feet smashing Dessalines's soil.

Was there, among these thousands of foreign soldiers, one who knew even the name of Dessalines? What brought them from their own poor countries to our Haiti? If they knew history, they would have been ashamed to treat our soil like this. They would be quietly and cautiously placing each foot on the ground so as not to dishonour Dessalines and his descendants. Instead, they were staring at us in ignorant defiance.

We were mesmerized by the marching soldiers when the officer brought us back to our rehearsal. He saw that we were discouraged. It was time for us to go home. We were not used to staying out so late. The parents of the children would be worrying. I felt ashamed when Annie called me to ask if I was close to home. I had to tell her I hadn't even left Tabarre! I lied that we were nearly finished, but in fact I didn't know what MINUSTAH had planned and I felt out of control. I should have told the officer that the hour was late and that the children should be returning home. But I didn't. There seemed to be no place for my own will in this big enterprise, no way to represent the real needs of the Haitian children.

It was nine o'clock in the evening when the officer called us to enter the dining hall. It appeared that most of the soldiers had finished. Some units were still eating. They put us on the opposite side of the dining hall. On those tables, there remained what other soldiers had left behind. We supervisors did not want to reveal our hunger. We thought it would be humiliating. But the children had no such inhibition. They were starving and they didn't care who knew it. They ravaged the tables, looking for whatever the overfed soldiers had left behind. They wanted to go to the tables that were still full of plates of food to eat, where the soldiers were sitting. I wonder if anyone in MINUSTAH asked themselves when was the last time that the children might have eaten. Did they assume that all of the children had eaten today? Did they care?

We were important enough that they had promised us medals, but they allowed us to eat only their left-overs.

No one could have controlled those kids. A couple of the supervisors made the mistake of trying to stop their kids from their frenzied feeding. One child set the tone by biting the hand of his supervisor when he tried to slow the kid down. We simply sat back and gave them full rein. The alternative was civil war.

The soldiers still eating in another part of the hall were transfixed by the scene. They stared wide-eyed, forks and spoons suspended before their opened mouths, as the children turned their dining hall upside down.

As the soldiers told us to hurry up, the children entered into an absolute frenzy. I saw one child devouring the powder used to make coffee. There was a basket of apples on each table. Perhaps MINUSTAH thought that the little children would never be able to eat them all. But, it was a miscalculation. The children were not about to leave something edible inside Tabarre. They tucked their t-shirts into their pants to make a sack. Then they filled the space between their skin and the t-shirt with apples.

The MINUSTAH soldiers were suddenly motivated to get the kids out of the base and back to Simon. The officer and another soldier stood at the door to exit the children two by two. The soldiers forced the children who had filled their t-shirt sacks with apples to empty them before they left the dining room. They said that each child could leave with one apple, no more. I don't think the soldiers understood the repercussions of that decision. The food would remain behind, in this country called MINUSTAH inside of Haiti, but guarded by armed soldiers. Now the kids knew for sure what those arms were protecting.

The kids filed into the buses in utter dejection to return to the base in Simon. It was nine-thirty when we left the base in Tabarre; the streets were almost empty. Without traffic, we made good time. As usual, there was still much activity in Simon. By candlelight, the merchants were still selling and their clients were still buying. We got the kids out of the base and to their parents.

I asked the driver who was returning to Tabarre if he would drop me off in Delmas 33. He agreed. I was now the only Haitian in the MINUSTAH bus with the soldiers. I was frightened. I did not want to be seen. I feared that someone might see me exiting the bus in Delmas 33. It could be a disaster. I would be taken as an accomplice, a spy. When we arrived in my neighbourhood, I descended from the bus and thanked them. I separated myself from them and flew through the alleyways to get home. There were a thousand dangers in being out at that time in Delmas 33. I just wanted to be in my room with Annie. Before long, that's where I was. Fortunately, Annie was fast asleep and so, by the next morning, her anger at my tardiness had lost its sting.

chapter thirty-nine

THE ELECTION HAD TAKEN PLACE on Sunday and the results were uncertain since all the candidates wanted to be winners. The population didn't know yet who would be president. In principle, the population that votes should be the first to know whom they have chosen. But it was clear that the ballots had been a formality. The powerful were clumsily deciding whom to declare the winner.

The results of the election were announced on the same day that MINUSTAH had scheduled the ceremony. The people were making their anger and disgust known all over Port-au-Prince. We had electricity that day. I was at home with Annie watching the protests on our little television when Ansel Herz, an American journalist, called me. He asked if I would join him at one of the protests to discuss what was happening. I agreed to meet him in Delmas 30, where a large group of people was heading toward the headquarters of the Electoral Council.

I arrived and looked for the journalist. Meanwhile, I followed the protesters on their mission. Among them were a number of presidential candidates. I walked along at the side. Sometimes, these protests turn violent and I didn't want to be in the centre. The people were angry and anything might have happened. They wanted to send some messages to those responsible for the farce of the elections. Many knew that the Electoral Council and the government were controlled by powerful interests hiding behind the United Nations, and so they had a hard time choosing a target for their anger. In fact, the machinations of the powerful are so devious that people often take intermediaries as the source of their troubles. They are just sell-outs. Moreover, it's not clear that the protesters actually have more courage than the sell-outs they protest. In any case, rocks register the message that something is rotten.

When they reached the Electoral Council building, the gates were closed. Sometimes the protesters were more or less calm. Other times, a wave of anger and frustration overcame them and they would throw rocks at the building and push against the gate to enter the grounds. The leader of the protest was standing in the back of a colourful vehicle using a loudspeaker to calm the crowd.

He spoke to the members of Electoral Council who were noticeably absent. "You see the violence of these people! This is just the beginning. The real army is amassing all over the country. If you make the wrong choice, you will see their power! If you want calm, do not be guided by the government or the United Nations. Do your job! ... Okay, that is all."

Perhaps for the leader, that was all; but the people had not yet begun. They wanted to vent their anger. There were some policemen whose job was to ensure that the protest not get out of hand. Some of the protesters who wanted to heat the protest up started to throw rocks at the policemen. Those who did not want to participate in violence dispersed in all directions. Only the fighters remained. The police tried to corner them. Those who had dispersed remained at a safe distance to watch the fight between the police and the violent protesters.

I kept a discrete distance, taking the side of neither the protesters nor the police. I didn't want to be a candidate for the protesters' rocks or the policemen's batons. The protesters began to construct barricades on the road to keep the police at a distance. They used the carts that the street vendors always leave behind. They piled the used tires that you can find on the side of the road anywhere in Port-a-Prince and set them on fire. They fed the fires with the garbage that is always at hand in the capital.

The protesters saw a United Nations SUV approaching. The UN personnel had probably been unaware of the protest growing in front of the Electoral Council headquarters. Nevertheless, it continued to advance at a more cautious pace. One of the protesters saw the vehicle approaching. He hid himself from the view of the driver with a big concrete block suspended above his head, hoping that the SUV would not veer from its route that was leading it directly into his trap. His luck held and, when it passed by him, he suddenly appeared and smashed his block flush on the roof of the SUV with all his force.

The SUV's windshields were tinted black so that it was impossible to see who was inside. It didn't matter for the protesters. The actual people who filled the positions for the United Nations were no more important for them than were the Haitians for the MINUSTAH authorities. The vehicle seemed to have its own inherent instinct for survival, in the absence of any apparent human direction. It bounced and then recoiled under the force of the concrete block. Then it searched for an escape route, moving desperately in a snakelike pattern. However, other protesters had seen it weaken and began to corral their prey.

The SUV swerved in one direction in order to distance itself from the man who had smashed its roof, but that diversion only served to make it visible to others who had not noticed the gift sent from heaven. They ran over from different directions, arming themselves with the biggest rocks they could find, to participate in the chase. Each time that the SUV swerved to avoid one group, it placed itself directly in the line of fire of another. It was panicking under the assault and the protesters were profiting. The SUV appeared to lift itself up and run away on its wheels.

I was increasingly concerned as I watched the SUV struggle to escape. I knew that there were real human beings inside even if they never wanted to reveal themselves behind the tinted windshields. I worried about what would happen if they could not get away. I knew the crowd. I knew its fury. I supposed that the SUV was headed for the ceremony in Tabarre. Of course, I had to get there myself and was running out of time because of this diversion to follow the protest. Under the circumstances, it didn't seem the right moment to ask the UN officials for a lift.

After it had fled and was out of danger, the protesters changed in their attitude towards the Haitian National Police that they had been fighting up until then. In their eyes, the real enemy had appeared and taken its rightful place in the protest. The pressure was off the Haitian police who were, after all, Haitians. The problem was the UN.

Perhaps the SUV had called for reinforcements. In the distance, we could see a couple of MINUSTAH jeeps that are used for carrying soldiers. They seemed to be trying to gauge the situation from afar. The protesters wanted to entice them to come closer. They started to walk calmly, as though they were out for a Sunday stroll, with not a malevolent intention among them, hoping to sucker the jeeps into a trap.

When the protesters were closing in, five well-armed soldiers jumped out of the back of each MINUSTAH jeep. They trained their rifles on the protesters. While the protesters continued on their way, under the menace of the soldiers' rifles, one decided to provoke a showdown. He picked up a healthy-sized rock and threw it at the soldiers. They prepared to fire. The other protesters responded by throwing rocks wholesale, singing, *Si yo tire sou nou, n'ap mete dife* — if they fire upon us, we'll start a fire.

It might have been wiser for MINUSTAH to teach its soldiers how to speak Creole instead of offering Portuguese lessons to Haitian children. For Haitians were never likely to chant Portuguese slogans during their protests. In any case, the soldiers understood the intentions of the protesters whatever language they were speaking and no matter what they were saying. The rocks spoke for themselves.

In response, one of the MINUSTAH soldiers fired teargas into the crowd of Haitians. I could see the exasperation in the eyes of the other soldiers. They were thinking, "What idiot fired teargas?! Is he trying to get us killed?"

But the protesters did not see that. They took up the volley of teargas as a declaration of war. They were happy to participate. From the distance, a mass of protesters ran all out to arrive at the fight before it was over. This cavalry, pouring down the hill, armed with rocks from the rubble that was everywhere, chilled the blood of the MINUSTAH troops, who scurried back into the jeeps. As they waited their turn to enter, each protected himself from the rocks with a plastic shield. But the Haitians were throwing big rocks with all their force. The plastic shields were not equal to the challenge. The people would not be stopped by plastic shields. Teargas was only an accelerant for the violence. The best option was a full retreat. The jeep driver hit the gas and burned rubber before all the soldiers had entered. It was now every man for himself. The MINUSTAH soldiers saw that their jeep was leaving with or without them. The quick-witted ones jumped aboard and held on to anything. One was not so lucky. He turned to see his buddies leaving him to the mercy of the crowd. He ran like the wind. A friend hollered to the driver to slow down. He obliged just enough for the straggler to catch up to the jeep, Haitians hot on his heels. He launched himself toward the jeep and grabbed onto a part of the frame. The jeep did not do him any favours. It sped up, dragging the poor soldier on the ground behind.

This small comedy defused the situation. Even the protesters who were chasing their prey started to laugh at the panic of the MINUSTAH soldiers. They threw their rocks with less force. Once the jeep was at a safe distance, the driver stopped for precisely the time it took to grab the soldier dragging along the ground and pull him aboard.

I was relieved. I had watched the little drama with increasing concern for the MINUSTAH troops. I was at least glad that the young soldier was well, even if his heart had had a good workout that day.

I was now running late to get to the MINUSTAH base in Tabarre for the great ceremony. I took a *taptap* to Simon to pick up my kids. On the way, I wondered how we Haitians would be received today in Tabarre. The MINUSTAH officials might be second-guessing their choice of "We Are the World" to mark the ceremony. I imagined the officer strumming his guitar and writing the lyrics for "Haitians Are Ungrateful Bastards" to sing before the United Nations' officials. Today, it was clear, was not a day for reflection. If MINUSTAH were to let the Haitians out of the Tabarre base alive, then maybe I would have time to reflect on these events sometime in the future.

I kept replaying the violent and ridiculous scenes from the protest in my mind as I headed to get the kids. I thought of an author who said that if ever the oppressed of the world were to unite and recognize their force, then they would overturn their oppressors that day. However, because people are oppressed and angry does not mean that they are not oppressors themselves.

I had almost arrived at the base. I did everything I could to wipe the morning from my mind and wrap myself up in innocence.

I was late getting to the base in Simon. My children were already there before the gates, waiting to be called. As soon as I arrived, they called my name. I immediately thought they were going to question me about my part in the protests. Instead, they patted me on the back and invited me to enter the base.

The two buses were there. After a few minutes, the officer arrived to give us our pep talk, followed by the driver to take us to Tabarre. I saw in the eyes of the officer that he was not happy. He spoke more severely than ever. The other Haitians present were probably unaware of the intensity of the protests. They would not have been able to understand the officer's unpleasant demeanour. But I knew what was eating him.

He told the children that he had been disappointed in them the previous week. They had behaved very badly by rushing to the toilets in disorder. And then, at the end of the day's rehearsal, their behaviour in the dining hall was reprehensible. After this motivational talk, we climbed aboard the buses. He said, "In order to assure our security, it is better that the children remain perfectly quiet on our way to Tabarre."

He didn't explain whose security he wanted to assure. But he knew the Haitians were targeting vehicles that belonged to the United Nations.

We all boarded the two buses to take us to Tabarre. Two jeeps filled with armed soldiers accompanied us for protection, one ahead and one behind. We left in time to arrive early, taking into account the normal traffic jams. At Tabarre, the officer brought us two bags of t-shirts with Brazilian logos. These were our uniforms for the ceremony. It was fitting that we, the children who were to represent Haiti, be clothed in the symbol of the lead country of the MINUSTAH occupation. The colour of our skin would be all that marked us as Haitian.

The officer had learned from the previous week the way to a Haitian heart. He wanted everything to proceed according to plan. And so I was not surprised to see him offer each Haitian an apple. But I knew the kids and their capacity. One apple was not going to run their motors for long when they knew what was on the dining tables of Tabarre. Anyway, they all ate their apples.

Then the children were all led to their place in the square. Their chairs were waiting for them. Around them, we were surprised to see other groups of Haitian children. They wore white t-shirts with red collars. I was told that they came from an orphanage. The dignitaries were all in place, in the first row, waiting for the ceremony to begin. We Haitians — the orphans and we from Simon — were sidelined from everyone of consequence.

For awhile, they projected images of Haiti and Brazil on the huge screen at the centre of the square. At seven o'clock, a Brazilian took the mic to introduce the countries that were present for the ceremony and the names of their representatives. It took forever, since each introduction that the Portuguese officer announced had to be repeated in the language of the country in question. Only Creole was missing from the line-up. Finally, when they had finished, everyone rose for the singing of the Brazilian national anthem. During the hymn, we watched all of the preferred images of the Brazilians: soccer games, parachutists, statues, and a number of military images to remind us who was speaking for Brazil. Then all we little Haitians got little Brazilian flags.

Then, they announced that we would sing the Haitian national anthem. The soldiers who were standing around us noticed that a number of the Haitian children were sleeping on the ground. It was late for the Haitian kids and, moreover, the ceremony was far from stimulating. Not surprisingly, they were already turning in for the night. All around the square, soldiers and officials were standing at attention. The soldiers got the kids up and asked them to sing their national anthem. Everyone started to sing the anthem, "Pour le pays, pour les Ancêtres, Marchons unis, Marchons unis. Dans nos rangs point de traîtres ! Du sol soyons seul maîtres..."

Some of the kids were singing, some not. Most Haitians don't know how to sing their national anthem. Most children don't learn it in school. Our school system is imported from France. The accent is, literally, not on Haiti and Creole speakers. As a result, only a few of the children were able to sing even the first stanza.

There are five stanzas in the national anthem. I sang the first. After that, the four stanzas only fill us with shame. Already after the first stanza, where we profess ourselves to be the masters of Haitian soil, I was starting to feel like a hypocrite. When we are supposed to sing about how we will fight to the death to defend our homeland, to protect it against all traitors, most of us didn't feel like even humming along. We had fought. We lost. We were singing to the victors.

While the national anthem was plodding along, the soldier who had first met us in Simon to explain the classes came to stand next to us. He managed to get through most of the first stanza. After that, he mouthed the words, pretending to be singing along with us, who were uninterested. For some reason he wanted people to believe that he could sing the anthem. In fact, the children and supervisors were the only people in the huge gathering capable of singing even a part of it... and we were not motivated. Still, he listened carefully to our mumblings and, if he could pick up a word here and there, chimed in on the last syllable. He looked daggers at the children, wanting them to help him out. The children yawned and rubbed their eyes while one or two of their partners carried the tune as if it was a block of concrete.

While my mouth was silent, my eyes were busy. There were a couple of soldiers standing at attention next to us, as usual, who taught me a valuable lesson. They also wanted to convince the dignitaries that they could sing our anthem. So, their tactic was to point their heads to the sky and simply mouth sounds. No one could tell what they were singing since their mouths were out of sight. But, for the record, they weren't singing the anthem.

After the national anthem, a dignitary took the stage and called a number of soldiers to come to the fore. He pinned medals on them for something. The kids arose from their torpor and sat up attentively. This was the famous medal ceremony. While the soldiers were being called, the children waited to hear their names over the loudspeaker. They were ready to walk to the front where a high official "from a great country" would pin medals on their chests. But the time passed and the medals all went to the foreign soldiers. The children understood that they had been passed by.

What were the soldiers being honoured for? What had they done? Some careers were advancing. I had the sense that some soldiers were profiting in direct proportion to our misery. Since they were here against our interests, any good they did in the eyes of their masters could hardly enthuse us. We could only think of them as people who wouldn't share their apples with us. And who fired on our families and friends.

But we hadn't yet sung "We Are the World." Maybe they were holding back our medals until we had presented the song.

The officials thanked all kinds of people. The international NGOs were all thanked, as well as the individuals who led them. Other foreign agencies and governments also merited special recognition.

The soldier closest to us noticed that the kids were either sleeping on the ground or fidgeting the way kids do when you tell them to be still and not fidget. He called to me. He could speak English.

He asked me, "Why are the kids behaving like this?"

I said, "They aren't used to being up this late."

He retorted, "But surely they can make a little sacrifice for a special occasion. Maybe they don't know why they have come here." Pointing to the stadium, he said, "Look at all of the dignitaries that have come from all over the world. That's because Brazil has respect for the children. That's why we have been presenting our country for them. The children are here for the same reason. They are representing their country. Everyone here wants to credit their nation in the face of the others. But the Haitians are making a very poor showing for Haiti."

I asked him, "Who chose children to represent Haiti?"

"That's what I'm telling you," he told me. "For us, children have much importance. We want to demonstrate that we value them by choosing them to represent their country.... I wonder if Haitians really believe that Haiti can change."

"Does change in Haiti depend upon the children or people or leaders?" I asked.

He said, "Change doesn't come from the leaders, but from the community. We, in Brazil, we believe in change for Haiti. Look at the program that we have introduced to educate the Haitian children. We already have done lots of work here in Haiti, but we took the time to try to educate the children as well. We would not have come to Haiti if we thought that it was not possible to change it. And so we are doing our best."

He said that he had noticed that Haitians misused their time. They spent time talking in the streets, playing dominoes, joking. "If all the Haitians had acted like we had in creating the classes for the students, imagine how the country would change. And we had to do that while we were working at our jobs for MINUSTAH!"

"I think Haitians see things differently," I said. "Understand that we live in a country with a very weak economy. If children go to school, it's to learn a trade of some kind. Do you think it's easy for students, after all their effort at school, after learning a trade or profession, to then work for no salary? For free? Haitians aren't poor because they don't work, but because they do. Working only makes us poorer. Don't forget that there are many trained people who are unemployed. There are no paying jobs. I think it would be easier if people had a job like you. In their free time, knowing that they had meaningful work, they would be happy to help their neighbours. Since you have a salary, you are better placed to coordinate lessons for children.... But I don't trust any other country saying that they are interested in helping Haiti to change. People are interested in their own advancement and that of their country. You didn't come here to help Haitians, but because you have a job with the Brazilian army. You are paid for that job. You did not come. You were sent."

I knew, because the *kokorats* who hang out at the gates of the MINUSTAH base had told me, how much the Brazilian soldiers are paid for their work in Haiti. For example, young men with nothing to do in Brazil join the armed forces to earn $1,000 US a month. They are the lowest-ranking soldiers. They don't have to spend any of that because their food and board are paid for. The next rank makes $2,000, and so on up to $5,000 a month for the highest ranks. Daily meal and gas allowances alone represent a monthly salary for a Haitian worker, if he could find work. The highest paid officers in the Haitian National Police do not receive as high a salary as the lowest paid soldiers in the Brazilian armed forces, who join up because otherwise they would be hanging around the Brazilian slums with nothing to do.

Maybe the soldier was right in speaking about change for Haiti. The question was what Haiti should change into. And, for the soldier, I was interested in what he thought it should change from.

So I said, "No, I don't believe that any country or any soldier comes here to change Haiti for the better. And I don't believe that anyone in MINUSTAH could change Haiti even if they wanted to. It's not from there that the change can come. In fact, it's exactly the opposite. MINUSTAH is here to keep things from changing. I know the effects of your work in Haiti better than you do. I have seen the changes that MINUSTAH has brought to Haiti since 2004. You have brought insecurity with you. Each time MINUSTAH's mandate is almost finished, we are used to an escalation in the violence that always results in the renewal of the mandate. One change that is clear is that the *kokorats* or *comida* are waiting in greater numbers before the gates of the MINUSTAH bases, looking for handouts. Of course, you take this as evidence of the need for your presence. It's the opposite. You create the need for your presence and then justify your presence based on the insecurity you provoke. Change in Haiti depends on God, the conscience of Haitians and all other nations who interfere to protect their own interests."

After our little conversation, the soldiers lined up to start smashing the Haitian soil for the benefit of the important dignitaries. They were even more severe than they had been the week before during the rehearsal. After this they called upon the Haitian representatives. We looked around, but it turned out that they meant us. A soldier was waving us forward. We lined up. The musicians were waiting. A microphone. All the thousands of soldiers that had grimaced at us as they marched past were now lined up behind us. The officer stood before us.

Everyone applauded for the little Haitians.

The officer sang his part. As usual, he pronounced the English words by way of Brazil so that there was little chance of a native English speaker understanding. The *kokorat* sang his line. The Haitian accomplices then sang their part. Then the rest of us started to sing the chorus. We managed the first two lines, "We are the world, we are the children," reasonably well. After that, the Haitian students garbled the lyrics so that they sounded much like the Brazilian officer had taught us. Behind us, the soldiers started to sing as well, but there was no recognizable English word in this mixture. Then we got to the Creole words that the officer had given us. As they had been told, the children sang, "Ayichi, Ayichi," instead of "Ayiti, Ayiti." That was the end of the ceremony. It was fitting.

When it was over, people applauded. Many soldiers shook our hands. No one offered us our medals.

It was nine o'clock. Some of the soldiers wanted to take some pictures of the little Haitians.

Relieved, the officer called us to board the buses for Simon. Soldiers had prepared a packet of two apples, a little piece of cake, and a soft drink for each Haitian. They were less thankful than the soldiers had hoped — because the soldiers had given them less than they had dreamed.

On the way back, I asked the driver to let me off at Delmas 33. He said that it was too late to stop on the way even for a second. He was under orders to deliver everyone to Simon. One stop. Everyone out.

I asked him again, "Could you drop me off at Delmas 33 on the way back to Tabarre?"

He said no. Strict orders. Only one stop allowed. So I had to walk all the way back to Delmas 33 while the city was at its most insecure. Because of widespread fear, no cars were moving that night. I was ready for anything that might happen. I tried to avoid the main routes, but wound up getting lost in the narrow alleyways of the slums that I didn't know. A stranger caught in such neighbourhoods at night can be taken as a thief and killed. I was frightened.

I understood that once MINUSTAH had no more use for me, they would simply throw me aside. I was on my own.

As I walked home through the shadows, I imagined MINUSTAH troops identifying me as a rebel and firing upon me.

chapter forty

THE MORNING AFTER he had spent the night in Ste Catherine Hospital, my father had an appointment at Gheskio medical clinic. He left one hospital for an appointment at another. I went with him. When we arrived, there were lots people waiting. Everyone took a number to have their consultation in turn. The waiting room was like a family conversation, flowing from one subject to another. There were those who spoke of MINUSTAH, how they had come to plant more misery, now including cholera. No one in MINUSTAH wanted to take responsibility for bringing cholera to Haiti. Some Haitians argued that cholera was part of a plan to increase the importance of NGOs in Haiti. They were working together.

While everyone was talking, a little street merchant entered the hospital to sell her pastries and water. The patients were hungry, but afraid to buy the pastries. They didn't want to compound their health problems. She kept hollering, "Eat pastries, drink water, it's good for your health."

A pastor answered, "It's true that we are hungry. But we've been advised not to eat in the streets."

"Of course they don't want you to eat. You're sick. They want you to die. Who can live without eating? The imbeciles speak and the idiots believe them."

Another patient spoke, "I would like to eat, but I have no water to clean my hands. We have to clean our hands before eating."

"It would be better if NGOs brought you rich hands. Rich hands are clean. Cholera is the disease of the poor. Listen to me! Since when have you listened to their advice? You all come from the countryside. You and your ancestors did your business in the open for centuries. And for water, you took it from springs. There were no tablets to put in water. If it was me, I would pay more attention to your face than your hands. Faces are always full of the dirt and dust of the streets, including dried poo-poo that blows around all the time. Sometimes, when your lips are dry, you pass your tongue over your lips like a mop and you collect all the microbes and then swallow them. Maybe some of you are tubercular. We know that the base of that disease is malnutrition. Now it's getting worse, because you're sick and you aren't eating. Better to eat my pastries and drink my water. You can find the real answers later."

Some of the patients were convinced by her arguments. She was a good saleswoman. Some of us were happy to be convinced. I bought two for my father and one for me. They were delicious.

After a few minutes, the doctor called Dad. I went with him. We explained to the doctor the effects that the medicines were having. He added to them a pill that would help Deland to sleep and also some other medicines. We were able to get them from a pharmacy in the hospital that gave free drugs.

In the *taptap* on the way back, Deland decided not to get off in Simon, but to keep going to Bon Repos. He decided to take up the offer of his godson, Lorès, to live there until he recovered. He asked that James bring some clothes for him to Bon Repos later.

We arrived at the rooms of my cousin Lorès. He gave my father a carpet to sleep in the dining room.

The wife of Lorès welcomed him and smiled. But she was not happy. She was pregnant. She thought it was a bad idea to welcome a person into the family while she was expecting. She took Deland for a mental case and feared that he would be violent.

James arrived with a bag of clothes and effects for Deland's stay.

Deland said to us, "Okay. Just don't abandon me. I know it's far, but from time to time come to see me."

So my brother and I organized a way to keep him from feeling abandoned. Every day, one of us would visit him and bring him something to eat. Monday, I went; Tuesday, James; Wednesday, me again, and so on.

He found a way to manage his drugs. After taking a pill, if he began to feel unwell, he would focus all of his attention on his Creole Bible. Sometimes, he concentrated so hard that he pushed his finger into the verse that he was reading, leaving imprints on the pages.

For the first two weeks, it worked well. He was calm. Lorès took care of his eating schedule. It was important that Deland eat well before he took the pills. However, Lorès and his wife began to lose patience. One day, my father took his pills without eating. Predictably, he lost control of his mind, as he had in Simon. Lorès' wife told people that she was frightened. She said that whenever she heard a sound at night, she jumped in fright for her safety. *Le ou vle debarase di yon vye chenn, ou di li gen raj* — when you want to get rid of an old dog, you say it has rabies. She turned my father into a problem to get rid of him.

James and I went to Bon Repos and I talked to Dad. He told me he was suffering from lack of food. Often, Deland's niece who was Lorès' sister, Christina, would prepare meals for her uncle and bring them to him. I went to see her since she lived nearby. She offered her own house if it was necessary. It was good to know.

−●−

At six o'clock one morning, my cellphone rang. It was Lorès.

He was so excited that he forgot to say hello. "Hurry, hurry! Come and get your father. I can't keep him here anymore," he said in a breathless voice.

"Calm down," I said. "What's going on?"

"I made my house! I'm not about to let anybody put me out on the street. Hurry! Hurry!" Then, click. He hung up without explaining.

I prepared myself quickly. I had only enough to take a *taptap*. Not even enough to leave something for Annie.

James had received the same phone call as me. We left at the same time. James got to Bon Repos first.

When I arrived, Lorès was speaking to James and Deland's little brother, Rico, in the yard. I greeted them and then went to see my father in the gallery.

"What's going on?" I asked Dad.

He told me that the previous evening, he had eaten late. Then he took his medicine. When it was almost morning, he had stomach cramps as though he had not digested his food. He had to go out to the toilet in the yard. But he had a difficult time opening the cast iron door to get out of the house. When he finally succeeded, it was too late.

He had already soiled himself.

He had just left the gallery. There was no use in proceeding further. He just took off his soiled pants.

Lorès and his wife came out of their room. Lorès began to holler at Deland. "What kind of idiocy is this?! If I had known that you were going to be this much trouble, I never would have let you stay here! That's it! This is the last straw! Your sons are going to have to come to get you!"

He made such a big deal of my father's humiliation, that the neighbours came out to watch the show. Fortunately, Christina also came to help care for Deland. She gathered some orange leaves to perfume water that she used to bathe Deland and clean his pants.

My father told me that he was surprised to see Lorès, his godson, speak to him with such venom. I asked him what he would like to do. Would he like to go back to Simon or to stay in Bon Repos?

"I'm not going anywhere," he said. "If Lorès came to get me, he has to assume his responsibility. To go back to Simon now would be humiliating."

Lorès overheard him. He said, "I'm not putting up with you here. Your sons are going to have to take you."

Christina arrived as Lorès was speaking. She announced before everyone that she was ready to take the responsibility for caring for Deland.

Lorès jumped at the idea, "If Christina wants to take responsibility for Deland, then let her! This is my house. I'm the boss here. And I've made up my mind."

My father said, "Okay. Since Lorès will no longer accept me here, I will leave. Maybe Lorès will be sorry someday . . ."

Deland hadn't yet finished. I interrupted, "Dad, I don't like this. Lorès is a member of our family. You are speaking as though you wish something bad should happen to Lorès. Don't forget that if Lorès has a problem, then the family has a problem. We are all branches on the same tree. If one branch is sick or disturbed, so is the tree. Lorès has reached the end of his patience. But only God is infinitely patient. We are only human; we all have our limits. Let's just thank Lorès for helping you for several weeks. He has done his best."

Christina took my father's things and we all walked to her place nearby. She was happy. She didn't see taking care of Deland as a burden.

She took over his care without complaining. James and I continued to alternate visits to Bon Repos to bring provisions when we could. Sometimes we were both without any means and couldn't help out.

When we needed to take him to Gheskio, I would leave before sunrise to pick Deland up in Bon Repos and take him in a *taptap* to the city. James would go directly from Simon to Gheskio to assure our place in line so that we could see a doctor.

Deland could not go more than two paces at a time without exhausting himself. He leaned against me. I was constantly prepared to stop so as not to push him beyond his ability. When we would finally arrive, James would hand us the number that assured his place in line and he would be ready when called for his consultation. They were always the same. The doctors just prescribed more of the same medicine. Then I would take him back to Bon Repos.

After a few weeks, Christina had to go to Jacmel to meet the parents of her fiancé. She didn't want to leave Deland alone. She asked James to come to take my father for two days. When she returned, Deland could come back. My father was now looking forward to visiting Simon and to seeing how everyone was doing.

chapter forty-one

FÉDRIK WENT WITH FRANCHESCA to SONAPI and joined the crowd of unemployed in front of the buildings. Eventually, he was chosen to work in Kay Morisette. As in the other sweatshops, work started at 6:30 a.m. He worked in a small module making pockets for men's trousers. A module is a group of people, normally four or five, who work together to produce a product. They work toward a quota, a certain number of the final product. If they achieve the quota, then everyone in the module makes a given amount; if they fail, then everyone makes approximately two-thirds of the quota salary. The quota is normally fixed at a rate just out of reach. Consequently, a module rarely succeeds. On the other hand, since it is within view, everyone is motivated to push the others so that all can reach the higher salary. The system is conceived to make workers police each other. If they try for the quota, they get angry at the weak link in the chain, whoever is unable to keep up. In SONAPI, a worker who is judged to be a drag on the module is called a *kokoye*: a coconut. It's a bitter epithet to swallow.

In Fédrik's case, the quota was required. Instead of rewarding the module for achieving its quota, it was punished when it didn't. The daily quota was 2,000 pockets. The module had to produce 1,000 pockets by eleven o'clock. If not, everyone risked being sent home. The members of the module worked hard to make sure they surpassed the quota. However, they got paid nothing extra when they did. They got paid nothing if they didn't make the quota. At Kay Morisette, Fédrik earned 3,200 gourdes ($80 US) every two weeks.

After three months in Kay Morisette, Fédrik got sick. He began to suffer from abdominal pains and couldn't keep up. He told the supervisor he needed time off. The supervisor brought him a pill. Fédrik said he was serious, that he needed a real diagnosis for his stomach cramps. The supervisor told him to get to work. Fédrik asked the bosses why he was having ONA deducted from his miserable salary if there was no healthcare. He asked whose pockets that deduction was lining. The bosses didn't like his questions any more than Fédrik liked their answers. They mocked him. They aimed at his masculinity, calling him a wimp, a crybaby, and finally, a *kokoye*. That was the last straw. He walked out on the job and went to recuperate in his tent in Delmas 31. Franchesca was angry. She had thought that maybe he would be able to keep his job this time. She pushed him to try again.

This time, he stood outside Building 43 to work for The Well Best. There, the manager was a harsh Korean woman named Jessica. Fédrik was hired as part of a module of thirty workers to begin production of a new product the company was launching: women's slacks. Jessica told them that the quota was 1,200 units per day. Pay was 3,200 gourdes ($80 US) every two weeks. The workers responded that the quota was unreasonable. They said that their module could manufacture a maximum of 600.

Jessica made two modules of fifteen workers each. Each was responsible for 500 pieces. She offered a bonus of 160 gourdes ($4 US) if they achieved the quota. The workers had seen this before; Jessica was testing them to see how much they could achieve if they worked hard. Once that was established, the bonus would be eliminated and the module would be responsible for the maximum.

The personnel officer has much power inside the SONAPI factories. He harasses, humiliates, and fires workers from time to time to control the group. The personnel officer needs to be seen to be ruthless. Fédrik's module was finding the quota impossible to attain. They were working at breakneck speed. If they had to use the toilets, they rushed in, took care of business, and then rushed back so fast that they left the paper towels on the floor. They knew that there was a janitor whose job was to clean the washroom. However, the personnel officer — a Haitian — came by to humiliate the workers very publicly. He called them *kabrit*, or goats, for the way they left the washroom.

Those kinds of words are meant to humiliate the workers. The personnel officer needed to be as loud and insulting as possible in order that his bosses register that he gave no quarter to the workers. Fédrik was supposed to recoil in the face of the insult. However, Fédrik responded in the tone that the personnel officer had chosen. He said that if they were indeed animals and coconuts, then there could be no question of them operating the machines, since everyone knows that goats can't sew. He said that all thirty workers were going to work like actual goats until the personnel officer and Jessica admitted they were human beings. Spontaneously, every one of the workers stood with Fédrik.

The apology was not forthcoming and they all walked out of the factory and loudly made known their insurrection. Other workers from the other sweatshops of SONAPI began to join them. They all threw stones at the factory, breaking the windows and frightening Jessica and the personnel officer who called the SONAPI guards. However, the guards were not strong enough to confront the growing crowd, so she called the police. They arrived and asked the workers why they were striking. The workers responded that they were underpaid and treated like animals. The police told the supervisor that it wasn't their business. They left.

The insurgents remained well past closing time, holding Jessica and the personnel officer hostage since they were afraid to present themselves to the crowd that the security guards and the police had decided were outside of their jurisdiction.

Jessica then called out to the workers using a loudspeaker. She said that they should choose three people to negotiate their grievances. The crowd began to calm down. They chose three people to speak for the whole module. The crowd then disbanded, deciding that they would withhold their decision until the following day. As soon as the crowd dispersed, Jessica left the building to go home, without exchanging so much as a word with the representatives. It had been a tactic to disperse the crowd. She had no interest in negotiations.

The next day, when Fédrik and the others arrived for work, they first learned of Jessica's treachery. Fédrik said that he had had enough. He handed in his badge and turned around for Delmas 31.

Franchesca called Fédrik later in the day, worried. She had stopped by The Well Best after work as usual to ride home with him, but he wasn't there. She said that there was a big crowd out front. She was afraid for what might have become of him. He explained that he had given up on the place.

chapter forty-two

IT WAS DECEMBER 2010. I had no money at all. I couldn't buy the fruits and other things that I had been getting for my father. I was ashamed and didn't want to go to Simon, where he was temporarily staying, without something to offer. That was a great error: imagining that I needed to have money to go to see my father. He was in the greatest need. I was only thinking of money.

On 30 December, I was leaving the church at eight o'clock in the evening. Something told me to call him. I struggled with shame for having nothing to offer him. Moreover, by now, weeks had gone by during which I had been unable to offer him anything. The shame built upon itself. Finally, I won the struggle and called him at nine o'clock.

I didn't know how to start the conversation. Finally I just said, "Hello, Dad."

He answered in a sad and discouraged voice, "*Bonswa*, my son."

"Dad, I feel really ashamed to call you. Things aren't going well for your son. I am hesitant to call you without being able to help you at all. I can't even offer you any lemons. But how is your health?"

"Ah, as you know, I'm not doing so well."

He didn't have anything else to say. I asked him if he had eaten. He mumbled that he had made an effort to eat something, but that he had no appetite.

"How is Annie?" he asked.

I told him that she was fine. I told him that we would come down to see him the next day.

"Okay, I'll see you then. Sleep well." I could tell that he was digging into his reserves for each breath.

I couldn't sleep that night. My body was in Delmas 33 and my soul in Simon with my father. The more I wanted the night to pass quickly, the longer it seemed to stretch out. I was thinking of Deland when James called me in the middle of the night to tell me that he had passed away. He was forty-eight.

chapter forty-three

I WENT TO SIMON before sunrise the next morning. I passed by Delmas 19 to tell Jelo the bad news. He came with me to Simon.

The neighbours were already gathered in front of my father's home, those who had been there when Deland arrived decades earlier, and those who had grown up with my father as a pillar of the community. Everyone was exchanging memories or thoughts about him. Those who didn't know he was dead found out as they passed by.

Jelo and I entered. We saw my father lying on a pile of fabrics inside his room. His face was calm and fresh as though death had wiped away his illnesses. He looked relieved and regretful at the same time: relieved to have been released from this world and regretful that he was leaving it to us. I guess that's what I projected onto him.

When Jelo and I were inside, some neighbours who had already seen the body entered again to show us that they were considerate — but really to see what I would do. I knew them. They had been unable to appreciate my father. Many of the neighbours had debts owed to my father. No one mentioned them. His death wiped the ledger clean.

Jelo and I went to see James, who explained to us the details of his death. I called my aunt, Deland's little sister, who lived in Delmas 33. She gave the news to her husband, who was at her house rather than with his mistress in Delmas 30. My uncle took the telephone. He told me that he had a friend who worked at the morgue at the General Hospital. He could plan the funeral. My aunt said she would come quickly to Simon to see Deland before the ambulance arrived.

The spectators were still walking in and out of the house. They decided that because I lived in Delmas, I must have money. That I lived in a little room without even a door was not of interest to them.

They were hanging around to see the plans that I would make for the funeral.

When my aunt arrived in the neighbourhood, she started to cry. People took her to where he was lying. She caressed his face. She started to cry loudly. "Look where he is lying. He came here before me, to Port-au-Prince. I never had the chance to do anything to help him. Now, he is gone forever. It's too late for me. How did I manage to lose a good brother like Deland?"

When she entered and started crying so loudly, the spectators ran back into the house. This was the show that they wanted to see. I had been a disappointment. I don't cry in public. As they were counting the tears streaming down my aunt's face, I took her hand and led her outside. The spectators followed. I wanted to get rid of them.

My uncle had given my telephone number to the ambulance driver. He called for directions. There are no street numbers in the poor areas. But it wasn't hard to find the place, I said, because there was a big crowd in front of the address. They found us and took Deland away.

Up until now, I didn't know what plans my uncle had made with the ambulance. He had told me not to worry; he would take care of everything. He said that he knew that we didn't have money and that he would be able to negotiate to keep the costs reasonable.

I talked to James. We had to plan. We had never faced such a responsibility. We had to make sure that we assumed it honourably for Deland.

James said that there was a man in the neighbourhood who had a hearse. He had organized funerals for people. He told James to find 30,000 gourdes ($755 US). He would take care of everything. James told him that the body would have to be buried in Saut d'Eau, not Simon.

I had doubts. People sometimes give a price just to get the body. Once they have it, they make the costs grow until the family is ruined. It wasn't clear that he knew how far Saut d'Eau was. The cost of a coffin alone was usually 15,000 gourdes ($377 US). The wake would also be a large expense. There would need to be chairs, refreshments for many people. The wake was an important ritual and would have to be done properly. Was this a serious offer or a trap?

I asked James to not give any answer. Our uncle had already taken the body. We'd have to see which was better. Our uncle had already organized funerals. Perhaps he would be a better choice . . . for once.

I was counting on the moral support of Jelo. He had been planning a trip to his home community in the mountains above Tigwav, but the moment that he learned of Deland's death, he told me that he would stay to help me get through the funeral. But when I passed by Delmas 19 after the ambulance had taken Deland, Jelo was already at the gate with his backpack, en route for Tigwav. He was embarrassed to see me.

"Oh Ti bòs. I decided I had better go after all. Everyone is waiting for me there. I'll just go and explain to them and then return right away."

That was the last I saw of Jelo until the funeral was over.

This would be a challenge. Would I be able to do this? What was I capable of?

I carried on to meet my uncle to go to the morgue at the General Hospital where his friend worked. He said to me, "I know that you don't have much money. I'll do whatever I can to make sure it doesn't cost more than 30,000 gourdes ($755 US)."

My uncle negotiated with his friend. "Here is my young nephew. It is his father's body that we're talking about. There is no mother and so he is responsible. But he has very little money. So, we want you to prepare the body and take it to the church for the funeral, and then the body will be interred in Saut d'Eau." The undertaker agreed to do this for 5,000 gourdes ($126 US).

"You see," said my uncle as we left the morgue. "Just leave things to me. I get things done. Everything's going to be fine. I have some coffins in the workshop and, since Deland was a good brother-in-law, I don't want anyone to exploit the situation."

When he said that Deland was his "good brother-in-law," I thought that maybe something was changing. Deland had indeed been a good brother-in-law, as opposed to my uncle. Perhaps he wanted to take this last opportunity to make things right, to reconcile with Deland and to make peace with his past. Maybe I wanted to believe that.

I went to tell James the good news. All that was left was to find the money.

As soon as the people in Saut d'Eau received the message that Deland was dead, my aunt called me. She was Deland's sister who, three decades earlier, had been victim of our family's *lwa* along with him.

"What will we do? How are you going to pay for the funeral?" she asked. "Your father still has a couple of plots of land in Saut d'Eau. Maybe we could find a buyer for them."

She knew that we had nothing in Simon. She also knew that my father's sickness would have eaten whatever money we may have had. Deland had stayed with her son Lorès and her daughter Christina. She was well aware that he and his family were broke.

Two days later, our aunt called to say that an agronomist had agreed to buy the land. Without having seen it, but on the assurances of the *koutche*, he agreed to pay 70,000 gourdes ($1,740 US). James met the agronomist in Port-au-Prince who made a down payment of 45,000 gourdes ($1,118 US) for the land. He would pay the rest after the funeral, once he had seen it in person.

When my aunt knew that we had money from the sale of Deland's land, she told us that we would have to send some of it to Saut d'Eau to receive the visitors and pay for the burial. Normally, as in this case, the wake and the funeral take place where the person died. As a matter of choice, Deland had not lived his life in Saut d'Eau. His church, his friends, his clients, his neighbours, and his family were all in Simon. So James asked what our aunt was planning for the countryside and how much money she needed.

Our aunt had the advantage of knowing how much money the sale would put in our hands. She said, "Well, we understand the situation. You don't have much money and you have lots of responsibilities.... Well, just try to send a little something for us to prepare for Deland the way we would have liked and in a way that would honour him.... There will be a lot of people who will want to pay their respects.... Well, let's see.... Just do your best and try to send about 25,000 gourdes ($621 US)."

James and I were amazed to hear a peasant pronounce such a figure. It used to be that a funeral in the countryside would cost 500 gourdes, altogether. We wondered if even our aunt might have been shocked to hear herself ask for 25,000 gourdes. We heard others whispering in the background. Our cousins. Were they all wondering whether they would get away with this or not?

James and I were thinking. That money could buy ten cows. If my father had had that money, he would never have come to the capital three decades earlier. He would have raised livestock as had once been his dream. If we passed all this money to the relations in Saut d'Eau, would we be able to have a proper funeral here in Simon, where it was needed?

We understood immediately that Deland's relations had one idea in mind and it was money. In Deland's youth, when there was a death, the relations got together, like a *konbit*, to plan the funeral. It was shared among all those concerned. But now, no one from Saut d'Eau offered to come to the capital to help with the plans and the organization. They simply wanted money. They would take care of the rest.

Deland had always cared about his larger family. He worried not only about us, but he wondered how he might be able to help his relations in Saut d'Eau.

Finally, we decided to make our relations aware of our expenses for the funeral in Simon. Beyond the funeral expenses, none of the children had decent clothes or shoes. We told her that we would send 15,000 gourdes ($373 US) to Saut d'Eau.

Our aunt started to complain. "No, no, no. That won't be enough. We'll have to buy rice, *pwa nwa*, meat, soft drinks."

James and I were both on the phone. We replied, "We understand. Since it won't be enough to do anything properly, maybe it would be better to forget about any ceremony at Saut d'Eau. We'll just plan for the capital and you can come down."

"Okay, okay, we'll just have to do what we can with 15,000 gourdes. It'll be tough."

We now had only 5,000 gourdes ($124 US) left from the sale of the land. With that, we needed to clothe all of the seven children. Not one of us had black clothes. But at least the costs of the funeral had been assured. All that remained was to confirm the date with the pastor of Deland's church. Once that was done, we announced the date of the funeral ceremony. But what people in Simon were really interested in was the wake that was always the night before the funeral. We would have to make a little money go a long way. There would be gossip. But there would be a wake.

A neighbour who used to use Deland's sewing machine found some black fabric in his workshop and made dresses for Christla and Gloria. Then, I bought whatever black *pèpè* I could find and managed to clothe the rest of us for the funeral.

A couple of days before the funeral, Deland's cousin Claude came by to ask if I needed any help. It was heart-warming. He was a painter and offered to help with the coffin if it was necessary. We told him that my uncle was taking care of the casket. He knew my uncle and didn't trust that he was atoning for his life of greed toward everyone. He suggested that we go to the workshop and make sure that it was acceptable.

Claude and I went to my uncle's house. I handed him the 25,000 gourdes ($621 US) for the morgue fees, including the casket. He took us to his workshop so that we could see it. He had moved from Delmas 19, where I used to work for him, to Titanyen, between Port-au-Prince and Saut d'Eau. When we arrived, we saw that he had made a few coffins years earlier. Insects had been gnawing at the wood. Around his shop were other craftsmen who made coffins of quality. Next to them, these of my uncle were unsaleable. They were painted white with sky blue borders. The colours were inconsistent with funerals. Worse, they were not well crafted. They were made to bury paupers.

Claude pointed to the one that was placed apart, as if ready to go. "Is that the casket?"

"Yes," said my uncle, "that's a good coffin."

"Okay," said Claude. He said no more. He hired a *taptap* to take it to Simon. There, he paid someone to rebuild the casket. He used his own money to buy the materials, including two tones of brown paint. He saved us from making a shameful mistake.

When it was finished, my uncle came by to see the renovated casket, "Look at it. Isn't that a beautiful coffin?" He took total credit for it in its renovated state, as if that was how he had offered it to us. "If I'd known it would be that nice, I would have brought a camera with me."

He continued, "Since the funeral is in two days, I'd better go to the morgue to pay the undertaker."

A short while later, he called from the morgue, with his voice full of outrage. "Joegodson! You know that this undertaker is a real bastard!? He's telling me that the 5,000 gourdes that we negotiated was just to keep the body in the morgue and prepare it for the funeral! He says that it was not to transport it anywhere! He says that we have to pay even more because the time in the morgue has been so long! I'm so angry I'm ready to leave this hospital. I don't want anything more to do with this *vakabon!*"

I tried to find out how bad the situation was, "And so, what have you concluded?"

"I don't want to be involved anymore. We have to bring the casket here, but I'm ready to wash my hands of the whole affair rather than deal with this bastard!"

"Haven't you negotiated to have the casket taken to the church?" I asked.

"That's what's making me so angry! He's not only refusing to go to Saut d'Eau, but to take the body to the church! . . . I'll get a *taptap* to take the casket to the morgue, but I won't enter. I don't want anything more to do with it."

I now could see no other options but to accept that plan. The body was in the morgue and my uncle had all the money for the funeral.

Before long, my uncle showed up with a *taptap*. A few friends came with us to the morgue to help carry the casket.

When we arrived at the General Hospital, my uncle handed me 1,500 gourdes ($37 US) — of the 25,000 gourdes ($621 US) that we had given him — to get from his "friend" in the morgue an official pass to transport the body. When I encountered the undertaker, he immediately took up his end of the argument.

"I won't have anything to do with that *vakabon*! What an arrogant bastard! He treats everyone as if they were *kokorats*! Who does he think he is? . . . Your uncle expects me to prepare the body, pay for its time in the morgue, take it to the church — which is already far enough — and then to Saut d'Eau! All that for 5,000 gourdes. Even my best price for a friend in need for all that is 30,000 gourdes. But your uncle is far from a friend and far from ever being one!"

"Okay," I tried to calm him. "I understand. I myself had been doubtful about the price of 5,000 gourdes. Just try to forget what's happened. I have 1,500 gourdes. Could you give me a pass for the body? Just forget about my uncle and deal with me."

He explained that he had sent the body to a private morgue. With the cholera epidemic, they were thoroughly cleaning the morgue in the General Hospital every few days. During the cleanings, they get rid of all the bodies in a common grave. "Your uncle wanted the body left here, but it would have been lost. The private morgue was more expensive. You have to pay for each day."

Finally, he gave me the pass and sent someone to show me the location of the private morgue. He warned me that, without that pass, I would not be able to transport the body anywhere.

As we exited the General Hospital, my uncle was engaged in a heated shouting match with the *taptap* driver who still had the casket in the back of his vehicle. My uncle had hired him principally to transport some corrugated iron to his workshop. After that job, my uncle offered to add another fifty gourdes ($1.24 US) to his fee if he would transport the coffin to a morgue. He had told the *taptap* driver that the morgue was close by, which was far from honest. Now, the driver was complaining. My uncle was calling him a *vakabon* and a cheat. The *taptap* driver was calling him an old bastard. There were lots of spectators. It was the travelling show that my uncle took with him wherever he went.

I approached the *taptap* driver with my job cut out for me. I began by saying that he was right. I didn't need to know the details. I threw myself at his mercy and asked if he wouldn't find it in his heart to carry the coffin for my father just a couple of blocks further. His blood pressure lowered and he agreed to help me out. But then he turned one last time to my uncle to holler that he would never deal with that old bastard again.

When we arrived at the morgue, the *taptap* driver helped the rest of us take the casket down. We arranged the time to pick up the casket and the body the morning of the funeral, the day after the next.

— • —

The day of the wake arrived. Everyone would be expecting something important. We had 2,000 gourdes ($50 US) left. I mulled over what I could do with that. James and I used 1,000 gourdes to buy soft drinks, chocolate, bread, and sugar to make tea with ginger, orange, and lemon leaves.

That would not be enough. I would have to do something to cut their appetites so they wouldn't start complaining. What could keep them so occupied that they wouldn't start looking for food? A couple of months earlier, I had been looking in a second-hand computer store when I found a DVD projector for a good price. I bought it, with the idea of showing documentaries and films. I didn't yet have the other equipment I would need to continue with my plan, but the projector waited in my room.

I borrowed a computer that could play DVDs and hooked my projector up to it.

The wake always starts after sunset of the night before the funeral and continues until sunrise. As usual, there were different groups. The Protestants came with their prayer and song books to pray and sing all night. Since Deland was Protestant, they naturally took the main place and set the tone for the wake. When adherents of the other religious sects pass away, their co-religionists likewise set the tone of the wake. Deland was also a tailor and his clients were as diverse as Haitian society. Some had been Vodouist and would ask Deland to make costumes for their rituals. The base of his business had been the Catholic school children who needed uniforms every year. They all came, and many others.

A wake is an occasion for anybody to say or do whatever he or she pleases. Some people take advantage of a wake to be foolish, to shout out nonsense, and even to insult the deceased and his family. Others come to pay their respects to the family. In any case, a wake is always a gathering together of all parts of Haitian society. There were the *vakabons*, for instance.

Among the *vakabons* could be people with some jealousy or resentment toward the deceased. They can use the wake to call out gossip or to denounce the family. When the house is open and the body on display, as was Deland the day of his death, anyone can enter. During the wake, people can yell out that they had seen a bucket of pee-pee in the corner, that Deland had never fixed his broken chair, or that the family never swept the floor. Sometimes, *vakabon* simply yell stupidities, "Deland used to steal his fabric from my shop." The *vakabon* section does not intend to comfort the family. But they are always there, as they were for Deland. I had to put up with them.

The earthquake had prepared the stage for Deland's wake. When the front wall of his house collapsed, Deland hung a sheet where the wall had been, to separate his home from the street. We took the sheet down, so that there was no division between inside and outside. We borrowed a few benches and chairs and placed them in the alleyway.

After the participants had all grouped themselves together, they played out their parts. While the Protestants chanted their songs, the *vakabons* tried to throw them off tune. They stood next to them, clapping and singing along but changing the tempo, the pitch, the lyrics, and the rhythm. They would sing "Where is the tea? Where's the food?" They would say, "It's a poor man who died. We can't smell the tea." "We want beer, not tea!" said others.

I knew that the tea and coffee and soft drinks would not stretch. There was not enough to even begin to calm the growing crowd. We brought out some small cups to serve everyone the tea and chocolate along with some bread. Some started to complain about the size of the cups. "No thanks. No tea! I'll wait for the beer!" "What kind of a wake is this without beer!? There's no respect for us here!"

When I heard this starting, I decided that the films would have to tranquilize the *vakabons*. While they continued to yell, I opened up a white sheet that I had placed in advance to hang from the wall inside the home and then began to project the first film.

As soon as they saw the Haitian film starting, they zipped their mouths shut and looked for a good spot to watch it. They immediately entered into the film. They shut up! No longer was there any distinction between the *vakabons* and the citizens. Even better, the film projected on a large screen quenched their appetites. As long as the film played, they were as quiet as mice and more polite.

As the night continued, and I played film after film, I passed out a few soft drinks. No one asked for anything. No one complained.

I had never seen a wake so quiet and so well-behaved.

When the sun rose, I was less proud of myself for having tranquilized the *vakabons* and satisfied the mourners than worried about how I was going to recuperate the body of Deland and get it to the church by seven-thirty in the morning. I confided in a neighbour who offered to take responsibility for finding a *taptap* to pick up the body at the morgue and take it to the church.

Once that neighbour had left to find a *taptap*, a church brother of Deland came up to offer his help. He had a truck, called a *kantè*, used to transport merchandise. It is larger than a *taptap*. There are two benches along the sides in the back for people to sit and room in the centre where merchandise can be piled or, in this case, people can stand. The problem is that there is nothing for people to hold onto to stabilize themselves. He offered his *kantè* to transport people from the wake to the church and, after that, to Saut d'Eau for the burial.

There were many people at the wake who wanted to attend the funeral. Now they could get there in the back of the *kantè*. There were also those who saw that this could be a good chance to travel to Saut d'Eau at our expense.

Two of my biggest problems seemed to have disappeared.

My brothers and sisters and I prepared. I had just finished dressing when I heard a strange noise outside. I immediately thought that it was the beginning of another earthquake. I rushed outside to see my neighbour calling to me while jumping down from an old dilapidated *taptap*, "Here we are! I found a *taptap* to go the morgue."

It was too late to start looking for another. I gathered some friends who could help me carry the casket. We got to the morgue early. I showed the pass that the undertaker had given me to the morgue officials. I verified that the body that I was recuperating was indeed Deland. Sometimes morgues switch bodies so that the funeral ceremony takes place over the wrong person. Sometimes, also, a malefactor could turn a person into a zombie. The family of the zombified person assumes that he is dead. Meanwhile, after the funeral, the sorcerer can take the body and reunite it with its soul. The zombie can then be under the control of the evildoer. If the zombie should awaken in the morgue and try to escape, the morgue workers can kill him for good in order to not lose the business. So, it is common practice to check the body for signs of violence. I recognized Deland by a mark on his face.

It was now seven o'clock. We had thirty minutes to get the body to the church and prepare it for viewing.

The *taptap* seemed ready to fall apart at any minute. It was fighting against itself, as though different parts of the vehicle wanted to go in different directions. The tires were worn. And it complained loudly about the state of the roads, sputtering invective out of its tailpipe.

And so it announced its approach to a commissariat of police. The police came out to see what was happening. A vehicle in Haiti has to be in an outrageous condition to attract attention. But this *taptap* was in a class of its own. It drew the attention of everyone, including the police. That there was a casket in the back added to the intrigue. Since the deceased is normally transported to a funeral in a hearse — and never in a *taptap* — the police had reason to be suspicious. The police asked the *taptap* driver for his licence.

"What are you doing with a casket in the back? Where are you going?"

We responded that we were taking the deceased to church for his funeral.

"A funeral! Who authorized you to carry a coffin around Port-au-Prince in a *taptap*?"

I said, "It's true, Chef. It's my father. We didn't have the money for a normal funeral. So, the *taptap* driver offered to help us to get our father to church, where people are waiting."

The policeman didn't believe me. "What kind of nonsense is this? You think I'm going to let you carry on like this?"

"Officer, you think that I am lying about the death of my father?"

"Are the police aware of this burial?" he asked.

There were many cholera victims at the time. The authorities had prohibited their transport around the country for fear of spreading the disease. Some families were defying the authorities in order to take their loved ones to the family burial site. It was likely that the police assumed that we were involved in that sort of scheme. If not worse. So, I handed the policeman the official pass that the General Hospital had given me, authorizing me to transport the body.

He accused me, "I don't believe this. You wrote this!"

What was the use of an official pass if no one believed it? While I was arguing with the policeman, the people in the *taptap* with the coffin climbed down. Among them was an elderly woman. She asked the officer to let us pass, since we were already late.

He looked at us, dressed for a funeral, and then looked at the state of the *taptap*, shaking his head between disgust and amazement. He decided to let us carry on, but said that there were other police up ahead that would surely stop us.

We were now late. I kept my eyes open for police along the route, praying that we not be stopped again. As the *taptap* chugged and puffed its way up the final hill, hundreds of people waiting in the courtyard of the church stared wide-eyed and open-mouthed. The vehicle had only barely outlived the person it was transporting. But it bravely inched its way into the courtyard of the church. People assumed that this old *taptap* was bringing some of Deland's pauper friends. But when they saw me jump down, they understood that it was Deland himself who had arrived.

Some of Dad's old church brothers were shaking their heads. They asked me if the morgue had not given me a gurney to wheel the casket into the church. I answered no, that was beyond our means.

The church had been rebuilt after the earthquake. It was clean and modern — even painted! Deland had worked hard, along with others in the congregation, to rebuild it after the earthquake. The *taptap* was a stark and noisy contrast to the church.

Some of them came to me and asked, "Who is responsible for the funeral? You?"

"Yes," I said.

"There aren't any others, older?" they asked.

"No," I replied.

"And the morgue didn't give you a gurney for the casket? If we had known that, we would have helped. Deland was a brother who had sacrificed and given a lot for the church."

These same brothers had known, as did anyone who opened his eyes, what the earthquake and illnesses had done to Deland. Now, the *taptap* was a visible symbol of Deland's troubles, and ours. They claimed that they would have helped. That was a tactic to hide their shame that they hadn't helped when it was needed.

I understood at that minute, with all of these grown men in front of me with one voice, that shame is the consequence of not sharing troubles and poverty. If poverty were shared, then there would be no more shame. The concept would disappear. Poverty would have no meaning either. However, when everyone tries to hide his and her poverty, it becomes shameful. People want to distance themselves from it. I had no intention of hiding my poverty. I was even starting to like the old *taptap* that had, against all odds, arrived at the church with the casket.

One of Deland's contemporaries asked me, "How many children did Deland have?"

"Seven."

"And his wife, she has been dead for a long time?"

"Yes."

"I'm sorry to see how things have gone. It's not like this we would like to have seen Deland's funeral. If Deland has some children who are not in school, I would be able to help. I have a school. We could offer scholarships for them."

He gave me his telephone number. I wondered why. In this case, it wasn't school scholarships that we needed, but food and clothes. I wondered why the offer was coming now, in these circumstances and in front of his church brothers. Years earlier, even months before, this offer — quietly and sincerely offered to Deland — might have been encouraging.

"Deland might have appreciated such an offer when he was alive," I said.

I thought out loud, "When we all aim to be rich and important, this is the result. When we share our poverty, then no one would ever be in this condition."

I asked them if they would help me to bring the casket into the church. Inside the church, someone had prepared two chairs to support the two ends of the coffin.

After the casket was in place, Mme Dieumerci, Mme Bolivar, and two other of Annie's sisters arrived. Since Annie was pregnant, it was customary that she remain at home. Her family came up to embrace me and offer sympathies.

When Annie's family went to see the body, our old neighbour Marie, the mother of my childhood friend Lòlò who had died in the earthquake, came to ask me if there was a way that she could accompany Deland to Saut d'Eau. I told her to stay close to me and I would make sure that she got aboard the *kantè*.

After the ceremony, everyone gathered in the courtyard of the church. I saw a cousin of my father who had brought his family in his minibus. He asked me if everyone was going to Saut d'Eau. The majority, I said, but we didn't have enough vehicles. I thought maybe he was going to offer us his minibus. Instead, he asked me if I could pay for his gas. How much, exactly? One thousand gourdes ($25 US), he answered. He had always said that my father was important to him. Deland had always helped him. An old neighbour of Dad's, his good friend, overheard and handed me the 1,000 gourdes to give to him. She said, "It's not a loan. Just keep it."

After I passed him the money, he asked how we were transporting the casket to Saut d'Eau. I pointed to the *taptap*. He laughed, "That's what you're using as a hearse?! Better to put the coffin on the top of my minibus," he boasted. "I have great doubts that that *taptap* can make it to Saut d'Eau."

He prepared to leave for the countryside, but in his minibus was simply his family. I had assumed that he was going to take others to Saut d'Eau. Instead, he had seen this as a good occasion to take a drive, which I would pay for, to his birthplace with his family.

I looked for the *kantè* that Deland's friend had promised. I asked one of his church brothers. He told me that the *kantè* had broken down and was in the shop. That was that.

I asked James to get started on the way. He and several friends put the casket into the *taptap* and then headed off for Saut d'Eau. Once they putt-putted out of sight, I turned to face the huge crowd waiting for their rides to Saut d'Eau. I felt like Moses in front of the Red Sea.

They were all looking directly at me. Everyone wanted to go to Saut d'Eau. I had no idea what I was going to tell them. I motioned to them to be patient a minute. Some understood my predicament and removed themselves voluntarily from the equation. There remained about thirty, asking me when the *kantè* would arrive, would there be room, and so on.

I simply waited for a miracle. I had no money and I knew that the *kantè* was out of commission. I held my head high . . . to avoid looking anyone in the eyes.

I didn't have the courage to tell the crowd that the *kantè* was no longer available, especially my new in-laws. Since Annie was pregnant, she remained at home, according to Haitian custom and practice. I wanted her family to see — and believe — that I was a responsible son who could organize his father's funeral. I also didn't want them to see that my relations weren't acting to help me out. Instead, they were profiting from me and waiting to see how I would manage. I wanted people, especially the Dieumercis, to think that I came from a noble, generous family. Unfortunately, the generous, noble member was now dead.

One of Deland's church brothers quietly called me aside. I knew him to be poor, even worse off than Deland had been. He passed 250 gourdes ($6.21 US) into my hand. He had seen what was happening and he understood. I'll never forget that.

I asked the crowd to follow me onto the street. I knew that 250 gourdes would not get us to Saut d'Eau. But it could get us to Titanyen, the large market well outside the city where the peasants from the north brought their products and the merchants from the city came to meet them. My own family in Saut d'Eau had brought their harvest to Titanyen for decades. Getting to Titanyen was a start. I would see where it led us.

The thirty people piled into two *taptaps* that took us to Titanyen. There, the vehicles dumped us in the middle of the market. The market operates on Tuesdays and Fridays. The funeral was on a Thursday, and so Titanyen was empty.

The *taptaps* dropped us off next to the workshop of my uncle. He was working. He had, needless to say, not attended Deland's funeral. He told us that he had seen the *taptap* with James and the casket pass by hours earlier.

"What's wrong?" he asked me.

I could see that he was plotting to "fix" whatever new problem I might have. "Everything's fine," I lied.

His nephew, my old friend Willy, was now a furniture maker with his own shop in another part of Titanyen. I went to see him. He loaned me 5,000 gourdes ($124 US) and helped me to find another *kantè*, much larger than the one we had initially hired, to take us to Saut d'Eau. The truck driver charged me 2,500 gourdes ($62 US) for a return trip to Saut d'Eau. The truck was so large that the thirty of us took up only a third of the space. Willy decided to come along.

We were in the middle of the dry season. The road that wanders through the mountains to Saut d'Eau was dry and the truck was kicking up all kind of dust. Before long, none of the mourners were wearing black. Everyone appeared to be white and in white. Our hair and even our skin was dusted white. This was the same route that Deland had initially taken to Port-au-Prince, with James and me in straw sacks across the back of a donkey. There had been no road then. This road was only a few years old. Peasants like Deland used to follow the mountain paths to the capital. This road was still mostly used by peasants and their donkeys carrying heavy loads.

After awhile, we passed a very old *taptap* that had broken down on the side of the road. Its right side was suspended in the air and resting on a pile of rocks. It appeared to have suffered a flat tire without the benefit of a jack to replace it. So the driver and passengers had lifted it by hand and held it in place with rocks. That's not unusual. On the ground, next to the *taptap*, was a coffin.

We saw James and our friends sitting on the exposed roots of a huge tree, laughing and joking. We have known this tree for decades. When Deland used to go to and from Saut d'Eau, we would stop here and sit under its shade for a rest before we continued on our way. The chauffeur was struggling alone with the flat tire. A tire lay on the ground next to him. He was putting on a good show, but it was clear to everybody that there was no way that the *taptap* could carry on. It had barely outlived my father. It had reached its final resting place, between Titanyen and Saut d'Eau.

James and I went to speak to the *taptap* driver. He said that the *taptap* wasn't in the best of health. We argued that that was his responsibility. Normally, people don't pay *taptap* drivers until they arrive at their destination since so much can go wrong. Drivers only collect their fees at the end of the route. In this case, his job was to get the casket to Saut d'Eau. Since he couldn't do it, then the contract was no longer valid. We suggested that he should return part of the 2,500 gourdes ($62 US) that we had paid him. But he said that he had no money left. He said he had spent it all on gas and preparing the *taptap*. He couldn't return what he didn't have. Moreover, he asked if we could help him out. He said it wasn't his fault, but the fault of the *taptap*. He gestured to it as though to plead for our compassion. The trouble that this damn *taptap* had caused him, we wouldn't believe! Couldn't we help him out with a little extra money?

Time was passing and the heat was mounting. The body was no longer on ice in the morgue. We knew we had to get going. We put the coffin into the *kantè* and left the driver and his *taptap* to reconcile their differences in peace. Then we all continued on our way to Saut d'Eau together.

Eventually, we passed Deland's property that we had sold for the funeral. Nearby was a river that we used to love in our childhoods. We would go there to bathe and to fish and to explore. But it was gone. Others were also reduced to tiny trickles, their water all diverted for various projects. I missed the vibrant and beautiful rivers.

Now, the *konbit* system that Deland grew up with is dead. Peasants work for each other, but they expect to be paid for the day, like any job. In Deland's day, the entire community loaned themselves out in *konbits*. As they loaned themselves to work for others, the *konbit* would come to work their land in turn. That community aspect has disappeared. Increasingly, each peasant is on his own.

The *kantè* went as far as it could. There was no way it could navigate to the burial place. After the road, it was able to follow the donkey paths for a little while. After that, we were on our own. My peasant relatives saw us and came over. Willy, who is strong, took the front of the casket and asked if someone would take the other end. One of the peasants stepped up and helped him. As they carried it, the others chanted along the way. The land was bumpy and I started to worry about the quality of the wood that my uncle had used. Claude had been able to do miracles as far as the appearance of the casket was concerned. But the planks used underneath were still rotting and unpredictable. I feared that they might give way before we arrived at the crypt. "Go slowly," I advised. "Take it easy."

We arrived in the *lakou* where my father had begun his life. As we approached, we heard people crying out. I wanted them to be the cries that I remembered from my childhood, the cries of *tet ansanm*, of unity. But these were cries of division. We passed the house that Deland had built for Cécile, that they had inhabited for a couple of unhappy years before Deland left for the capital. Now, his little sister lived in it. She wept loudly and paced from one side of the little *kay* to the other. Never did she move beyond the limits of her own residence.

In the past, death surmounted divisions among families and friends. Feuds were put on hold in the case of death. Now death had amplified the feuds.

We descended to the *kay* of Deland's elder sister, she who had asked us for 15,000 gourdes ($373 US). About a hundred people had assembled there. Even the family of my mother, Cécile, had come. We opened the coffin so that they could pay their respects. A few people were sobbing. The majority were piling their plates with rice and tiny pieces of pork or complaining that they hadn't yet got anything.

After we closed the coffin, a peasant led us to the tomb where my father would be placed next to Cécile. He told us that there was no more money to complete the work. I asked what work he was talking about. All that had to be done was to close the tomb with cement once the coffin was placed inside. I could see that the cement was waiting.

"How much money do you need?"

"Well... if you have 2,500 gourdes ($62 US), that would be enough," he said. "We know that you don't have any money."

"Really?" I said. "All we have is 1,000 gourdes ($25 US). Take that and see what you can do. Maybe in the future, we'll find a way to give you the rest."

He took the money and put the coffin in its place in our presence. Then he filled the opening with cement to close it. We went to see my aunt before returning to Port-au-Prince. She and her children were waiting for us. She said that we needed to discuss the outstanding issues. We asked what else there was now that the burial was over and the people were finishing the rice.

My aunt said, "No, no. We have to observe the Last Prayer."

I was confused. "Last Prayer?"

One of her daughters reacted to my surprise, "Yes! Yes! We have to say the Last Prayer. If we don't, the soul will never join the body. It will always remain in the *lakou*."

This was a Catholic custom that had a price tag. We weren't sure that it was relevant for us. "Send the soul where exactly? What are you proposing?"

The daughter defended the custom, "Yes. All funerals say the Last Prayer." She led me outside to see the "tunnel" that the peasants had constructed in front of the house. A number of long branches had been cut down and placed to make the tunnel about six metres long. On top was a roof of straw and coconut leaves. Until the Last Prayer had been said, people thought that the soul of the deceased was still in the *lakou*. They would come to play dominoes or other games in the tunnel to be with the deceased. Once the Last Prayer had been pronounced, then the tunnel would be taken down.

Our relatives told us that, for them, the funeral ceremony was secondary, and that the Last Prayer was all-important. They would have to slaughter livestock and prepare a large feast.

"Without the Last Prayer, we can't remove the tunnel," they told us.

"Well, we could take it down now and see what happens," we offered.

"No! No! No!" replied our cousin. "If you were to do that, we will have to pay the price. The soul would be forever in the *lakou*. If you can't offer much, okay. You could just buy a case of soft drinks. That's all."

My aunt was silent in the background. Her children were leading this charge for an expensive ceremony of Last Prayer. Of all people, my aunt knew of my father's beliefs. Thirty years earlier, she had been stricken with the same insanity that had almost killed Deland. Together, and with the rest of the family, they became Protestant. But this ceremony was Catholic and Vodou. Both used the tunnel and the Last Prayer. I wanted to know why they wanted to revive this for Deland, of all people.

"I understood that you were Protestants. Why are you planning this ritual for my father? He was Protestant, like you."

"Yes, we are Protestants. But everyone knows that it's a custom. If we don't do it, people will say that the funeral was poor and that we didn't care for the soul properly. We don't want to give them the chance to gossip like that."

I said, "Okay. I get it. You would rather please people. For whatever reason, I don't understand. We have lost our mother and now our father.... Yes, I understand. I thought that you were going to help us. We aren't foreigners. We aren't *blan*. You know we have nothing. You know that! And now you want to see what else you can take from us while you have the chance. Now you want us to pay for a Vodou and Catholic custom that Deland had renounced. You say you reject it too. You say that you want to do this for some nameless neighbour who may not like your beliefs.... I wonder if it isn't because this custom is also expensive.... I imagine that you will be able to show others here how generous you are. But the opposite is true. You want us to pay for your generosity. What kind of generosity is that? Even if it weren't the case that we are poor, that we have debts, that Deland's children are all in real danger in Simon. Alone. And you want to take their money to show off to your neighbours?"

Someone interrupted us tell me that the driver wanted to get back to Titanyen.

"Okay, listen. If someone wants to criticize, tell them to criticize James and me. I'm going to take down the tunnel now."

James and I went out and started to pull out the branches. There were a few people under it. There was a Protestant peasant who had been following my conversation with my aunt and cousins. He came to me anxiously, "Okay, Joegodson. Just leave the tunnel for now. What you said is true. But there are people under it now. Just leave them and I'll take it down later tonight."

We left it to him.

James told me to wait for him. He was thirsty and, before we left for Titanyen, he wanted to get a drink of water. He entered my aunt's *kay*. There, he saw a cat sitting next to a huge metal tub, a *kivèt*, which was partly protruding from under my aunt's bed, munching on a big piece of meat. James was curious. He pushed the cat aside and pulled the tub out from under the bed. Inside the tub was three quarters of a pig. She had served the mourners one quarter of the beast and cached away the rest. All with the 15,000 gourdes that she insisted she needed for the burial. Of course, she had asked for much more, and used much less.

James had wanted to believe that his aunt was fond of Deland and solicitous of his children. He was unhappy to find that she had betrayed him in death while his family was in distress. It hurt.

He came to tell me in secret what he had found. He took me by the hand to the room to see three-quarters of a pig in the tub. We both stood over it dumbfounded. My aunt entered and saw us.

She said, "Oh, I forgot to tell you. We had some meat here. We were going to give you some to return to Port-au-Prince. It might be helpful."

She cut off a little piece for James and another for me.

I said to James, "You can take it, James. I don't have the stomach to eat that. It would be like insulting our father."

James accepted the little insult. My aunt was half ashamed and half relieved.

We left to board the *kantè* for Titanyen.

Waiting in front of the *kantè* were more people than we had brought for the funeral. A number of others had decided to take the opportunity to visit the capital. Others had been in the region and heard that there was a free ride available to Port-au-Prince. When James and I approached the *kantè*, my cousin in the minibus was just arriving. He had taken 1,000 gourdes ($25 US) from me to pay for his petrol to bring his family to Saut d'Eau in his minibus. Along the way, he had had two flat tires. Since there was little chance of getting back to Port-au-Prince with his tires, he also decided to leave his minibus in Saut d'Eau and put his family into the *kantè*.

Everyone climbed aboard. It was now full. When we had originally boarded in Titanyen, we had taken up only a third of the space. We were thirty then. Now, we were one hundred. And we were squished.

The driver called me. "I negotiated for 2,500 gourdes ($62 US). That was for one way. I never agreed to carry a coffin. I never agreed to return. And I never agreed to carry half of Saut d'Eau back to Titanyen."

I was totally disoriented by this new challenge. He was right of course. Things had changed just as he argued. However, it wasn't true that he had not agreed to return to Titanyen. That was why he was still there waiting.

"Okay, tell me what you want."

He said, "You should pay me the same amount to return, of course! 2,500 gourdes."

All that I had left was 1,500 gourdes ($37 US). While he and I were engaged in this tricky negotiation, the people inside the *kantè* started to pound against the railings and the floor, "Come on, chauffeur! Let's go!" This was not helping my end of the negotiations. I was expecting him, at any minute, to yell at everyone to get out of his truck and then take off for Titanyen alone.

I made the mistake of telling him the truth. That I needed to get these people back to the capital, that I had 1,500 gourdes, and that I would need 500 of that to pay for the *taptaps* from Titanyen to Port-au-Prince. I could only offer him 1,000 gourdes ($25 US). I may as well have poured oil on a fire.

"What! That's it!" He said as he charged to the back of the *kantè* and started clapping his hands together in frustration. "Everybody! Get down! Get down from the *kantè* right now!"

No one got down. Everyone started whining. I stood to the side. This spectacle was just what I had been trying to avoid in front of the Dieumerci family who had come to Saut d'Eau in the group of thirty.

Willy was in the cabin of the *kantè*. He had driven out with his friend the driver and would go back in the cabin as well. He told me that he judged the driver to be right. He advised me to find a way to solve the problem amicably.

"It's not because I'm trying to be difficult. I think he's right too. I'm just telling the truth. I'm not holding any money back somewhere. I'd give him more if I had more. I don't," I said.

Willy asked how much I had. I brought him up to date. He said that I didn't have nearly enough. That's what I'd been trying to tell everyone.

Willy said, "Give me your 1,000 gourdes. I'll add another 1,000."

He called the driver over, who accepted the new offer. He was so riled that he took the money from Willy, jumped up into the driver's seat, started the *kantè*, and took off while I was still standing there. I didn't run after him. I just calmly walked behind as he sped off. He knew I was there. He saw me in the rearview mirror if he hadn't seen me standing next to the truck's cabin. Anyway, he decided to give in and stopped twenty metres ahead. I walked to get aboard the back with the rest of the world.

As I climbed aboard, I felt satisfied. Of course, we live in Haiti and it is always foolish to assume that nothing more can go wrong. But, when this *kantè* arrived back in Titanyen, I would have succeeded in my goal of giving my father a funeral. It didn't matter how many people had tried and succeeded to screw me along the way. I breathed calmly.

Mme Dieumerci and three of her daughters — Annie's elder sisters — were there. They were content. They had seen that I had the competence to get through a number of obstacles. Of course, the *kantè* swayed and rolled backed to Titanyen. Mme Dieumerci, seventy-three years old, had to stand up and try to keep her balance like everyone else. But, in Haiti, that is normal. That is success.

When we arrived in Titanyen, I split up the 500 gourdes ($12.50 US) into two parts. I gave 250 to James to take a *taptap* to Simon. He took all of that group. I hired two other *taptaps*, one to take people back to Bon Repos and another to go to Silo to drop off the Dieumercis and to carry on to Delmas 33. When I arrived home, Annie was waiting. "Did everything go all right?" she asked.

"Better than I expected," I said.

chapter forty-four

THE DEATH OF MY FATHER discouraged me about my future. What would my generation face? What about those being born? What was in store for them? Did my father have such thoughts in his youth? Could he ever have imagined how he would leave the world? And what he would leave behind? He had arrived in Simon and worked so hard to make a family and a business. He died in despair.

My concerns were urgent, not at all philosophical. Annie's doctor advised her that she would give birth on the fourth of February. I had no means to care for the baby. Deland's funeral had added more debts to my account. I had a month to prepare.

On 25 January, after I had returned from church in the afternoon, Annie said that she was feeling unwell. I wasn't too worried. I had the doctor's date in my mind. At eleven o'clock at night, she woke me to tell me that she was having cramps. I could see that the baby had dropped. I had little experience in this area, but I knew that midwives massaged the stomachs of women in childbirth with the oil from the *maskriti* plant. It is helpful to relieve pain. From time to time, Annie felt pain and then, a few minutes later, she was able to fall asleep again. However, near midnight, she was struck by a pain that would not subside.

I didn't want to leave Annie alone. I called Mme Bolivar, who lived close to us. Mme Dieumerci was staying there at the moment. They, of course, had firsthand experience in childbirth. They arrived and quickly determined that the birth was imminent. I needed to find a vehicle to get her to a hospital.

I called a church brother but he had taken his car to the garage for repairs. Then I called my uncle, although I knew that even if his car was working, he would make me pay for gas.

"Who is this!?" growled my uncle, registering his reaction to being called during the night.

"It's me, Joegodson."

"What do you want?!"

I had only one hundred gourdes in the house. It wasn't mine, but the payment from my friend Mardi to Mme Dieumerci for a jar of *manba* she had made. "It ... it ... it's about Annie ... she's giving birth. I wanted to know if you would help her to the hospital with your car."

My uncle didn't hear the last word. Maybe he heard in my voice my financial situation. He replied, "My car is broken down. You'll have to find another way to get to the hospital."

I wasn't surprised. I had known what his response would be. Mme Bolivar and her husband said that they would go to ask a neighbour who had a vehicle. They left. The neighbour had been sleeping like everyone else. He asked no questions, but got dressed and prepared.

We had intended to go to the Doctors Without Borders clinic in Delmas 31. We got there at one o'clock in the morning. When we entered the courtyard of the clinic, a security guard directed us to a big tent. Annie was beginning to feel the pain intensely. Some nurses came. "What's happening? What is it?"

"We have a woman here who is giving birth."

"Sorry," they said. "We don't deal with pregnancies here. Just accidents — broken arms and legs and gunshot wounds."

We told them that we just needed help. The baby was almost delivered. But they offered their regrets and left us in the courtyard, alone.

We piled back into the car. Annie was in the back, with her mother on one side and me on the other. The night was dark. There was no electricity. The road was bumpy and there were big potholes. The headlights of the car couldn't illuminate all of the obstacles. Consequently, the car was surprised by each bump and every descent. So was Annie and, I'm sure, our baby.

Despite the shocks, we set out for Chansrèl, a hospital along the Route Nationale. The car ride could not have been better designed to provoke the birth. Annie wanted to stop the car to simply get it over with. She preferred just to push the baby there, as we passed the broken-down Imperial Cinema on Delmas. But the driver continued toward the hospital.

While the car continued along, we shifted our positions in the backseat. Annie leaned her back against me on one side and her two feet against the door of the car, on either side of Mme Dieumerci who waited for the birth almost as though she was playing goal, not sure how it would arrive. The baby cried and Mme Dieumerci said, "Ah, it's a girl."

The driver stopped the car after the population of the backseat had gone from three to four. If he had been a *taptap* driver, he would have insisted on another five gourdes.

Some police were on patrol. When they saw the car stopped, with the interior lights on, they assumed that we were thieves or kidnappers. They surrounded us. They were afraid of us. They had their hands on their hips, ready to pull their guns. They could have fired upon us to save their lives.

"Look at this!" I said, "Everyone is afraid except our baby."

They had their flashlights trained on us as they hollered, "What's going on here?!"

Mme Bolivar responded, "It's a childbirth."

They weren't buying it, "Where is this baby?!"

They continued to surround us. One of the cops leaned forward; his feet firmly planted a safe distance from the car as he stretched his head like a giraffe to peer into the backseat. He seemed to be willing to lose his head, as long as his body could escape in case of foul play.

Fortunately, the baby cried. The officer relaxed. The others also loosened their tensed bodies. "Okay, okay," he said and stood at ease. Our daughter had already defused a tense situation. Only three minutes old!

"Now where are you going?" he asked.

Mme Bolivar told them we were going to continue on to Chansrèl to have the umbilical cord cut. They found that reasonable. They let us carry on.

We got to the gates of Chansrèl Hospital at two o'clock in the morning. We asked the security guards to let us enter. We told him that it was a childbirth.

"No, we aren't accepting any more women. It's already full inside," he said.

"It's not to give birth. The baby is already here. We just want help to cut the umbilical cord," said Mme Bolivar.

He let us enter. In the courtyard were hundreds of people who had accompanied other women who were giving birth that night. They were sleeping on the ground.

Annie and the baby were not separated yet. So Mme Bolivar went to get a doctor to come to the car. He cut the cord. Then Mme Dieumerci and I accompanied Annie and the baby into the hospital. At the entrance, they had us wash our hands with bleach to protect against cholera.

All of the pregnant women were pacing, praying, and chanting to relieve the stress and pain of childbirth. I thought that three-quarters of Haiti's women were giving birth that night.

They left my daughter on a table, without any covers or any supervision. They put a bracelet on her wrist so as not to confuse her with the other babies. I asked the doctor if I could take the baby in my arms. He asked Annie if she knew me. They then took Annie into another room for stitches.

Mme Dieumerci and I dressed the baby for the first time.

When Annie returned, the staff led her and the baby into a big room that was both happy and sad. It was full of the women who had given birth and some who had lost their babies trying.

At daybreak, a couple of nurses came by to register the births. While Annie was giving the information, a young man who had come with his wife came up to me. He wanted to name his baby after a German soccer coach. He asked me how to spell it. I had no idea. I asked him what it meant. He said he didn't know, he just liked the sound. It sounded like "wokinlaw." I suggested that he call the baby "Walk-in-law" in order to get the same sound. I told him what it meant. He thought it was a great idea and he registered his little boy as Walk-in-law. Often, parents choose names strictly on the sound. I have a neighbour whose boy is called Hitler, because his father thought it sounded nice.

Annie, with the nurses in front of her, forgot the name we had chosen. She called me over and I wrote it on a piece of paper so that they would get it right: Naara. They gave us a birth certificate. We went home.

It was thanks to the hundred gourdes that Mardi had given me that I was able to get a *taptap* to return to Delmas 33. We three entered our little room for the first time.

chapter forty-five

AFTER THE EARTHQUAKE, Paul created a website so that I could post blog entries about what was going on in Port-au-Prince. When Naara was a few months old, we thought about writing a book. We wrote a proposal and sent it to some publishers. When they accepted the project in principle, we decided to put our website on hold. Now Paul and I would have to get together again to talk and write full time.

Since Paul had already lived in Haiti in 2006, he preferred that I come to Canada for the work. I went to the Canadian embassy to inform myself about how to enter Canada to work temporarily.

I went to the big Canadian embassy on the main avenue that cuts through Port-au-Prince, Rue Delmas. The embassy was closed for a holiday. But in front there was a board with some announcements along with brochures that explained the services offered. I took the relevant ones: instructions for applying for a temporary visa along with the Internet address for more information. While I was reading the information, a number of people came to see what I was looking at. I had a pen and was taking notes. They lived nearby and passed every day this huge building with the white (actually grey thanks to Haitian dust) and red Canadian flag flying above. But that another poor Haitian was taking notes might have prompted them to stop to consider its potential value for them. When I went up to the board, I was alone. When I had my information and left to go home, there was a small crowd searching for what it was that had so interested me.

Paul called me in the evening for an update. I told him that everything was on the Internet. Since he had access and I didn't, we decided that it made more sense for him to do the research and report back to me. We could see that the Canadian government intended to make the process difficult for the poor. First, the rate of illiteracy is high in Haiti. A bulletin board is already a challenge for many people. For those who pass that obstacle, there is next the problem of the Internet. Few Haitians have computers. We have to pay at an Internet cafe for a connection. The service is outdated and unreliable. Few poor Haitians see the value in wasting money — that they could otherwise use to buy food — to learn to surf the Web. By sending Haitians to the Internet, the Canadian government is saying that it is either insensitive or doesn't want the poor to even apply for visas.

Paul found the requirements for entering Canada from Haiti on the government site. I needed a passport, a bank account at least six months old with evidence of activity, photographs, a certified cheque for $75, letters from my employer, and a letter from my Canadian sponsor.

I had opened an account in 2006, but it had lapsed from lack of activity. My passport too was within a month of expiring. Paul sent me money to renew my passport and another $500 to open a bank account. He sent me the forms by email. I went to an Internet cafe to print them. Often, the Internet cafes have no service during the days because there is no reliable electric current. If you do find electricity, the signal is so tenuous and slow that much time and money can be wasted. Every thirty minutes, I had to pay again to keep trying to download the documents. Finally, I had them.

On the day before I had to submit the documents, I went to the Capital Bank, where I had opened an account, for the certified cheque for $75. They said that it was not possible. The teller said that I needed to have an account for six months before they would issue me a certified cheque. I was discouraged. I told the teller that I had a rendezvous early the next morning. The embassy would not accept cash. It needed to be this cheque. *Zafè kabrit pa gade mouton* — a sheep doesn't care about a goat's problems. I called Paul in Canada. He said it made no sense that they would not give me a certified cheque. He checked their website to see that the service was offered. So I called the manager. He repeated what the teller had said. And there it ended. I just took out $100 with the hope that I might find another institution to write me a certified cheque.

I walked the streets without any clear objective. Which of these banks would write me a cheque? Finally, I tried my luck at the Banque Nationale de Crédit. It was my last chance, since time was running out.

I asked the receptionist. She asked if I had an account in the bank. No. She said that I would need to have an account there. When I explained that it was urgent, she said that I could open an account and come tomorrow for the cheque. But the rendezvous at the embassy was set for eight o'clock in the morning. Was there anything that she could do for me? She said that the charge for a certified cheque was twenty dollars and that the account would need to have twenty dollars in it after the cheque was issued to remain open. That meant that I would need to have $115 to get my cheque. All I had was $100. It seemed hopeless. There were only ten minutes left until the bank closed its doors on my chance to realize my goal. Just at that moment, a member of my church choir entered the bank. I quickly explained the situation and he handed me the fifteen dollars. I would repay him later. I had my cheque.

I returned home in triumph. I thought that for once things were changing for me. I wondered if this was a sign that it was God's will that I succeed in getting to Canada to finish our work. It seemed a miracle that my friend from church should appear at that precise moment.

My head was alive all night long. I couldn't sleep. I projected myself into the near future. If this worked, I would be in Canada. What would it be like? How would people see me there?

The day arrived after a long night. My fantasies seemed out of place in the harsh reality of our little room in Delmas 33.

The rendezvous was for eight. I arrived before that, but there was already a long line-up in front of the embassy. Some were tired. They were crouching on the ground. A security guard was giving instructions. He called to me and asked what I was doing here. I explained that I had a rendezvous. He wanted to see the documents that I had brought with me. He told me that I needed to have copies of my passport and my national identity card. I scurried around looking for a place that made copies. I returned with them and saw that the people who were scheduled for the first rendezvous were already entering. I followed them into the big building.

A security guard took my identity card and noted my presence in a book. He gave me a key to a locker where I had to leave my cellphone. I followed the others up to the second floor.

Inside was a big room with comfortable chairs. There were a number of places where we could speak to people through slits in windows.

A guard asked if I was there for an interview. I said yes. So, he showed me where to sit.

After a few minutes, I heard a voice call out the names of those who were there for an interview. Mine wasn't among them. So I asked the security guard for help. He asked again if I was there for an interview. I said yes, but since it was my first time, I wasn't really sure about the procedures. He took my passport and went to find out where I should be. He returned to tell me that I was simply there to hand in my documents. That wasn't, it turned out, an "interview." Who knew? He led me to another office where I was to hand in my documents. He introduced me to the woman there, saying condescendingly, "Here's a young man who thinks that everything is simple. He thinks you just walk into the embassy and they send you to Canada."

I didn't think that.

I waited in line. When it was my turn, the clerk told me that I was missing a document. She didn't tell me what it was, just that there should be another document. She said that if I could get it and bring it back by noon, then she could accept it. She never suggested that the document was available in the embassy. Why would the embassy not just hand me the form? I didn't ask even such logical questions. I had to go to an Internet cafe to find it, download it, fill it in, and return it. I called Paul and he discovered that there were new documents required now. Applicants from Haiti now had to give a detailed description of their work history for the last ten years and, in another document, they had to list all of their brothers and sisters along with their jobs and criminal records.

I went to all the Internet cafes in the area. None of them had the program that could download the document I needed. It was the rainy season and, as usual, it was coming down in torrents as I searched for an Internet cafe that could print the document. I finally was able to download the document, but, by now, I was so far away from the embassy that there was no way to return before noon.

When I arrived, the security guards at the main gate said that it was too late.

I walked home in the pouring rain, having no more money for a *taptap*. I had all my documents with me, including the cheque. I was more than discouraged. I didn't want to go to Canada. That meant that I wouldn't finish the project. I was feeling very low.

I called Paul to explain. "Isn't there another way we can finish our book?"

Paul reprised what had become a common theme, "You are discouraged. It's obvious. They are putting you through nasty hoops. The treatment at the embassy has been conceived to discourage you. To make you give up. But, especially because it is uncomfortable for you, you should keep going to the end. To see what happens. Don't give up. We'll make another chapter of our book describing your experiences at the embassy. But you have nothing to apologize for. You have done everything they ask, even where it's humiliating. You have a letter from Canadian publishers saying that they are waiting for the manuscript. You will be contributing to the Canadian economy. It makes no sense that this particular government, obsessed with economic growth, should discourage you. Just try to get through this. Take it like another obstacle. Think of all you've been through. Finish with the embassy and we'll decide what to do after that."

I agreed. But Paul's pep talk hardly softened the unpleasantness of dealing with the embassy. It was clear that they were trying to humiliate me. It was working. I felt ashamed. They asked me every question that might demonstrate that I was poor and that my family was poorer. Why did they want to know that my brothers and sisters were all unemployed? Why did they need to know their level of education? It seemed that they wanted me to say it. Why did they ask for the criminal records of each of my brothers and sisters? Why did they want to know whether I had a good job? Would they acknowledge that I was a skilled furniture maker? Would they acknowledge that I was creating my own employment by writing about life in Haiti? Why did I feel so debased, miserable, and utterly hopeless every time I approached the embassy now? I felt like they were trying to prove that, on paper, I was worthless. It was demeaning. The security guards snickered and made fun of me. But I decided to carry on as Paul suggested. He said to try to keep my distance from them. From now on, I should think of the Canadian embassy as an experiment. I should have no expectations. The goal was now to put them under the microscope, to judge them while they were judging me. I would try.

I got another interview for the following week. I knew now that I had all the documents required and that they were filled in. I also had letters from Paul in Montréal and his mother in Toronto who would sponsor me while in Canada. And the letter from the publisher; though, not ultimately, the actual publisher. I took everything to the embassy for the second time. This time, the receptionist took all my documents. She kept my bank account book and my passport along with all the forms. She set up a rendezvous for the following week.

This time, I started to think that the answer would have to be affirmative. I had fulfilled all the requirements. I had filled in all the forms. I had sponsors in Canada. I had a bank account that had recently had 500 Canadian dollars in it. I had a letter from Canadian publishers. The more I thought of it, the more I realized that they would have to agree to my request. I was asking to visit Canada for only three months to complete our project. Especially after we talked and they understood, Canada would open its doors to me.

I arrived the following week an hour before my rendezvous. There was already a large crowd in front of the embassy. There wasn't a hint of shade and the sun was pitiless.

I started to forget about my humiliations and think about the poor people in line who would be disappointed. I thought about how these people, standing out in the open like they were, would be vulnerable to thieves who could target people in front of the embassy. If they were asking for visas, then they had some wealth. But, talking with the people in the crowd, I came to see that they were just like me. They had spent their money to buy some humiliation from the Canadian embassy.

In my first conversation, I met some people who had left from the countryside before sunrise. They had sold land and livestock to find the money to go to Canada. Unfortunately, they wore their poverty on their Creole faces. They were not visa material.

From inside their air-conditioned embassy, the functionaries would have seen us all wiping the sweat from our brows. We couldn't keep ourselves dry and our handkerchiefs were drenched.

Many in the crowd hadn't had the time to eat before beginning their trek to the embassy. They bought little things from the passing street merchants. Not real food, but soft drinks and candies to keep from fainting. The boys who sell packets of water surrounded us, singing out *"Dlo, dlo, dlo."* We were easy marks, and they stayed close by to make a gourde from us when we could no longer stand the sun.

Finally, the security guards came out in front of the gates. They asked us to form two lines: one for those like me who had come to receive their results; the other for those who were handing in their documents, as I had done the previous week. Our line was allowed to pass the gates and enter the grounds and then the embassy. They gave us our responses. Everyone separated him or herself from the others to go into a quiet corner to read the results of their requests for visas to enter Canada. There was a general hush of anticipation.

On my document was written that I hadn't "convinced" the authorities that I would leave Canada at the end of the time permitted under my visa application. So, my request was rejected. However, I had no idea what arguments would have "convinced" them of my integrity. My visa application was for three months, the time it would take to complete our work. They assumed that I would stay in Canada after that date. Why? Did they assume that only a fool would remain in Haiti to work for Canadian clothing manufacturers for three dollars a day under the conditions I knew only too well? Did they know that only a masochist would accept living in a country whose economy was conceived to enrich a minority of Haitians and their Canadian and American collaborators? In fact, they had me wrong. I would have returned to my life in Haiti, such as it was. But it did tell me something about what the Canadian authorities thought about people like me. The entire process had been about discovering what class I belonged to. Then, they argued that my class would stay put.

chapter forty-six

IN JULY, I HAD TO TRAVEL TO SAUT D'EAU. It was during the time when pilgrims start to arrive for the big festival, but for me it was not a celebration.

Suzanne, my grandmother, was very old. She was Deland's mother. She had saved him and my aunt in their youth when our family *lwa* turned against us. Now she was blind. She needed an arm to hold on to even to move across the room. She lived alone. Her little house in Saut d'Eau was falling apart; the mortar that the peasants concoct to hold the stones in place had been disintegrating for some time. It was getting dangerous. Dad and I had been planning to repair it. Then Deland died. As for me, I had so many concerns when Naara was born that I pushed my grandmother's need into the background. But I knew that she was there and that she needed me.

Burying her son Deland was unbearable for her. She suffered a stroke and stopped speaking. Then she stopped eating until her body expired. She couldn't see. She couldn't walk. She couldn't speak. But I fear that she could hear. It was what she heard as she was dying that ate away at me.

She had six children. Five were still alive. The youngest daughter, the aunt whom I had lived with after my mother died, lived in Port-au-Prince; four others lived in Saut d'Eau. She had dozens of grandchildren. When she was a young woman, Suzanne bought a piece of land for seventeen gourdes — just a few pennies. Now it was valued at 60,000 gourdes ($1,486 US). She wanted the plot to go to her youngest daughter in Port-au-Prince who otherwise would have no land in Saut d'Eau and would lose her connection to her birthplace. The other plots of land that Suzanne had owned were in the possession of her other children.

This final plot was especially valuable. It is centrally located and fertile as well. It could be profitable for tourism or for agriculture, or both.

My aunt, Deland's eldest sister, wanted it for her family. And so my relatives divided into camps, each vying for the property. The struggle for the plot of land had become so acrimonious that no words passed between the two groups. When Deland was buried, his eldest sister watched the funeral from her yard because she refused to be in the presence of those who refused to accede to her claims to the property. My grandmother was too disheartened to enter the argument raging around her. Literally, dis-heartened. Her blood pressure rose to cause the stroke. She stopped eating. I think she wanted her heart to stop beating.

There are no morgues in the countryside and so funerals have to take place soon after death. Such was the case with Suzanne. Normally, the plot of land should have been sold to pay for the funeral if no other means were available. That was the case. But the plot was neither sold to pay for the funeral nor left to the youngest daughter.

I travelled to Saut d'Eau on the morning of the funeral and returned to Port-au-Prince in the evening.

I couldn't bear to see my grandmother disrespected in death. The funeral was stingy. There were two groups. One group of forty people was present as the body was buried. The other group, including my father's eldest sister, was a distance away looking on. I knew that my grandmother had been aware that her children were fighting over the property as she lay dying. People were now at her funeral but were focused not on Suzanne but on the land.

There was no ceremony. I insisted that everyone sing the traditional hymns for interment. A couple of people were crying. They started hollering that it was the other group that had caused the situation. It was a mess.

I had not planned to speak, but I couldn't stand the atmosphere around me. I asked people to stop hollering recriminations. I told them that these were battle cries whereas they should be tears of respect for Suzanne who had done so much for us all during her life. I chastised all of my relatives for their avarice and their inhumanity toward their mother and grandmother. I told them that I would take no side in the coming war over the land.

They had divided themselves and they were all the poorer for it. I told them so. They had taken a beautiful place and turned it into hell. No one denied it. No one said anything. Everyone looked at the ground until I had finished. Then they put my grandmother in the ground. No one spoke. At best, my words will remain suspended in the air of Saut d'Eau.

Then I returned to Delmas 33 to be with Naara and Annie and to wonder whatever would become of us.

I have found it hard to live with the tragedy of Suzanne's final passage. After all her life, a simple gesture of paying someone seventeen gourdes for a plot of land overshadowed raising children and grandchildren, keeping us all alive and healthy through sometimes desperate situations. I will always be haunted by the likelihood that she heard her children fighting over her little plot of land at her deathbed.

My aunt was separated from her mother's burial. She stood with her group in a valley in Saut d'Eau. Her future, she thinks, depends upon that plot of land. She thinks that she can build a future that ignores the past. She can't.

chapter forty-seven

IF CANADIANS WOULDN'T LET ME enter their country, I refused to work in their sweatshops. But the double rejection soon turned into a positive experience for me. I had to lay a better foundation for my life in Haiti.

We had the chance to rethink the status of my little property in Canaan. It was suffering. I had given my phone number, along with a few gourdes, to a woman who lived in the area and asked her to keep an eye on my land and call me if there was something I should know. She did call to say that the squatters on each side kept moving their property lines, squeezing me from each direction.

If I had gone to Canada as planned to work on this book, maybe my heart would have remained behind in Haiti, worried about what was happening to Annie, Naara, and my land. When the Canadian government refused me entry, they allowed me to focus on my worries here in Haiti.

After the news from the embassy, Paul advised me to use the rest of the money in my account to make my presence clear in Canaan. If time went by and there were no signs of construction, someone else might claim the land. And, depending on the decision of the local committee, they might succeed. Marking my presence on the land was important.

I had already started to prepare for my home in Canaan. In the summer of 2010, we received an anonymous gift of $500 Canadian from someone who followed our writings. The person said I was to use it to develop the plot in Canaan that I had written about. I immediately called my cousin Lorès, who lived in Bon Repos. He was a metalworker and skilled in construction. He advised me to go to Site Solèy to buy my reinforcement bars. He said that he bought materials there and the locals sold their stuff cheaper than the construction stores. He told me that it was better that I prepare a solid foundation even if I didn't have enough money to finish. I should build something durable, the opposite of the flimsy wooden shacks that the NGOs were throwing up. The NGOs gave these structures to Haitians and imagined that they were satisfied with them. Lorès didn't have to convince me that I should work toward a stable, solid home.

Lorès set aside a day to accompany me to Site Solèy to get the reinforcements. I bought twenty-five half-inch iron bars. Then we rented a *taptap* to take them to his property in Bon Repos. Lorès prepared the posts for the construction. Then one of Annie's sisters advised us to not go further with the construction. There were still doubts about the future of Canaan. Would the government allow construction there? Would a bourgeois family succeed in claiming the land as its own? It wasn't clear. Better that we survey the situation and wait until the signs were clearer. She worried that my money and effort would be wasted if the state prohibited construction. We decided that she was right. We left the steel bars on Lorès' property to go to Canaan when the time was right.

Instead of tracing the foundation of the building on the property, I decided to buy a truckload of sand. That would cost 4,000 gourdes ($100 US) and would be a clear sign that someone serious had claimed the property. At the same time, it wasn't too great an expense. It was a good balance.

I used the rest of the money from the donation to finish the furniture for my marriage.

My friend Louise had sent Annie and me a wedding gift of one hundred English pounds ($162 US). I received it in November of 2010. I decided to use it to buy a truckload of stones. My pile of sand would have a friend. I went to Canaan and found trucks lined up, waiting for someone like me who wanted a load of rocks. One of the drivers agreed to allow me to travel with him to the quarry where the rocks were mined.

When the driver arrived at the quarry, I found a community of male peasants who had created a world of their own. They were materially poor, far below the standard of Port-au-Prince. They were cheerful and happy in their work. I spent the afternoon talking and joking with them.

They had peasant names. Haitian peasants distinguish their offspring with names that refer to the conditions of their birth. I began by chatting up a man in his forties named Lamizè (Misery). His story was similar to the others. He had four children. They lived with his wife in Croix-de-Bouquets so that they could attend school. A couple of times a month, they came to visit their dad in his quarry and he would pass along the money he had earned so that they could pay their teachers and buy food. Otherwise, the quarrymen lived apart from their families. They lived and worked hard from sunrise to sunset in their quarries.

Each peasant mined his own quarry. I bought a truckload of stones from Tinonm (Little Man) who had a shipment ready to go. All four of the peasants who worked in that area came to help Tinonm and me load the truck. They joked and laughed together and then went back to their separate quarries. I was exhausted just watching Tinonm pound the wall of rock into blocks of stone. They told me that when sunset comes, they were physically exhausted and slept well. They lived in *ajoupas* (a hut built of branches covered with palm leaves that allows breezes to circulate inside the structure, typically built to last for several years).

When I asked Tinonm how long he had worked in the quarry, he replied that he had been there since a truckload cost 100 gourdes ($7 US). Now, it fetched 3,000 gourdes ($75 US). The peasants did not use the same references as I: they did not calculate in years or hours, but followed events that had meaning for them. I tried several other approaches until I figured out that Tinonm had been working there since 1995. Others had been there longer. Tinonm used to make charcoal for the Port-au-Prince market before that, but since there were no more trees to be transformed into charcoal, he decided to get into the quarry business.

There was no water in the neighbourhood. They looked forward to the passage of a truck, like the one that brought me to them, so that someone could hitch a ride back to Canaan and fill up the jugs with water. Otherwise they had to walk and it was a long way. I looked at the dirty water containers and asked about their precautions since Haiti was dealing with the cholera crisis.

"Aren't you afraid of cholera?" I asked.

"What's that?" they all asked.

They were all in good condition, of course, although their skin was burnt by the sun. They worked constantly, always making sure that someone had a shipment of rocks ready in case a truck came by. There was no telling when the next truck might appear.

They knew little about what was happening in Port-au-Prince. While only kilometres away, it was not easily accessible. They made their own community, dependent on the urban economy, but otherwise isolated from the city.

My spirit lightened during the afternoon. They were unpretentious and evidently content with their lives and comradeship. Once they made enough cash to support their families, their own material needs were minimal and almost completely independent of money.

Their simplicity was inspiring. Port-au-Prince — greedy, anxious, egotistical, unhappy — seemed far, far away. The constant struggle to earn enough of the little money in circulation to assure our survival seemed artificial in the face of this community of men who happily allowed money to slip through their fingers.

We returned to Canaan and piled the rocks next to the sand. They could serve as a solid foundation.

A few months later, a number of people were building homes to last, not *ajoupas* or tents. This increased activity fed upon itself. Before long, it was clear that the state had no choice but to recognize the new community of Canaan and those who were building even farther up the mountains. When policemen started building and the state recognized the committees, it was clear that we were safe to continue. People were setting up businesses. Once a new development takes off, the question is who will profit from it. The powerful would come to get their piece of the Canaan action.

The money that remained in my bank account would allow me to complete the foundation. That would solidify my claim to the land. First, my land was on a slope. That meant that I would need two other truck-loads of rocks and twenty-five bags of cement to lay a solid foundation. Fortunately, a few of the new settlers had already dug water reservoirs. Water had been scarce only a few months earlier. Now, I would have access to what I needed to mix the cement.

In Canaan, I found a couple of masons who were experts at tracing and digging the foundation. They traced two rooms, each four metres square. So, my house would be four by eight metres. I chose the crest of the hill, overlooking the valley below, and cooled by the perpetual breeze.

My future neighbour who watched over my land in my absence lent me a few drums to fill with water. I hired her young son as the water boy. Each bucket of water cost five gourdes (12 cents US). His job was to carry buckets of water from the nearest basin and fill up the drums. I was there just to oversee the work. I helped the masons with whatever they needed, carrying rocks and mixing mortar.

As we worked, masons passed by continuously asking for work. There was no lack of work to be done. There was no lack of skilled people to do it. There was only a pitiful lack of money to meet everyone's needs. I was privileged to be in the situation of laying a foundation. It had taken me a year to get this far. The other plots had nothing but sticks.

After two and a half days, the foundation was laid. The sand that I had bought a year earlier was the best quality. It helped the work go smoothly and it meant that the foundation was solid. Others, cutting corners, were using coarser sand. The mortar that resulted from using the coarser sand and cement was less reliable, less secure. I wanted to be sure that my little home would withstand the next earthquake, whenever it came.

It took time, but I could see my home literally rising out of Haitian soil. I was very happy.

chapter forty-eight

AFTER THE CANADIAN EMBASSY REFUSED ENTRY, I was discouraged about this project. I suggested to Paul that the only way we could continue was by telephone. Seeing how unwelcome a poor little Haitian like me was in the Canadian embassy in Haiti, I wondered what it would be like if I had been accepted. Was Canada not just a big version of the embassy? Would I not be humiliated everywhere? My curiosity and excitement was replaced with apprehension and acrimony. I feared that I understood Canada through its embassy.

Why had the Canadian embassy not accepted me? Everyone was seeing me as a furniture maker, a manual worker who is little respected in Haiti. That I was most happy and satisfied when I was crafting furniture was irrelevant to authorities. They scoffed at the idea that I could also be a writer. Maybe they were right. Maybe they knew me better than I knew myself. I shared those thoughts with Paul. I told him that we could just continue to write articles on our website and talk on the phone. Paul heard the resignation in my voice. He said that what I was feeling was just what the authorities had been hoping for. Both in Haiti and in Canada, the powerful are very happy when the poor, whether Haitian or Canadian or other, believe they are powerless. When we resign ourselves to the lowest rung of the global ladder, they profit. Their great fear is that the ladder might be disassembled. Those at the top would have a long way to fall. We had to decide how to respond to the humiliations and rejections that I had faced.

Paul argued that these experiences that had got me into a funk were inevitable. If things had been easy — if people could move between these borders as easily as money and corporations — then we would have to rethink how we understood the world. We had to keep supporting each other in the face of the obstacles that people, and the system in which we all live, put in our way.

Paul's mother, who was eighty-two years old, was angry to find that her government had refused me entry into her country. She had been willing to welcome me not only into her country, but into her home. She told me to not let them bully me. That showed me that the government didn't speak for all Canadians. But the rejection by the Canadian government helped us to understand how the rich and poor countries of the world were working together to manage things.

After my embassy nightmare, Paul asked me to think about what I wanted to do. He said that he would call me after three days and we could talk about it. He said that if I was really still too dejected to continue, he would let our project die. I asked him if he was willing to continue by telephone. He said no, that it would not be possible to write unless we sat together and reflected in depth. Were we to continue with our challenge, we would simply have to find a way around the Canadian government.

Three days later, he called as promised. I told him that I still wanted to continue our work. I agreed that we needed to have both courage and truth together. But how to write our book together? Paul said, "If Mohammed can't go to the mountain, then the mountain must go to Mohammed."

And so he planned to arrive as soon as he had finished a contract in Canada. We needed to have two laptops that we could recharge whenever electricity flowed. That way, we could usually keep working until the batteries ran out. So he bought an extra laptop for me.

Meanwhile, things around me continued to change all the time. My little sister Gloria was now eighteen years old. All her life, she had been dependent on Deland who had cared for her in the face of her constant seizures. We worried about whether we would be able to care for her without Deland — and how Gloria would respond to life without Deland. She couldn't understand his final illness and death. Sometimes, she would ask the neighbours where her father was. When they told her that he had died, she asked when he would come back. On 24 October, Gloria came down with a fever and was dehydrated. My sisters in Simon took her to the hospital where they put her on intravenous fluids. But she had a seizure and pulled the tubes out. Soon after, she died. Since they suspected that she had died of cholera, they disposed of her body in a common grave.

As I prepared for Paul's arrival, therefore, I was a strange mixture of sadness and excitement.

My room was already too small for three Haitians. Unless Paul had shrunk to nothing since 2006, he wouldn't have been able to fit into it with us. I called Annie's sister and brother-in-law who were renting two rooms in Silo. I told them of our situation and that I would like to stay with them for two months to write our book. I told them that, during the time we spent with them, we could pay for the food for everyone. They didn't hesitate. They agreed right away to the proposition. All was settled.

We decided that we would try to be liquid and to fit into whatever situations came along. Paul happily agreed that he would follow my counsel while he was here.

And so the day arrived, 31 October. My cousin Claude agreed to drive his *taptap* to meet Paul at the the airport. I wanted to make sure that I had someone I could trust. We arrived after Paul's plane. That made sense. It's easier to get to Toussaint Louverture Airport from Canada than from Delmas 33.

To see what we did next, go back to chapter 1.

COMMENTARY

Joegodson often frames his critique of modern-day imperialism in terms of the national hero, Jean-Jacques Dessalines, a central figure of the revolution and first ruler of an independent Haiti in 1804. As we will see, Joegodson is not alone among Haitians in calling upon the spirit of Dessalines, who is both an historical and a mythical figure. Scholars work to understand the historical Dessalines, both the person and his actions. However, the mythical Dessalines fulfils an important role in present-day Haiti. It is that Dessalines that Joegodson invokes.

The mythical and historical Dessalines are not distinct phenomena that can be definitively separated. In the first place, there is more than one mythical Dessalines. The imperialist, slave-owning countries created their own mythical Dessalines who was as ignoble as the mythical Dessalines of Haiti's struggling classes is noble. The hero of the successful Haitian Revolution was the villain of its opponents. American and French leaders defamed Dessalines as an illiterate savage. Contemporary documents prove otherwise. As there is no such thing as an unmediated fact, we should see that evidence comes to us through agents already embedded in systems of power. How we receive "facts" tells us about our own relationship with those systems.

I leave it to readers to determine what Dessalines means to Joegodson; however, he is often explicit. And, in those cases, the mythical and historical Dessalines are consistent. Dessalines fought bravely and, as general, inspired the ex-slave soldiers. As the first ruler of Haiti, Dessalines tabled a constitution that prohibited foreigners from owning Haitian land. He ordered the execution of the French colonists. He fought with great determination and secured the avowal of the revolutionary generals to fight to the death all attempts to recolonize Haiti. Like many

Haitians, Joegodson believes that he was assassinated by mulatto generals whose ambitions as landowners he obstructed.

Do these references to Dessalines — whether mythical or historical — imply that Joegodson accepts the Great Man theory of history? Or that he worships Dessalines who, alone among the revolutionary figures, found a place among the pantheon of Vodou *lwas*? Precisely the opposite is true. For Joegodson, Dessalines represents a standard of behaviour in the face of imperialists to which all Haitians are subject. Joegodson is concerned with (and judges) his fellow Haitians. He is looking for neither leaders nor followers. Similarly, we can tell the story of the revolution from the perspective of the ex-slaves who fought throughout Haiti in small formations of which Dessalines was surely unaware. Historian Carolyn Fick argues that those ex-slaves understood liberation to mean the freedom to cultivate plots of land free from the slaveholders. They largely succeeded. However, the revolution could not make the world outside of Haiti go away. And it was there that the landowners and merchants could make their fortunes, from what they appropriated from the peasants. The ex-slaves became tenant farmers, giving rise to a semi-feudal system in which they grew their own food but also cultivated cash crops that they owed to their landowner. If they could grow a surplus of coffee, sisal, or cacao, they could sell it to a speculator, thus earning a small amount of money to buy items that they could not produce. The speculator, in turn, sold his cash crops to the merchants for export to the United States, Europe, and Canada. That culture still persisted until the period when Joegodson's story begins. However, in Saut d'Eau, no landowners imposed obligations on the peasants who cultivated the land much as the ex-slaves intended.

In discussing Haitian symbols, we risk assuming that we — who are putting Haiti under a microscope — do not mythologize the past. Many scholars ask why Haiti was unable to integrate into the capitalist world system on more favourable terms. Some blame Haitians for their supposed failure; others blame the Western powers. In either case, the failure of Haitians to join the Western liberal democracies needs to be explained. In reality, neither the United States, France, nor Canada attains the ideal of democracy as rule by the people. The philosophers and founding fathers of modern nation-states rejected democracy in favour of representative government, whereby citizens choose professional politicians to govern them. Democracy means, literally, that that the people govern themselves. In other words, our modern languages give the place of democracy to something that is not democracy and and leave us no term to describe what they have taken away. That is a remarkable achievement of the ruling class.

Political scientist Bernard Manin shows how key figures among the founders of representative government in the seventeenth and eighteenth centuries were aware of the historical precedents of democratic government. In Athens, for example, citizens were chosen by lot to serve terms on key institutions. (Similarly, our jury system calls upon citizens at random. It is accepted that all qualified citizens have the capacity to judge once they are informed of the issues involved.) Consequently, the system nurtured a sense of accountability among the citizenry. Athenian democracy was inherently proportional of the society it served. (The exclusion of women and slaves from the *demos* was a self-imposed constraint on Athenian democracy. The *demos* can be as inclusive as we choose.) In contrast, representative governments have resulted in cultures of powerlessness and frustration throughout the world. The founding fathers assumed that citizens would elect an elite, which they called the "natural aristocracy." The subsequent changes to the system — the rise of political parties, the struggles for universal suffrage, the current cult of celebrity leadership — have consolidated the power of the "natural aristocracy" over the people, all the while laying the responsibility on the electors. If you do not like the state of the world, it is your own fault for voting wrong.[1]

1 Bernard Manin, *The Principles of Representative Government* (Melbourne: Cambridge University Press, 1997); Lucia Boia, *Le Mythe de la démocratie* (Les Belles Lettres, 2002); Moses Finley, *Democracy Ancient and Modern* (New Brunswick, New Jersey: Rutgers University Press, 1985); Claude Mossé, *Regards sur la démocratie athénienne* (Paris: Perrin, 2013), reviews the debates that Finley's critique of modern democracy — as compared to Athenian — precipitated in the United States and Europe in the later twentieth century; Francis Dupuis-Déri, *Démocratie: Histoire politique d'un mot aux États-Unis et en France* (Montréal: Lux Éditeur, 2013), traces the transformations in the meaning of the term *democracy*, especially since the eighteenth century. Étienne Chouard sponsors a discussion of how to transform representative government into a realizable, actual democracy at http://etienne.chouard.free.fr/Europe/.

In what follows, we will break from the custom of confusing democracy with representative government. When "democracy" is used to mean representative government, it will appear in quotation marks, as in this sentence. Athenian democracy describes only one system in which people govern themselves. Anthropologists have documented countless traditional cultures that achieve that end without a state or elections. While the United States claimed to be spreading "democracy" during the Cold War, it was doing precisely the opposite: destroying all traditional systems in which people governed themselves. Article twenty-one, section three of the Universal Declaration of Human Rights imposes representative government on the entire world: "The will of the people shall be the basis of the authority of government; this will shall be expressed in periodic and genuine elections which shall be by universal and equal suffrage and shall be held by secret vote or by equivalent free voting procedures."

Citizens in "democracies" are responsible for electing politicians to represent them in the international system. However, production proceeds on a transnational basis. Each nation assumes a part of the process that culminates in a product for sale in the global marketplace, from which the poor are excluded. The system has been constructed, and is maintained, by a transnational capitalist class. Politicians become a part of that class when they sign trade agreements and pass domestic legislation. The nations that constitute the transnational system are unequal in the economic, diplomatic, and military pressure they can bring to the negotiating table. Since World War Two, the United States has pursued a strategy of ensuring that no other nation can challenge its role as the centre of the capitalist world system. What, then, are citizens outside of the core capitalist countries authorizing with their votes?[2] Why would Haitians ever vote their approval of the system that relegates them to the economic role described in Joegodson's story?

---

2 The following works describe the system of transnational production and the class that manages it: Robert W. Cox, "Multilateralism and World Order," *Review of International Studies* 18, no. 2 (April 1992): 161–80; William I. Robinson, *A Theory of Global Capitalism: Production, Class, and State in a Transnational World* (Baltimore: Johns Hopkins University Press, 2004); Leo Panitch and Sam Gindin, *The Making of Global Capitalism: The Political Economy of American Empire* (London and New York: Verso, 2013).

It is unsurprising that Haitian elections are at the centre of the history reviewed in the following pages.

Undoing the Revolution

The first American invasion of Haiti occurred in the context of American expansionism at the turn of the twentieth century. An American named James P. McDonald initially secured the concession from the Haitian government to build a railroad from Port-au-Prince to Cap-Haïtien under the charter of the National Railways of Haiti. City Bank of New York (which would become Citibank) issued bonds in France, guaranteed by the Haitian government at 6 percent. Roger L. Farnham, vice-president of the City Bank, became the president of the National Railways of Haiti, which proceeded to construct only those sections that passed across flat ground, ignoring the difficult mountainous passages.[3] Even the work completed was shoddy. Nevertheless, Farnham demanded that the Haitian government pay in full for the contract. When it refused, he sought to force the Haitian government into receivership and to take over the customs revenue, citing the debts allegedly owed to the National Railways. By 1914, Farnham was the adviser on Haiti to the American Secretary of State, William Jennings Bryan.

When the Haitians refused to give up their economic sovereignty to the American bank, in 1914 President Woodrow Wilson and Secretary of State Bryan sent the Marines to steal $500,000 in gold from the Banque Nationale in Port-au-Prince and transfer it to the vault of City Bank in New York.[4] The Americans invaded Haiti in 1915 and imposed their laws and a constitution, all illegal and against the will of Haitians of all classes. A key provision of the new constitution was the right of foreigners to own Haitian land, undoing the central achievement of the revolution. This would ultimately weaken the Haitian landowning class that depended on the peasant surpluses; that power would be transferred not to the peasants, but rather to American

---

3   Hans Schmidt, *The United States Occupation of Haiti, 1915–1934* (New Brunswick, NJ: Rutgers University Press, 1971), 37.
4   Ibid., 60–61.

corporations. In 1922, Louis Borno, Washington's choice, was inaugurated as president of Haiti and days later the National City Bank of New York was awarded the contract to refinance the Haitian debt. It sold thirty-year Haitian government bonds on the American market. The bonds were backed by Haitian government revenue, ensuring that very little capital would be available for domestic development, but that whatever surplus Haitian peasants might produce should go to profit the National City Bank and its bondholders. Consequently, Americans playing the market had a reason to demand that Washington protect "American interests" in Haiti. The proceeds of the peasants' work had been appropriated twice: once by the Haitian bourgeoisie and then by the Americans for Citibank. The occupation collected all revenues and decided how to disperse them.[5] Not only did the Americans order all Haitian newspapers to refrain from criticizing the occupation and the government but they were prohibited from printing the fact that they were prohibited from criticizing. Many Haitians joined an armed resistance movement under the leadership of Charlemagne Péralte who was betrayed, captured, tortured, and killed to dissuade potential resistors. American Marines killed thousands of Haitian peasants who fought with the resistance.[6] This occupation lasted until 1934.[7]

5 Ibid., 133; *Inquiry Into Occupation and Administration of Haiti and the Dominican Republic*, 67th Congress, 2nd Session, Senate Report no. 794, http://www.history.navy.mil/library/online/haiti_inquiry.htm.
6 Roger Gaillard, *Les blancs débarquent: Charlemagne Péralte le caco* (Port-au-Prince: L'Imprimerie le Natal, 1982). From a critical American perspective, see Mary Renda, *Taking Haiti: Military Occupation and the Culture of U.S. Imperialism* (Chapel Hill: University of North Carolina Press, 2001).
7 The occupation altered domestic class relations. The Haitian landowning class was weakened when the United States rewrote the constitution allowing foreigners to own land. Americans established HASCO, a large-scale sugar manufacturing plant, and other capitalist ventures that exploited Haiti's fertile soils and cheap labour. The Haitian landowning class and merchants depended on the peasants cultivating small plots. The capitalist penetration under Jean-Claude Duvalier spawned a new bourgeoisie that subcontracted assembly work. Their interests were fundamentally different from the landowning class, except insofar as both groups exploited — in their own way — poor Haitians. The comprador bourgeoisie that controls the import-export business in Haiti is described by Fred Doura, *Économie d'Haïti* (Montréal: Les Éditions Dami, 2002), 78–82.

"Democracy" as a Strategy of Control

Wall Street conspired to control Haiti through debt. It then used Washington and the Marines when force was required to take over the state and subdue the population. Forcing Haiti into debt was especially offensive. Haiti was coming to the end of paying the odious debt imposed by France in 1825, compensation for the loss of its plantations and slaves as a result of the Haitian revolution.

To protect their investment in Haiti, the Americans established and trained the Gendarmerie d'Haïti. Replacing American Marines with Haitian soldiers allowed Washington to conceal its role in Haiti's affairs. As long as Washington had the allegiance of key officers, it could manipulate Haitian politics when necessary. Moreover, it could leave the impression that military violence and political instability were endemic to Latin America. Stability appeared to belong to the rich liberal "democracies" of the North. However, the racism and chauvinism inherent to the occupation spawned a movement of pride in Haiti's African heritage aligned with the international movement called Négritude. A key contributor to the movement was François Duvalier, who established his credentials as a defender of black peasants, the Creole language, and the Vodou religion.[8]

In the 1957 elections, Washington supported François Duvalier (later known as Papa Doc) for president, not because of his strengths, but rather his apparent weakness. It appeared he would be easily manipulated. However, to outfox the Americans, Papa Doc created a new security force that operated at a local level. All over the country, he authorized otherwise uneducated and unqualified men and women to act on his behalf locally. The *tontons macoutes* owed their power and loyalty to Papa Doc.[9] Often tyrants in their dealings with the local

---

[8] Rémy Bastien, *Le paysan haïtien et sa famille* (Paris: Éditions Karthala, 1985). See the preface by Professor André-Marcel d'Ans for a discussion of the ethnographic tradition in Haiti, including the place of François Duvalier.

[9] Bernard Diederich, *Le prix du sang: La résistance du peuple haïtien à la tyrannie* (Port-au-Prince: Éditions H. Deschamps, 2005). Nicolas Jallot and Laurent Lesage argue that Papa Doc channelled his discretionary funds into the *macoutes*, rather than into his own personal coffers. See their *Haïti: Dix ans d'histoire secrète* (Paris: Éditions du Felin, 1995), 50.

inhabitants of both rural and urban parts of Haiti, they sidelined the Army as the main instrument of coercion. They were drawn from the very parts of Haitian culture that had been oppressed historically and that the ethnographic movement had tried to validate: black, Vodouist, and Creole-speaking. Through them, Papa Doc had consolidated his power by 1963.[10]

Papa Doc legitimated his hold on power by staging celebrations in his own honour. From the early 1960s, local authorities were responsible for rounding up some peasants in their sections and busing them into Port-au-Prince every year on 22 May. There, they were the backdrop for a public display of their supposed devotion to Papa Doc. After they had served their purpose as a mass of devoted subjects, Papa Doc lost interest in them. Many remained stranded in the capital that was foreign to them. Papa Doc's wife, Simone Duvalier, convinced François to clear the peasants out of sight. They were displaced to the north of the city on swampy, mosquito-infested land. The neighbourhood was christened Cité Simone. The state took no interest, but the Salesian Brothers attempted to bring rudimentary services to the displaced peasants. The *tontons macoutes* called it Cité Interdite, meaning the Forbidden City. After the fall of Duvalier, the *macoutes* were replaced by petty criminals and their gangs. But there was also a religious authority that grew in importance. Evidence of this transition can be seen in the renaming of Cité Simone as Cité Soleil, after the Catholic radio station that broadcast there.[11]

By the late 1960s, resistance to Papa Doc's repressive regime was growing. He agreed to the terms offered by the Nixon administration for America's support in protecting his regime. He would have to accept American investment, against the interests of his main allies, Haiti's big landowners. American investment in agribusiness and assembly plants would mean the end of the semi-feudal system. Before his death in 1971, Papa Doc arranged for his son, nineteen-year-old Jean-Claude, or Baby Doc, to succeed him as president-for-life.

10 Elizabeth Abbott, *Haiti: The Duvaliers and Their Legacy* (New York: McGraw-Hill Book Company, 1988).
11 Werner Kerns Fleurimond, *Haïti de la crise à l'occupation: Histoire d'un chaos (2000–2004)* (Paris: L'Harmattan, 2009), 170–72.

The State in the Transnational Economy

By moving production offshore, American industrial capitalists reduced their labour costs substantially. That required changes in both the core and the peripheral countries. Capitalists assured consumers in the core countries that their objective was to lower the price of goods. Instead, they eliminated jobs and increased profits. By 1980, multinational corporations had opened 200 assembly plants next to Cité Soleil to take advantage of the poorest people in Haiti.[12]

Until the 1980s, Haiti was almost entirely self-sufficient in rice production. The domestic industry employed 20 percent of the population. After the fall of Baby Doc in 1986, the Haitian military government under General Namphy lowered the tariffs on imported American rice from 35 to 3 percent. Meanwhile, Washington subsidized American rice production throughout the 1980s and 1990s at a rate between 35 and 100 percent. The World Food Program calculated that Haiti's food self-sufficiency ratio deteriorated from 85 percent in 1980 to 50 percent by 1995. By 1996, an American monopoly named The Rice Corporation of Haiti controlled the importation of 2,100 metric tons of American rice into Haiti every week. Haitian cultivators lost $23 million a year, at precisely the moment that they needed money to buy imported rice. The policy was justified on the grounds that Haitian farmers could not feed the nation. Augustin Antoine Agustin, a Haitian-born professor at Tulane University with business interests in Haiti, helpfully penned a report to justify the policy, arguing that, without imported American rice, Haiti faced increasing malnutrition. In fact, his report was fabricated out of whole cloth. At that time, no one had monitored food production in the remote areas of Haiti. In 1994, USAID would

---

12 Timothy T. Schwartz, *Travesty in Haiti: A True Account of Christian Missions, Orphanages, Fraud, Food Aid and Drug Trafficking*, (Lexington, KY, 2010), 108. Robert W. Cox, "Labor and the Multinationals," *Foreign Affairs* 54, no. 2 (January 1976): 344–65, describes the new global production regime emerging in the 1970s. Jacques Arcelin's documentary, *Bitter Cane* (*Canne amère*, Haiti Films, 1983) offers readers invaluable access to the conditions that Deland faced as he moved from Saut d'Eau to Port-au-Prince. The documentary contains footage of the American managers of the new factories and the people — mostly women — who worked in them.

establish the Interim Food Security Information System precisely to "collect, analyze and monitor food security indicators." They spoke of the need to "begin to address this critical area of agricultural data collection." Years later, they were still talking about beginning the research. The goal of USAID was to make Haitians dependent on American rice. First, they had to present Haitians as victims of their own incompetence as cultivators. In reality, by destroying Haitian agriculture and manipulating Haitians into dependence, USAID created the situation they claimed to be resolving.[13]

The Resilience of Class Structures

Duvalier had been forced out of the country as a result of the growing pressure from the popular classes. The world revolution that crested in 1968 also left its mark on Haiti. Slowly, inspired by liberation theology imported by local priests into every corner of the country, peasants reconsidered their place in society. In the urban slums and in the countryside, they became increasingly conscious of the oppressions they lived daily. They called the process of learning about the economy and politics *lave je* — cleaning the eyes. By the 1980s, such local consciousness-raising groups had evolved into the Ti Legliz (Little Church) movement. All over Haiti, small local churches and peristyles, or Vodou temples, were the centres of communities. Local people spoke of their place in heaven and earth in a new way. Many leaders arose in the face of the backlash from the Duvalier regime. Father Jean-Bertrand Aristide spoke eloquently about the inherent equality of all human beings. That proposition was radical and powerful in the context of Haiti's class relations. At the same time, Aristide fiercely condemned the capitalist world order under which poor Haitians suffered. His interpretation of Christ's message inspired the poor, but disturbed and insulted the oligarchy.

[13] Schwartz, *Travesty in Haiti*, 109–10; Food for the Hungry International, "Haiti Food Security Needs Assessment," PL 480, Title II Institutional Support Assistance Program, January 1999, http://pdf.usaid.gov/pdf_docs/Pnacr821.pdf, 5; World Food Programme, "*Rapport complet de l'evaluation du programme de pays en Haiti (1998-2002)*," September 2001, http://www.wfp.org/content/rapport-complet-de-levaluation-du-programme-de-pays-en-haiti-1998-2002.

The notion that the poor had dignity, let alone rights, was offensive to the rich. They armed groups to violently put down all attempts to alter existing power relations.

The military maintained control of government for five years after the flight of Duvalier, protecting corporate America and the Haitian oligarchy against the interests of poor Haitians. In 1990, former President Jimmy Carter summarized their approach to "democracy" in these words: "As recently as Nov. 29, 1987, an election was called to fulfill promises made in their post-Duvalier constitution. Citizens who lined up to vote were mowed down by fusillades of terrorists' bullets. Military leaders, who had either orchestrated or condoned the murders, moved in to cancel the election and retain control of the Government."[14] In 1987, Father Aristide was preaching fiery sermons at Saint Jean Bosco Church in one of the slums of Port-au-Prince. On 11 September 1988, his parishioners filled the church despite the threat of violence. When the *macoutes* attacked, many were massacred. Aristide survived.[15]

Haiti's first free and fair elections were scheduled to be held in 1990. Washington was confident that its candidate, Marc Bazin, a World Bank official, would be elected president and oversee the continued integration of Haiti into its plan for a world system of American-led transnational capitalism. But, at the last minute, Aristide was persuaded to run for president as the representative of the Lavalas movement. Lavalas was the successor of the Ti Legliz movement. *Lavalas* means flood. Each person is a drop of water. As they all come together to achieve a common goal, they become an unstoppable force of nature, like the flash floods that carry everything along with them during Haiti's torrential rains. When Aristide agreed to run for the presidency, Washington's plans were swept away with the tide. Candidates identifying with Lavalas and Aristide were virtually assured of victory. Many senators and deputies saw Aristide as a convenient stepping stone to government, one of the few sources of income in Haiti. By the constitution of 1987, political power was shared

---

[14] Jimmy Carter, "Haiti's Election Needs Help," *New York Times*, 1 October 1990.
[15] Amy Wilentz, *The Rainy Season: Haiti Since Duvalier* (New York: Touchstone, 1989).

among the three levels of government: the presidency, the senate, and the legislature. Haitians had long lived with the reality of a president with total control, however. They assumed, as have analysts and casual observers, that Aristide had that power. In reality, Haitian presidents must work with the other two bodies of government, not to mention the external sources of power. The minister who had overseen the *tontons macoutes* under Duvalier, Roger Lafontant, attempted a coup on 17 January 1991, a couple of weeks before Aristide's inauguration. Thousands of people left the poorest neighbourhoods to place themselves between the guns of Lafontant's thugs and their president-elect. This time, they were victorious.

Aristide proceeded cautiously to soften the harshness of life among the poor without challenging the system. Nevertheless, USAID criticized his policies on labour and foreign-exchange controls as inhibiting growth. While USAID funnelled $26.7 million to the business sector in 1991, it opposed both a rise in the minimum wage from thirty-three to fifty cents an hour as well as the government's attempt to stabilize food prices.[16] USAID was a branch of the State Department whose mission is to support American business internationally. Even a modest rise in the minimum wage could mean that transnational corporations would locate their assembly plants in countries where the state could better control the workforce and assure business a supply of cheap electricity. For that segment of the oligarchy whose revenue depended on sub-contracting work from transnational corporations, the poor were Haiti's most attractive resource. Policies that improved the conditions of the poor threatened their interests.

General Cédras took power on 30 September 1991 in a military coup. This time, the Army was prepared when the poor came to protect Aristide. They opened fire; many were killed. Thousands would be slaughtered by the reactionary forces in the months that followed. Aristide escaped assassination. For the next three years, Aristide would search for allies in the United States to help lobby the administration on behalf of his, and the Haitian people's, presidency. Meanwhile, the CIA worked with the coup to destroy Lavalas. CIA assets were paid to

---

[16] Peter Hallward, *Damming the Flood: Haiti, Aristide, and the Politics of Containment* (London: Verso, 2007), 36.

organize death squads, weapons were funnelled into Haiti from Miami, and Washington protected the assassins from prosecution when the coup ended in November 1994.[17] Those in the slums who could not escape or go into hiding formed themselves into gangs to defend themselves against the death squads.[18]

For three years, Presidents George H. W. Bush and Clinton negotiated with Aristide in Washington while they supported the Army that gunned down his supporters in Haiti, especially Cité Soleil. Aristide would be allowed back into Haiti only when Washington was convinced that he no longer posed a threat to its interests. Clinton attempted to manipulate Aristide into implementing a neoliberal program upon his return. But Aristide negotiated cleverly. He agreed to drastically reduce tariffs on rice, but only if accompanied by investment in that sector. Bush and Clinton insisted that Aristide grant amnesty for the authors of the coup. When Aristide insisted on holding the assassins accountable, President Bush called him "vindictive." Finally, Aristide did agree to the condition, but framed it in terms of the actual coup of 30 September. In that way, all of the crimes that preceded or followed the coup would be open for prosecution. (In fact, when he returned to Haiti, Aristide established the Bureau des Avocats Internationaux, which, along with colleagues from the Institute for Justice and Democracy in Haiti, helped to successfully prosecute members of the death squads for a massacre in Raboteau during the coup.) Washington also required that Aristide sell state assets. Clinton wanted to force Aristide to betray himself and the Haitian people who had elected him. Aristide finally agreed to this demand on the condition that part of the money from the sale be put in trust and used for housing, education, and health.[19]

---

[17] Kathleen Marie Whitney, "Sin, Fraph, and the CIA: U.S. Covert Action in Haiti," *Southwestern Journal of Law and Trade in the Americas* 3, no. 2 (1996): 303–32.

[18] Ken Bresler, "If You Are Not Corrupt, Arrest the Criminals: Prosecuting Human Rights Violators in Haiti," Project on Justice in Times of Transition, Harvard University, Spring 2003. Bresler's summary of the process of defending the victims of the Raboteau massacre will help readers understand conditions in Haiti and shed light on both parts of this book.

[19] Hallward, *Damming the Flood*, 56–58.

The most extraordinary thing about this agreement — the Paris Plan — is that it existed at all. Washington first sponsored a coup, then negotiated the conditions under which it would allow the elected president to serve out what remained of his term. Washington assigned a number of technocrats to accompany Aristide back to Haiti and to "help" him implement the Paris Plan, which Lavalas supporters called the Plan of Death, meant to control every aspect of the transition from military dictatorship (for which Washington was responsible) to "democracy" (which it would not allow). In 2009, the United Nations would name the man responsible, Bill Clinton, its special envoy for Haiti. After the earthquake of 2010, he would attempt to implement the same policies.

At the time, in the mid-1990s, there was a campaign in North America to sensitize the public to the working conditions in the peripheral countries where transnational corporations were transferring manufacturing jobs. The Clinton administration was aggressively pursuing a global restructuring of class relations in favour of transnational capitalists. Workers in the core countries like Canada and the United States discovered that they were in direct competition with the poorest peoples in the world for their jobs. However, the sweatshop campaign addressed North Americans not as workers, but as consumers. The campaign asked them to petition certain corporations to improve the conditions of Haitian workers.[20] Corporations like Disney and Nike responded by transferring production to China.[21] In response, the Clinton administration, together with the biggest corporations, established a monitoring agency controlled by the garment industry.[22] Many student organizations in North America uncritically accepted the "solution."

---

20 Institute for Global Labor and Human Rights, see Eric Verhoogen, "The U.S. in Haiti: How to Get Rich on 11 Cents an Hour," 1 April 1996, http://www.globallabourrights.org/reports/the-u-s-in-haiti; Charles Kernaghan et al., "Behind Closed Doors: The Workers Who Make Our Clothes — University Students Investigate Factories in Central America," 28 April 1998, http://www.globallabourrights.org/reports/behind-closed-doors.

21 Campaign for Labor Rights, "Disney/Nike Contractor Leaves Haiti for China," Action Alert, 8 August 1998, http://www.hartford-hwp.com/archives/43a/263.html.

22 The Fair Labor Association documents its successes at http://www.fairlabor.org/. FLA Watch documents its failures at http://flawatch.usas.org/.

A more astute World Bank official advised the industry not to worry about Aristide's attempt to increase the minimum wage because "in a country like Haiti the government's enforcement capacity is nil."[23]

In the parliamentary elections of June 1995, Aristide's group, the Plateforme Politique Lavalas, won seventeen of twenty-seven Senate seats and sixty-seven of eighty-three seats in the Chamber of Deputies. However, inside the Plateforme, the largest group was the Organisation Politique Lavalas, led by Gerard Pierre-Charles, an economist who had returned from exile after the fall of Duvalier. He now represented the interests of the oligarchy. Since the Chamber of Deputies has as much power as the president, the government was deadlocked. In 1996, the confusion inside of Lavalas was resolved. Those like Aristide who were fighting for the poor founded the political party Fanmi Lavalas, which drew its support from local groups all across Haiti called the Organisations populaires (Popular Organizations). The OPL of Pierre-Charles renamed itself Organisation du peuple en lutte. By suggesting a people in struggle, it attempted to retain the allegiance of the same constituency as Fanmi Lavalas; however, the people it was struggling for already owned Haiti. Once the electorate knew who was who, they voted overwhelmingly for Aristide's Fanmi Lavalas in the legislative elections of 1997. After the first round of voting, the OPL could see the writing on the wall and refused to participate in the second round so that the legislature would not be swamped with FL deputies. They persuaded the UN to validate their boycott. Their terms expired in January 1999, but they delayed organizing elections until May 2000. As long as they sat in the Assembly, they could block the FL program that President Préval supported.

After disbanding the Army (that had carried out the coup) on his return to Haiti, Aristide established the Haitian National Police (PNH) in July 1995. To run the PNH, Aristide trusted an ex-Army officer, Dany Toussaint, who had been loyal to him on a number of occasions, even refusing orders to assassinate Aristide in 1988. However, Washington clandestinely took control of the new police force. It sent a dozen soldiers from the disbanded Haitian Army and the coup death squads, including Guy Philippe, to its base in Ecuador for paramilitary training.

[23] Hallward, *Damming the Flood*, 63.

It sent police recruits to Fort Leonard Wood in Missouri for training. Any officer who supported Aristide was systematically denounced by the US as untrustworthy, a drug dealer, and a human rights abuser. Since American officials refused to disarm the members of the death squads and Army responsible for atrocities under the coup, the most disloyal paramilitaries were well armed. In 1996, Bob Manuel, the chief of security under President Préval, uncovered coup and assassination plots among the Presidential Guard. Both Préval and Aristide were targeted for assassination. When Manuel began a purge of the Guard, the American State Department sent forty security agents to oversee the changes.[24]

The core capitalist countries, under the direction of Washington, worked to control Haiti's economy through political and military interventions. What role, then, did non-governmental humanitarian and developmental organizations play? When the American organization CARE wanted to expand its aid programs in 1999, it contracted anthropologist Timothy Schwartz to evaluate its existing distribution process. Schwartz discovered that the massive amounts of food aid that CARE sent to Haiti each year were being embezzled and sold on the market. CARE had no idea what had been happening to its food aid. The promotional material describing its school feeding programs was simply cooked up by public relations personnel. Meanwhile, food aid arrived at times when it did the most harm to Haitian cultivators. Schwartz compiled data to discover that, in periods of bountiful harvests, NGOs distributed more food than during droughts. When Schwartz reported his research to CARE, the assistant director told him candidly that they were aware that their aid was in fact subverting Haitian agriculture. However, they had no money to buy local Haitian products for their food aid programs. Their funding from USAID comes in the form of subsidized American food to be sold on the Haitian market. That aid further weakens the local cultivators. Whether imports entered Haiti as humanitarian aid and were then embezzled and sold for profit, or were sold on the market by the NGOs to fund their programs, the effect was the same: the subversion of Haitian agriculture. The system that finances humanitarian organizations, in other words, sets up a dilemma. They are structurally

[24] Ibid., 64–72.

compelled to fail in the stated goal of helping the poor. In fact, they are part of a system that creates the poor, which then justifies their presence as humanitarian workers. Their employees are left to their own devices to resolve the moral issue, if they can see it.[25]

"Democracy" in a Transnational Economy

By 2000, the divisions within Lavalas were more clear than a decade earlier. The opportunists — Dany Toussaint, Serge Gilles, Evans Paul, Gerard Pierre-Charles — appealed to the poor who, in every election that followed, showed that they did not believe them. The overwhelming majority of the poor continued to trust Aristide, whose party, Fanmi Lavalas, tabled a program of egalitarian development. Aristide represented, both to the rich and to the poor, a pole in the Haitian class struggle. The oligarchy could never hope to win power in an electoral contest. Aristide would be in the way. The oligarchy and their transnationalist allies in the core capitalist countries could govern Haiti only by manipulating elections. The subsequent history of chaos and terror in Haiti is the details of that manipulation.

The May 2000 parliamentary elections would loom large in the struggle between "democracy" and class rule. The Organization of American States observed and sanctioned the elections as free, fair, and peaceful.[26]

---

25 Schwartz, *Travesty in Haiti*, 103–6. When Schwartz tabled his report that demonstrated the devastating effects that food aid has had on Haitian agriculture and society, some experienced executives in the development industry privately acknowledged his findings. Others went on the attack, threatened both professionally and personally by his claims that aid actually harms Haitians. A German nutritionist who had just arrived in Haiti was outraged at his survey report. She had invested a doctorate and her identity in the prospect of making a difference in the world. If the development industry was misguided, then so was her career.

26 The OAS press release issued on 21 May reads: "The Mission has noted that Haitian voters showed their strong desire to go to the polls by the relatively high participation in the elections. The EOM congratulates the voters, the Government, the police and the political parties for having worked together to create the climate necessary for the vote." http://www.oas.org/OASpage/press2002/en/Press98/Press2000/haitielections.htm.

Sixty-five percent of eligible Haitians voted, an impressive turnout in the context of intimidation and violence that had marked each election since Duvalier's departure. For many people, casting a ballot was an act of defiance and courage. Fanmi Lavalas won 72 of 83 seats in the House of Deputies and 16 of 17 seats in the Senate. Around the country, Fanmi Lavalas won 89 of 115 mayoralty positions.[27] The people had unequivocally chosen Fanmi Lavalas, which was now in a position to implement its program to redress the huge inequalities and to establish a viable system of justice. The state would have to belong to the people who elected this government. The oligarchy would have to step aside.[28]

Meanwhile, the American Deputy Secretary of State Roger Noriega called the elections a farce.[29] Noriega was Washington's most accomplished saboteur of Latin American democracy. On 2 June 2000, he enlisted the help of the OAS, which suddenly questioned the methodology that the Electoral Council used to calculate the vote percentages for Senate candidates. In fact, the Electoral Council had followed traditional practices.[30] While all Fanmi Lavalas candidates had won handily, an alternative method would have forced run-off elections in two of the Senate races. Even in those two cases, the Lavalas candidates received twice the votes of their closest rivals. This belated challenge to the calculation methodology by OAS was first rejected by the head of the Electoral Council, Léon Manus. However, after he was flown to Washington on 21 June 2000, he returned to Haiti claiming that Aristide and Préval had pressured him to overlook "massive electoral fraud" and that they had threatened to engulf

---

[27] Hallward, *Damming the Flood*, 76.
[28] Michel-Rolph Trouillot, *Haiti, State Against Nation: The Origins and Legacy of Duvalierism* (New York: Monthly Review Press, 1990), identifies the problem of states struggling within the context of the world order at the same time that they have domestic responsibilities. Consequent contradictions arise most markedly in peripheral states.
[29] Hallward, *Damming the Flood*, 78.
[30] Irwin P. Stotzky, "Democracy and International Military Intervention: The Case of Haiti," in *Democracy and Human Rights in Latin America*, ed. Richard S. Hillman, John A. Peeler, and Elsa Cardoza Da Silva, 125–178 (Westport, CT: Greenwood Publishing, 2002).

the capital and departments in "fire and blood" unless he approved their fraud.[31]

Washington used the OAS claim of fraudulent elections to impose an embargo on all foreign aid to Haiti. Haiti, like all countries heavily indebted in a foreign currency, faced a dilemma. It was dependent on the international financial institutions to meet its basic operating expenses. The structural adjustment programs that the Clinton administration had attempted to force on Aristide as a condition of his return to Haiti stripped the state of its meagre domestic sources of revenue. So it needed to take out more loans. These loans drive countries deeper into debt and dependence. But to not take the loans means that governments cannot operate. The people will revolt. And if they are ignorant of how the system operates, they will blame their domestic governments for incompetence. The role of Washington and the international financial institutions is obscured.

Since the fall of Duvalier, no opposition had formed to challenge Lavalas. There were two poles in Haitian politics: representative government or authoritarian rule. The politicians who lost the May 2000 elections banded together to create the Democratic Convergence, funded by Washington through the National Endowment for Democracy, established by President Reagan in 1983 to obscure Washington's aggressive, anti-democratic foreign policy.[32] The Democratic Convergence was composed of two separate groups: the upper class, who simply loathed the poor, and vindictive rivals jealous of Aristide's stature among the people.[33]

[31] Hallward, *Damming the Flood*, 78–80. Manus appealed to newly appointed Secretary of State Colin Powell in December 2000, describing how "ballot boxes were stolen and replaced with stuffed substitute boxes," all in favour of Aristide. If true, the logistics would have been impressive. A copy of Manus's letter to Colin Powell is posted at http://www.corbetthaiti.org/archive/archive7/msg06504.html.

[32] For a brief critique of the National Endowment for Democracy, see Jonah Ginden and Kristen Weld, "Benevolence or Intervention? Spotlighting US Soft Power," *NACLA Report on the Americas*, 1 January 2007, 19–21. Sourcewatch offers a critique and numerous sources documenting NED's work in the world at http://www.sourcewatch.org/index.php?title=National_Endowment_for_Democracy#Fostering_.22Free_Press.22.

[33] Fleurimond, *Haïti de la crise à l'occupation*, 70.

Given that Fanmi Lavalas had swept the legislative elections in May, it was clear to all that Aristide would win the presidential election in November 2000. Since the Democratic Convergence was arguing that those elections had been rigged, they risked being discredited by an Aristide win. Their only option was to boycott the election and claim they had the support of the public. In fact, their support was located outside of Haiti, among the power elite of the core capitalist countries that mediated events in Haiti (and everywhere) for their domestic audiences. In fact, some elements within the diaspora initiated a campaign in Miami and New York in support of Jean-Claude Duvalier. Baby Doc, from France, took the opportunity to criticize Lavalas and to hint that he was still available to serve his country. Meanwhile, in October 2000, Prime Minister Jacques Edouard Alexis uncovered a plot against the Préval government. The conspirators had sent their families to France months earlier. Their goal was not to take power, but to assassinate a number of Lavalas leaders. Then, an emergency government would be put in place. At the centre of the intrigue was a group of thirteen police commissioners, all of whom had worked under Duvalier or in the Army and had been trained at the American Military School in Ecuador.

During the week prior to the presidential election of 26 November 2000, bombs exploded throughout Port-au-Prince. While that may account in part for the low turnout in the capital, the provinces were equally unenthusiastic. With a turnout of between 10 and 15 percent, Aristide was elected with 92 percent of the vote.[34] In response, the Democratic Convergence announced that Gérard Gourgues would act as a parallel president. He operated out of the offices of the Organisation du peuple en lutte that had lost the legislative elections of 1997, then denounced them as fraudulent and blocked the legislative process. The Democratic Convergence, in naming him the actual president of Haiti, demonstrated that there was nothing behind their posturing.[35]

The US ambassador, Dean Curran, advised Aristide that the US would not normalize relations until the problems of the May 2000 elections were resolved. From 2000 to 2003, USAID continued to give an average of $68 million a year to American NGOs that helped to undermine

[34] Ibid., 37–50.
[35] Ibid., 68–69.

Aristide and the authority and legitimacy of the government. Washington also blocked $145 million in loans from the Inter-American Development Bank that had already been approved. Although the loans were frozen, the Bank demanded that the Aristide government pay the interest. By 2003, the Aristide government had a budget of $300 million for the entire country, of which $60 million had to go to service the debt. Forty-five percent of that debt had been incurred by the Duvaliers and was now being squandered on the French Riviera while Joegodson was putting grains of salt on his tongue to ward off hunger pains. In November 2000, the IMF required that the government reduce subsidies on essential commodities such as fuel. Between 2002 and 2003, consumer prices rose by 40 percent. By 2004, Haiti's GDP was about half of what it had been in 1980, measured in constant 2000 dollars.[36] But this contraction of the economy, measured in dollars, was taking place as the percentage of Haitians dependent on money for their survival was increasing. In summary, the actions of Washington and the international financial institutions undermined any chance that the Fanmi Lavalas government would be able to implement a meaningful program of governance at the same time that they increased the resources available to the Democratic Convergence and drove the poor deeper into poverty. They blamed everything on Aristide.

The Convergence refused to cooperate with Aristide, no matter how much he conceded. In fact, Aristide became undemocratic only insofar as he seriously negotiated with the Democratic Convergence over the will of the electorate that had given Fanmi Lavalas a huge majority at all levels of government. He asked them to join his government. They refused. He agreed in November 2002 to name them to a new Electoral Council. They refused. He offered them a majority of positions in the government. They refused. He proposed dates for new elections. They refused. For all of this, Aristide was consistently called intransigent in the Western media. He was said to be refusing to work with the opposition. This "opposition" was unelected and unpopular with the electorate. Aristide lost a number of key supporters when he bothered to talk to the Democratic Convergence at all. In the face of intense criticism at the OAS Assembly in Québec City, Aristide proposed organizing legislative

---

36 Hallward, *Damming the Flood*, 82.

elections in November 2002, two years before the mandate. Not only did he not have the constitutional authority to dissolve the legislature, but the proposal gave credence to the idle claim that the May 2000 elections had been fraudulent.[37] The only way that Aristide could prove his commitment to "democracy" was to become anti-constitutional. Journalists in both English and French Canada uncritically accepted the mantra that Aristide was corrupt and dictatorial and had stolen the elections.

The assault on Lavalas intensified when Aristide signed a number of bilateral agreements with Castro, all to Haiti's benefit. Aristide's visit to Cuba in July 2001 prompted American Congressman Peter Goss to call for the restoration of "democracy" in Haiti.[38] American Ambassador Curran became a spokesman for the Democratic Convergence.

In late 2001, Haitians protested the Lavalas government to do something about the deteriorating living conditions. The Democratic Convergence took advantage of the protests to foment as much discontent as possible. But when CIA asset Guy Philippe led an armed attack on the Presidential Palace on 17 December 2001, people from the poor neighbourhoods, including armed gangs, came to aid the National Police in retaking the Palace. The poor supporters of Aristide attacked the headquarters of the Organisation des peuples en lutte in retaliation, remembering that it was there that the farcical parallel government of Gérard Gourgues had been installed by the Democratic Convergence at the investiture of Aristide as president in February 2001.[39] Throughout the country, people rose up in support of the elected government. The

[37] Fleurimond, *Haïti de la crise à l'occupation*, 84.
[38] Ibid., 113–14.
[39] Kim Ives, "'*Mafia boss . . . Drug dealer . . . Poster-boy for political corruption*': WikiLeaked U.S. Embassy Cables Portray Senator Youri Latortue," *Haïti Liberté*, vol. 4, no. 50, (29 June 2011). Ives reports that, according to a high-level government security source, Youri Latortue used his contacts in Palace security to ensure that Philippe was admitted to the grounds. Latortue would play an important part in the coming coup, helping to coordinate the paramilitaries led by Philippe and Chamblain. The focus of Roger Noriega's OAS inquiry into the events of 17 December 2001 is the reaction that the attempted coup d'état provoked among the poor. Nowhere in the report is the connection drawn between the OPL's attempt to install a parallel government in February 2001 and the retaliation against the OPL offices, which the people naturally understood to be at the centre of the attack on their elected government.

Democratic Convergence consistently signalled its intentions by giving pride of place to the collaborators of Haiti's past dictators. The people understood.[40]

Through the Democracy and Governance Program, USAID funded any Haitian journalist who criticized Aristide. The professed interest of the American State Department in a critical, independent media in Haiti would come to an abrupt end when Aristide was forced out of the country and Fanmi Lavalas violently repressed.[41] USAID also funded the International Foundation for Electoral Systems that organized lawyers, magistrates, and human rights groups to protest Aristide's supposed abuses and corruption. In reality, Washington frustrated every attempt by Préval and Aristide to reform the corrupt judicial system.[42] Nevertheless, in Haiti, where few opportunities exist to earn money, such programs were received with enthusiasm. The money was contingent on protesting the government. Washington funded protest groups of all kinds and blocked money that would have helped Fanmi Lavalas to implement the programs the protesters were calling for.[43] The International Republican Institute and the Haitian oligarchy funded the Haiti Democracy Project through which money was made available to women's and students' groups who would protest Lavalas. One of

---

[40] Fleurimond, *Haïti de la crise à l'occupation*, 95–100, 1313.

[41] Dan Whitman, *A Haiti Chronicle: The Undoing of a Latent Democracy*, available at http://www.scribd.com/doc/117997669/A-Haiti-Chronicle-the-Undoing-of-a-Latent-Democracy-Dan-Whitman. Whitman discusses his role with the American embassy in implementing the program. He sees himself as a defender of the goodwill of the American State Department in helping Haitians to advance.

[42] Hallward, *Damming the Flood*, 92–94. The Institute for Justice and Democracy in Haiti and the Bureau des Avocats Internationaux document their approach, which seeks justice and attempts to empower victims of human rights abuses in Haiti. Their legal work exposes the collaboration between Washington and the Haitian oligarchy: http://www.ijdh.org/about/#.UvzVw2Jdwso. They successfully helped to convict fifty-seven defendants, including the leaders of the Cédras coup, the subject of a Harvard University case study: see Bresler, "If You Are Not Corrupt, Arrest the Criminals."

[43] Hallward, *Damming the Flood*, 98; Max Blumenthal, "The Other Regime Change: Did the Bush Administration Allow a Network of Right-Wing Republicans to Foment a Violent Coup in Haiti?" *Salon*, 16 July 2004.

the avowed concerns of the Haiti Democracy Project was an enquiry into the assassination of the investigative journalist Jean Dominique, a champion of the Haitian poor who relentlessly exposed the corruption of Haiti's richest families. Now, those families promoted the project called "Justice for Jean," committed to finding his killers. When Aristide was removed from power, the "Justice for Jean" project died a quiet death. The oligarchy lost interest in exposing Dominique's killers the moment that it took control of the justice ministry.[44]

The Haitian oligarchy was speaking primarily to the populations of France, Canada, and the United States, not the Haitian poor who already knew them. Their goal was to convince those peoples of the core capitalist countries that opposition to Aristide was broad and progressive. In December 2002, the Group of 184 was created to coordinate that opposition. The Group of 184 was supported by almost all of the groups getting CIDA, USAID, or IRI money. All were outspoken in their opposition to Aristide. Middle-class Haitians, funded by Washington and the Haitian oligarchy whose fortunes derived from the exploitation of the poor, would be the public face of Haiti abroad. The main spokesman for the Group of 184 in North America was Andy Apaid, whose father had established sweatshops under the name of Alpha Industries during the regime of Jean-Claude Duvalier. The overthrow of Aristide and Fanmi Lavalas would have to appear to come from within Haiti. The conspirators were also finding and motivating young men to carry out the military arm of the coup. Paul Arcelin, a professor at the Université du Québec à Montréal), together with Guy Philippe and Louis-Jodel Chamblain, two death squad leaders during the Cédras dictatorship, would lead the paramilitary forces.

When Fanmi Lavalas supporters fought back, their opponents condemned what they characterized as unprovoked attacks on the helpless victims of the Aristide dictatorship. One of the leaders of the Democratic Convergence, Gerard Pierre-Charles, said in March 2003 that the Aristide government was behind the so-called rebel incursions "to justify its permanent and institutionalized violence against the Haitian people." In Washington, Roger Noriega blamed Aristide for

---

[44] Jonathan Demme, *The Agronomist* (Jonathan Demme, 2004); Hallward, *Damming the Flood*, 157–58.

not "healing the wounds" caused by the attack of Guy Philippe on the Presidential Palace of 17 December 2001. There was nothing that could not be blamed on Aristide. Every shot they fired at him was evidence that he had been unable to stop the violence. It was a bold strategy whose success rested on the conviction, if not the certainty, that the media would report the story exactly as it was framed by Washington.

Throughout his presidency, Aristide had to deal with the fact that all of his enemies had power while his supporters were poor. That was true inside Haiti and globally. Lavalas opponents had the arms and connections to mount constant paramilitary attacks from the Dominican Republic, while starving his government of operating funds. They disseminated venomous propaganda. They made life as difficult as possible for Lavalas activists. Both in Haiti and abroad, Lavalas supporters were forced to react to attacks, to deny accusations, to plead for funds, and to defend a counter-hegemonic perspective. Nevertheless, the Fanmi Lavalas government managed to advance its program as much as possible, build public schools and hospitals, institute a school lunch program, double the minimum wage in 2003, implement extensive adult literacy programs, create public spaces and low-cost housing projects, and raise taxes on the rich. All would be lost after the coup d'état.

In July 2003, Andy Apaid, the head of the Group of 184, met with a number of gang leaders in Cité Soleil, offering them financial support if they would agree to take up arms inside the poor neighbourhoods against the defenders of the democratically elected government. Only Labanye, a gang leader in the Boston neighbourhood, accepted the offer. In response, gangs in the other neighbourhoods of Cité Soleil joined together to fight Labanye. Between Boston and the rest of Cité Soleil was Simon, where Joegodson's family lived. It would become a battleground. Since the poorest neighbourhoods were also the most passionate supporters of representative government, the oligarchy needed to neutralize them. Apaid and Reginald Boulos (who owned many sweatshops located at the edge of Simon) chose to bribe the criminal element to support their political and economic interests. They blamed the ensuing violence on Aristide.[45]

---

45 Thomas M. Griffin, "Haiti Human Rights Investigation," Center for the Study of Human Rights, University of Miami School of Law, 11–14 November 2004, 4–11.

As a result of the infiltration by the Democratic Convergence, the CIA, DEA, and State Department, Aristide could not depend on the Haitian National Police to protect the elected government. In fact, Andy Apaid, an unelected businessman, acknowledged that he gave direct orders to the Haitian National Police to not arrest Labanye, but to "work with him." At the same time, the police were targeting other gang leaders and killing civilians at will in Cité Soleil, Bel Air, and the other slums.[46] The poor would never be able to compete with the firepower of the rich. Nevertheless, controlling the airwaves, the Democratic Convergence made much of the fact that Aristide's "regime" rested on the violence of criminal gangs. This propaganda did much to discredit Aristide and Lavalas in the foreign media.

President Aristide accepted the continuation of imported American rice and the extension of the assembly plant system into a new "free trade zone" in Ouanaminthe, next to the Dominican border in the north of Haiti. These compromises earned Aristide the enmity of some Lavalas supporters who charged him with compromising with the imperialist, neoliberal enemy. But Aristide's compromises were irrelevant to the transnational capitalist class. Their goal was to establish as fact that Aristide was a dictator and a tyrant. Once that proposition was accepted among the "informed" public in the core capitalist countries — those who took the time to keep up with world events through the corporate mainstream media — the groundwork would be laid for the "liberation" of the Haitian people. Anyone challenging that truth would be dismissed as having entered the dark, dodgy world of conspiracy theory.

Throughout the fall of 2003 and into 2004, the Democratic Convergence merged with the protest groups that it was funding. Now called the Democratic Platform, they maintained that they were living in a dictatorship. This was a dictatorship in which the political opponents of the government controlled the airwaves, were given full access to the streets to protest, and were never jailed as political prisoners even as they openly called for the overthrow of the government voted into office with a huge majority. The Democratic Convergence used the crisis it had manufactured to break off, once again, negotiations over elections. The United States scaled back its diplomatic presence. CARICOM also withdrew from

46 Ibid., 51.

negotiations, but it cited the lack of will of the Democratic Convergence, not Aristide. The Inter Development Bank withheld $200 million promised to the Aristide government. Throughout all this, huge rallies continued in support of the government throughout January and February 2004.[47]

On 21 February 2004, American Deputy Secretary of State Roger Noriega arrived in Haiti to give the appearance of an attempt to negotiate with Aristide. He laid down a number of outrageous propositions, designed to be rejected by any responsible politician. In fact, the conditions he presented to Aristide to assure American support for his government were beyond the constitutional authority of a Haitian president. Noriega insisted that Aristide accept a cabinet filled with unelected representatives chosen by the Democratic Convergence. But, according to the constitution, Aristide's nomination for prime minister would require the confirmation of the two other chambers, overwhelmingly Lavalas. Remarkably, Aristide accepted all of Washington's demands. In response, the Democratic Convergence refused anything short of Aristide's resignation. They argued, in effect, that Aristide's complete capitulation to the unconstitutional demands of a foreign power was further evidence of his dictatorial methods. Noriega would later argue that it was Aristide's refusal to compromise in any way that caused his downfall.[48] Canadian and French politicians followed the same line, as though it had been decided at a board meeting.[49]

As the paramilitaries ravaged the north of Haiti, killing Lavalas supporters and over two hundred police officers loyal to the government, the Security Council of the United Nations issued a statement on 26 February 2004. In view of the increasing tensions, and in the interests of creating "a secure environment in Haiti and the region that enables respect for human rights, including the well-being of civilians, and supports the mission of humanitarian workers," the Security Council called "upon the Government and all other parties to respect human rights and

[47] Hallward, *Damming the Flood,* 192–223.
[48] Ibid., 224.
[49] Yves Engler and Anthony Fenton, *Canada in Haiti: Waging War on the Poor Majority* (Vancouver: Red Publishing, 2005), 41–45, discuss the Ottawa Initiative, in which officials from Canada, France, and the United States appear to have planned their collaboration in the overthrow of the Aristide government a year prior to Aristide's removal.

to cease the use of violence to advance political goals. Those responsible for human rights violations will be held accountable." In other words, the Security Council seemed to take the time to call upon Aristide to refrain from doing something he was not doing: using violence to advance political goals. In fact, he had used the electoral process to advance political goals and the defenders of "democracy" were refusing to cooperate. (The convoluted grammatical formulation suggests the authors understood the need for ambiguity.) The Secretary General warned that Haiti could destabilize the region, which laid the groundwork for intervention.[50]

When Aristide was finally abducted on 29 February 2004 and flown out of the country, the people who identified with Lavalas were left completely undefended. The Democratic Convergence claimed that "freedom fighters" were liberating the people and ridding the country of criminals. Spokespeople in Washington, Paris, and Ottawa claimed that Aristide freely resigned and that the United States kindly flew him to the safety of a repressive French client state, the Central African Republic.[51]

The Proprietors of the World Take Haiti, Once Again

Within hours of the abduction of President Aristide, the United Nations Security Council adopted Resolution 1529. The phrasing of the resolution was ambiguous, "*Taking note* of the resignation of Jean-Bertrand Aristide as President of Haiti and the swearing-in of President Boniface Alexandre as the acting President of Haiti in accordance with the Constitution of Haiti." In fact, only if Aristide had resigned voluntarily would the swearing-in of the Chief Justice of the Supreme Court of Haiti have been constitutional. If, however, the American government had threatened Aristide that, if he did not sign a letter of resignation, they would kill him and his family and then launch a bloodbath against his supporters — as Aristide and his American security guards avow was the case — then all subsequent actions of the Security Council would

---

[50] United Nations, Statement by the President of the Security Council, S/PRST/2004/4, 26 February 2004.
[51] Kim Ives and Ansel Herz, "WikiLeaks Haiti: The Aristide Files," *The Nation*, 5 August 2011.

be in violation of the Charter of the United Nations. Remarkably, the Security Council did not consult President Aristide in any way before validating the change in government. (This is great news for aspiring putschists the world over.) In order to justify intervention in Haitian affairs, the Security Council needed to show that Haiti represented "a threat to international peace and security," a phrase that was included in precisely those words, with no explanation as to how international peace and security were at risk from a tiny impoverished country that did not possess an army. Under Chapter VII of the Charter, the Security Council authorized the deployment of a Multinational Interim Force for a period of three months, after which it would be ready to establish a stabilization force "to support continuation of a peaceful and constitutional political process and the maintenance of a secure and stable environment." In violation of the constitutions of both the United Nations and Haiti, the Security Council called for the respect of the constitutional process. Canadian and American forces were already on the ground in Haiti. Canada would contribute 450 troops to the Multinational Interim Force.[52]

At the moment that Aristide was being flown to central Africa, a number of countries sympathetic to Lavalas were considering their support, exposing the division of the world into core and peripheral nations. The heads of the Caribbean countries held an emergency session, claiming their "dismay and alarm over the events leading to the departure from office by President Aristide and the ongoing political upheaval and violence in Haiti. They called for the immediate return to democratic rule and respect for the Constitution of Haiti."[53] The African Union Commission, representing fifty-three states, issued a similar statement: "The African Union expresses the view that the unconstitutional way by which President Aristide was removed set a dangerous precedent for a duly elected person and wishes that no action be taken to legitimize the rebel forces."[54] Venezuela refused to

---

52 UN Security Council resolution 1529, 29 February 2004.
53 Statement issued by CARICOM heads of government at the conclusion of an emergency session on the situation in Haiti, 2–3 March 2004, Kingston, Jamaica.
54 "Aristide's 'Removal' from Haiti 'Unconstitutional': African Union," *Agence France Presse*, 9 March 2004.

recognize the replacement government, which President Hugo Chavez qualified as "illegitimate" and the result of a "coup d'état." Chavez said, "The President of Haiti is called Jean-Bertrand Aristide, and he was elected by the people."[55] Military aid had been shipped from South Africa that would have arrived within days to arm the government supporters. Cuba, Jamaica, and Venezuela could have been drawn into an armed conflict. Washington's recent covert interventions in those countries, using "democracy" as a code for class rule, might have prompted some people to reconsider its intentions in Haiti.[56] At best, it would have been a diplomatic disaster for Washington and NATO, already overextended in wars of expansion in Iraq and Afghanistan, based on equally fraudulent claims. So it was urgent to get Aristide out of the country before a real military confrontation clarified who was behind the paramilitaries. Instead of receiving weapons to fight their enemies, those who wanted to defend their elected government confronted paramilitaries, backed by American and Canadian troops. In case the popular classes responded by fleeing the coming terror, three American Coast Guard cutters were stationed off Port-au-Prince. As if anticipating the need, the Security Council added a clause validating their presence: "To facilitate the provision of international assistance to the Haitian police and the Haitian Coast Guard in order to establish

---

55 Venezuelanalysis.com, "Venezuela Won't Recognize Haiti's New 'Illegitimate' Government," 17 March 2004, http://venezuelanalysis.com/news/419.

56 Washington had attempted to coordinate the overthrow of Hugo Chavez in 2002, with the same American agencies using the same tactics in league with the same class interests in Venezuela as in Haiti: N. Scott Cole, "Hugo Chavez and President Bush's Credibility Gap: The Struggle Against US Democracy Promotion," *International Political Science Review / Revue internationale de science politique* 28, no. 4 (September 2007): 493–507; Ronald D. Sylvia and Constantine P. Danopoulos, "The Chávez Phenomenon: Political Change in Venezuela," *Third World Quarterly* 24, no. 1 (February 2003): 63–76. Joshua Kurlantzick, "The Coup Connection: How an Organization Financed by the U.S. Government Has Been Promoting the Overthrow of Elected Leaders Abroad," *Mother Jones*, November–December 2004, describes how the same people were involved in both coups, namely Bush advisers Roger Noriega and Otto Reich. Haitian Stanley Lucas, who would become an adviser to President Martelly, was also involved in both the attempted coup in Venezuela and the successful coup in Haiti.

and maintain public safety and law and order and to promote and protect human rights." Up to 1,000 Lavalas supporters were killed in the first few days after Aristide's abduction.

Once president, Boniface Alexandre named economist Gérard Latortue, managing director at the United Nations Development Organization, as prime minister. A cousin of Youri Latortue, he had lived in Miami for the previous twenty years. No member of Fanmi Lavalas or any organization connected with Aristide was included in Latortue's government that, instead, succeeded in buying off several FL politicians who, in the process, destroyed their credibility with the electorate.

While $1,200,000,000 in conditional aid finally arrived, all of the social programs, job creation, and public works projects that Fanmi Lavalas had intended to use it for were shelved. Latortue unconstitutionally fired five justices from the Cour de Cassation and named five replacement justices. That meant that Haiti's ultimate appellate court would not undermine the new Interim Government of Haiti.[57] Latortue fired several thousand public service employees and published their names on lists of *chimères* which, in the circumstances, was a death sentence. (*Chimère* is a loaded term, used by the Haitian oligarchy and their transnational allies to smear active supporters of Aristide and Lavalas. It accomplishes the same objective as did "communist" during the Cold War, "terrorist" in relation to the Middle East, and "democrat" in eighteenth-century France, England, and United States.)

Many of those dismissed had worked as policemen or in security and they retained their firearms to defend themselves. Meanwhile, the National Police, now fully under the control of the oligarchy, staged raids into the poor neighbourhoods where the strongest support for Lavalas was located.[58] A reign of terror descended throughout Haiti. Local Lavalas leaders were assassinated or forced into hiding once their opponents realized that the oligarchy and their *blan* allies had finally

---

[57] Working Group on the Universal Periodic Review Human Rights Council, "Republic of Haiti: Submission to the United Nations Universal Period Review," 3–14 October 2011.

[58] Interview with Samba Boukman, Haiti Analysis, http://haitianalysis.blogspot.ca/2012/03/samba-boukman-on-his-life-and-necessity.html,

eliminated Aristide. Those who had public profiles and could inspire poor Haitians were silenced rather than killed.[59]

While it imprisoned people guilty of supporting Lavalas, the Latortue government overturned the convictions of those who had carried out the massacre in Raboteau in 1994, during the Cédras regime. The trials that led to those convictions had been based on painstaking investigations and courageous testimony. They represented a watershed in Haitian history. Moreover, the convictions rested on the judgment and intelligence of ordinary Haitians who sat on the jury: the core concept of Athenian democracy.[60] They were a triumph of Préval's government and had shown that Haiti could have a functional justice system. The capricious decision to release the convicts told poor Haitians — in the words of Joegodson — that they were as vulnerable as cockroaches in the face of hens.[61]

MINUSTAH

On 1 June 2004, the United Nations Security Council transferred authority from the Multinational Interim Force to the United Nations Stabilization Mission in Haiti, henceforth known by its French acronym

[59] Harvard Law Student Advocates for Human Rights, Cambridge, Massachusetts, and Centro de Justiça Global, Rio de Janeiro and São Paulo, Brazil, "Keeping the Peace in Haiti? An Assessment of the United Nations Stabilization Mission in Haiti, Using Compliance with Its Prescribed Mandate as a Barometer for Success." The people of Joegodson's birthplace, Saut d'Eau, also testify to a reign of terror: Association of University Grads for a Haiti with Law, "Central Plateau: Mirebalais-Lascaobas-Belladère, Former Soldiers and Armed Civilians Enjoy Complete Impunity, the Current Situation of the Victims of Former Soldiers and Armed Civilians from 2002–2005," August 2007. For a focus on the popular neighbourhoods of Port-au-Prince in the aftermath of the coup, see Griffin, "Haiti Human Rights Investigation"; and Kevin Pina, *We Must Kill the Bandits*, documentary, Haiti Information Project, 2007.

[60] Bresler, "If You Are Not Corrupt, Arrest the Criminals," 22. In the Haitian justice system, jurors can ask questions of the defendants. The lawyer for the victims, Mario Joseph and Brian Concannon, reported that the jurors' questions showed that they had followed the details and implications of the testimony, even where the prosecutors had been lax in their presentation of the case.

[61] Hallward, *Damming the Flood*, 275. *Ravet pa gen jistis devan poul* — the cockroach is never in the right before the hen.

MINUSTAH. It was initially established to serve for six months, but with the explicit intention of being renewed indefinitely, as has been the case. MINUSTAH included both civilian (up to 1,622 police) and military (up to 6,700 troops) components. The Security Council, while affirming its "strong commitment to the sovereignty, independence, territorial integrity and unity of Haiti," endowed MINUSTAH with extraordinary powers divided into three separate areas: to establish a secure and stable environment; to support the political process; and to monitor, protect, and report on human rights. It was specifically mandated to protect civilians under imminent threat of physical violence, to monitor, restructure, and reform the Haitian National Police, and to assist the transitional government in bringing about elections at all levels at the earliest possible date.[62] On 9 July 2004, Prime Minister Latortue, representing Haiti, signed the agreement legalizing the existence of MINUSTAH. The agreement included an immunity clause that released MINUSTAH from legal accountability for its actions in Haiti. However, as prime minister, Latortue did not have the constitutional authority to sign an international treaty on behalf of Haiti. Consequently, the MINUSTAH presence violates both international law and Haitian sovereignty.[63] During the first year of its mandate, researchers from the University of Miami, Harvard University, and the Centro de Justiça Global from Brazil all found that the United Nations forces were instead contributing to the deterioration of conditions for the majority of Haitians. The latter two institutions reported in March 2005,

> These violations span a gory spectrum, from arbitrary arrest and detention, to disappearances and summary executions, to killing of scores of hospitalized patients and the subsequent disposal of their bodies at mass graves. As this report details, MINUSTAH has effectively provided cover for

---

[62] United Nations Security Council Resolution 1542, 30 April 2004.

[63] This argument is advanced by Ricardo Seitenfus, the special representative of the secretary general of the Organization of American States in Haiti from 2008 to 2011. See Dan Beeton and Georgianne Nienaber, "Haiti's Doctored Elections, Seen from the Inside: An Interview with Ricardo Seitenfus," *Dissent*, 24 February 2014.

the police to wage a campaign of terror in Port-au-Prince's slums. Even more distressing than MINUSTAH's complicity in HNP abuses are credible allegations of human rights abuses perpetrated by MINUSTAH itself, as documented in this report. MINUSTAH, however, has virtually ignored these allegations as well, relegating them to obscurity and thus guaranteeing that abuses go uncorrected. In short, instead of following the specific prescription of its mandate by putting an end to impunity in Haiti, MINUSTAH's failures have ensured its continuation.[64]

All subsequent critical analyses of MINUSTAH would confirm and elaborate on that judgment. If MINUSTAH were to actually fulfil its mission responsibly, it would need to investigate and report on the illegal activities of those who brought it into existence and who profit from its continuation. Spokespeople from Haiti's poor neighbourhoods explicitly and vocally denounce MINUSTAH as a continuation of the coup d'état and an assault on Haitian democracy.

The people from the poorest neighbourhoods organized a march on 30 September 2004, to mark the anniversary of the first coup against Aristide in 1991. They demanded the return of Aristide and their elected government. The Haitian Police opened fire on the huge crowd, killing a number of people. Then, along with Labanye's gang, the police attacked the centres of Fanmi Lavalas support, killing eighty people over the next couple of weeks and imprisoning influential radio personalities on specious charges of complicity in attacks on the police. Prime Minister Latortue ordered the United Nations forces to mount operations against the poor whom he classified as terrorists. The terror was most pronounced in slums like Bel Air and Cité Soleil. In one instance, the Haitian Police forced eleven young men to lay on the ground and then shot them each in the head. They burned homes. MINUSTAH troops looked on. In December 2004, the interim government of Prime Minister Latortue paid former members of the armed forces the first of three instalments in compensation for Aristide's disbandment of the Army in

---

[64] Harvard Law Student Advocates for Human Rights and Centro de Justiça Global, "Keeping the Peace in Haiti?" 1.

1995. The indemnities amounted to $29 million and were intended to reach between 5,000 and 8,000 ex-soldiers, who would not be required to hand in the arms they kept when Aristide disbanded the army in 1995. The targets of these ex-military and death squad agents were the poor who were supposed to be protected by MINUSTAH.[65]

In December 2004, the oligarchy's paramilitaries, the National Police, MINUSTAH, and Labanye's gang fought to demoralize those loyal to Aristide and Lavalas. Finally, in March 2005, Dred Wilme's gang defeated Labanye, who was killed. Labanye's gang dispersed. The people of Cité Soleil rejoiced at the defeat of Labanye. Interim Prime Minister Gérard Latortue publicly mourned his death.

Upon the death of Labanye, the oligarchy directly armed the police to defend their interests. Reginald Boulos asked Washington to support their vision of a private police force. Fritz Mevs, a member of one of Haiti's wealthiest families, told the American ambassador that he worried "that funneling the arms secretly would only serve to reinforce [accurate] rumors that the elite were creating private armies." Instead of supporting that initiative for a police force directly and explicitly under the authority of the oligarchy, Juan Gabriel Valdes, the United Nations mission chief, committed MINUSTAH to taking over the role that the Labanye gang had fulfilled on behalf of the business class. The American embassy in Port-au-Prince cabled Washington that, "In response to embassy and private sector prodding, MINUSTAH is now formulating a plan to protect the area." The American ambassador praised MINUSTAH for showing "backbone" by incursions into the slums that killed and wounded large numbers of men, women, and children.[66] By shifting the responsibility for repression onto MINUSTAH, the Haitian oligarchy and their Washington allies obscured their role. Brazil accepted the offer to act as the lead nation of the MINUSTAH

---

[65] Griffin, "Haiti Human Rights Investigation," 4–13. Harvard Law Student Advocates for Human Rights and Centro de Justiça Global, "Keeping the Peace in Haiti?" 10. Wadner Pierre, "Why Bernard Grousse Shouldn't Be Haiti's Next Prime Minister," http://www.dominionpaper.ca/weblogs/wadner_pierre/4063.

[66] Dan Coughlin and Kim Ives, "WikiLeaks Haiti: Country's Elite Used Police as Private Army," *The Nation*, 22 June 2011. Also see Professor Keith Yearman, The Cité Soleil Massacre Declassification Project, College of DuPage, http://www.cod.edu/people/faculty/yearman/cite_soleil.htm.

mission in the interests of realizing its geopolitical ambitions. Brazil wanted to be recognized as a regional power in Latin America and, more specifically, to secure a permanent seat on the Security Council. At home, Brazil's leaders appealed to Brazilian nationalism. Leading the stabilization mission in Haiti was proof of their increasing prestige on the world stage. Brazilians should be proud of their country as it joined the ranks of the United States, France, Canada, the Vatican, the United Nations, the Organization of American States, the World Bank, and the International Monetary Fund. Together, they formed the "core group" that controlled Haitian "democracy" on behalf of the transnational capitalist class.[67]

New Elections: Préval

Haiti's interim government had to organize elections. For years, the Democratic Convergence had claimed that Aristide was a dictator held in place by criminal gangs. According to that logic, the "resignation" of Aristide should have set the stage for immediate elections. But it would take two years to organize those elections. The oligarchy and their transnational allies were well aware that Fanmi Lavalas would have, once again, won any election by a large majority. Consequently, they needed first to demoralize the poor, to imprison Lavalas candidates who could take the place of Aristide, and, finally, to manipulate the elections.

In 2005, as a result of the widespread attacks, repression, and imprisonment of political leaders, Fanmi Lavalas supporters declared their intention to boycott the coming elections. The oligarchy and Washington appeared to have won. By their standards, and for propaganda purposes, there would be "democratic" elections and their candidates would control the government and the presidency. However, a wild card appeared that changed the complexion of the elections for the poor classes. Since leaving the presidency in 2001, René Préval had dedicated himself to the development of his hometown of Marmelade and

[67] Tullo Vigevani and Gabriel Cepaluni, "Lula's Foreign Policy and the Quest for Autonomy Through Diversivication," *Third World Quarterly* 28, no. 7 (2007): 1309–26.

had not been involved in national politics. The Democratic Convergence and the coup leaders had largely ignored him, and he them. Now, as the elections approached, he presented himself as a candidate for his new party, called Lespwa, meaning Hope. His candidature was accepted by the Interim Government. But then the popular classes claimed him as their candidate. In Haitian culture, twins are thought to have a spiritual significance. It was believed that Aristide and Préval were twins: two people who shared one soul. A vote for Préval was, therefore, a vote for Aristide. Moreover, Préval promised the people that, if he was elected, he would allow Aristide to return to Haiti. The people saw their chance to prevail over their enemies who had stolen Aristide and destroyed their government. By the time the oligarchy understood what was happening, it was too late. In the death sport of Haitian politics, the people had scored a short-handed goal.

As the elections approached, relations between MINUSTAH and the police deteriorated. MINUSTAH officers understood that they were being used as a police force of repression in the service of the Haitian oligarchy. At one point, MINUSTAH troops blocked Haitian police from gaining access to a demonstration in Bel Air. The commander of MINUSTAH, General Ribeiro, resigned and a Brazilian general, Urano Teixa da Matta Bacellar, took his place. But the tensions remained. On 7 January 2006, Bacellar was found shot dead in his room at the Hotel Montana. The official explanation was that he had committed suicide. Many speculated that he had been murdered as a result of his unwillingness to use MINUSTAH to invade and pacify the poor neighbourhoods in advance of the elections. The Brazilian investigation and autopsy have never been released.

Boulos and Apaid favoured an invasion of the slums before the elections on the usual pretext of pacifying the bandits. But the assault was not authorized and, in its place, the residents of Cité Soleil and Bel Air organized massive nonviolent rallies in support of Préval. The armed gangs from the slums announced that they would protect voters. That exposed the fallacy at the heart of the oligarchy's narrative; the gangs and the poor formed a block in opposition to the rich. However much they hated gang culture, the people from the poor neighbourhoods relied on the gangs to protect them from the oligarchy and their transnational *blan* allies in the exercise of "democracy."

When Préval organized the last elections in November 2000, he had set up 10,000 voter registration centres throughout the country. In contrast, Latortue installed 500. Given the terrain and lack of infrastructure in Haiti, it is difficult to get around. In Cité Soleil, there were approximately 150,000 voters, but the Electoral Council sent only 52,000 voting cards. Even at that, only 30,000 votes from Cité Soleil were counted. In 2000, Préval had set up 12,000 polling stations. Latortue had 800. The poorest neighbourhoods had none. No polling station was located in Cité Soleil. When a number of polling stations did not open on the morning of the vote, the people began protesting loudly. When the foreign press began to cover the story, they eventually opened.[68]

Despite all of the obstacles, there was a 65 percent turnout. On 9 February, with a quarter of the votes counted, it was announced that Préval was leading with 62 percent. But on 11 February, the Electoral Council lowered his total to 49.6 percent, which would have necessitated a run-off election. Then, tens of thousands of charred ballots, cast mostly for Préval, were found in a garbage dump in Port-au-Prince. They apparently had been set alight, but a rainfall kept the fire from consuming them. The Electoral Council also found that 4.3 percent of the total ballots were blank. It was presumed they had been inserted in order to dilute Préval's percentage to under 50 percent. By whom? American Deputy Secretary of State Roger Noriega encouraged the Electoral Council to resist the demands of the mobs that were clamouring for the declaration of Préval as president.

The people erupted in controlled but passionate and menacing protests. They knew that the Interim Government was trying to cook the elections and steal the presidency from them. Huge protests consumed Port-au-Prince, literally threatening to lay waste to the country if the election was stolen from them.[69] Sociologist Alex Dupuy describes the reaction of the transnational ruling class:

68 Hallward, *Damming the Flood*, 300.

69 We observed the huge protest marches. The people chanted "Pa gen Préval, pa gen Ayiti" which is ambiguous but can mean, "If we don't get Préval, you don't get Haiti." Thousands of poor from Cité Soleil climbed the mountain to the luxurious Hotel Montana where they entered *en masse*, jumped in the pool, lounged on the chaises longues, and otherwise hobnobbed with the rich. When they left everything just as they had found it, the message was not lost on the oligarchy. The price for fixing the elections was going to be high.

At that point, ambassadors from the United States, Canada, and France who had initially insisted that the CEP [Provisional Electoral Council] continue to count the votes that would have forced a second round reluctantly agreed to join with their counterparts from Brazil and Chile and meet with UN, interim government, and CEP officials to come up with an acceptable legal solution that would grant Préval a first-round victory. The solution was found in the so-called Belgian Option suggested by the Brazilian and Chilean diplomats. According to Article 185 of the Haitian electoral decree, blank ballots must be included as part of the total votes cast, but the article does not stipulate how the votes are to be counted. The Belgian Option consisted of distributing the blank votes proportionally to each candidate rather than adding them to the total. While this solution raised everyone's percentage, it also put Préval over the 50 percent plus one vote he needed to win in the first round. In the early morning hours of February 16, eight of the nine members of the CEP signed the agreement that declared Préval the winner.[70]

American ambassador Tim Carney candidly said that the validity of the election would be judged according to Préval's cooperation in office.

The people, said to have been held in terror by Aristide, overwhelming elected the man they called his twin who promised to allow Aristide to return to Haiti. And then they rejoiced. What happened to the candidates who had rid the country of Aristide and Lavalas? Manigat received 12.4 percent of the votes. Baker, widely trumpeted as Washington's favourite, got 8.2 percent. The paramilitary leader, Guy Philippe, who fancied himself the liberator of Haiti, managed 1.9 percent; Evans Paul, 2.5 percent. Dany Toussaint, a key traitor of Aristide, polled

---

70 Alex Dupuy, "Haiti Election 2006: A Pyrrhic Victory for René Préval," *Latin American Perspectives* 33, no. 3 (May 2006):135.

0.4 percent. Gérard Gourgues, whom the Democratic Convergence had named as the head of the parallel government in 2004, refusing to recognize Aristide, got 0.3 percent of the vote. Washington's World Bank candidate Marc Bazin, claiming to represent Lavalas, got 0.7 percent.[71] Remember that these results represent the totals after the Interim Government had done all in its power to undermine Préval and push the oligarchy's candidates.

The Limits of Transnational, Capitalist "Democracy"

Upon taking office, Préval worked to strengthen Haiti's relationship with Venezuela and Cuba. Venezuela offered Haiti a steady and reliable source of energy through PetroCaribe. To complement that policy, Cuba offered Préval its medical expertise. Short on money, Cuba was strong in human resources. Both Aristide and Préval had strengthened ties to Cuba in the past. Now, Préval deepened relations with an agreement that would see Cuban medical practitioners work with the Haitian state to improve health services in the most remote communities in Haiti. These initiatives, that brought Haiti into the Bolivarian Alliance for the Americas, directly threatened Washington's regional political agenda. Préval attempted to assuage Washington's concern at the same time that he worked to integrate Haiti into the Alliance that could benefit the Haitian poor over the interests of the transnational capitalists. This put Préval on a collision course with Exxon-Mobil and Chevron, which had control of the Haitian market. Under the deal, they would have to answer to the governments of both Haiti and Venezuela. Chevron appealed to Washington for help. President Bush warned Préval against aligning Haiti with Hugo Chavez. Finally, by agreeing to a complex agreement whereby Chevron would ship PetroCaribe oil from Venezuela to Haiti, Préval managed to conclude the deal.[72]

---

[71] See Georgetown University, Political Database of the Americas at http://pdba.georgetown.edu/Elecdata/Haiti/06pres.html.

[72] Dan Coughlin and Kim Ives, "WikiLeaks Haiti: The PetroCaribe Files," *The Nation*, 1 June 2011.

Préval — like all political leaders in the current context of transnational capitalism — had to choose between two constituencies: on one side, the poor of Haiti who had elected him as president and, on the other, the transnational capitalist class represented by the Haitian oligarchy and their powerful allies in Washington, Paris, and Ottawa. (Betraying the electorate can make a "democratically"-elected politician unpopular; betraying the transnational capitalist class is often fatal.) Préval managed to negotiate deals, such as PetroCaribe with Hugo Chavez, that were favourable to the Haitian people. But, once in office, he reneged on his promise to allow Aristide to return to Haiti, until the very end of his mandate. Washington and its allies worked to keep Aristide in Africa; Préval could not have prevailed without opening himself to Aristide's fate. But Préval further excluded Lavalas from the political process. In its place, he offered a new party, Inite (Unity). Since he could not run for a third term as president, Préval's son-in-law Jude Célestin would be the Inite candidate for the country's highest office. Practically, Préval needed to control the Provisional Electoral Council to assure the outcome. Whatever his motivations, the consequences of his authoritarian actions in breach of his promise earned him the lasting enmity of poor Haitians.

According to the Haitian constitution of 1987, elections are to be overseen by a Permanent Electoral Council composed of three representatives from each of Haiti's nine departments. (A tenth department was added since the constitution was written.) The smallest geographical level of government — the communal section — chooses representatives to send to the larger geopolitical divisions. Finally, the Departmental Assemblies are supposed to nominate thirty candidates for the Permanent Electoral Council. From that list, the President, the Supreme Court, and the National Assembly each choose three members to form the actual Permanent Electoral Council. The Departmental Assembly has never been implemented as a level of government, however. Consequently, there has never been a Permanent Electoral Council. The Provisional Electoral Council, created after the flight of Duvalier to oversee the first elections based on the new constitution, remains in place. It has always had full independence to "organize and control" the complete electoral process in the absence of a permanent body. Instead of implementing a system of oversight consistent with the constitution insofar as that was possible in the absence of Departmental

Assemblies, President Préval chose several groups to propose to him a number of candidates from which he then selected the Provisional Electoral Council. In that way, Préval retained substantial control over the composition of the Electoral Council, contrary to both the letter and the spirit of the constitution.[73]

In April 2009, Haiti held elections for twelve of the thirty Senate seats. The Provisional Electoral Council required that all candidates submit an original signature from the party leader. Knowing that Aristide was in South Africa and would not be able to send it in time, the *ad hoc* requirement was clearly designed to exclude all Fanmi Lavalas candidates. Voters boycotted the elections in protest. Most observers estimated a turnout of approximately 5 percent of the electorate.[74] Next, elections for all ninety-nine seats of the House of Deputies and ten Senate seats were rescheduled from November 2009 to February 2010. The Electoral Council again rejected the participation of Fanmi Lavalas candidates, but this time offered no coherent explanation. In fact, Fanmi Lavalas had met all the legal requirements, including authorization from Aristide, still in South Africa. When the earthquake struck on 12 January 2010, the elections were called off, leaving Haiti without a functioning parliament.

Préval called an election for 28 November 2010 to fill the positions of president, the entire House of Deputies, and one third of the Senate. Préval declared that the candidate list agreed upon for the November 2009 elections, postponed already once, would be carried over to 2010. That meant that Fanmi Lavalas would remain banned from participating, as a result of the earlier unconstitutional and capricious ban.

---

[73] Lamp for Haiti, "The Right to Vote: A Report Detailing the Haitian Elections for November 28, 2010, and March 2011," Bwa Nef, Cité Soleil, 2010, http://ijdh.org/wordpress/wp-content/uploads/2010/11/LAMP_HR_Program_Right_to_Vote_Rep_2010_2011.pdf; "Reconstructing Democracy: Joint Report of Independent Electoral Monitors of Haiti's November 28, 2010 Election," 7, http://ijdh.org/wordpress/wp-content/uploads/2011/02/Haiti-Joint-Observer-Report-FINAL.pdf.

[74] Institute for Justice and Democracy in Haiti and Bureau des avocats internationaux, "The International Community Should Pressure the Haitian Government for Prompt *and* Fair Elections," 30 June 2010, http://www.ijdh.org/wp-content/uploads/2010/04/Elections-Process-6-30-10_final-1.pdf.

The United States, Canada, the OAS, and the UN all made a show of cautioning Préval for this anti-democratic lapse. Meanwhile, Washington and its imperialist allies invested $30 million in the election; Canada contributed $5.8 million of that total. With Lavalas banned, no candidate posed a threat to the transnational capitalist class. They were ambiguous toward Préval, who had made enemies of Chevron and Exxon-Mobil while keeping the lid on Lavalas. Patrick Elie, a political scientist who had been the defence minister in Aristide's second government, speculates that the elections were scheduled to take place in devastated, post-quake Haiti precisely to take advantage of the chaos and a traumatized electorate. The political arm of the transnational class would be able to claim success in bringing "democracy" to Haiti, while blaming the exclusion of Fanmi Lavalas on Préval.

Electoral Shamming

During the months preceding the November elections, large crowds protested the exclusion of the country's largest political party, Fanmi Lavalas. According to its mandate, MINUSTAH was responsible for assuring lawful and orderly elections. The same protesters who promised to boycott the elections, however, also called for the expulsion of MINUSTAH from Haiti. An outbreak of cholera erupted and rumours spread that the Nepalese contingent of MINUSTAH had been dumping raw sewage into a tributary of the Artibonite River. The cholera bacteria thrived in the conditions of post-earthquake Haiti. Victims of the quake lived in close quarters with inadequate hygienic facilities. Water was untreated and most people could ill afford bottled water, itself not always reliable. Among the poor, rumours spread that MINUSTAH had introduced the bacteria on purpose to kill them off.

Then came election day, 28 November 2010. Many who tried to vote were simply turned away from the voting stations, if they could find them. Observers documented a level of incompetence on the part of the Electoral Council hard to explain were it not deliberate. Foreign news agencies filmed people stuffing handfuls of ballots into boxes while other ballots blew in the wind. At some voting stations, potential voters were turned away at gunpoint. People were directed to nonexistent voting stations. Between the boycott and logistical chaos, the participation rate was only 20 percent of registered voters. In any case, behind closed doors, the head of MINUSTAH was deciding the outcome of the elections long before the polls closed.

Early in the morning of election day, the head of the MINUSTAH mission to Haiti, Edmond Mulet, told the international press that he was impressed with the desire of Haitians to vote and that the day was "an electoral celebration." Several hours later, Mulet convened a meeting of the representatives of the guardians of Haiti, including the United States, Brazil, Canada, France, Spain, the UN, the OAS, and the European Union. Mulet told the special representative of the OAS, Ricardo Seitenfus, that he had just informed President Préval that an aeroplane had been arranged for him to leave Haiti within forty-eight hours. He confided in Seitenfus that Jude Célestin appeared to be on track to win the elections and that was unacceptable. Mulet, apparently acting on behalf of the core countries that controlled Haiti — the United States, France, and Canada — had decided to repeat the same tactics that had forced Aristide out of the country in 2004. This time, Préval would appear to have left in response to the mounting protests against the undeniable electoral farce. However, the representatives from Latin America at the meeting refused to sanction the proposed coup d'état. Consequently, Canada, France, and the United States were forced to back down. Instead, they transformed the Observation Mission from the OAS-CARICOM into a Recounting Mission of nine persons, which they stacked with seven members from the United States, France, and Canada. It proceeded to capriciously tally the votes until Célestin was in third place, behind Myrlande Manigat and Michel Martelly. Consequently, he was eliminated from the second round to determine who would become president.

The run-off election between Myrlande Manigat and Michel Martelly took place in March 2011. Martelly, under the name of Sweet Mickey, had been known for his vulgar — sometimes obscene — musical performances, in the course of which he championed Haiti's dictators: Jean-Claude Duvalier, General Cédras and his death squads, the *tontons macoutes*, and the oligarchy. He berated Lavalas and Jean-Bertrand Aristide. As the run-off election proceeded, Joegodson posted articles on our website describing the gangs of *vakabons* that marched through the streets of Port-au-Prince, threatening violence against those who did not support their preferred candidate. Martelly had promised them that, as president, he would reinstate the Haitian army. His followers were called Tèt Kale (Bald Heads) and stood for nothing more noble than their own advancement. Although he won the presidency, the Electoral Council refused to validate the results. Martelly's presidency is not constitutionally valid.[75]

The Transnational World and the Transnational State

Although Jean-Bertrand Aristide had returned to Haiti two days before Martelly gained the presidency, he has withdrawn from public life. The current leadership of the political party he founded, Fanmi Lavalas, represents less and less the poor and oppressed of Haiti.[76] But that constituency — growing and increasingly desperate — continues to call upon the spirit of Dessalines. The seventeenth of October 2013 marked the two hundred and seventh anniversary of the assassination of Jean-Jacques Dessalines. Tens of thousands of people marched in Port-au-Prince and Cap-Haïtien to commemorate the man who symbolizes the liberation of Haiti from both imperial domination and Haitian sedition. As Dessalines had forced the imperialist countries out of Haiti — and as his successors had expelled Jean-Claude Duvalier in 1986 — the protesters demanded the unconditional departure of both Martelly and MINUSTAH. The police opened fire on them. In Port-au-Prince, the police blocked them from gaining access to Place Dessalines, where MINUSTAH troops were holding a military parade.

---

[75] Center for Economic and Policy Research, "Reconstructing Democracy: Joint Report of Independent Electoral Monitors of Haiti's November 28, 2010 Election," n.d.; National Human Rights Defense Network, "RNDDH Presents Its Report on the 2nd Round of the Presidential and Partial Legislative Elections of March 20th, 2011," 23 March 2011; Lamp for Haiti, "The Right to Vote,"; Center for Economic and Policy Research, "Haiti: From Original Sin to Electoral Intervention — An Interview with Ricardo Seitenfus by Dan Beeton and Georgianne Nienaber," 24 February 2014.

[76] Kim Ives, "The Split in Fanmi Lavalas: How It Came About and What It Portends," *Haïti Liberté*, vol 7, no 22, 11–17 December 2013.

Diverted to the Champs de Mars, they took up a variation on the chant that Joegodson had heard similar crowds shout as they forced Duvalier to flee to France: "*Grenadye alaso, sa ki mouri zafè a yo. Si yo tire sou nou, n ap mete dife. Nou pa pè, nou pap janm pè, wè pa wè fòk Martelly jije pou krim li fè sou jij la, pou manti li bay pèp la.*" Thus, they claimed that they were unafraid, but would bring Martelly to justice for both his crimes and his lies, some of which they enumerated: violating the constitution, destroying democratic institutions, manipulating the judiciary and the police, assassinating Judge Jean Serge Joseph, refusing to organize elections, refusing to support the legal claim brought forth by the victims of cholera against MINUSTAH, refusing to enact the Senate resolution demanding the departure of MINUSTAH by May 2014 at the latest, attempting to erect a totalitarian regime against the will of the people, manipulating the media, and persecuting critics.[77]

Inside of government, Senator Moïse Jean-Charles has accepted the role of denouncing the crimes, hypocrisy, and lies of the powerful in Haiti and in the international arena. He has appeared on Brazilian television to represent the will of the Haitian majority — and legislature — for the departure of MINUSTAH. Other deputies and senators have revealed to him the nature of the Martelly presidency and Jean-Charles has been sharing those confidences with the people of Haiti over the radio, much as Jean Dominique had done before his assassination. Jean-Charles is not the only voice. Kòdinasyon Desalin (Coordination Dessalines) comprises a number of articulate spokesmen and -women who defend the poor, the Haitian constitution, and international law against the transgressions of the transnational capitalist class. They argue that there can be no justice for imperialist crimes against them as long as Martelly, in collaboration with the bourgeoisie, neo-*macoutes*, and Duvalierists, holds onto the presidency. Not only does KOD call for his resignation, but also his arrest and trial for overt participation in the coup d'état of 2004. Likewise, FOPARK (Patriotic Force for Respect of the Constitution) has brought tens of thousands of Haitians into the streets to vigorously protest developments under

---

[77] Yves Pierre-Louis, "17 Octobre 2013: Commémoration sur fond de manifestation anti-Martelly," *Haïti Liberté* vol. 7, no. 15, (October 2013), 4.

Martelly. On 29 November 2013, they organized a march from the slums of Bel Air and La Saline to the American embassy, under the slogan, "Dessalines is going to visit Uncle Sam." Their goal was to protest American machinations that brought Martelly to power in 2011.[78]

These analysts, mostly from Haiti's poorest neighbourhoods, describe how Martelly is capturing the Haitian state to impose a dictatorship. Martelly has refused to call elections since his unconstitutional entry into the presidency. Mayoralty terms expired in 2011. Instead of holding elections, Martelly replaced all elected mayors and county officials with personal appointments. Throughout Haiti, individuals loyal to Martelly now hold power locally, much as was the case under the Duvalier dictatorship. Thirteen Haitian congressmen have tabled a resolution enumerating Martelly's offences against the constitution — grounds for his trial by a High Court. With no legal basis, he imposed taxes on both telephone calls to Haiti and money transfers from abroad. The fund has collected hundreds of millions of dollars and is under the exclusive control of Martelly and his prime minister, Laurent Lamothe. Martelly unconstitutionally designated his wife and son to manage hundreds of millions of dollars of public funds with no oversight. Two lawyers brought an extortion case against Martelly's wife and son before Judge Jean Serge Joseph, who was in turn threatened by Martelly, Lamothe, and Minister of Justice Jean Renel Sanon. Two days later, Joseph died in suspicious circumstances. The lawyers who brought the case have subsequently been harassed by the police. Only by the intervention of the poor of Port-au-Prince did lawyer Michel André escape arrest. Meanwhile, the average time elapsed between arrest and charges being laid is almost two years. That time is spent in inhuman prison conditions. Martelly's closest political allies in the Senate and legislature are accused of drug trading,

---

[78] The press conferences of both KOD and FOPARK are available on the YouTube channel of frantzetienne1: https://www.youtube.com/user/frantzetienne1. "Deklarasyon KOD sou 10zyèm anivèsè koudeta 2004 la!" *Haïti Liberté* vol. 7, no. 33, (February 2014), 6. The Sentinel Staff, "FOPARK Announces March to U.S. Embassy on November 29," http://www.sentinel.ht/news/articles/community/5198-fopark-announces-march-to-u-s-embassy-on-november-29#ixzz2wFdpwsEN.

arms dealing, the execution of political and criminal competitors, and other crimes.[79]

Haiti is no longer a problem for the core capitalist countries. The president is operating blatantly outside of the constitution to consolidate power in his office; in other words, he is reconstructing a dictatorship that was defeated when the great majority of Haitians forced Jean-Claude Duvalier to flee the country. Electoral results are now assured by the arbitrary prohibition of parties that represent those Haitians

---

[79] These claims are only a small summary of the accusations against the Martelly government. Many are repeated and elaborated independently in various human rights, Senate, and legislative reports. Réseau National de Défense des Droits Humains, "Situation Générale des Droits Humains dans le pays au cours de la deuxième année de présidence de Michel Joseph Martelly," 18 June 2013, 6–7; Statement of Senator Benoit to the American Congress, http://www.ijdh.org/2013/10/topics/politics-democracy/senator-benoit-statement-to-congress/; Kim Ives, "Arrestation de Me André Michel!" *Haïti Liberté* vol. 7, no. 15 (October 2013), 4; Kim Ives, "Outspoken Senator Charges: Martelly Government, a 'Cesspool' of Corruption and Nepotism," *Haïti Liberté* vol. 5, no. 25 (January 2012); United States Department of State, Bureau of Democracy, Human Rights and Labor, Country Reports on Human Rights Practices for 2013; Réseau National de Défense des Droits Humains, "Trafic illicite de drogues: Le Gouvernement Martelly/Lamothe met tout en oeuvre pour protéger les narcotrafiquants proches du Pouvoir," 18 September 2013. One of the most disturbing revelations is the testimony of Sherlson Sanon, who describes how Senator Joseph Lambert enrolled him into his criminal gang at age eleven. Lambert and Senator Edwin Zinny paid him to carry out executions of criminal and political competitors, run drugs, and frame political opponents, such as Senator Moïse Jean-Charles. See Emmanuel Saintus, "Affaire Lambert: Al Capone haïtien?" *Haïti progrès*, 11 July 2013. One of the most tenacious journalists in Haiti, Jean Monard Métellus, exposes the workings of the Martelly government. In October 2013, Justice Minister Jean Renel Sanon published a press release revealing that Métellus was the target of an assassination plot. He claimed that two motorcyclists had been engaged to kill the journalist in a drive-by shooting, a common tactic in Haiti. Jean Dominique had been assassinated in precisely that manner. Journalist Francklyn Geffrard questions the purpose of a press release announcing the assassination plot rather than a police investigation to find the conspirators based on whatever information the justice minister possesses. The announcement had the effect of communicating to journalists the price that accompanied criticism of the Martelly regime. Francklyn B. Geffrard, "La vie de Jean Monard Métellus en danger!" *Haïiti Liberté* vol 7, no 15 (October 2013), 7.

who expelled Duvalier. The political elite are, once again, known to be deeply implicated in criminal activity. They use the state to ensure that Haitians do not, once again, interfere with the interests of the transnational capitalist class. The police and judicial systems are tools to silence critics. Washington accepts that the head of the Senate has personally murdered Haitians who tried to peacefully defend the rights of the poor. Washington knows that he is building a criminal network in the Gonaïves region, based on the drug trade. The president is personally tied to another drug ring, operating out of the south of Haiti, which has been credibly accused of a culture of murder, extortion, and terror. UNICEF does not express concern aroused by the testimony of children who claim that the current political leaders have recruited them to commit murder and other criminal actions. The judicial authorities who have attempted to bring charges for embezzlement and extortion against the family of the the president have died in suspicious circumstances or been harassed by the police. When Mario Joseph, the lawyer who defends the victims of Duvalier and the current despotic regime, accuses the current mayor of Montréal of having facilitated the illegal abduction of President Jean-Bertrand Aristide in 2004 in the capacity of his role as Minister of the Francophonie, Denis Coderre responds that Joseph is simply trying to bring Haitian domestic politics to Canada.[80]

Representative government — almost universally called democracy — is not compatible with the needs of transnational capitalism. The global division of paid labour and pauperism, in a system where everyone needs money to survive, means that majorities of people in peripheral countries — and increasing numbers in the core capitalist nations — are expected to vote for their own subjugation. The majority of Haitians see little choice but to fight those who present themselves as the political class. The transnational ruling class offers them Michel Martelly as their representative on the international stage. Those Haitians who fought and suffered to rid themselves of Duvalier only to witness a transnational class destroying their chosen governments, now see President Martelly working with those same putschists, with Jean-Claude Duvalier, with ex–death squad killers granted amnesty for having murdered their

[80] "Un avocat haïtien réclame des excuses de la part de Coderre," *La Presse*, 27 February 2014.

friends and relatives to protect Haiti from poor Haitians. Martelly's job is to deliver Haiti to Washington, Paris, and Ottawa. Together, they represent the "natural aristocracy" that the founders of "democracy" assumed would take control of the world in the course of time. They were prescient, but there is nothing "natural" about the transnational aristocracy. It is a product of the imperialist, capitalist world system. It is as "natural" as the slavery against which Haitians revolted more than two centuries ago.

Glossary of Haitian Terms

ajoupa   A temporary structure used as a home.

annavan   Forward march.

blan   White. In the first place, all foreigners in Haiti. Secondly, Haitians who are light-skinned can also be called *blan*. However, a very dark-skinned foreigner is also *blan* because he or she is not a native Creole speaker.

bòs   Boss: a master in any vocation.

bourèt   A large wheelbarrow with one single wheel used by sturdy men to transport heavy loads in the cities.

comida   A *kokorat* who waits in front of a MINUSTAH base for a handout. *Comida* is the Portuguese word for street kid.

degoche   The first step in an apprenticeship; a small course to learn the basic principles of any discipline.

ebenis   Cabinet maker, furniture maker.

houngan   A male Vodou priest.

kafou   An intersection of streets.

kantè   A truck designed to transport merchandise.

kay   A home.

kivèt   A tub for washing clothes.

klarin   An alcoholic beverage made from sugar cane.

kokorat   A street kid. *Kokorats* search through garbage piles for food and anything that they might be able to sell. They have no home. They live outside of families and are unemployed.

konbit   A peasant work collective for a full day.

konpa   Style of Haitian music.

koutche A person who brings together buyers and sellers for a range of products, including real estate, employment, car rental or purchase. A business person touching all interests.

kout lè The fatal breeze that the San Pwèl blow on their victims.

lakou A group of several small houses belonging to members of an immediate family.

lougarou Vodouists who can transform into any animal during the night. They can stay in human form and fly as a result of a fire that burns in their buttocks. They search babies and either steal their soul or suck their blood. In both cases, their little victims die.

lwa A Vodou spirit.

madriye Thick planks of wood used in the crafting of furniture and construction.

mambo A female Vodou priest.

marinad A spiced dumpling.

mason Mason.

mawon During the time of the French colony, a slave who escaped his owner to live free in the mountains. Today, anyone who flees from his or her responsibilities. Also, the colour brown.

mekanik A mechanic.

mera A peasant work collective for a half day.

ofis A piece of furniture like a china cabinet, but with sliding glass doors instead of doors.

pèpè Second-hand goods from North America sold by street merchants throughout Haiti. Although most commonly used to describe second-hand clothing, it refers generally to all second-hand goods sold in Haiti.

plasaj Common-law marriage.

ranyon Clothes and other fabric too worn, stained, and ripped to be of further use.

rechau A small oven that uses gas or coal, hammered out of scrap metal by travelling artisans called "recholye."

restavèk A child given to another family who is victim of abuse and exploitation.

San Pwèl A kind of Vodouist who circulates during the night. When they meet people in the streets, they emit a breeze that will be fatal within hours. They also have a magic rope made with human intestines and fibres from the sisal plant with which they lasso their human victims to transform them into animals, such as cows and horses. They can even eat the people that have been transformed into cows.

sòs pwa nwa A sauce made out of black beans passed through a strainer or a blender or a mortar and served with rice or cornmeal.

sousou A sycophant; a yes-man.

taptap A transportation service. A pick-up truck transformed to carry approximately a dozen passengers along specified routes. It is private business in the place of public transportation.

tayè Tailor.

tet ansanm "Heads together." A term to call for unity or cooperation.

ti bourik A chair used to aid mothers in childbirth (literally, "little donkey").

tikounouk A very little house, often squeezed among others, as in slums; a shanty.

tonton makout A soldier in the service of the Duvalier regime.

vèvè Symbols to communicate with the Vodou spirits. Each *lwa*, or spirit, has its own *vèvè*.

viejo Haitians who spend many years in the Dominican Republic.

Pawol Granmoun / Haitian Sayings

Zafè kabrit pa gade mouton.
A sheep doesn't concern itself with a goat's problems.

Bourik travay pou chwal galonnen.
The donkey works so that the horse can prance.

Si ou pa pwason, ou pa dwe antre nan nas.
If you aren't a fish, you shouldn't enter the net.

Tout otan tèt ou poko koupe, espere met chapo.
As long as you still have a head, you can hope to wear a hat.

Sak vid pa kanpe.
An empty sack cannot stand.

Marengwen ap vole ou pa konn mal ak femèl.
While mosquitoes are flying, you can't tell male from female.

W'ap kouri pou lapli, ou tonbe nan gran rivye.
While you're running from the rain, you fall in the river.

Se le ou nan male w'ap konn kiyes moun ki zanmi w.
When you are in trouble, you find out who your friends are.

Nan chemen jennen, yo kenbe chwal malen.
In a tight space, you rein in a wild horse.

Bourik fè pitit pou do li pose.
A donkey has foals to lighten his load.

Tout sa'k pa bon pou youn, li bon pou yon lòt.
Things that are not good for one person are good for another.

Chat brule nan dlo cho, le li wè dlo frèt, li pè.
After a cat burns itself in hot water, it is then afraid when it sees cold water.

Twòp magi gate sòs.
Too much seasoning ruins the sauce.

Responsab se chaj.
The person responsible is also accountable.

Le ou bezwen debarase yon chen, ou di li gen raj.
If you want to get rid of a dog, you say he has rabies.

Ou jamn tande pòt an bwa goumen avèk pòt an fè?
You ever hear of a wooden door fighting an iron door?

Men anpil chay pa lou.
Lots of hands make light work.

Makak sou konn sou ki bwa li fwote.
A drunken monkey knows what tree he is rubbing against.

Se kondisyon ki bat kòk.
You can't change the rules in the middle of the game.

Se sòt k'ap soti, lespri ap antre.
Each trial makes us wiser.

Domi pa konn mizè malere.
The wretched can sleep anywhere.

Woch nan dlo pa konn mizè woch nan solèy.
Rocks in the water don't know the misery of rocks in the sun.

Chants

Si yo tire sou nou, n'ap mete dife.

If you fire upon us, we'll start a fire.

—●—

Lafanmi Chilè siye dlo nan je'w,
Chilè pa mouri, se nan plàn li ye,
demen a katrè al telefòne'l,
al devan Sen Jan Bosko w'a jwenn Chilè.
Lafanmi Toto siye dlo nan je'w,
Toto pa mouri, se nan plàn li ye,
demen a katrè al telefòne'l,
al devan Sen Jan Bosko w'a jwenn Toto.

Wipe away your tears, Chilè family,
Chilè is not dead, he is at the pawnbrokers,
At four o'clock tomorrow you should telephone him,
In front of Saint Jean Bosco Church you will find Chilè.
Wipe away your tears, Toto family,
Toto is not dead, he's at the pawnbrokers,
At four o'clock tomorrow you should telephone him,
In front of Saint Jean Bosco Church you will find Toto.

—●—

Grenadye alaso! sa ki mouri zafè a yo!

Charge grenadiers! Those who die, that's their own business!